CONTESTING EARTH'S FUTURE

CONTESTING EARTH'S FUTURE

RADICAL ECOLOGY AND POSTMODERNITY

MICHAEL E. ZIMMERMAN

1994

UNIVERSITY OF CALIFORNIA PRESS   BERKELEY   LOS ANGELES   LONDON

University of California Press

Berkeley and Los Angeles, California

University of California Press, Ltd.

London England

Copyright © 1994 by The Regents of the

University of California

Library of Congress Cataloging-in-Publication Data

Zimmerman, Michael E. 1946–

    Contesting Earth's future : radical ecology

and postmodernity / Michael E. Zimmerman.

      p. cm.

    Includes bibliographical references

and index.

    ISBN 0-520-08477-2 (alk. paper)

    ISBN 0-520-20907-9 (pbk; alk. paper)

    1. Environmentalism. 2. Deep ecology.

3. Social ecology. 4. Ecofeminism. I. Title

GE195.Z56 1994

304.2—dc20   93-21431

                  CIP

Printed in the United States of America

  2 3 4 5 6 7 8 9

The paper used in this publication meets the

minimum requirements of American National

Standard for Information Sciences—Permanence

of Paper for Printed Library Materials, ANSI

Z39.48-1984. ∞

I dedicate this book
to two groups of people
with whom I have been
fortunate enough to have
engaged in such stimulating
dialogue over the years:

the students in my
Humanity's Place in Nature
course at Tulane University

and my friends
in radical ecology

CONTENTS

- ACKNOWLEDGMENTS

I would like to thank the following for contributing to the successful completion of this work. John Clark, J. Baird Callicott, Gus
diZerega, Donna Haraway, George Sessions, Charlene Spretnak, and
anonymous reviewers provided very helpful criticism of all or part of
various drafts. Edward Dimendberg of the University of California
Press encouraged me to write the book and supported it at every stage.
The philosophy faculty of the Seattle University invited me to give
the Michael J. Toulouse, S.J. Memorial Lecture in April 1989. In that
lecture I offered the initial statement of the book's major themes. For
this opportunity and for their hospitality, I am grateful. Portions of
chapter 3 originally appeared as "Rethinking the Heidegger–Deep
Ecology Relation," *Environmental Ethics* 15, 3 (Fall 1993): 195–224.
My thanks to that journal's editor in chief, Eugene C. Hargrove, for
permission to reprint those portions here. Harald Mesch offered good
conversation and bibliographical suggestions about German aspects
of radical ecology. Tulane University provided me with a leave of
absence in 1991–1992, when I wrote much of the book while living
in Munich. I was supported financially by my wife, Teresa A. Toulouse, who was then a Fulbright Fellow at the Amerika Institut of
Universität München. Her intellectual and editorial efforts signifi-

cantly improved the introduction to this book. Above all, however, I am very grateful to her for having once again displayed such patience, forbearance, and love while I wrote yet another book.

Most people know about radical ecology from headlines featuring Greenpeace members risking life and limb to confront polluters and whalers; from stories about the women of Greenham Common spending years in a vigil next to a British air base to protest nuclear weapons; or from reports of Earth First!ers resisting attempts to log old-growth forests in the Northwest. This book, although acknowledging the importance of such groups, concerns itself with the less publicized work of radical ecological *theorists* who represent three major branches of radical ecology: deep ecology, social ecology, and ecofeminism. To be sure, in addition to writing essays, these theorists also take other political steps to protest and to alter ecologically destructive practices. In what follows, however, I focus on analyzing, comparing, and evaluating their attempts to provide philosophical frameworks to justify and guide such activism. Although initially attracted to deep ecology, I have learned much from social ecology and ecofeminism. Hence, my intention is to offer an equitable reading of all three branches of radical ecology, though I acknowledge that my reading will inevitably be colored by my own perspectives. Let me begin by briefly sketching some of the basic concerns of each.

Deep ecology explains the ecological crisis as the outcome of the anthropocentric humanism that is central to the leading ideologies of modernity, including liberal capitalism and Marxism. Hoping to free humankind from material deprivation by controlling nature, modern societies tend to overlook the fact that humans, too, are part of nature. Hence, attempts to gain control of nature have also led to attempts to control human behavior in ways that limit freedom and prevent "self-realization." In general, deep ecologists call for a shift away from anthropocentric humanism toward an ecocentrism guided by the norm of self-realization for all beings.

Social ecology explains the ecological crisis as the outcome not of a generalized anthropocentrism, but rather as the result of authoritarian social structures, embodied most perniciously in capitalism but also present in state socialism. Wanton destruction of nature reflects the distorted social relations at work in hierarchical systems, in which elites subjugate other people while pillaging the natural world for prestige, profit, and control. Maintaining that humans *are* nature rendered self-conscious, social ecologists call for small-scale, egalitarian, anarchistic societies, which recognize that human well-being is inextricably bound up with the well-being of the natural world on which human life depends.

Finally, ecofeminists often explain the ecological crisis as the outcome of the patriarchy that follows the "logic of domination." According to this logic, whatever is defined as superior to something else is entitled to use the "inferior" thing in any manner the superior so chooses. Under patriarchy, maleness, rationality, spirit, and culture have been regarded as superior, whereas femaleness, emotion, body, and nature have been regarded as inferior. Members of the allegedly "superior" gender, males, have traditionally felt justified not only in subjugating women, but also in abusing nature. The logic of domination also works by forcing the "other" to conform to the categories that define the masculine, patriarchal subject. Wild nature, then, like "headstrong" women, must be tamed, ordered, and otherwise rendered pliant to masculine will. According to ecofeminists, only dismantling patriarchy will free human relations and nature alike from the dark consequences of the logic of domination.

Despite a number of internal disputes, all radical ecologists attempt to distinguish themselves from "reform environmentalists," who seek to curb industrial pollution and to use natural resources more wisely, but who do not call for basic alterations in modernity's instrumentalist view of nature. Radical ecologists insist, however, that unless far-reaching changes *do* occur in this and related views, as well as in authoritarian political and socioeconomic arrangements associated with them, modernity's attempt to gain wealth and security through technological control over nature could trigger off ecological catastrophes capable of destroying humankind and much of the rest of terrestrial life. Rejected twenty years ago by mainstream society, some of the claims of radical ecologists are being examined more carefully by a number of contemporary economists, scientists, and politicians, who concede that ecological problems cannot be solved simply by tinkering with the attitudes and practices that generated those problems.

The task of analyzing, comparing, and evaluating these three types of radical ecology has proved to be more complex than I thought it would several years ago, when I first envisioned writing a book on this topic. Let me explain by referring to my own personal and intellectual path to one branch of radical ecology, deep ecology. Like many students during the 1960s, I vilified industrialism and other aspects of the modernity that I held responsible both for ecological violence, and for personal alienation and social disintegration. At the same time that I admired the apparently simpler and more satisfying life of premodern peoples, however, I internalized many of modernity's emancipatory goals, a fact that led me to support the civil rights movements of the 1960s and 1970s. The counterculture of this period reflected my own ambiguous attitude toward modernity. On the one hand, counterculturalists condemned the dark consequences of modernity, including urban alienation, a control-obsessed technological culture, widespread social violence, and ecological destruction. On the other hand, counterculturalists often used their own version of modernity's rhetoric of freedom, emancipation, and self-determination. Hence, despite their "back to nature" tendencies, exemplified by experiments with countryside communes, and despite their critique of many features of modernity, many counterculturalists understood themselves far less as politically conservative than as progressive, in the sense that they envisioned the advent of a "new age," characterized by dramatic improvements in personal, political, ecological, and spiritual conditions. Counterculturalists, however, believed that this new era could not arise in the context of modernity's dualistic, control-oriented, hyperrational outlook, but instead would require insights and practices drawn from premodern tribal peoples, from the world's wisdom traditions, from contemporary visionaries attuned to the complex relations between humankind and nature, and from the best of modernity's democratic traditions. The radical ecological movement, in which I began taking part in the 1970s, is an offshoot of the counterculture; hence, radical ecologists criticize *some* aspects of modernity, while appropriating and transforming *other* elements of its emancipatory vision.

It was during the time that I was adopting the counterculture's ambiguous attitude toward modernity that I encountered the writings of Martin Heidegger. Attracted to his critique of technological modernity's diminishment of humankind and destruction of nature, I was also drawn to his idea of a "new beginning" that would renew human existence in a way that would also halt humanity's baleful treatment of nature. In the mid-1970s, I began interpreting Heidegger as a forerunner of deep ecology.[1] Like his former student, Herbert Marcuse, I read Heidegger as a sophisticated counterculturalist whose views could somehow be reconciled with my own hopes for a politically and socially liberated, but ecologically sound society.[2] My original plans for a book on radical ecology, with special emphasis on a Heideggerian deep ecology, began to change in the late 1980s, however, when Victor Farias and Hugo Ott disclosed that Heidegger's life and thought were far more involved with National Socialism than I had previously believed.[3] In 1933, Heidegger viewed Hitler's revolution as constituting the "new dawn" that would make possible a "complete transformation" of human existence. What had long seemed apparent to the promodernity critics of Heidegger now became clear to me. Because he used rhetoric consistent with the antimodernist, antidemocratic, antiegalitarian rhetoric of Nazism, Heidegger could not be understood, as I had thought, as a progressive thinker. In view of these disturbing revelations about the link between Heidegger's thought and his politics, I came to write two books, in which I reexamine in an interrelated way my attitude both toward modernity and toward movements, such as radical ecology, which sharply criticize aspects of modernity.

The first of these two books is *Heidegger's Confrontation with Modernity*.[4] In this text and in the one that follows it, I define "modernity" as the socioeconomic arrangements legitimated by political ideologies arising from the European Enlightenment, including Marxism and liberal capitalism. Insofar as they criticize authoritarian social structures and promote egalitarian doctrines, Marxism and liberalism are both progressive ideologies, despite important differences. Heidegger's critique of such modernity and the technology accompanying it was, I came to see, one voice in a cultural conversation in which Spengler, Jünger, and other "conservative revolutionaries" took part. Rejecting the progressive interpretation of history offered by proponents of Enlightenment modernity, including Hegel and Marx, these Nietzsche-influenced authors maintained that history lacked any direction. Rather, history for them was simply a series of temporary power constellations that could best be appreciated as aesthetic phenomena with no hidden "meaning" or "purpose." Significant features of such Nietzscheanism, including a kind of "antihumanism," are discernible in Heidegger's radical critique of modern concepts of truth, subjectivity, freedom, and history.

Elements of this critique appear in the work of a group of contemporary French philosophers, such as Jacques Derrida and Michel Foucault, whom I call "postmodern theorists."[5] Postmodern theorists reject the totalitarianism that they associate with modernity, while emphasizing political pluralism and cultural difference. Yet these theorists do not always seem to appreciate the extent to which adopting Heidegger's blanket critique of modernity can lead to dangerous political positions.[6] In *Heidegger's Confrontation with Mo-*

dernity, I thus had a double intention. Although acknowledging the importance of postmodern theory's critique of modernity's totalizing ideologies that cannot tolerate uncertainty, ambiguity, difference, and otherness, I also warn of the reactionary potential of a postmodern theory that completely rejects modernity, especially its positive emancipatory goals.

If the first book examines Heidegger's thought in terms of the complex promodernity versus antimodernity dispute, the present work—now before you—analyzes radical ecology in terms of that dispute. Having once read Heidegger's thought as partly compatible with deep ecology, I now ask whether deep ecology in particular and radical ecology *in general* are in fact compatible with a reactionary type of antimodernism. Defenders of the progressive project of modernity, including Marxists and liberal democrats, have answered this question affirmatively. They contend that the mood of radical ecologists and many other counterculturalists recalls the cultural despair and loss of nerve that helped to pave the way for the dismal "new age" of National Socialism. Progressive theorists suspect that radical ecology's critique of modernity's aim of conquering nature must go hand in hand with reactionary, antidemocratic views that propose to justify authoritarian measures to solve an allegedly universal ecological crisis. Because Nazi racism linked the "blood purity" of the *Volk* to a healthy natural environment, an entire generation had to pass after World War II before environmental movements could gain prominence in Western countries.

Denying such oppressive aims, many radical ecologists envision the emergence of nonauthoritarian, nonoppressive, nonhierarchical, "postmodern" societies in which free, playful, decentered, heterogeneous people live in small, bioregionally oriented, technically efficient, democratic, ecologically sound communities.[7] Realizing this vision, which is undeniably attractive to many contemporary people, would require an enormous shift in contemporary attitudes, practices, and institutions. My increased understanding of the link between Heidegger's thought and his politics, however, along with my study of postmodern theory after Heidegger, have led me to be more skeptical of grand proposals for revolutionary change, including those based on fears of an ecological crisis. Many radical ecologists have charged that this crisis arises from modernity's obsession with control and power. But since they themselves were raised within and are thus inevitably influenced by modernity, questions arise as to whether they are sufficiently free from this control obsession, and whether—in attempting to save nature from further destruction—they will repeat the errors that undermined modernity's positive emancipatory aims and led to such ecological destruction.

Because "nature" and the "natural" are to such a large extent socially mediated, threats to nature can be (and, in fact, have been) interpreted by unscrupulous people to mean that "unnatural" outsiders are threatening cultural, political, and socioeconomic arrangements that are supposedly "natural," but which in fact are historically constituted, and often authoritarian and exploitative. In stressful times, people are all too willing to surrender to leaders promising to end humanity's alienation from nature. Hence, one aim of this book is to encourage radical ecologists to take into account not only the political dangers facing every revolutionary movement, but also the specific dangers posed by movements seeking to improve humanity's relation to "nature." A related aim is to examine the extent to which the views of radical ecologists are consistent with emancipatory political orientations, the definitions and even the possibility of which are themselves hotly contested questions.

Although taking seriously the political risks of radical ecology's critique of modernity and its attitude to nature, I nonetheless explore ways in which radical ecology's yearning for a "postmodern" ecological age can be read as being somehow in accord with an emancipatory, progressive vision. Denying that their aims are either totalitarian or reactionary, radical ecologists usefully reveal the social and ecological wrongs committed in the name of progressive modern worldviews. Many radical ecologists believe that the ecological crisis stems from the fact that modernity's proponents have simply assumed that human emancipation and well-being can be achieved only by somehow "mastering" the natural world. Here, I join radical ecologists in arguing that this idea is both nonsensical and self-defeating, since humankind itself is not merely a historical being, but arises through, participates in, and depends on natural processes.

Though they agree with postmodern theory's critique of modernity's totalizing control obsession, many radical ecologists are also like progressive critics in suspecting that postmodern theory can be neoconservative, since it renounces the possibility of a general critique of the conditions generating social and ecological problems.[8] One progressive critic, for instance, asks whether it is any accident that, at the very moment in which capitalism is transforming the planet into a homogenized production unit, many postmodern theorists encourage students "to reject global and universal narratives in favor of fragmentary conceptions of the world as 'text'."[9] Postmodern theorists reply, however, that their work criticizes oppression and encourages freedom, even if the latter can be both construed and achieved only in limited ways and then under particular circumstances.[10] Moreover, postmodern theorists, along with some radical ecologists influenced by postmodern theory, remain skeptical of large-scale, radical ecological narratives that are reminiscent of the metaphysical foundationalism characteristic of modern ideologies and their countercultural cousins. According to these skeptics, yearning for a new age in which social antagonism and humanity-nature dualism will finally be overcome may in fact lead to new forms of social oppression that may also, paradoxically, *worsen* the ecological situation.

To facilitate my analysis of radical ecology in terms of the complex dispute between modernists and antimodernists, progressives and postmodernists, I focus on how deep ecology is contested, in different respects, by social ecology and by ecofeminism. In part because of my attempts to link Heidegger and deep ecology, many social ecologists have come to maintain that the latter's critique of anthropocentrism tends to promote an "ecofascism," that is, an authoritarian antihumanism wrapped in ecological garb. Hence, social ecologists maintain that deep ecology should be excluded from the ranks of radical ecology, especially if the latter term has anything to do with human emancipation. Attempting now to mediate the dispute between deep ecology and social ecology, I want to explore whether the former's ideal of "self-realization" for all beings can be regarded as consistent with an expanded and transformed version of modernity's emancipatory aims.

If social ecologists consider deep ecology as dangerously anti-modernist, many ecofeminists believe that deep ecology remains promodernist, though in a way that fails to nurture true liberation. Since feminism has played such an important role in postmodern theory's critique of the *patriarchal* dimension of modernity, it should come as no surprise that ecofeminists have complained that male deep ecologists are blind to the masculine bias inscribed into their supposedly universal ideal of "self-realization." In 1984, eco-feminist Ariel Kay Salleh published a stinging critique of deep ecology.[11] According to Salleh, the sincere efforts of deep ecologists like Arne Naess, Bill Devall, and George Sessions were compromised by their masculinist blindness to the connection between patriarchy and the domination of nature. Convinced that ecofeminism's critique of deep ecology merited serious consideration, but hoping to avert a crippling factionalism within the ranks of radical ecology, I wrote essays seeking common ground in the dispute between deep ecology and ecofeminism.[12] In what follows, I explore this dispute in more detail.

Many ecofeminists agree with deep ecology's critique of modernity's oppression of many women and men, and its destructive treatment of nature, but they disagree with deep ecology's contention that humanity-nature dualism can be overcome by a process of "wider identification," which I read as a progressive dimension of deep ecology. Deep ecologists maintain that today nature is treated almost exclusively instrumentally because modern people often regard nature as radically other than or separate from themselves. People who allow their sense of "self" to expand, so as to include other people as well as animals, plants, and ecosystems, achieve a wider sense of identity. Such wider identification presumably allows people spontaneously to care for animals, plants, and ecosystems, instead of treating them either indifferently or as mere commodities. Yet ecofeminists read "wider identification" not as a progressive concept, but rather as both the self-expansion of the modern masculinist ego, and as the echo of patriarchal modernity's totalizing attitude that seeks to erase difference in order to attain a problematic unity. Although deep ecologists concede that patriarchy has justified vast social and ecological destruction, they reply that freeing society from patriarchy would not necessarily end attempts to dominate nature, for such attempts are manifestations of a general anthropocentric humanism.[13]

My attempt to interpret deep ecology's ideal of self-realization in progressive terms will be met with skepticism not only by most social ecologists, who view deep ecology as a reactionary movement, and not only by many ecofeminists, who view deep ecology as unwitting patriarchal modernists, but also by some deep ecologists themselves, for whom the idea of "progress" is tainted with modernity's Promethean ideals. To be sure, some radical ecologists offer a more nuanced critique of modernity, for they are cognizant of the perils of a wholesale condemnation of it. Others, however, seem to agree with those postmodern theorists who assert that modernity's supposedly emancipatory, universally valid narratives turned out to be simply power motivated, Eurocentric stories that justified social horrors ranging from concentration camps to Third World colonization. For such theorists, as one critic notes, modernity is solely "the termination of a terrible mistake, a collective madness, a relentless compulsion, a deadly illusion."[14]

As one might expect, many progressive theorists repudiate postmodern theory's critical analysis of modernity. Indeed, some of them regard "postmodern theory," "postmodernism," and "postmodernity" as virtually meaningless terms, since such terms refer to a host of apparently conflicting phenomena. Other critics regard postmodernism as a concept that fails to understand how capitalism remains responsible for many of the cultural changes to which postmodern theorists often point as evidence of the end of modernity.[15] In spite of my appreciation for such objections, I nonetheless believe that "modern" times *are* undergoing significant change, not least because the ecological crisis constitutes a potentially insurmountable obstacle to modernity's dream of infinite material growth. The words "postmodern" and "postmodernity" are often used to refer to the complex social and cultural permutations that are now occurring. In this essay, I use "postmodernity" specifically to refer to the unstable contemporary situation in which many modern socioeconomic structures remain in place, but in which modernity's progressive ideologies and many of its basic assumptions are being challenged from a number of different angles.[16]

For example, in addition to the fact that many people now question modernity's assumptions that incessant economic growth is both possible and desirable, other significant events are taking place: Third World peoples are challenging Eurocentric historical teleology; the relentlessly self-critical character of modern theorizing is undermining assumptions about rational foundations and metaphysical foundationalism; those for whom truth is a perspectival, power-oriented affair are questioning assumptions about "objective" or "eternal" truth; and those who emphasize the relational, decentered, and heterogeneous character of human "identity" are questioning the primacy of the centered, self-controlled, patriarchal ego.[17] Concomitant with such challenges are the questions that postmodern theorists are raising about the relationship between representation and "reality."[18] In describing modernity's major ideologies as "grand narratives," postmodern theorists such as Jean-François Lyotard have emphasized that those ideologies are not statements representing or corresponding to an absolute truth, but are rather akin to literary fictions or to artistic constructions, whose validity is measured by their efficacy and durability, not by their alleged "correspondence" to an independently existing "reality."

Yet in spite of the trenchant critiques offered by postmodernists of various stripes, many radical ecologists refuse either to abandon their own broad narratives, or to concede that those narratives are simply useful fictions that express nothing "true" about humankind, nature, and their appropriate interrelationship. In these respects, these radical ecologists often have more in common with what I am calling *counterculturalism* than with postmodern theory. I define "counterculturalism" broadly to include not only the New Age movement of the 1970s and the New Paradigm movement of the 1980s, but also the worldwide Green movement, of which radical ecology at the broadest level is a manifestation. Despite agreeing with postmodern theory's critique of the dark consequences of modernity's grand narratives, most counterculturalists still persist in exhibiting their own versions of modernity's optimism. Hence, for example, many counterculturalists believe that humankind is evolving to a "higher" consciousness that will mitigate not only personal problems, but social and ecological problems as well. Some counterculturalists articulate their evolutionary narratives in terms drawn from sources that most modernists would regard as "irrational" and "mystical." Yet other counterculturalists seek to ground their views just as proponents of modernity have so often done: by appealing to the findings of contemporary science, especially the increasingly popular view that, despite important regularities, natural events involve an inherently unpredictable dimension that makes possible novelty, spontaneity, and even "freedom."

Although apparently offering a new way of explaining the possibility of freedom—an ideal defined somewhat differently by radical ecologists, counterculturalists, and modernists—such new scientific theories also pose challenges to radical ecology. For instance, a number of contemporary ecologists appeal to chaos theory in order to contest the once-established view, favored by a number of radical ecologists, that natural systems are "healthy" when "stable" and "ecologically balanced." Rejecting the idea that individual organisms are temporary manifestations of enduring, overarching ecosystems, these new ecologists suggest that such "systems" are merely the unintended results of interactions among countless individual organisms. If natural "order" is best understood as a temporary stabilization of processes that are primarily chaotic and dynamic, what sense does it make to speak of an ecological balance? For radical ecology, the potential implications of this shift in ecological theory arc important. If in fact there is no such balance, and if natural processes are constantly in flux, why should anyone take seriously radical ecology's warning that the practices of advanced technological societies are throwing nature "out of balance"?

In some ways, chaos theory seems compatible with postmodern theory's critique of modernity's search for a univocal, stable structure that organizes all phenomena. Assuming that there is no such structure, postmodern theory asserts that truth claims are best understood as perspectival, heterogeneous, mutable, and differential. This idea of "truth" also poses certain problems for radical ecology. Of course, many radical ecologists agree that modernity's quest for "totalizing" truth has justified destructive social and ecological projects, and that recognizing the perspectival character of knowledge claims may promote a healthy skepticism regarding ideologies that promise freedom, but which often end up oppressing people and devastating ecosystems. But if truth is merely perspectival, there would seem to be no basis for the assumption made by some radical ecologists that their views involve higher, eternally valid truths about humankind, nature, and their "proper" relationship. If there are no privileged moral, epistemological, or metaphysical perspectives, radical ecologists have no choice but to enter into a *contest* to determine which of many competing views will shape the future of human society and the living Earth.

A number of ecofeminists take postmodern theory's perspectival view of truth more seriously than do either deep ecologists or social ecologists. Hence, as we noted earlier, many ecofeminists contend that deep ecologists and some social ecologists promote ideas that are supposedly universal, but which in fact reflect the attitudes of white, Western males. But other ecofeminists make a more general claim: that ecological destruction and social domination are manifestations of the power interests of patriarchal "man," who denies his mortality, finitude, and limitation.[19] The idea that man's rage against finitude leads to so many of modernity's problems, including ecological devastation, would appear to be part of a grand narrative claiming to be "true," in the sense of somehow disclosing or corresponding to major features of human history.

Still intrigued by the possibility that some such narratives may not only be useful, but also in some sense true, I explore by way of example the grand narrative offered by the deservedly noted "transpersonal" theorist, Ken Wilber. His narrative of the evolution of human consciousness from prehistoric times to the present is consistent with and can be read as harmonizing important elements of all three branches of radical ecology. Moreover, his narrative also offers a perceptive way of addressing the promodernity-antimodernity debate. According to Wilber, humankind is in the process of evolving beyond the constricted, dualistic mode of "mental-egoic" consciousness celebrated by many proponents of modernity. Denying that post-egoic consciousness involves psychological regression, Wilber defines such consciousness as an advance toward a less dualistic and more integrated, yet also highly differentiated awareness that would be compatible with nonauthoritarian, postpatriarchal, ecologically sane societies. In Wilber's view, achieving such nondual, transpersonal awareness makes possible the affirmation of one's mortality, and thus the cessation of resentment against finitude. Nondual awareness purportedly reveals that one already participates in an eternal domain that simultaneously embraces and transcends spatiotemporal phenomena.

As a progressive thinker, Wilber maintains that modernity is an important phase of human history, in that it represents the fullest development of what he calls mental-egoic subjectivity. Modernity's political ideals and institutions, including the rights of persons, constitutional guarantees of liberty, democratic principles, and egalitarianism, are important achievements that need to be broadly consolidated. Wilber further asserts, however, that criticism of modernity is justified not only because it has helped to generate such social oppression and ecological destruction, but also because neither modern ideologies nor the modern ego subject are "final" stages in human evolution, but instead are temporary moments along the way toward nondualistic, "postmodern" consciousness. Despite their progressive aspirations, neither liberalism nor Marxism can avoid generating social and ecological problems, because both ideologies reflect dualistic, anthropocentric consciousness. According to Wilber, modern humanity's socially violent and ecologically destructive behavior will only diminish when, in the process of evolving to "higher" stages, consciousness reintegrates what it had once dissociated from itself, including nature, corporeality, emotions, and the female.[20]

To be sure, any theory that attempts as much as Wilber's invites criticism. Postmodern theorists, for instance, object to Wilber's evolutionary theory because it is another grand narrative that pretends to say something true about the ultimate meaning of human history. Taking into account such objections, I nevertheless widen my search for conceivably progressive accounts of humanity's future by examining the work of certain theorists whom I call "critical postmodernists." Although they are neither radical ecologists nor transpersonal theorists, these critical postmodernists envision ecologically sustainable, ameliorative futures that may in fact have a greater chance of realization than the futures envisioned either by modernists or by radical ecologists and other counterculturalists. Critical postmodernists are concerned about the perils of naive utopian yearnings and totalizing truth, but retain countercultural hopes that new technological developments, especially when utilized by a less dualistic humankind, will make possible increased political freedom, material satisfaction, and ecological well-being. Unlike proponents of modernity, these theorists believe that it is possible to forego modernity's metaphysical foundationalism and historical teleology, without inevitably lapsing into reactionary politics.

One critical postmodernist, Gus diZerega, maintains that an "evolutionary liberalism," informed by chaos theory, could lead to a technologically advanced, though more harmonious humanity-nature relation. Another, Alexander Argyros, holds that the cybernetic future will bring greater human freedom, though perhaps at the cost of increased risk of ecological calamity. Finally, for Donna Haraway, overcoming humanity-nature dualism would involve adopting "monstrous" new identities, part human, part animal, part machine. Unwilling to concede that the mere "drift" of chaotic social interactions can lead to an ecologically sustainable future, critical postmodernists urge progressive people actively to *contest* wantonly destructive social and ecological practices, while simultaneously avoiding naive primitivisms and antitechnological attitudes.

Supporting modernity's contention that freeing people from illegitimate authority should not be purchased at the cost of wrongfully subjugating other people, critical postmodernists nonetheless question modernity's willingness to "subjugate" nonhuman forms of life. It is because modernists deny to nonhumans the status of subjects that they protest against using terms like "domination" and "exploitation" to describe relations between humans and nonhumans. Presumably, such terms should only apply to practices that may obtain between conscious agents. If nature is in fact inert and insentient, this protest has validity. But if, as many radical ecologists and critical postmodernists suggest, nature is an active, creative, self-organizing process that generates life and self-conscious forms of life, then nonhuman beings (including organisms and perhaps ecosystems as well) *cannot* properly be regarded simply as passive stuff. In critical postmodernism, I discern an intriguing intersection of modernity's emancipatory goals, postmodern theory's decentered subject, and radical ecology's vision of an increasingly nondomineering relationship between humans and nonhumans.

This book examines debates—"contests"—now occurring among a number of different approaches to today's ecological and social problems. The term "contest" often refers to a struggle in which one of the contending parties becomes the "winner," while the others become "losers." Although not pretending that hegemonic aims will soon disappear from political-ideological contests, I wish to highlight an important dimension of "contest" that is often overlooked in the winner-versus-loser, us-versus-them conception of contest. In my view, a contest is most successful if it encourages the best—whatever this may be—in all contenders. In the process of explaining and taking part in the contests among deep ecology, social ecology, and ecofeminism, I have learned a great deal about the limitations and strengths of each of those positions. Likewise, in examining how the dispute between defenders and critics of modernity sheds light on the contest within radical ecology, I have come to a more nuanced appreciation of modernity and postmodernity. In what follows, then, I have tried to avoid simply defending one viewpoint against all contenders; instead, I have sought to provide an adequate, even sympathetic voice for each of them. I do not end by claiming that one position is the overall winner, though the reader should be able to discern where my own (sometimes conflicting) sympathies lie. My analyses are inevitably colored by my own interests and limitations. Were I not concerned about what is happening to life on this planet, for example, I would not write a book on radical ecology. Moreover, were I not concerned about the political dangers of such radical movements, I would not contextualize my account of radical ecology in terms of the political issues raised by the broader modernity–postmodernity debate.

I do not conceive of this book as the product of a solitary intellect propounding "truth," but rather as the tentative expression of ongoing conversations among many different people. Unfortunately, I have not always been able to discuss in detail and sometimes even to mention some of those conversations. But I am now more aware than ever of the extent to which "my" voice is not singular and fixed, but rather multiple, open-ended, and malleable. Although entertaining so many contending perspectives has the virtue of providing a more nuanced and critical understanding of complex affairs, such understanding can also persuade one indefinitely to defer taking action.[21] In these pressing times, however, I feel obliged to act politically, despite the fact that what I choose to do based on one viewpoint will often seem inconsistent with another viewpoint that I also admire. Tolerance for such ambiguity and uncertainty is a prerequisite for taking action in this promising and perilous era.

I invite the reader to enter into the conversation in which this book engages, to contest the claims made herein, and to help negotiate alternative ways of addressing the challenges facing the human and nonhuman world at the beginning of a new century.

1 ▪ DEEP ECOLOGY'S WIDER IDENTIFICATION WITH NATURE

Though sometimes sounding like contemporary Jeremiahs, proclaiming to a wayward humankind the spiritually devastating and
potentially suicidal consequences of practices that are destabilizing
the ecosphere and threatening millions of species (possibly including
humankind) with extinction, deep ecologists offer a positive message:
humankind can become more integrated and mature, thus outgrow-
ing the fearful posture that leads to such aggressive treatment of nature. In celebrating and protecting Earth's life community, of which
humanity is but a part, people would fulfill themselves and thus serve
their own best interests. Seeking to protect all life, which they regard
as inherently valuable, deep ecologists also stress that ecological
devastation diminishes the human spirit.[1] Freely conceding that there
is nothing new about the idea that human fulfillment requires aligning oneself with cosmic laws transcending human control, deep
ecologists claim to be drawing upon a variety of sources including:
the science of ecology, Asian religions, the perennial philosophy,
leading Western philosophers (including Spinoza, Heidegger, and
Whitehead), Norwegian and American naturalism and pastoralism,
countercultural ideals, creation-centered spirituality, and the practices and attitudes of primal peoples (especially Native Americans).[2]

Though some postmodern theorists might praise deep ecology's pluralism as a sign both of its commitment to diversity and of its rejection of modernity's disastrous quest for certainty, others would argue that deep ecology exports unrelated ideas from their original contexts and forces them into a unified conceptual scheme. Deep ecology's eclecticism might seem similar to the pastiche style of postmodern architects who—influenced by electronic media that have made virtually every historical tradition available for consumption—ransack the building styles of previous epochs for new vocabulary in order to add historical "density," playfulness, and irony to their structures. Leading deep ecologist, Arne Naess, however, celebrates cultural and intellectual pluralism both as an end in itself and because it strengthens the deep ecology movement, defined in terms of the Deep Ecology Platform (DEP) that was devised by Naess and George Sessions in 1984. Seeking to be as inclusive as possible, the DEP is stated in terms sufficiently general that people from many different religious and philosophical traditions—such as Christianity, Buddhism, Spinozism—can join the deep ecology movement. Hence, Naess emphasizes the distinction between deep ecology as a dynamic *social movement* guided by the DEP and his own explicit *philosophical worldview*, Ecosophy T.[3] Echoing postmodern theory's concern about totalizing narratives, Naess asks: "Why *Gleichschaltung?* Why monolithic ideologies? We have had enough of those in both European and world history."[4] Preferring a pluralism that allows for deep cultural difference, he fears that establishing one philosophy or religion for all humankind would be "a cultural disaster."[5]

Naess describes deep ecology as "deep" in part to contrast it with "shallow" environmentalism, which seeks only to reform certain socioeconomic practices (e.g., curtailing industrial pollution) without altering modernity's anthropocentric attitude, which is held to be largely responsible for the growing ecological crisis. The more important reason for calling deep ecology "deep," then, is that it poses deeper questions about the normative and descriptive premises of modernity.[6] Is the way of life made possible by the norms of anthropocentric modernity truly satisfying? Can one's own well-being be purchased at the expense of that of another, whether that "other" be human or nonhuman? In seeking answers to such questions, Naess believes, people will discover that the norms of technological modernity not only promote biospheric catastrophe, but are also inconsistent with the ultimate norms of many spiritual and philosophical traditions. In light of this discovery, people will call for major changes, both personal and socioeconomic, regarding how humans treat each other and the natural world.[7] Although at the level of ultimate norms many religious and philosophical traditions may be incompatible with one another, few have an ultimate norm compatible with the view that people should devour the planet in an orgy of private gratification.

The primary norm of Naess's Ecosophy T is self-realization. A major hypothesis is that all beings are manifestations of the great Self, Atman: all things are interrelated. Hence, the possibility for self-realization ought not to be restricted to humans alone. Developing a wider sense of identification with all beings is crucial for self-realization. Deep ecologist Warwick Fox observes correctly that most deep ecology theorists adhere to some version of Ecosophy T.[8] Further, he argues that wider identification is linked to nondualism, the insight that there is no ultimate divide between things. Nondualism is central not only to Ecosophy T, but also to the above-mentioned diverse traditions to which it appeals for support. Although Naess wants to distinguish between Ecosophy T and the DEP-guided deep ecology movement, Fox maintains that the DEP is so general that it conceals what is *distinctive* about deep ecology: the norm of self-realization, which is to be achieved through nondualistic wider identification. As we see later on, Fox recommends that deep ecologists change the name of their shared philosophy to reflect its distinctive approach, while letting "deep ecology" refer to the social movement guided by the DEP.

Since most deep ecology expositors share some variation of Ecosophy T, however, most people simply *identify* Ecosophy T with deep ecology. For this reason, many ecofeminists and social ecologists neither embrace the DEP, nor call themselves deep ecologists, despite Naess' efforts to distinguish between deep ecology, a *collective* term for all movements capable of agreeing with the DEP, and Ecosophy

T, a name for a *specific type* of ecosophy that justifies adhering to the DEP. In what follows, I use the term "deep ecology movement" to refer to the movement that includes all supporters of the DEP; and I use "deep ecology" and "deep ecologists" to refer to Ecosophy T and its supporters. My account of deep ecology inevitably conflates some issues and blurs certain distinctions that are important to various deep ecology theorists. I ask their forbearance, just as I ask for the forbearance of social ecologists and ecofeminists in later chapters.

This chapter begins by examining the DEP. The second section analyzes the distinction between deep ecology and reform environmentalism. And the third section considers in more detail Ecosophy T, the leading version of deep ecology theory. Finally, the last section considers Fox's suggestion that deep ecology change its name to "transpersonal ecology," to reflect what is intellectually distinctive about deep ecology theory.

THE DEEP ECOLOGY PLATFORM   Naess uses a four-level "apron chart" to model the process by which, beginning with ultimate norms, one may loosely derive increasingly more particular principles and recommendations for treating all life in a respectful manner. Such ultimate norms, and the principles and attitudes derived from them, constitute an ecosophy, that is, a total ecological worldview, which is useful in guiding decision-making in a complex world. Most deep ecologists assert that the DEP—whose position in deep ecology's conceptual scheme is visible on the apron diagram—provides common ground for people with diverse backgrounds.[9] Almost as important are deep questioning, which helps to disclose ultimate norms, and derivational processes—represented by the apron diagram—which help both to develop and to show the applicability of one's own ecosophy.

The first level of the apron chart represents one's own ultimate norms, which may be drawn from various religious or philosophical traditions, and which should also express one's own intuitions about the inherent worth of all life. The DEP, the second level of the chart, is loosely derivable from those ultimate norms. The third level concerns general consequences derivable from the DEP, including

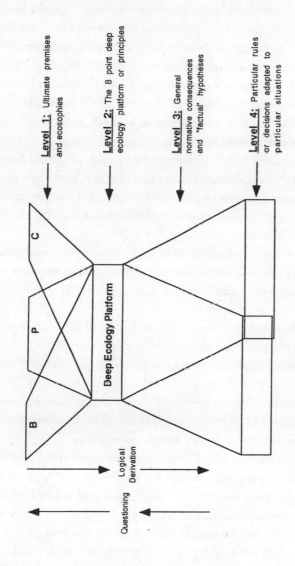

APRON DIAGRAM

Level 1: Ultimate premises and ecosophies

Level 2: The 8 point deep ecology platform or principles

Level 3: General normative consequences and "factual" hypotheses

Level 4: Particular rules or decisions adapted to particular situations

C

P

B

Deep Ecology Platform

Logical Derivation

Questioning

Examples of kinds of fundamental premises:
B = Buddhist
C = Christian
P = Philosophical (e.g. Spinozist or Whiteheadian)

broad policies. The fourth and most concrete level concerns specific ways to implement such policies. The direction of flow of the apron chart is both top-down and bottom-up. Starting from the bottom in the domain of the concrete practices of everyday life, one begins a process of questioning that leads toward ultimate premises and norms. Starting from such norms, at the top of the chart, one works one's way down, loosely deriving the DEP, along with general and specific recommendations. The diagram needs some clarification, however. For example, the difference between levels three and four is not altogether clear, nor is the process of "loose derivation" by which one moves from ultimate norms to the DEP and beyond.[10]

The DEP itself has eight planks. The first three are the most general norms and hypotheses, whereas the final five paragraphs are hypotheses and norms "loosely derived" from the first three. The eight principles are:

1. The well-being and flourishing of human and nonhuman life have value in themselves (synonyms: intrinsic value, inherent worth). These values are independent of the usefulness of the nonhuman world for human purposes.

2. Richness and diversity of life forms contribute to the realization of these values and are also values in themselves.

3. Humans have no right to reduce this richness and diversity except to satisfy vital needs.

4. The flourishing of human life and cultures is compatible with a substantially small human population. The flourishing of nonhuman life *requires* a smaller human population.

5. Present human interference with the nonhuman world is excessive, and the situation is rapidly worsening.

6. Policies must therefore be changed. These policies affect basic economic, technological, and ideological structures. The resulting state of affairs will be deeply different from the present.

7. The ideological change will be mainly that of appreciating life quality (dwelling in situations of inherent value) rather than adhering to an increasingly higher standard of living. There will be a profound awareness of the difference between bigness and greatness.

8. Those who subscribe to the foregoing points have an obligation directly or indirectly to try to implement the necessary changes.[11]

Though the DEP is supposedly consistent with different ultimate norms, the DEP may be read as having significant parallels with Ecosophy T. Supporting, in effect, the contention that Ecosophy T—not the DEP derived from it—is what is distinctive about deep ecology, one critic notes that the DEP's first paragraph, which speaks of the "flourishing" of all beings, is consistent with Ecosophy T's ultimate norm: self-realization for all beings.[12] If the DEP is in fact a shorthand version of Ecosophy T, this helps explain why the DEP, originally presented as "revisable," has assumed a more authoritative status among most deep ecology theorists. The increasingly fixed status of the DEP leads some radical ecologists to view it as the expression of a few like-minded eco-philosophers, concerned less with an open contest of views and more with promulgating their own ideas.

Concerning the first paragraph of the DEP, Naess comments that all life is bound together by "all-pervasive intimate relationships." "Life" refers not only to humans and other organisms, but also to "rivers, landscapes, ecosystems."[13] Because life is defined so broadly, and because all life-forms are said to have value in themselves, nothing can be regarded solely instrumentally: everything deserves respect. Hence, "ecological processes on the planet should, on the whole, remain intact."[14] The second paragraph notes that diversity and richness not only contribute to the realization of life-values, but have "value in themselves." Hence, the DEP opposes monoculture in farming and homogeneity in culture. Complexity and symbiosis, at work in the extraordinary web of relationships constituting the soil of old growth forests, foster greater diversity, which is a good in itself. Microbes, bacteria, tiny insects, and other "lower" forms of life are *not* less valuable than higher forms, though other life-forms may be more complex and in various ways richer. Praising the work of conservation biologists Michael Soulé and Edward O. Wilson, George Sessions notes that destruction of wildlife habitat and the ensuing mass extinction of species are such portentous phenomena that reputable scientists are forsaking scientific "objectivity" to lobby openly in favor of the claim that humanity *ought* to protect species diversity not only for prudential reasons, but also because biotic diversity is good in itself.[15]

Although deliberately vague, because "vital needs" differ in different circumstances, paragraph three implies that the rampant consumerism of industrial nations does *not* satisfy vital needs. Indeed, such consumerism indicates that people are not realizing authentic needs, for spiritually unsatisfied people try unsuccessfully to fulfill themselves with material goods. Insofar as consumer goods are substitute satisfactions for a sense of connectedness and union, paragraph seven holds that a higher material living standard is not necessarily compatible with "appreciating life quality."

From the fourth paragraph, which hypothesizes that humans *can* flourish with a much smaller population, and that the flourishing of nonhuman life *requires* a smaller human population, and from the fifth paragraph, which makes the factual claim that human interference is seriously damaging the nonhuman world, the DEP concludes that major social policy changes are needed. Further, human population must be decreased to protect wildlife habitat and to allow room for speciation.[16] Done humanely, as deep ecologists insist, reducing population to a desirable level—numbers ranging in the one billion range have been mentioned—might take up to one thousand years. On occasion, Naess has suggested that the planet be zoned into three different regions. The first would be areas that are now densely populated by humans; the second would have a limited population, perhaps engaged in relatively nonintrusive forms of agriculture; the third would be allowed to return to its wild state and would be inhabited primarily, though not exclusively, by nonhuman beings.

Although population reduction in First World countries is crucial, because their citizens consume vastly disproportionate amounts of Earth's resources, population reduction is also important in Third World countries where remaining rainforests are being cut down by ever-growing numbers of poverty-stricken people. For the poor, numerous children are a form of old-age insurance. Deep ecologists generally favor economic development and education, since these often lower birthrates, but they urge that such development occur without creating further ecological problems and especially without destroying more wildlife habitat.[17] Talk of population control and reduction has provoked objections from some ecofeminists and social ecologists, for whom it smacks of racism, shows a lack of understanding of the role played by First World countries in the "population bomb," and reveals the same mentality of domination responsible for the ecological crisis. In reply, deep ecologists emphasize that they do acknowledge the social roots of poverty, and that they call for a reduction of human population over the long run, according to methods that are both humane and just. They agree, however, with those professional ecologists who assert that unless current human population growth is curbed, the results may include not only the loss of remaining wildlife habitat, but also the deaths of billions of people by disease, starvation, and war.

On the basis of principles three and four, which emphasize the intrinsic value of diversity in nonhuman life and in human culture, and from principle seven, which emphasizes life quality, some deep ecologists look favorably upon bioregionalism, though this is *not* a logical outcome of the DEP. Bioregionalism maintains that a culture is most healthy when its practices, myths, and norms are tied up with the natural character of the culture's geographical region. Because bioregional cultures would presumably be concerned with the flourishing of all life in the region, not just with human life, concern about short-term profit would be replaced by concern with long-term issues, ranging from protecting wild areas to developing ecologically compatible agriculture and manufacture. Personal satisfaction would follow from more profound personal relationships and self-expression within the context of a life-celebrating culture. Global consumerism would give way to widely differentiated cultures, as people from different regions take direct action to protect the planet from further devastation. There are clear parallels between these ideas and postmodern theory's celebration of cultural diversity.

Direct action can take two forms: personal and political. The latter can involve anything from lobbying for new environmental protection legislation, to risking life and limb to protect old-growth forests from being clear-cut. Personal direct action includes bringing one's lifestyle into conformity with one's deep ecological attitudes. A true believer could condemn people for failing to conform to an ecologically correct lifestyle. Hence, Naess—concerned as usual to forestall orthodoxy—cautions that in developing criteria for a deep ecology lifestyle, "one should not look for 'complete consistency,' whatever that would mean. Every formulation would have to be vague and highly dependent upon technological idiosyncrasies."[18]

Some of the countercultural lifestyle changes recommended by Naess include: choice of simple over complex means; avoidance of activities without intrinsic value or far from basic goals; hence, anticonsumerism; appreciation of cultural differences; concern for improving the situation in Third and Fourth world; affirmation of depth and richness of experience, as opposed to intensity; appreciation of meaningful work over just making a living; cultivation of life in community (*Gemeinschaft*) instead of in society (*Gesellschaft*); satisfaction of vital needs through primary production on a small scale; avoidance of tourism; appreciation of all life-forms, not just those that are beautiful or useful; respect for intrinsic value of life-forms; tendency to protect wild species if their interests come into conflict with pets; concern for protecting local ecosystems; tendency to condemn and to deplore as excessive interference in nature, without simultaneously condemning those responsible for the interference; support for nonviolent direct action when other means fail.

In addition to lifestyle changes, deep ecologists call for structural changes in social, economic, and political institutions. Sessions proposes that the United Nation establish an Environment Council, analogous to the Security Council, which would provide an integrated ecospheric-protection approach to population issues, Third World economic development, and wildlife habitat preservation.[19] Unfortunately, Sessions notes, many Third World countries are now embracing American-style capitalism's gospel of growth, which deep ecologists regard as incompatible with an ecologically sustainable, long-range future. He describes the "new world order" as an "octopus" intertwined with multinational corporations and markets, and lacking any allegiance to any country, "as the working classes of America and the world are now beginning to realize to their dismay."[20]

Naess proposes the following axiom for deep ecological politics: "Long range, local, district, regional, national, and global ecological sustainability is the criterion of ecologically responsible politics as a whole."[21] Though attracted to the Green movement, which links social justice for Third World countries, global disarmament, and ecological concerns, Naess says that accelerating ecological destruction makes it "acceptable to continue fighting ecological unsustainability, whatever the state of affairs may be concerning the other two goals of green societies."[22] Without a viable ecosphere, peace and social justice issues will be irrelevant, for the human species may become extinct. Still, says Naess, humans are our "nearest, in terms of identification with all life, and green parties should include political plans for participation in the fight against world hunger and for basic human dignity."[23] In my view, militarism, colonialism, and poverty are so closely linked to ecological problems that all these issues must be addressed simultaneously.[24] Hence, I agree with Fox that deep ecology is but one of several voices in the overall Green movement.[25] Many Greens share with deep ecologists the conviction that revolutionary social changes, including respect for nonhuman life, requires an "inner change" or personal transformation. Presumably, were such a conversion to occur among sufficient numbers of people in the First World, technological society would shift from reform environmentalism to deep ecology.

DEEP ECOLOGY VERSUS REFORM ENVIRONMENTALISM   In 1972, when he first spoke of shallow versus deep ecology, Naess articulated an old distinction, perhaps best exemplified by the turn-of-the-century quarrel between Gifford Pinchot, first head of the U.S. Forest Service, and John Muir, nature writer and wilderness advocate. Pinchot voiced the aim of shallow or reform environmentalism: to make the most efficient use of natural resources for human ends. Condemning Pinchot's anthropocentric "resource conservationism," Muir helped found the "wilderness preservation" movement, which defends wild nature from mammon-bewitched entrepreneurs. Muir fought many battles, including the famous, though unsuccessful, national campaign to halt plans to dam the river in beautiful Hetch Hetchey Valley, located in Yosemite National Park.[26] Shortly after the death of the heartbroken Muir, world war erupted and eclipsed environmental concerns. During the Great Depression, President Roosevelt supported a wave of conservation efforts to prevent soil erosion, to improve management and productivity of national forests, and to enhance national parks. World War II and the postwar emphasis on economic recovery again pushed environmental concerns to the back burner of the public agenda.

In the 1960s, there rose a new wave of environmentalism, which began to replay the Muir-Pinchot debate. On the one hand, biologist Rachel Carson, in her dramatic bestseller, *Silent Spring*, revitalized the wilderness preservation movement and opened the way for the radical ecology movement by warning that widespread use of DDT was killing birds and other wildlife (hence, the "silent" spring). On the other hand, authors like Barry Commoner and Ralph Nader conceived of environmentalism primarily as the struggle against industrial pollution and other threats to *human* health. These "man-centered," antipollution reformers had little sympathy with "nature-lovers" like Carson, Gary Snyder, and David Brower, who emphasized that human population growth and industrialism threatened not only humankind, but wild nature as well.[27]

Responding to public alarm about environmental deterioration, the U.S. Congress passed the Clean Air and Clean Water acts in the early 1970s. By also passing the Endangered Species Act and laws to protect wilderness areas from development, Congress gave a nod to deeper ecological concerns. In 1980, with the election of President Reagan, federal commitment to environmental concerns declined, but membership in mainstream environmental groups soared. In the mid-1980s, with scientists warning of global ecological calamity, some political leaders, including then-Senator Albert Gore, began trying to shift the focus of public debate from pollution control to ecosystem protection.[28] Some deep ecologists suspect, however, that in using the language of politicians and experts, one fails to "think with a heart" and thus helps the system continue its deadly work.[29] Christopher Manes warns that by working from *within* to reform the technological system, one allows that system to continue its deadly work. At the end of the Reagan administration, feeling seduced and stymied by the system, Dave Foreman resigned his position as Washington lobbyist for a national environmental group, and cofounded a leading radical ecology group, Earth First!, whose slogan reads "No Compromise in Defense of Mother Earth!" Taking immediate action to save remaining wilderness areas from destruction, Earth First!ers sometimes commit acts of civil disobedience and "ecotage," that is, sabotage of equipment used to cut old-growth forests or otherwise to damage wilderness. To those accusing them of criminal behavior, Earth First!ers, Greenpeace members, and Sea Shepherds reply that the *real* criminals are corporate bosses who insolently order the clear-cutting of old-growth forests or who pollute oceans with toxic wastes.

Though generally agreeing with this assessment and supporting frontline efforts to halt ecological destruction, not all deep ecology theorists would support ecotage. Although ecoactivists maintain that resisting the technological juggernaut allows no time for theorizing, deep ecology theorists insist that critical reflection is crucial for guiding action. Overcoming this simplistic opposition in his own life, Naess has committed acts of civil disobedience against ecological atrocities such as damming a beautiful and ecologically vital Norwegian river, *and* he has written the most important deep ecology literature. Influenced by Gandhi, he insists that nonviolent action is most effective in stirring the conscience of the larger public. To the extent that destroying property is an act of violence, Naess would have reservations about it, though the issues involved here are subtle. In general, it is advisable to distinguish between deep ecology *theory* and its propagandistic *application* by nonphilosophers with little concern for nuanced expression. Failure to make such a distinction has led critics wrongly to link deep ecology theory with racist, sexist, and misanthropic remarks made by a handful of Earth First! activists.

Naess says that reform environmentalism is limited "not due to a weak or unethical philosophy, but due to a lack of explicit concern with ultimate aims, goals, and norms."[30] Guided by such concerns, deep ecology challenges the political, economic, and metaphysical presuppositions of technological modernity. Insofar as the ecological crisis is a crisis of character and culture, reforming existing practices without changing self and culture will not suffice in the long run, since such reforms only address certain symptoms (e.g., health-threatening pollution), and not the *roots* of ecological devastation. George Sessions says that "an ecologically harmonious social paradigm shift is going to require a *total* reorientation of the thrust of Western culture."[31] Maintaining that "progress" purchased at the expense of the natural world is "unequivocal *regress*," Devall and Sessions take "an uncompromising stand against the main thrust of modern, technocratic culture."[32] They call for a spiritual transformation that will give rise to an "ecological sensibility," which will make possible joyful relationships among people and with nonhuman beings. Such relationships will in turn lead to life-enhancing social and political changes. Faced with the inertia of technological modernity, deep ecologists are at times skeptical about making the transition to an ecological society. Naess once wrote that "the most probable course of events is continued devastation of conditions of life on this planet, combined with a powerless upsurge of sorrow and lamentation."[33] But deep ecologists are often more upbeat about the future.[34] Retaining countercultural optimism, they envision the possibility that a mature humankind will generate "a new metaphysics, epistemology, cosmology, and environmental ethics of person/planet."[35]

But critics like Charles Krauthammer, charging deep ecologists with being immature and, worse, with engaging "in earth worship to the point of idolatry," assert that a "sane" environmentalism must be "entirely anthropocentric" and must declare "unashamedly" that "*nature is here to serve man*."[36] Deep ecologists retort that it is usually not "man" in general, but industrial elites who benefit most from ecologically devastating technologies.[37] Further, unless people respect life for its own sake, not merely for its utility, technological civilization will ultimately destroy itself. Some say the choices facing us are limited: either retain the industrialism model and watch the planet die, or hope that model collapses so that the earth may live. David Ehrenfeld asks: "What is the gentlest Gollum [sic]—one that in the final act of self-destruction will take with it merely a finger

of civilization, not the whole body?" His answer: "[G]lobal economic depression, coming soon, without war if that is possible, and
resulting in *a collapse of the present world economic system* and along
with it the collapse of exploitative industry."[38] Though his hope is
that economic collapse would allow earth's ecosystems to recover,
such a social calamity might not foster ecological well-being, but
might well pave the way for authoritarian leaders who would wreak
even greater ecological havoc. Since total economic collapse would
probably trigger off war, starvation, and disease that would kill
hundreds of millions of people, one may detect a hint of misanthropy in the hope that industrial collapse would save life on earth.
Tending to agree with Ehrenfeld that "the true misanthropists are
those who are struggling to hold to the mad course that we are now
pursuing with such relentless enthusiasm and such little heed for the
ultimate cost,"[39] however, many deep ecologists would say that a
measure of human suffering in the short term must be weighed
against the possibility of tremendous long-term suffering if present
practices are not changed. Of course, deep ecologists hope that the
transition to an ecological age will *minimize* suffering for all concerned.[40] Hence, they envision what Theodore Roszak has called the
"*creative* disintegration of industrial society."

Yet friendly critics like Martin W. Lewis argue that in calling for
the end of industrial civilization, deep ecologists "reduce their own
potential bases for political power to ever more minuscule, and
powerless, groups."[41] Similarly, Robert Paehlke holds that real
progress can be made in dealing with ecological problems only by
working *within* existing political arrangements.[42] Despite their own
rhetoric to the contrary, deep ecologists in fact often recommend
working from within to change the system, while simultaneously
working for personal and social transformation. Increasingly, moreover, deep ecological attitudes are being embraced by people who once
scoffed at saving forests for reasons other than prudential ones.
Reformist views may fade into deep ecological views. For example,
anthropocentric reformers want to preserve rainforests because they
are: a *silo* (a source of genetic diversity for medicine agriculture); a

laboratory (for biologists and ecologists); a *gymnasium* (for human recreation and refreshment); a *life-support system* (sustaining the human species); a *cathedral* (a source of religious awe and inspiration); and an *art gallery* (source of aesthetic pleasure).[43] Though the silo and laboratory arguments seem plainly anthropocentric, the life-support, cathedral, and art gallery arguments can be read either in anthropocentric terms or in deep ecological terms. If Earth is viewed as a kind of human spaceship in need of oxygen, one could offer anthropocentric reasons for saving oxygen-producing rainforests. But if Earth is viewed in terms of the Gaia hypothesis, as the self-organizing home for *all* life, and if life itself is intrinsically valuable, one could argue that rainforests should be saved both as ends in themselves and because they help sustain the interconnected web of life.[44]

A similar reading can be given of the view that rainforests are like a cathedral or an art gallery. John Muir's experience of the "sacred" beauty of wild nature *may* share aspects of Pinchot's utilitarianism.[45] Rainforests should be saved, in other words, not because of their intrinsic worth, but because of their religio-aesthetic "use-value." Hence, John Rodman reads "this once world-historical schism [between Pinchot and Muir] as a family quarrel between advocates of two different forms of human use [of nature]—economic and religio-aesthetic."[46] Rodman criticizes aesthetic utilitarianism for two reasons. First, claims about natural beauty are open to dispute, thus making aesthetics an unsatisfactory candidate for revealing nature's *intrinsic* value. Second, European-American aesthetic sensibility, shared by Muir, leads people to save scenic wonders like Yosemite Valley while ignoring the less attractive marshes and brushland that may have greater ecological importance.[47]

Defending Muir, deep ecologists argue that his utilitarian aesthetic appeals are usually found in writings connected with political debates.[48] Elsewhere, he gives voice to his nature mysticism, according to which nature's beauty is not *projected* onto it by the human perceiver, but is an aspect of nature that humans are *capable* of perceiving. That people often experience a healing pleasure in the face of nature's awesome beauty and complexity may mean that they are directly apprehending nature's inherent worth. In saying that appreciating such beauty is important for human well-being, Muir anticipated other instrumentalist-sounding arguments advanced by deep ecology sympathizers like Paul Shepard and Edward O. Wilson, who maintain that the human psyche *needs* wild nature.[49] Deep ecologists stress that all life is to be protected not only because of its instrumental value, but also because it has a worth of its own.

Although useful in some ways, the reform versus deep ecology distinction seems inconsistent with deep ecology's nondualism and often generates needless controversies between deep ecologists and reformists.[50] Furthermore, deep ecology's anti-anthropocentrism has encouraged the rise of radically anthropocentric groups, such as the "Wise-Use Movement," which condemns deep ecology as a pagan ecofascism that calls for outright appropriation of private land. Insisting that national security rests on easy access to natural resources, Wise-Use members call for dismantling legislation that established wilderness areas and forbade practices such mining in national parks.[51] Further, as Earth Firstlers have aggressively defended wilderness areas, opposing groups—such as the "Sahara Club"—have aggressively defended *their* right to motorcycle wherever they please. Despite such countermovements, the corporate and political mainstream is beginning to take ecological issues into account in a way that would have been unimaginable twenty years ago. For instance, the idea of sustainable development, though it admits of widely varying definitions, has become a buzzword at high levels of corporate society.[52] Many radical ecologists fear, however, that so-called sustainable development will simply slow the rate at which wildlife habitat is destroyed and general environmental quality is degraded.

Some ecological reformists maintain, however, that liberal democracy is flexible enough to further economic growth in an environmentally sustainable fashion. "Free market environmentalists" argue that new forms of property rights can help alleviate many ecological problems.[53] Scarcity of desirable natural resources will raise prices to the level that ecologically sounder alternatives will become economically attractive. And increased costs associated with safe disposal of toxic products will create a demand for innovations that minimize environmental problems, while sustaining or even enhancing productivity. Although Bill Devall states that "privatization of some aspects of land can further the long-term environmental quality of the land, if the stewards of the land respect its integrity,"[54] he also notes that the privatizing approach defines the value of nonhuman according to *human* interests, even if such interests include having unspoiled land in which to hike. Free market environmentalism's problem-solving approach also conceals the fact that many of yesterday's "solutions" are today's "problems." In the 1950s, for instance, nuclear-generated electricity was to said to be too cheap to meter. Today, not only is such nuclear-generated electricity very expensive, but the waste stemming from producing it poses perhaps the gravest, humanmade, long-term threat to ecological well-being. Deep ecologists conclude that anthropocentric attitudes must shift if humankind and the rest of the living earth can flourish. According to Ecosophy T, this shift involves attaining a wider identification with the nonhuman.

ECOSOPHY T   According to Naess, deep questioning of basic beliefs may be motivated by the intuition of *identification* with nonhuman beings. For him, this intuition occurred when, as a child playing in the Norwegian fjords, he was struck by the fantastic variety of life forms, particularly tiny, "useless" ones.[55] Though these little organisms were *different* from him, he felt they were not *radically* other. His sense of identification with all life was strengthened when he became a helpless witness to the suffering of an insect.[56] But he emphasizes that

> [S]uch experiences are enough. No definite Buddhist or other cultural phenomena are strictly necessary to start developing the basic attitude expressed, among other ways, by the term the greater Self, and the norm "Self-realization!" This is only to fight the idea that there is something extraordinary and culturally sophisticated involved. Just the ordinary sensitivity of a loving child.[57]

Although seeking to preserve wilderness, Naess also urges that urban parks be maintained, because encounters with birds, squirrels, insects, plants, and other organisms afford the possibility for a life-changing intuition about one's relationship to other life forms.[58] Since one cannot argue for one's intuition, Naess expresses his in terms of an ultimate norm, self-realization, from which he derives an internally consistent total view capable of addressing concrete ecological problems. Trained as an analytic philosopher and influenced by Spinoza's method, he uses a deductive model—complete with numbered axioms and derived theorems—to articulate this total view, Ecosophy T. Though *not* expecting others to use this method, Naess starts with an axiom, that is, the ultimate norm of self-realization, grounded on his own intuition and influenced by Gandhi, among others. In light of this norm, Naess posits three hypotheses that, taken together, form an argument that concludes that self-realization for one requires self-realization for all. On the basis of this conclusion, he posits a new norm: self-realization for all beings. Subsequently, he adds further hypotheses, for example, concerning the sorts of behavior that promote the norm of self-realization of all beings.

Acknowledging recent criticism of the identitarian logic of metaphysical system-builders from Aquinas to Hegel, Naess asserts that Ecosophy T is *not* a modernist system purporting to deduce the purpose of world history—and justifying violence to realize that purpose—but instead is a structured, dovetailed "assemblage of statements, all provisional and tentative."[59] Such an ecosophy, "a philosophy of ecological harmony or equilibrium" helps orient praxis in the face of intricate ecological and social problems.[60] An ecosophy can also "provide a single motivating force for all the activities and movements aimed at saving the planet from human exploitation and domination."[61] Naess calls his total view "Ecosophy T" to emphasize that other possible ecosophies range from "A to Z," the "T" supposedly referring to his mountain hut, Tvergastein ("cross the stones"). Refusing to privilege his ecosophy, and encouraging a Socratic process of critical self-inquiry, he wants to eliminate "absolutisms, arrogance, and 'eternalism' with regard to validity [of basic principles and norms] in time and in social and physical space."[62]

Developing a revisable total view is consistent with Naess's quest to become more mature or integrated. Such integration does not mean becoming isolated or self-encapsulated, but instead means discovering how one is related to and constituted by the larger ecosystemic context.[63] Far from being an impenetrable ego demanding that things conform to his abstract schemes, a mature person is attuned to and prepared to enter into relationships—sometimes contradictory—with many human and nonhuman beings. Such a relational self benefits from a total view, which helps to guide action in the multifarious relationships constituting an ecological community.

Gandhi inspired Naess's conviction that personal fulfillment can only occur in connection with the fulfillment of all beings. Naess cites Gandhi:

I believe in *advaita* (non-duality), I believe in the essential unity of man and, for that matter, of all that lives. Therefore I believe that if one man gains spiritually, the whole world gains with him and, if one man falls, the whole world fails to that extent.[64]

Following Gandhi's assertion that "self-realization" involves attaining "*Muksha*" (liberation) and seeing God "face to face," Naess regards deep ecology not only as a campaign to save wilderness and to protect biodiversity, but also as a movement to liberate humanity from enslaving attitudes and practices.[65] Naess and George Sessions also appeal to Spinoza's thought to support their nonanthropocentrism and nondualism. Combining a concern for human freedom with an interest in modern science, Spinoza viewed humanity in terms of its relation to the cosmos, instead of conceiving of the cosmos as an instrument for human ends.[66] According to Sessions, Spinoza's purpose in philosophizing

is to break free from the bonds of desire and ignorance which captivate and frustrate most men, thus standing in the way of what real happiness is available to them, and to attain a higher Self which is aligned with a correct understanding of God/Nature.[67]

For Spinoza, Nature and God are identical. Since all individuals are modes of the infinite attributes of the one Substance/God/Nature/Being, individuals manifest the attributes, including thought and extension, in ways appropriate to their own being. Combining mystical intuition with scientific insight about the interrelatedness of all things in the rational cosmos, Spinoza contended that human bondage ensues from ignorance about the necessity at work in the interrelated self-manifestation of God/Nature, whereas human freedom arises from intellectual intuition about such necessity. For Spinoza, all things are characterized by *conatus,* the striving for self-preservation. Unlike Hobbes, who conceived of conatus passively, as a fearful struggle for survival, Spinoza conceived of conatus actively, as the joyful process of self-realization. He posited an

inner relation between joy (*laetitia*) and increase of power of realization, and sorrow (*tristitia*) and decrease of power of realization (*potentia*). Joy is not felt *because of* the realization of a potential, but it is part of the very process of its realization.[68]

For Spinoza, true freedom means acting according to and persevering in one's own nature; actively expressing and fulfilling one's essence. The more one acts according to one's own nature, the more one acts from love and generosity and also from the highest level of reason: the wisdom of *amor intellectus Dei.* Revealing that all things are interrelated manifestations of God/Nature, such wisdom inspires compassion for things stymied in their attempts at self-realization. My own self-realization is enhanced by the self-realization of others with whom/which I am internally related.[69] Because exploitation reduces the potential for self-realization on the part of exploited beings, and because it thus reduces my own capacity for self-realization, exploitation is to be avoided.

Naess and Sessions concede that Spinoza had an instrumental attitude toward animals (he considered vegetarians to be naive sentimentalists), though Naess denies that such instrumentalism was integral to Spinoza's thought.[70] Although agreeing that Spinoza did not view humans as privileged or separate from the rest of nature, and that he regarded our noblest emotions and thoughts as "on a par with rainbows and snakes," Yirmiyahu Yovel, however, insists that Spinoza accorded no inherent value to particular entities. In the final analysis, God/Nature is "beyond good and evil." Values are human projections that weigh things in relation to our own desire or conatus. Thus it is *humanity* that evaluates pollution as "bad" and pristine nature as "good." At a more fully actualized level of awareness, where we attain "God's understanding love" (*amor intellectualis Dei*), we may begin saying "yes" to nature (and humankind) not only when it pleases us or serves our interests, but also in all its ambiguity, ugliness, and destructiveness. Further, a growing understanding of the lessons of ecological science may lead us to treat the biosphere better in order to enhance our own striving and also to avoid doing serious harm to ourselves. Yovel, then, supports the view that Spinoza offers an affirmative, but utilitarian, reading of the cosmos, a reading not shared by Naess and Sessions.[71]

The concept of interrelatedness, promoted by deep ecology theorists as an alternative to modernity's atomistic-anthropocentric paradigm, helps to justify Ecosophy T's norm of self-realization.[72] Naess rejects "the man-in-environment" image

in favour of *the relational, total-field image.* Organisms as knots in the biospherical net or field of intrinsic relations. An intrinsic [internal] relation between two things A and B is such that the relation belongs to the definitions or basic constitutions of A and B, so that without the relation, A and B are no longer the same things. The total-field model dissolves not only the man-in-environment concept, but every compact thing-in-milieu concept—except when talking at a superficial or preliminary level of communication.[73]

In line with this total-field image, Australian deep ecologist John Seed intuits that his identity is bound up with the tropical rainforests:

When I realize that I don't have any independent existence, that I am part of a food chain, for instance, then at a certain point Me-first and Earth-first become inseparable. I feel that's the best position to be coming from—to realize one's identity with the Earth. "Myself" now includes the rainforest, it includes clean air and water.[74]

In the process of wider identification, one discovers that the self is not an ego encapsulated inside a skin bag, but is an event constituted by a complex network of relations.[75] Appealing to Leopold's land ethic and ecosystem ecology, a leading environmental ethicist, J. Baird Callicott, argues that individuals are not independent units, but are constituted by a network of internal relationships. Since no part can be valuable independent of the ecological whole of which it is an integral aspect, Callicott regards bioregions and species as more valuable than individual organisms.[76] Critics attack such interrelational holism for at least two reasons.[77] First, the ecosystemic approach to ecology, often appealed to by deep ecologists as evidence for their ideas about interrelatedness, has been challenged in recent years by a new approach to ecology, developed by population biologists, which explains ecosystemic phenomena as the unintended by-products of the interactions among *individual* organisms. (Though postponing examination of this approach to chapter 3, I wish to note here that systemic and individualist ecologies need not be mutually exclusive: they may simply be different ways of approaching complex phenomena.) Second, the concept that individuals are constituted by internal relations leads some critics—including a number of radical ecologists—to conclude that holism promotes a type of ecofascism, in which individuals may be sacrificed for the good of the larger whole. Sensitive to this political problem, deep ecologists acknowledge the inherent worth both of individual organisms and of the ecosystems of which they are a part.

Appealing to scientific hypotheses to support one's ethical and political views is an old practice. Hobbes and Locke explicitly modeled their individualistic social theories on the atomism of early modern science. Despite subsequent warnings against deriving is from ought, or fact from value, such derivations are still often made. Nacss says, however, that "all the sciences are fragmentary and incomplete in relation to basic rules and norms, so it's very shallow to think that science can solve our problems."[78] Nevertheless, deep ecologists at times proclaim that modernity's mechanistic-atomistic materialism is giving way to a new interrelational cosmology, according to which the idea of "dominating" or "conquering" nature seems suicidal.[79]

Recently, Freya Matthews has appealed to holistic trends in physics to justify Ecosophy T's concept of self-realization, interconnectedness, and wider identification.[80] In her view, human flourishing requires a cosmology that is both consistent with modern science and that portrays the universe as compatible with human interests. Such a cosmology must reconcile our intuitions about the quasi-independent character of individuals, with the view that things are constituted at all levels by interrelated, holistic, dynamic processes. Matthews argues that the "substance monism" of geometrodynamics (GED), which is linked to general relativity theory, is such a cosmology. GED is consistent with the intuition of interconnectedness, capable of justifying the principle of wider identification, and also able to be reconciled with the view that individuals have a measure of inherent worth. As Matthews concedes, however, because GED is a troubled theory, she does not want to make her *metaphysical* postulate of cosmic interrelatedness entirely dependent on the problematic status of an *empirical* hypothesis. All too often, radical ecologists make unjustified leaps from contested scientific claims to bold metaphysical assertions. Nevertheless, Matthews rightly contends that contemporary physics suggests that relations obtain among events that were once regarded as utterly separated by space and time.

GED views Einstein's spacetime as the generative matrix from which all things emerge. C. J. Graves remarks that this matrix

is not a passive arena, but the source and medium of all interactions, its parts both acting on and being acted on by each other; and . . . spacetime is a unified whole, with global and topological as well as local characteristics. It is not a collection of things, but a single thing—the only thing that is really real. One could call it by such names as pure substance, or being as such.[81]

According to GED, an individual entity is not precisely localizable, but instead "there is a sense in which each body or source is everywhere, and at the same time."[82] Matthews maintains that GED can be reconciled with Spinoza's monism, but she concedes that his tendency to discount the reality of time poses a problem not only for such reconciliation, but also for her own effort to conceive of the cosmos as a self-realizing, dynamic system. Like Hegel, Matthews faults Spinoza for not endowing God/Nature with its own conatus, that is, with a teleological, temporal drive that mirrors the teleological striving of individuals which are modifications of God/nature's. Although maintaining that the organism is the paradigmatic instance of an individual self, Matthews maintains that GED justifies viewing the cosmos itself as a kind of dynamic self, with which each individual self—ranging from amoeba to whole ecosystems—is bound up in complex sets of interrelationships. The value of selves stems from their activity of self-realization, but since all selves are interconnected, the self-realization of any particular self is somehow bound up with the self-realization of all other selves, including the cosmic Self. The cosmic whole conditions individuals, whereas individuals condition the cosmic whole through a serious of feedback loops.[83] Since the individual has so many interdependent relations with the whole, "the individual is thus in a very real sense a microcosm of the wider self in which it occurs."[84] The psychological process of identifying with ever wider wholes, a process in which "my" interests are aligned with the interests of that larger whole, is "grounded in a recognition of the metaphysical fact of interconnectedness."[85] Matthews concludes that being part of cosmic conatus may be the source of spiritual feelings, which involve "faith—trust in the order of things, an affirmation and surrender of the ego to a wider reality."[86] Though in some ways appealing, this conclusion has problems. For one thing, most deep ecologists do not seem to read the cosmic Self as being apart from the individuals comprising it; hence, they would probably not concur with Matthews's idea that there is a "cosmic conatus." For another, critics would say that in addition to not having established a "cosmic Self," Matthews has failed to secure the autonomy of individuals over and against the purported holistic Self.

Hence, a number of environmental ethicists remain unconvinced that deep ecologists really respect the worth of individual organisms. Often influenced by modernity's moral individualism, environmental ethicists ask: if a class of nonhuman individuals can be shown to have inherent value, such as a good or an interest of their own, why not extend moral considerability and even rights to that class of individuals?[87] To those critics who contend that animals and plants cannot have rights because rights are always correlated with responsibilities for which nonhumans have no capacity, "moral extensionists" reply that just as brain-damaged or otherwise incompetent humans are accorded moral standing and/or legal protection, so interest-bearing nonhuman beings also deserve moral considerability and legal rights.[88]

Deep ecologists suspect that the noble goals of moral extensionism may be colored by a subtle version of anthropocentric individualism. John Rodman argues that modern natural rights theory is a contraction of the Roman doctrine of *ius naturae,* which applied to all animals and which expressed "a cosmic order of right and duty."[89] Grotius, Locke, and Kant turned this cosmic law into a right belonging only to self-conscious individuals capable of entering into contracts. In expanding the scope of moral standing, moral extensionists tend to include only those entities that share some aspect of a property recognized as essential to human life: sentience or consciousness. Hence, Rodman asks: "Is this, then, the new enlightenment—to see nonhuman animals as imbeciles, wilderness as a human vegetable?"[90] This patronizing attitude fails "to respect [nonhumans] for having their own existence, their own character and potentialities, their own form of excellence, their own integrity, their own grandeur."[91] Instead of intellectually colonizing things that seem like us, Rodman urges us to appreciate their *otherness.*

Rodman also asserts that moral extensionism's criteria for moral considerability are drawn from the modern concept of self as a *separate* ego-subject. In extending moral considerability to individual organisms, such as plants, animals, and insects, environmental ethics often ignores the moral standing of *collective* factors—soil, rivers, mountains, and other constituents of the interrelated life community (Leopold's "land")—so crucial for individual life-forms. Callicott and many deep ecologists suspect that the moral atomism of modern ethical theories—rights-based, utilitarian, and Kantian—is incompatible with a truly *environmental* ethic, according to which "things" are at least in part manifestations of the internal relationships constituting the larger biotic community.[92]

The fact that deep ecology literature is peppered with terms such as intrinsic value, inherent worth, and rights, however, has led some people to regard it as a version of environmental ethics. Though employing terms such as "rights," deep ecologists use such terms in a nontechnical, shorthand way to indicate that nonhumans deserve respect. Moreover, deep ecologists are *primarily* concerned not with formulating an environmental ethic, but rather with developing an ecocentric sensibility, from which nature-respecting attitudes and practices would presumably flow spontaneously. Fox says that this sensibility involves a psychological shift following from cosmological identification, inspired by the realization that all life is one.[93] Others including the present author, suggest that the shift is ontological, leading to a different sense of what it means for something "to be." If the natural phenomena that once manifested themselves solely as raw material began to reveal themselves as inherently valuable, we could expect significant changes in humanity's treatment of such phenomena.[94]

Critics insist, however, that the egalitarianism following from wider identification offers no criteria for resolving difficult moral conflicts, for example, regarding whether to save a human being or a fly. Deep ecologists recommend only an egalitarianism "in principle," however, which does not equate humans indifferently with caterpillars. If an arguably vital need of a wild species comes into conflict with an arguably nonvital need of some human group, deep ecologists and environmental holists such as Callicott say that we are morally obligated to tip the scales in favor of wild nature. Naess insists that "the more vital interest has priority over the less vital. The nearer has priority over the more remote—in space, time, culture, species. Nearness derives its priority from our special responsibilities, obligations and insights."[95] Naess has said that if someone were faced with the unfortunate choice of saving the earth's last tiger or his or her own daughter, he or she ought to save the child.[96] It is not clear, however, that this decision can be squared with the idea that saving a rare species is more important than saving individuals from heavily populated species.

Insisting that a relative individuality is possible even if interrelatedness obtains at many levels in ecological webs, deep ecologists argue that their emphasis on *self*-realization reveals their concern for individual as well as for communal well-being. Though in hiking Naess inevitably steps on tiny organisms clinging to rocks, he continues to hike, though seeking to avoid treading on rare flowers. If one identifies with other living beings, Naess remarks, one will take into account their own striving for self-realization when one is faced with making decisions about altering an ecosystem or killing living things. To justify their consumption of other organisms, deep ecologists appeal not to a hierarchy that puts humankind at the top, but rather to the fact that satisfying their hunger or other vital needs is necessary for their own self-realization. As Naess admits, however, deep ecologists have not provided a satisfactory account of how to reconcile the competing claims of striving individuals.[97]

When emphasizing the rights of individual organisms, deep ecologists are in general agreement with moral extensionists. As inherently worthy beings, humans have a right to flourish, but so do other forms of life. When people begin speaking of the rights of ecosystems, however, they may stretch to the breaking point a concept originally intended for individuals. This is one reason deep ecologists use the concept of "rights" not in a technical sense, but only to convey the idea that nonhumans deserve respect and admiration. Before concluding that ecosystems are not individuals, however, we must note that no one knows what counts as a living "individual."[98] A human organism is composed of many complex organic and cellular systems; moreover, the same organism is dependent on larger organic, ecosystemic, and social systems. Such larger systems are usually ignored when liberal theorists define "individuals." Holmes Rolston III has explored with great sensitivity the ontological and ethical issues involved in differentiating among parts and wholes. What may be described as an individual at one level may be considered an aspect of a more encompassing system at another level. Hence, decisions about how to treat someone or something is to some extent dependent on the point of view from which the decision is being made."[99] The moral problems posed by conflicts between individual and group are hardly restricted to deep ecology.

As noted above, deep ecologists hope that an ecological sensibility would help to dissipate such dilemmas. Wider identification involves nondualistic experience, which reveals that there are no ultimate boundaries between self and other: all living beings are reciprocating, interrelated manifestations of the same cosmic Self. Wider identification elicits compassion for those with whom one identifies, without the need for moral imperatives and ethical duties. One cares for others just as one cares spontaneously for one's own ego, one's body, and one's family. If "I" expand so as to embrace other beings, then "their" interests become "mine" as well; I care for them spontaneously, rather than because of some onerous moral duty. Naess says that "through identification, [people] may come to see their own interests served by conservation, through genuine self-love, love of a widened and deepened self."[100] By virtue of a widened sense of self, people will engage in what Kant called "beautiful" actions, not merely dutiful ones.[101]

The idea of spontaneously caring for that with which one identifies frees deep ecologists from the daunting task of proving that nature is intrinsically valuable, that is, valuable apart from the evaluative activity of a conscious being.[102] Some deep ecologists do maintain a kind of value objectivism. For instance, Naess rejects the view that value is projected by valuing subjects onto a world devoid of intrinsic value.[103] One critic, however, says that deep ecologists are like ventriloquists projecting their own voices onto nature and then pretending that what they say is nature itself speaking. They talk of natural goodness or natural beauty "as though it were a self-presenting absolute, rather than a post-Enlightenment invention that happened to require subduing the wilderness and becoming bourgeois to appreciate."[104] But Fox maintains that deep ecologists have never argued for their assertion that things have intrinsic value because their major concern is not with axiology, but rather with developing—by way of wider identification—"a vision of reality as 'unity in process.'"[105] Someone endowed with ecological consciousness would care for nonhuman beings for the same reason that parents care for their child: not because moral reflection reveals that the child has intrinsic value, but rather because the parents *identify* with the child.

Fox would seem to agree with Callicott who, following sociobiology, argues that it is "adaptive" for parents to care for and to have strong emotional ties with their offspring. When cultural evolution begins to shape human ethical attitudes, the family circle gradually expands to include members of one's tribe, members of other tribes, and even humanity in general. This circle of concern can grow beyond the human to embrace the land, as people become aware that human survival depends on a fit habitat.[106] In fact, however, Fox does not agree with Callicott's sociobiological explanation of widened identification. The guiding principle of sociobiology is inclusive fitness, which holds that an organism seeks to pass on its own genes or those of its closest kin (the "selfish gene" hypothesis); hence, one's most important concerns are one's own children and relatives. Some sociobiologists believe that a positive concern for the environment *may* be derived from the human organism's effort to maintain its own genetic lineage. But Fox maintains that according to sociobiology's idea of "inclusive fitness," any organism invests primary importance in its own survival, then in the survival of its closest kin, and so on. Thus, far from supporting ecological identification, "a sociobiological approach clearly represents . . . a biological underpinning for *personally* based identification."[107]

Despite the merit of Fox's argument, at least two objections may be raised against it. First, the leading deep ecology theorist, Arne Naess, seems to agree with Leopold and Callicott about the evolutionary sequence of wider identification, beginning with family and extending outward. Naess says that

from identifying with "one's nearest," higher unities are created
through circles of friends, local communities, tribes, compatriots,
races, humanity, life, and, ultimately, as articulated by religious and
philosophical leaders, unity with the supreme whole, the "world" in
a broader and deeper sense than the usual.[108]

Second, Callicott's approach to increased identification has the advantage of offering a hypothesis about *how* wider identification may come about: by way of a process of biological and cultural evolution. Some deep ecologists shy away from such evolutionary and progressive accounts, because they are shared by social ecologists, modernists, New Ager counterculturalists, and others whom deep ecologists suspect of anthropocentric bias. Though there are problems associated with progressive views of human history, neither Spinoza nor Heidegger—both of whom have been important for deep ecology theory—offer a satisfactory account of how the shift to self-realization and wider identification is possible. In the next part of this chapter, which considers Fox's suggestion that deep ecology change its name to "transpersonal ecology," we examine in more detail the question of the "evolution" of ecological sensibility.

FROM DEEP TO TRANSPERSONAL ECOLOGY?   Fox says that deep ecology's name should reflect what is distinctive about deep ecology theory: the ultimate norm of self-realization. In reply to Naess's claim that deep ecology means any ecosophy that questions deeply to develop ultimate norms, Fox says that from *some* ultimate premises one may derive principles that are inconsistent with the DEP.[109] For example, if to the ultimate norm, "Obey God!", one adds two hypotheses: (1) that "man" is given "dominion" over Creation (Genesis); and (2) that "man" is supposed to "develop his talents," then one may derive a subsidiary norm: "Develop Creation!" If one interprets "dominion" as "having total authority over," and if one interprets "develop one's talents" as consistent with exploiting nature, one ends up with the contemporary view that Earth is human property.

Fox may be right that one can arrive at anthropocentric attitudes by starting with ultimate norms derived from major religious traditions, but one critic says that from the ultimate norm "Obey God!", and from a disputed view of the "dominion" theme in Genesis, Fox has derived a straw-man version of a Christian attitude toward nature.[110] Other Biblical passages commend an attitude toward Creation more consistent with the deep ecology movement.[111] Fox would probably reply that even though one *may* derive a deep ecological attitude from Christianity, the fact remains that over the centuries Christian theologians *have* derived attitudes that justify an exploitative stance toward Creation. To claim that they did not question "deeply" enough is, in effect, to beg the question.

Even if Naess is wrong in assuming that deep questioning of religious traditions leads to attitudes consistent with the DEP, however, does this fact justify discarding the name "deep ecology"? With certain reservations, the deep ecology movement could still be the blanket name for various DEP-consistent movements. Disagreeing, Fox distinguishes between a formal, a popular, and a philosophical sense of deep ecology. The *formal* sense, which Fox believes he has undermined, describes deep ecology as "deep questioning" to ultimate norms. The *popular* sense refers to the DEP, but within the larger Green movement there is nothing particularly distinctive about the DEP's affirmation of ecocentrism and its criticism of anthropocentrism. Hence, Fox concludes that what *is* distinctive about deep ecology is its *philosophical* sense, which holds that self-realization leads beyond egoistic identification and toward a wider sense of identification.[112] Since this view and the notion of wider identification are both compatible with transpersonal psychology, Fox proposes that deep ecology change its name to *transpersonal ecology.*[113]

Because most deep ecologists do agree with Ecosophy T, which Naess himself admits is compatible with transpersonal psychology, why not follow Fox's suggestion? One answer is that doing so would undermine Naess's commitment to diversity in the deep ecology movement. That the DEP lacks a philosophically distinct position is consistent with its pluralistic aim of including people with many different ecosophies. By arguing that what's really distinctive about deep ecology is the norm of Self-realization, Fox privileges Ecosophy T, a move tending to alienate radical ecologists, such as Jim Cheney, who are wary of the masculinist implications of "Self-realization," but who might agree with much of the DEP.[114] Cheney says that most radical ecologists agree that humans are "bound up with the rest of the world," but in passing from this fairly neutral description to "an anything-but-neutral metaphysics" of Self-realization, Fox purports to provide "a privileged account of the experience underlying a great multiciplicity of differing voices."[115] In so doing, Fox *supposedly* follows modernity's "logic of identity," which cannot tolerate diversity and difference.

If deep ecology wants broad agreement on midlevel principles, I believe that it should stick to Naess's pluralism regarding ultimate norms and premises. Although I am attracted to Fox's transpersonal account of Ecosophy T, I prefer using "deep ecology," rather than his "transpersonal ecology," when referring to Ecosophy T. Moreover, I find it preferable to keep the distinction between the deep ecology *movement,* which is primarily defined by the DEP, and *Ecosophy T,* the basic norm of which is self-realization through wider identification. I should like to add the following qualifications. First, the DEP itself should *not* be presented as received truth, but as a set of negotiable principles. As members of the deep ecology *movement,* deep ecology theorists may be expected to support its principles; as *philosophers,* however, those same theorists should invite criticism of those principles. Second, deep ecology theorists should follow Naess's advice and develop their *own* ecosophies, rather than elaborating Ecosophy T. Doing so would not only demonstrate that Ecosophy T is *not* the official theory of the deep ecology movement, but would give the deep ecology movement the benefit of theoretical diversification.

Now a word about the relation between transpersonal psychology and transpersonal ecology. Like deep ecology and the larger countercultural movement, transpersonal psychology draws upon ancient esoteric traditions, nondual Asian religions, and radical trends in Western psychology, including the work of Abraham Maslow. As Fox has pointed out, Maslow's notion of self-actualization contributed not only to psychology's "third wave," humanistic psychology, but also to its "fourth wave," transpersonal psychology, whose idea of self-actualization approximates Ecosophy T's notion of self-realization through wider identification. Though Maslow said that the transpersonal is "transhuman, centered in the cosmos rather than in human needs and interests, going beyond humanness, identity, self-actualization and the like," he also claimed that "identification love," which transcends the "selfish" self, is limited to *human be-ings*.[116] Later, however, transpersonal psychologists such as Roger Walsh and Frances Vaughn showed an increasing appreciation of the interrelationship of all life, thereby moving transpersonal *psychology* toward transpersonal *ecology*. The latter holds that the ecological crisis stems from subject-object dualism, in which consciousness identifies itself with the ego-subject. The ego-subject seeks to control everything, including nature, in order to guarantee its own security.

Fox argues that there are three different and poorly integrated aspects to the modern ego: desiring/appetitive, rational/judgmental, and moral/evaluative, which roughly correspond to Freud's id, ego, and superego.[117] This tripartite division of the "normal" Western ego-structure corresponds to three widespread attitudes toward nature: resource exploitation, resource conservation, and environmental ethics. The id-like self, dominated by the pleasure principle, desires to consume nature without any constraints; the ego-like self, governed by the reality principle, counsels that it would be better to consume resources wisely, with an eye to the future; the superego-like self imposes moral constraints on human treatment of nonhuman beings. Transpersonal ecologists maintain that human maturity and ecological sanity require identifying with what lies beyond the personal ego-structure. Such wider identification brings about a new field-like sense of self and a nondomineering attitude to what formerly seemed "other." Fox argues that Buddhism and Taoism, tribal traditions and the new physics, pastoral literature and Spinoza's metaphysics all share the "central intuition" of a deep, transpersonal ecology:

This is the idea that there is no firm ontological divide in the field of existence. In other words, the world simply is not divided up into independently existing subjects and objects, nor is there any bifurcation in reality between the human and nonhuman. Rather all entities are constituted by their relationships. To the extent that we perceive boundaries, we fall short of a deep ecological consciousness.[118]

As noted earlier, Fox distinguishes between cosmic identification and ontological identification.[119] In my view, the latter type of identification seems most consistent with transpersonal psychology, especially as articulated by its leading theorist, Ken Wilber. Ontological identification is made possible when the ego-subject is revealed not as a solid entity, but rather as a shifting and changing phenomenon that is merely one among the countless manifestations arising and passing away, moment by moment. Often associated with this revelation is the insight that all spatiotemporal phenomena arise "within" an all-encompassing, generative, "emptiness" (*sunyata*), sometimes called "absolute nondual consciousness." Mystics from many different traditions assert that "enlightenment" involves identifying with this generative nothingness, thereby ceasing to identify with spatiotemporal phenomena, including the ego-subject. If identification with the ego-subject ceases, there is no longer any need for defending it against phenomena that seem to threaten its existence. Instead, by identifying with generative, absolute nothingness, it becomes simultaneously possible both to affirm and to show compassion for all phenomena that arise and pass away "within" such nothingness, or absolute consciousness. Generative, nonthing-like, absolute consciousness both transcends and embraces all the spatiotemporal phenomena arising and passing away "within" it.

Although sharing postmodern theory's critique of modernity's grand narratives, which have often justified ecological destruction, deep ecology's hope for a "paradigm shift" to an ecocentric sensibility would seem to have something in common with modernity's utopian aspirations. In the next chapter, I read deep ecology as an aspect of the counterculture which, despite criticizing modernity, seeks both to fulfill and to transform its emancipatory aims. Fox says that because deep ecology emphasizes types of identification "that tend to promote impartial identification with *all* entities, Robyn Eckersley . . . has appropriately described the political upshot of this orientation as 'emancipation writ large.'"[120] Historian Roderick Nash argues that because deep ecologists use the vocabulary of "rights" and seek to extend rights to nonhuman organisms and ecosystems, deep ecology is a revolutionary extension of American liberalism.[121] Naess views self-realization in terms of the gradual maturation or evolution of human sensibility. And Christopher Manes has described deep ecology as "the last reservoir of revolutionary energy in industrial society,"[122] a statement plainly indebted to modernity's progressive heritage. Elsewhere, however, Manes says that deep ecology is far more subversive than traditional civil rights movements, since deep ecology's biological egalitarianism is more connected with Pleistocene "tribal law" than with liberal political formations.[123]

Though Manes rightly suggests that deep ecologists wish to recover ancient tribal wisdom, his tendency to engage in a total critique of modernity affirms the suspicions of deep ecology's critics: that it is a psychologically and socially regressive movement that ignores the dangers of tribalism and which demands that people conform to "nature's laws." As I noted earlier, however, if deep ecologists do admit to utopian-progressive expectations for the future, they then invite criticism from postmodern theorists. Hence, although modernists fear that deep ecology risks promoting ecofascism by dismissing modernity's progressive narrative, postmodern theorists fear that deep ecology risks promoting authoritarianism by adopting even a transformed version of that narrative.

If deep ecology ends up accepting postmodern theory's view that there is no historical direction either to human or to cosmic evolution, however, to what theoretical principles can deep ecology appeal to explain the possibility of a paradigm shift to a nondualistic ecological sensibility?[124] In my view, deep ecologists discount this question, in part because they have not examined sufficiently the enormity of the obstacle impeding such a shift. By ignoring this obstacle, deep ecologists who yearn for an ecocentric society risk falling into some of the same oppressive and destructive patterns as modern revolutionaries who longed for a postcapitalist society. The obstacle I have in mind is the interrelated phenomenon of death anxiety and death denial which accompanies the emergence of increasingly individuated forms of consciousness. Arguably, such death denial has played a crucial role in two phenomena that have accompanied the historical development of urban civilization during the past several thousand years: social authoritarianism and attempts to subjugate nature. By controlling other people and nature alike, that is, by gaining power and wealth, the anxious ego gains an illusory security against mortality.

Postmodern theorists often argue that modernity's revolutions went astray because they sought the impossible: to close the permanent fissure between subject and object, to achieve the unrealizable unity of humankind with nature. As we see in a later chapter, however, Ken Wilber maintains that modern revolutions often led to oppression *not* because they sought a higher unity, but rather because they sought it without coming to terms with humanity's mortality, finitude, and radical dependence on what transcends the human. Wilber also maintains that, despite deep ecology's rhetorical support for individual self-realization, some deep ecologists risk political disaster by allegedly suggesting that humanity-nature unity be achieved by regressing to the preindividualistic levels of consciousness which presumably characterized preagricultural peoples ten thousand years ago. Hence, progressive social revolutions, on the one hand, and reactionary fascist revolutions, on the other, may be read as political manifestations of the two most popular ways of denying death: self-assertion and self-effacement. The self-assertive person denies death by affirming that his or her specialness, power, knowledge, attractiveness, and so on will protect him or her from dying. By way of contrast, the self-effacing person denies death by abandoning anxiety-provoking individuality, by submerging himself or herself into another person.[125] Powerful revolutionary leaders sometimes utilize both methods of death denial: asserting their chosen status as the leader of the revolution, they simultaneously proclaim that they are merely the instruments of higher cosmic purposes.[126]

Wilber supports deep ecology and modernity insofar as their ideals of self-realization and progress, respectively, can be read as consistent with what he means by the evolution of consciousness. As we see later on, Wilber affirms death denial's historical role in social oppression and ecological destruction, but also asserts that death denial plays a crucial role in motivating the evolution of consciousness through the millennia. In Wilber's view, which I find persuasive in many respects, only by positing that consciousness can develop do deep ecologists have any reason to expect that the modern ego will eventually "mature," in the sense of ceasing to dissociate itself from nature. Explaining that death anxiety leads the patriarchal ego to deny its relationship to nature, to the body, the female, and other symbols of mortality and finitude, Wilber rejects the option of overcoming death anxiety by a regressive merger with unself-conscious nature. Instead, he maintains that death denial loses its grip only when people recognize their participation in that which transcends but embraces all spatiotemporal phenomena. The Vedantic tradition uses the term *Atman* to name this eternal, transcendent, nondual, generative, and absolute consciousness. Even though deep ecologists speak of self-realization as the movement toward Atman, Wilber suspects that deep ecology's ecocentrism has ties with materialistic, nature-worshipping attitudes that are ultimately incompatible with the notion of Atman as that which both transcends and generates the spatiotemporal world.

Deep ecologists and postmodern theorists alike are suspicious of Wilber's view about human evolution, because his neo-Hegelian theocentrism (the goal of human history is attainment of absolute consciousness) is all too reminiscent of totalitarian and ecologically destructive regimes, which assert that they are the historical mani-festation of the iron laws and goals of cosmic evolution. Some postmodern theorists acknowledge the role played by death denial in modern authoritarianism, but confronting the issue of death denial alone is insufficient to avoid the dangers of such authoritarianism. As we see in chapter 3, Heidegger maintained that authentic existence requires affirming one's own mortality. But in rejecting the view that the transcendent domain can be understood as the eternal Alpha and Omega explaining the progressive dimension of history, Heidegger ended up promoting a disastrous reactionary movement. In some ways, as we see in the next chapter, New Age counterculturalism seems to agree with Wilber's transpersonal view of progress as the process by which Atman realizes itself through history. But if deep ecologists protest that New Age is modern anthropocentrism in counterculturalism clothing, Wilber fears that New Age goes astray by naively overlooking the staying power of death denial and by underestimating the extent to which human history is part of a process that transcends human concerns.

Drawing on imagery from occult, astrological, mystical, pagan, Christian, anarchistic, and modern revolutionary sources, the counterculture that emerged in the 1960s was a reprise of an old theme: the longing for a new age of harmony, unity, and purpose, to replace an old age of conflict, fragmentation, and nihilism.[1] Millennial movements, inspired by esoteric teachings promising the dawn of a glorious culture and a peaceful era, have long attracted significant followings who have sought an alternative to the militaristic, patriarchal cultures of Europe and America.[2] As William Irwin Thompson has observed, the esoteric teachers of the 1960s, including Alan Watts and Norman O. Brown, were recent representatives of traditions that can be traced back to D. T. Suzuki, Jean Gebser, C. G. Jung, W. B. Yeats, Rudolf Steiner, Wassily Kandinsky, William Blake, Freemasons, Rosicrucians, Swedenborg, Boehme, Paracelsus, Bosch, Pico della Mirandola, Ficino, Cabbalists, Sufis, Cathars, Neo-Platonists, Gnostics, Essenes, Pythagoreans, and beyond.[3] With the help of mass media, counterculturalists made these esoteric traditions available to more people than at any time in world history. Unfortunately, some esoteric traditions have been violently repressed by mainstream cultures, and some millennial movements have themselves been characterized by violence, paranoia, and apocalyptic fantasies.

Much of the rock music of the 1960s, which both expressed and influenced the counterculture, exhibited aspects of the esoteric longing for celebration, abundance, sacred experience, sexual freedom, and liberation from hierarchy. Two extraordinary musical happenings from that era, Woodstock and Altamont, revealed the bright and the dark side of countercultural millennialism. Woodstock took place in the late summer of 1969 on a New York farm some miles from the town of Woodstock. The event is remembered by many as a spontaneous, euphoric celebration of life and a moment of generational solidarity, pointing toward a New Age. The following year, at the infamous Rolling Stones concert in Altamont, California, brooding violence and nihilistic self-indulgence revealed that things would not change as easily as many counterculturalists had hoped. The difficulties involved in passing from the conflictual Piscean Age to the harmonious Aquarian Age were underscored by the physical violence and scapegoating that marred so many antiwar protests during the same era.

There was nothing new to the naïveté of hippies and other counterculturalists regarding the prospects for a congenial New Age. Two centuries ago, many spokesmen for Enlightenment modernity promised that a new age—free from despotism, social strife, natural and material want—would be achieved by redesigning society according to reason, as embodied in science, technology, and economics. These idealistic expectations were soured by the social, political, military, and ecological horrors of the twentieth century. Defenders of modernity attribute these phenomena to outbreaks of unpacified irrational forces, whereas critics insist that it was precisely modernity's quest for total control that led to mechanized warfare, concentration camps and Gulags, and ecological disasters. These conflicting explanations may be reconciled by viewing them as different dimensions of widespread death denial. When the quest for a measure of control is warped by the irrational project of making mortal creatures immortal, dark consequences inevitably follow.

Though inheriting modernity's hopes for a New Age, the counterculture may also be understood as the recent expression of a vocal minority that has always protested that the freedoms purchased by

Enlightenment modernity's rational project have been too costly. Protesting against the alienating effects of industrial labor and market economies, European romantics and American transcendentalists demanded personal fulfillment and communal transformation. In the early twentieth century, Germany's youth anticipated aspects of the 1960s counterculture by promoting social harmony, "natural" expression of emotion and sexuality, folk mores and practices, occult and paranormal practices, and the sacredness of nature, while opposing modernity's nihilism, class strife, artificiality, industrialism, gospel of efficiency, worship of calculating rationality, and violations of nature.

The fact that National Socialism was in part a perverted expression of this prevalent desire for social harmony does not make such desire illegitimate, but does require that critics of modernity—including counterculturalists and radical ecologists—proceed carefully in calling for alternatives to it. As we see later on, National Socialism may be understood, at least in part, as an attempt to overcome mortality by identifying with the immortal forces of nature. This movement, with its goal of achieving an immanent harmony of *Volk* and nature, proved particularly attractive to those who shunned the heavy moral responsibilities conferred by the Jewish and Christian traditions, according to which humans are not merely "natural" creatures, but instead exist within a history that is tied to the transcendent. Any revolutionary movement that fails to take into account death denial's role in that movement risks creating situations that are worse than those supposedly being overcome.

In this chapter, I divide counterculture roughly into three interrelated movements in the 1960s, 1970s, and 1980s. The counterculturalism of the 1960s saw at least three different types of protest against "the system" of mainstream industrial culture. The civil rights movement demanded greater political freedom *within* the system for oppressed minorities (blacks, Native Americans, women); the antiwar movement was an increasingly violent protest *against* the system, especially its authoritarianism and militarism; and the hippie movement sought to *replace* the existing culture with a simpler, unalienated, nature-loving, decentralized culture that was in many ways antimodern. There were conflicts among these three movements. Civil rights advocates, for example, criticized flower children for "dropping out" of the struggle to win freedom for the oppressed. But in calling for an alternative to modernity, hippies used not only the language of Asian religions and millennial traditions, but also the vocabulary of modern emancipatory movements. In my account of the 1960s counterculture, I focus particularly on the hippies' call for a dramatic cultural shift.

From the complex interactions among these movements there gradually emerged not only various radical ecology movements, but also the New Age movement of the 1970s and the New Paradigm Movement of the 1980s. New Age sought to transform the system from within, by translating countercultural ideals into an idiom more acceptable to business, industry, and politics. New Paradigm, which is more self-critical than New Age, shares certain themes both with postmodern theory and with deep ecology. Despite differences, New Age and New Paradigm agree that "progress" must be defined less as growing technical mastery over nature and more as the evolution of consciousness.

Though once tempted to describe all three phases of the counterculturalism as "countercultural postmodernism," since all three seek to replace modern culture, I eventually realized that the same term could refer to efforts by postmodern theorists to establish cultural alternatives to modernity. Despite sharing certain attitudes and mutual influences, New Age/New Paradigm and postmodern theory differ in that the former harbors aspects of modernity's utopian hopes, whereas the latter regards such hopes as dangerous. To mark this difference, I use the term "counterculturalism" to refer only to the utopian/progressive New Age and New Paradigm movements. Charles Jencks views this more affirmative counterculturalism as double-coded: simultaneously honoring *and* subverting, embracing *and* criticizing both traditionalism (including the "old ways" favored by deep ecologist poet, Gary Snyder) and futurism (including technological and managerial practices consistent with ecological harmony, decentralization, and democratic pluralism).[4]

The first section of this chapter describes links between the 1960s counterculture and deep ecology; the second section examines deep ecology's critique of New Age anthropocentrism; the last part examines New Paradigm's attempt to combine postmodern theory, modernity's emancipatory ideals, and deep ecology.

DEEP ECOLOGY AND THE 1960S COUNTERCULTURE   Two bestselling authors, Alan Watts and Rachel Carson, helped to insure that 1960s counterculturalism would have an ecological flavor. In several books, including *Nature, Man, and Woman* (1957), Watts anticipated deep ecology's contention that since aggressive, dualistic, anthropocentric attitudes justify the practices that are destroying nature, only a dramatic spiritual shift will save humankind and nature from destruction. Similarly, in *Silent Spring* (1962), Carson argued that the dramatic loss of songbirds due to the overuse of pesticides was an example of Western humanity's misguided attempt to dominate nature: "The 'control of nature' is a phrase conceived in arrogance, born of the Neanderthal age of biology and philosophy, when it was supposed that nature exists for the convenience of man."[5] Another influential counterculturalist, Herbert Marcuse, argued that since efforts to dominate internal and external nature had led not to freedom, but to new forms of enslavement, humanity had to reconcile itself with nature. Although at times maintaining that the one-dimensional technological system was all-embracing, Marcuse saw in the counterculture—with its revolutionary music, consciousness expansion, affirmation of eros, celebration of previously marginalized peoples and lifestyles, universal brotherhood, anarchistic individualism, and ecological concerns—the possibility not only of resistance, but of a new beginning. His leftist counterculturalism led some to conceive of nature as a new dimension of the class struggle.[6] Although appreciative of Marcuse's critique of technological modernity, however, some budding deep ecologists viewed him as promoting Hegel and Marx's view that nature achieves its highest potential when "pacified" by humankind.

During the 1930s, Arne Naess—skeptical about the "man-perfects-nature" ideology of industrial modernity, captivated by Gandhi's nonviolent method of social transformation, fascinated by Spinoza and Eastern religions, and enthralled by the beauty and worth of nature—had anticipated the attitudes of the 1960s counterculture, especially as it unfolded in California. Discussing the counterculture-deep ecology connection, George Sessions notes that both beatniks and hippies rejected the "mindless goal of consumerism and endless materialistic progress of the emerging urban-industrial society."[7] Their experiments with the "spirituality and self-knowledge techniques of Zen Buddhism and other 'esoteric' religions" were an effort to prevent their own wildness from being tamed.[8] Poets Gary Snyder and Allen Ginsberg urged people to abandon the confining attitudes of bourgeois modernity and to forge a freer, more authentic, more self-expressive life, which does not depend on dominating anyone or anything. Contending that "the recent dramatic rise in movements for self-discovery and personal autonomy" is "paralleling the equally dramatic rise of the contemporary environmental movement," Sessions singles out the "brilliant" writings of Theodore Roszak for discussing "most of the concerns of deep ecology."[9]

Roszak's idea that the needs and rights of the person are bound up with the needs and rights of the planet confirms Sessions's idea that "the key to contemporary ecological consciousness is to see the diminishment of man and the diminishment of the planet and its nonhuman inhabitants as essentially one and the same problem."[10] Criticizing technological society, Roszak called for a "resacralized nature and sacramental perception," as well as for "decentralization and for new democratic ecological/spiritual/anarchist communities."[11] Anticipating the shallow versus deep ecology distinction, Roszak differentiated between the reformist political strategy of "countervailing expertise," on the one hand, and the complete transformation of culture, on the other. Despite its good intentions and occasional successes, countervailing expertise,

does not challenge the universally presumed rightness of the urban-industrial order of life. Therefore it cannot address itself to the possibility that high industrial society, due to its scale, pace, and complexity, is *inherently* technocratic, and so inherently undemocratic. At most, it leaves us with the hope that the bastardized technocracies of our day might yet be converted into ideal technocracies.[12]

In the late 1960s, Roszak focused on liberating *humans* from technocratic culture, but soon began exploring the connection between the domination of humanity and the domination of nature. In *The Unfinished Animal* (1975), he argued that as they regained hidden wisdom about the interrelationship of all things, counterculturalists realized that human emancipation cannot occur without emancipating the rest of nature.[13] *The Unfinished Animal*'s subtitle, *The Aquarian Frontier and the Evolution of Consciousness*, suggests that the emancipation of humanity and nature (1) is *underway* in the shift from the conflicted Piscean Age to the harmonious Aquarian Age; (2) is the new *frontier* for Americans accustomed to being renewed through entering the "wilderness"; and (3) is the consequence of the progressive spiritual *evolution* of humankind. (Leading deep ecology theorists have never endorsed these astrological notions, however.) In *Person/Planet* (1978), he argued that human personhood will not be safe until the personhood of Earth is respected: "There is no way to treat the planet and the nonhuman things upon it as our disenfranchised proletariat without perpetuating the exploited human proletariat."[14]

In *The Voice of the Earth* (1992), Roszak outlines "ecopsychology," which "seeks to heal the more fundamental alienation between the person and the natural environment."[15] The "ecological ego," we are told, "matures toward a sense of ethical responsibility to the planet that is as vividly experienced as our ethical responsibility to other people." According to ecopsychology,

there is a synergistic interplay between planetary and personal well-being. The term "synergy" is chosen deliberately for its traditional theological connotation, namely that the human and divine are cooperatively linked in the quest for salvation.[16]

Protesting modernity's spiritual poverty and materialism, many counterculturalists of the 1960s favored a demodernizing process to recover lost primal wisdom so as to live more in harmony with nature.[17] Arguing that social misery, the nuclear arms race, ecological devastation, and power politics resulted from constricted awareness, many counterculturalists believed that only "consciousness expansion" could bring the radical social changes needed to heal the planet. To explain such an expansion, counterculturalists concocted an eclectic mix of occultism, postmodern science, irrationalism, millennial fervor, utopian aspiration, and valuable insights.

For example, millions read Carlos Castaneda's accounts of himself as an arrogant, anthropocentric, and ecologically ignorant Western "man" taught by native American *brujo* don Juan Matus that, to become a spiritual warrior, he must forsake his narrow cultural categories and respectfully acknowledge his limited place in a vast, enigmatic, and beautiful natural world. Heeding the widespread message that drugs can help open the constricted Western mind, countercultural youths enthusiastically ingested mind-expanding drugs and "dropped out" of a materialistic, hypocritical society. Psychotropic drugs can trigger ecstatic, mystical, and a sometimes terrifying sense of interrelatedness with the living universe. Fritjof Capra's account of an experience in the late 1960s seems to have been influenced by a psychotropic substance:

I suddenly became aware of my whole environment as being engaged in a gigantic cosmic dance. . . . As I sat on that beach my former experiences [as a physicist] came to life; I "saw" cascades of energy coming down from outer space, in which particles were created and destroyed in rhythmic pulses; I "saw" the atoms of the elements and those of my body participating in this cosmic dance of energy; I felt its rhythm and I "heard" its sound, and at that moment I *knew* that this was the Dance of Shiva, the Lord of Dancers worshiped by the Hindus.[18]

Although not all counterculturalists took drugs, most were convinced that only by changing perception could alienated Western people reestablish their lost relation with nature. Paul Shepard says that this loss began ten thousand years ago with the shift to agricultural civilization in which people no longer acculturated their children with the requisite sense of relatedness to wild nature.[19] The growing sense of alienation from nature was voiced both in Greek philosophy and the New Testament, which Shepard calls "one of the world's most antiorganic and antisensuous masterpieces of abstract ideology."[20] Otherworldly Christianity, influenced by Greek mind-body dualism, lacked the rites of passage needed

to translate [the adolescent's] confidence in people and the earth into a more conscious, more cosmic view, in which he broadens his buoyant faith to include the universe. The amputation of nature myths causes a grievous dislocation, for which he will seek, in true questing spirit, an explanation in terms of 'ultimate' reality.[21]

In 1967, Lynn White, Jr. added to growing mistrust of mainstream institutions by charging that Christian anthropocentrism is responsible for the ecological crisis.[22] A monotheism teaching that God is wholly "other" than Creation, early Christianity extirpated pagan groups and cut down their sacred groves. Centuries later, now conceiving of Creation as raw material to be "developed" by those willing to utilize their God-given talents, Puritan settlers in the New World set out to convert the savages and to tame the wilderness. While he was Secretary of the Interior, James Watt maintained that Christians were bound to "develop" the land (including wilderness areas) in anticipation of Jesus' imminent return.[23] Given Christianity's problematic attitudes toward nature, one can understand why many deep ecologists believe that the views of Henry David Thoreau and John Muir are inconsistent with that religion. Like Shepard, deep ecologist Dolores LaChapelle stresses the need for nature-affirming rituals.[24] Similarly, in seeking to regenerate "ecological unconscious" and "innate animism," Roszak appeals to many sources, including the healing practices of primary peoples, nature mysticism, wilderness experience, and deep ecology.[25]

Unknown to most deep ecologists, however, is the fact that an influential minority in Puritan Christianity adhered to something akin to nature mysticism. This mixed religious heritage explains why the same contemporary American who regards the "purple mountain majesty" as a potentially lucrative ski resort may affirm that his or her own personal freedom and salvation somehow depend on preserving the wide open spaces. That American deep ecologists regard their movement primarily as a spiritual revival, rather than as a secular political movement, indicates the unspoken influence on their work of the nature-mystical strand of Puritan Calvinism—a strand ignored by Max Oelschlaeger when he describes young Muir's Calvinist God as a "cosmic Hitler."[26] In *Wilderness Lost,* David Williams explains that for the early Puritan settlers the term wilderness at first meant the *internal* wilderness, and only secondarily untouched wild nature:

They came to the literal wilderness . . . for the express purpose
of entering the *mental wilderness* and being converted in the fires
of conversion from ego-centered stupidity to the regenerate perception of infinite self-less love. Those first settlers understood that
the experience was *spiritual* and that their sojourn in the literal wilderness was but a symbol of a spiritual state. . . . Their goal was
a spiritual freedom toward which political freedom was only a
means.[27]

Entering the wilderness meant surrendering the control-craving ego and enduring the purifying fire of existential terror, which alone could prepare one for receiving saving grace. Increasing material comforts and a growing sense of security, however, led many second-generation colonists to confuse the *wilderness of the mind* with the *geographical wilderness* of the New World, so that settling in literal wilderness came to be seen as a sufficient measure to gain "justification." Concluding that they were *already* in the New Jerusalem, later settlers perceived a garden where their forebears had spoken of a "howling wilderness." Nevertheless, Puritanism was always both pessimistic and optimistic, warning of human depravity and rejoicing in "being one with God in the sunny vineyard of Canaan." Williams notes that "the struggle between doubt and affirmation, protest and celebration, denial and devotion has been an integral part of American culture ever since."[28]

In the 1750s, preacher, theologian, and nature-mystic Jonathan Edwards helped lead the Great Awakening, the spiritual revival that played such an integral role in the American Revolution. Country people, suspicious of the urban materialism and capitalism, were swept up by Edwards's contention that colonists had fallen victim to pride by presuming that they had been redeemed without making the terrifying journey into the *spiritual* wilderness, that is, without surrendering the ego.[29] Like Calvin, Edwards argued that the self-worshiping ego's craving for control and independence predetermines behavior and constricts perception. In their "vision quests," many Native American tribes seem to acknowledge that a terrifying ritual of self-surrender is required to gain access to mysterious sacred powers. According to Edwards, despair was replaced by ecstasy as one abandoned "the finite self for *identification* with the eternal glory of God. Self no longer mattered, only God did, and only after conversion had occurred could all of God's creation be appreciated in its true divine beauty."[30] Freed from overweening self-love, one spontaneously loves all things, or "Being-in-general." When individuals are awakened to their participation in the glorious whole, the corrupt and sinful world will be transformed into a loving and caring world, in which *all* things are recognized as inherently valuable and extraordinarily beautiful. Thus Edwards, like Muir and deep ecologists after him, asserted that surrendering control lets one discover the profound interrelatedness and worth of all Creation.[31]

Edwards's brand of Calvinism, which asserted that nature's divine beauty is visible only to those who are saved from sinful egocentrism, may be at work in Thoreau's assertion that "in wildness lies the preservation of the world." Though in part he may have meant literal wilderness, he may also have had in mind the importance of experiencing the wild, infinite power of that which gives birth to the ego. Thoreau's terrifying experience on Mount Katadin revealed to him the indifference of wild nature to his own concerns and jolted him from the subjectivistic tendencies of his nature romanticism. Thereafter, he purged his nature writings of stylistic embellishment and increasingly sought to give immediate "voice" to what manifested itself through him.[32] Further, Edwards's condemnation of human arrogance seems to be echoed not only in John Muir's frequent rebukes of "Lord Man's" aspirations to conquer nature, but also in his view that selfish conceit blinds us to the

rights of all the rest of creation! . . . Though alligators, snakes, etc., naturally repel us, they are not mysterious evils. They dwell happily in the flowery wilds, are part of God's family, unfallen, undepraved, and cared for with the same species of tenderness and love as is bestowed on angels in heaven or saints on earth.[33]

At times, Christians have used the assertion in Genesis that God gave man "dominion" over Creation to justify abusive treatment of the nonhuman world. Yet Christianity's hope for a New Jerusalem, in which humanity-nature harmony would be restored, has influenced deep ecology's hope for a cultural paradigm shift, just as that same hope—in secularized garb—inspired Enlightenment revolutionaries who believed that humanity could transform earth into a paradise.[34] The parallels between Edwards's Great Awakening and the counterculture of the 1960s revolt two centuries later are striking. Just as young colonists, feeling that modern materialism had stripped their lives of meaning, "thirsted for the heavy sense of purpose that had sent their great-grandparents into the wilderness one hundred years before," countercultural youths in the 1960s rebelled against the spiritual bankruptcy, complacency, materialism, and hypocrisy of their parents, and explored drugs, meditation, transformational workshops, and other avenues that promised an encounter with the wildness beyond the ego and an ecstatic identification with the Divine.[35] Williams notes that as Puritan society,

divided into two antagonistic groupings, young persons at the stage of adolescence . . . had to choose between their parents' worldly Armenianism [uninspired, legalistic Christianity] or the original identity that their culture seemed to be abandoning. They had to choose between a worldly ethic devoted to material gain and a theistic world view centered on the demands of spiritual regeneration. . . . The abandoning of the old self and the assumption of a new personality paralleled the experience of identity-loss and acceptance of a new identity.[36]

Despite such parallels between the Great Awakening and the counterculture, some deep ecologists remain suspicious of Christianity, though Naess emphasizes Christianity's potential for affirming the DEP. In *The Turning Point,* which argues that Western culture is moving away from anthropocentrism, dualism, and abstract rationality and turning toward biocentrism, nondualism, and interrelational thinking, Fritjof Capra does not mention any positive aspects of Christianity.[37] Instead, like many other deep ecologists, he appeals to Asian nondualism and to ideas drawn from contemporary science as the basis for reenchanting a nature stripped of mystery by otherworldly Christianity and mechanistic science. According to Capra, the paradigm shift will not occur because of miraculous intervention by the Divine in historical affairs, but rather because the cosmos is a self-organizing and quasi-sacred process that is developing greater complexity and freedom.

DEEP ECOLOGY AND NEW AGE   During the 1970s, countercultural dropouts and visionaries initiated the complex New Age movement. To be sure, even though allegedly protesting against modern materialism, many hucksters have cashed in on New Age interest in reincarnation, organically grown food, ethereal music, channeling, crystal power, astrology, and the like. Nevertheless, New Age's sometimes contradictory, sometimes flaky, but often suggestive ideas about human development have influenced many modern institutions. Hardly monolithic in terms of ideology, many New Agers emphasize that decentralized networking, individual transformation, self-empowerment, and self-realization are crucial for achieving a "soft" revolution, "a vast metamorphosis of human consciousness and behavior" that is rivaled only by the shift to agriculture ten thousand years ago.[38] Humankind is now moving, we are told, from an era of strife (the Piscean Age) to an era of cooperation and interdependence (the Aquarian Age). Though often criticizing the oppressiveness of modern science, New Agers reveal lingering ties to modernity's confidence in science by appealing to "postmodern" science in order to legitimate their own views and products. Criticized by leftists for supporting an allegedly conservative individualism, New Agers reply that the left failed because it ignored that people yearn to assert their own individual worth, influence, and abilities.[39] Individuals who have taken responsibility for their own lives recognize that they must also take responsibility for their communities.

New Age seems to agree with deep ecology that transforming the humanity-nature relationship requires attaining transpersonal awareness, in which the isolated atomistic self becomes related to the larger whole. Such awareness is supposedly consistent with aspects of "postmodern science," including quantum theory, chaos theory, and ecology. Moreover, the current social and ecological crisis is indicative of an evolutionary shift involving personal transformation, social liberation, and ecological harmony. Despite such congruencies, and despite the ecological concerns of many New Agers, however, deep ecologists generally regard New Age as unecological, both in failing to understand the ecological importance of wilderness and in viewing evolution as culminating in humankind.[40]

Deep ecologists see New Age anthropocentrism in the work of Hazel Henderson, who agrees with deep ecology's criticism of global monoculture and emphasizes cultural, productive, and species diversity, but who describes Earth as a "planetary storehouse" whose genetic resources must be managed "cooperatively, *for the benefit of all the human family.*"[41] Sessions argues that Marilyn Ferguson, author of the bestseller, *The Aquarian Conspiracy,* shares the anthropocentric views of Fichte, Hegel, Marx, Marcuse, Buckminster Fuller, and Teilhard de Chardin, according to whom man "perfects" nature by making it more suitable for human well-being.[42] Fuller proclaimed that human evolution on "Spaceship Earth" requires the "metaphysical mastering of the physical."[43] The Jesuit theologian Teilhard said that since the goal of evolution is the development of divine consciousness in humanity, evolution will culminate in the "noosphere," in which Earth becomes self-conscious through humanity. One Teilhard scholar says that humanity will eventually take charge of terrestrial evolution.[44] New Ager Peter Russell asserts that global networking, electronic communications, and technological achievements that let us view Earth from outer space are leading Gaia into a revolutionary era of self-awareness.[45]

A critical admirer of Teilhard and a deep ecology sympathizer, Father Thomas Berry has concluded that the Jesuit scholar was heir to the "imperial tradition in human-earth relations," according to which humanity's evolutionary advance was to be supported by scientific and technological domination of nature.[46] Though Teilhard could accept neither the spontaneity of the natural world, nor the idea of humanity living lightly in "intercommunication with the total earth community," he believed that humanity is destined not only to redeem a fallen humanity, but to heal a fallen nature as well.[47] Sessions prefers Berry's creation-centered Christianity in contrast to other worldly Christianity. According to the latter, nature is "fallen" and thus in need of redemption or improvement. "As the American Indians and other primal cultures found out to their dismay, it was God's work for Europeans to 'redeem' the vast wilderness and 'undeveloped' land by converting them to town, factories, and farms."[48]

Many New Agers call on the Gaia hypothesis, coauthored by James Lovelock and Lynn Margulis, to support their views about human evolution. The Gaia hypothesis says that life on Earth (Gaia) operates as a self-regulating feedback system that maintains global temperature, gaseous composition of the atmosphere, sea water salinity, and other crucial factors at the precise levels needed to sustain life.[49] Although generally supportive of the Gaia hypothesis, some deep ecologists fear that its use of cybernetics and systems theory can be used to prop up New Age's illusion that humankind can understand and control Earth's complex processes.[50] Describing the Gaia hypothesis as "an updated version of Gifford Pinchot's 'scientific management' of the national forests," for instance, Bill Devall once said that the Gaia hypothesis might justify greater interventions in the ecosphere to offset problems created by industrialism, thereby forestalling changes in attitudes and lifestyles.[51] David Spangler maintains, however, that New Age responds to the "archetype or myth of the sacred planet" and seeks a mutually empowering, cocreative relation between humankind and earth.[52] Further, Lovelock says that humanity is not to be seen as dominant over Gaia, but rather as a partner with her in a coevolutionary process that resembles deep ecology's idea that humanity is maturing toward ecological sensibility:

[I]t may be that the destiny of mankind is to become tamed, so that the fierce, destructive, and greedy forces of tribalism and nationalism are fused into a compulsive urge to belong to the commonwealth of all creatures which constitutes Gaia. It might seem to be a surrender, but I suspect that the rewards, in the form of an increased sense of well-being and fulfillment, in knowing ourselves to be a dynamic part of a far greater entity, would be worth the loss of tribal freedom.[53]

Nevertheless, just as some deep ecologists suspect that Lovelock's talk of "coevolution" masks a hidden agenda of human domestication of nature, others suspect that Réné DuBos's phrase, "Think Globally, Act Locally," calls for humanity to turn Earth into a garden. The hermeneutics of suspicion lead others to read E. F. Schumacher's search for appropriate technology as a way for humans to increase their control of the planet.[54] Even though deep ecologists generally favor small-scale technology, they fear that fascination with high-tech tempts some New Agers to explore schemes for dominating the earth and planets beyond. For instance, New Agers such as Gerard O'Neil and Timothy Leary say that humanity will colonize the Solar System and the universe, whereas Gaia-hypothesis coauthor Lovelock has written about "terraformation," the process of turning Mars into a home suitable for human life.[55] Though terraformation may one day be technically possible, deep ecologists join Edward O. Wilson in wondering whether "the psychic thread of life on Earth [can] be snapped without eventually fatal consequences."[56] Such concerns will not likely hinder those technological innovations, including genetic engineering, that further the goal of manipulating nature in even more extensive ways. New Ager J. Peter Vayk asserts that as "legitimate children of Gaia," humans can remake Earth according to their own dreams.[57] To be sure, Vayk quickly adds that we must respect Gaia's handiwork, including other species of life, but deep ecologists view such remarks as window dressing to soften the real anthropocentric message, which refuses to let all creatures realize their evolutionary destinies without undue human interference.

A consideration of systems theory and cybernetics reveals the complex relation between deep ecology and New Age. Some deep ecologists say that ecological science now relies so much on cybernetics and systems theory that it marginalizes the language of "community" emphasized by earlier ecologists like Aldo Leopold.[58] And Morris Berman argues that systems theory, cybernetics, artificial intelligence, and other scientific approaches favored by many New Agers disclose the planet as a giant abstract system of which humans may be a part, but which they can also control.[59] Such reservations notwithstanding, Fritjof Capra appeals to systems theory as a metaphor for the interconnected, dynamic web of the biosphere. Deep ecology, we are told, recognizes that "ecological balance will require profound changes in our perception of the role of human beings in the planetary ecosystem. In short, it will require a new philosophical and religious basis."[60] Though appealing to the nondualistic aspects of quantum theory and ecology, deep ecology goes beyond such theory

to an intuitive awareness of the oneness of all life, the interdependence of its multiple manifestations and its cycles of change and transformation. When the concept of the human spirit is understood in this sense, as the mode of consciousness in which the individual feels connected to the cosmos as a whole, it becomes clear that ecological awareness is truly spiritual.[61]

Capra believes that systems theory can provide a scientific metaphor for this intuited interconnectedness:

Systems are integrated wholes whose properties cannot be reduced to those of smaller units. Instead of concentrating on basic building blocks or basic substances, the systems approach emphasizes basic principles of organization. . . . The same aspects of wholeness are exhibited by social systems—such as an anthill, a beehive, or a human family—and by ecosystems that consist of a variety of organisms and inanimate matter in mutual interaction. What is preserved in a wilderness are not individual trees or organisms but the complex web of relationships between them.[62]

At all levels, from subatomic phenomena to whole ecosystems, reality seems to involve systemic, self-regulating processes. Following the *I Ching*, Capra maintains that ecologically destructive practices result from an unbalanced society, driven by masculinist, aggressive, competitive, analytic *Yang* tendencies, which must be counterbalanced by feminist, conservative, cooperative, intuitive, and synthesizing *Yin* tendencies.[63] Influenced by Gregory Bateson, Capra views individual minds as nested within larger social and ecological systems, which in turn participate in the Divine, understood not as a personal entity, but rather as "the self-organizing dynamics of the entire cosmos," and thus as infinite, formless, nothingness: cosmic consciousness or mind.[64]

Like many deep ecologists, Capra criticizes modernity because it interferes with the smooth functioning of the Earth's *ecosystem;* hence, he suggests that *systems* theory is not intrinsically domineering, any more than quantum theory, which is so useful for the computers and other electronic equipment on which systems theory applications are so dependent. Deep ecologists warn that despite supercomputers, scientists cannot fully predict the consequences of their actions. Chaos theory, though not mentioned by Capra in *The Turning Point,* argues that this lack of predictive capacity is due to the fact that most natural phenomena, including weather, are nonlinear systems, which are *in principle* unpredictable beyond the short term. Very small-scale perturbations can trigger off a vast, system-altering event. Hence, although some people may wish to use systems theory and cybernetics to support schemes for domination, chaos theory shows the limits to such aspirations.

The debate about photographs of Earth taken from outer space also reflects the debate between New Agers and deep ecologists. The technical accomplishments required to build the spacecraft from which to take those photos, regarded by some ecological activists as inspiring images of the living Earth, were made possible by the same objectifying attitude that discloses Earth as a stockpile of raw materials for enhancing human power. Hence, Yaakov Garb has argued that although those photos may seem to disclose the interconnectedness of life, they may also be read as symptoms of Western "man's" drive to escape from his dependence on Earth.[65] By achieving a perspective that reduces Earth to an image reproducible on a postcard, "man" gains the illusion of control over the planet. Recoiling against his organic origins and his mortality, man begins conceiving of himself as godlike and as radically other than nature. Satellite photos of Earth may be instances of that "high altitude thinking" (Merleau-Ponty) which conceives of itself as pure spirit rising above the natural world. In such photos, we see Earth reflected in the rearview mirror of the spaceship taking us away from our home in order to conquer the universe. Heidegger warned that in the technological era, for something "to be" means for it to be an "image" (*Bild*) projected by and constrained in accordance with the demands of the power-craving subject.[66] In 1966, he remarked that "I was frightened when I saw pictures coming from the moon to the earth. We don't need any atom bomb. The uprooting of man has already taken place. . . . This is no longer the earth on which man lives."[67] Garb argues that the same environmentalists who charge that the objectifying technological attitude that reduces natural phenomena to indistinguishable raw material sometimes fail to notice that high-altitude photos of Earth also erase difference and reduce the planet to two dimensions. Garb notes that immersing oneself in wild nature for an extended period lets one experience the multi-layered complexity and specificity of the living Earth, as well as one's dependence on it.

Though deep ecologists, New Agers, and many postmodern theorists extol the virtues of the local, the particular, and the different, the very idea of the "local" becomes problematic as the socioeconomic world becomes increasingly interdependent. Consider the following scenario: rising global oil prices make cooking fuel too expensive for many Third World people, who then cut trees for fuel. The felled trees no longer absorb carbon dioxide and give off oxygen, thus exacerbating the global warming that may trigger climate changes that devastate midwestern American agriculture, while at the same time melting polar ice caps and thus flooding New Orleans and Miami. Further, felled trees may contribute to local topsoil erosion, but may also cause erosion that silt up rivers, thereby causing massive flooding downstream. Complex socioeconomic events thus can set off a chain of events with catastrophic consequences at local and global levels.

Garb's views about satellite imagery of Earth agree with postmodern theory's contention that the logic of identity erases difference and reduces everyone and everything to homogeneous raw material. According to Jean Baudrillard, however, clinging to ideas of "difference"—including the metaphysical difference between appearance and reality—indicates a failure to appreciate the metaphysical change brought about by the pervasiveness of electronic media, which reduce everything to superficial phenomena: hyperreality. Even to speak of "superficial" is to use the outmoded language of "surface" and "depth." In hyperreality, according to which there is no "thing in itself" behind the representation, what does experiencing "nature" mean? Seeing photos of Earth taken from outer space? Watching videotaped images of a Brazilian waterfall in a "National Geographic Special"? Recalling memories of viewing time-lapse photography of the unfolding of a flower's petals? In hyperreality, could ecological problems be "solved" in the same way that political problems were "solved" in the Reagan years by cleverly manipulating images and narratives to make viewers "feel good" about nonexistent solutions?[68] If what matters (assuming anything "matters" at all) is the surface, the image, the appearance of things, what is wrong with plastic trees or "designer genes," organisms engineered according to exact specification?[69] And what, if anything, is problematic about efforts to create "virtual reality," artificially induced but "lifelike" experiences, whether they involve diving into a cool mountain stream or fighting Klingons for control of the galaxy? Many deep ecologists would answer such questions by saying that the electronics revolution is but another stage in the quest by anthropocentric humanists to control the planet.

Deep ecologists hold that the writings of Henryk Skolimowksi exemplify such humanism.[70] Sounding like a deep ecologist in calling for a paradigm shift away from industrial modernity's ecologically destructive worldview, Skolimowski calls for a new paradigm that is spiritually alive, active in the pursuit of wisdom, ecologically conscious, politically aware and socially concerned, conscious that economics must be linked to life-quality, vocal about individual responsibility, tolerant of transphysical [and transpersonal] phenomena, health-mindful, and life-oriented. Skolimowski says that humanity is taking part in a cosmic evolutionary process leading to "ecological humanism," which has three major principles: (1) in the coming stewardship age, humans will further evolution by creatively transforming nature, not by dominating it; (2) the world is a sanctuary, both in the sense of being a habitat for humankind and other species, and in the sense of being a site for religious sensibility and awe that we—as priests of the sanctuary—are to cultivate; (3) knowledge is an intermediary between humans and the creative force of evolution, not a set of tools for analyzing the world so as to facilitate our exploitation of it.

According to Skolimowski, humanity's project of transcendence becomes perverted when aligned with a mechanistic-materialistic cosmology, but can be liberating when aligned with a creative evolutionary cosmology.[71] Affirming the value of Teilhard's work, Skolimowski asserts that since humans are the crown of creation, "an understanding of the nature of the human being is tantamount to an understanding of the fundamental structure of evolution itself."[72] Yet humans are of utmost importance *not* in their own right, but rather as "a shining particle of the unfolding process of evolution," an intelligent "sacred vessel" responsible for furthering divine evolutionary processes.[73] Ecological humanism requires people to enhance evolution, life, the ecosystem, and the creative human consciousness "in which the most precious achievements of evolution are bestowed."[74] Although some progress is being made toward the new cosmology, some are still hubristic enough to regard Earth as property to be used however they see fit, without regard to the well-being and potential of *all* its components.

In my view, Skolimowski's writings are insightful, though they would be strengthened by acknowledging the obstacles that death denial poses for the evolution of consciousness. Moreover, I am sympathetic to his complaint that by focusing exclusively on terrestrial issues, and by ignoring cosmological, eschatological, and theological concerns, deep ecologists do not always think "deeply" enough.[75] Arne Naess replies, however, that Skolimowski prefers that his own ecosophy, evolutionary humanism, become identical with deep ecology, instead of letting people adhere to many *different* ecosophies, all of which may be reconciled with the DEP.[76] George Sessions admires aspects of Skolimowski's critique of modernity, but rebukes his "virulent" Teilhardian anthropocentrism. Sessions concludes that "the choice between New Age versus Deep Ecology futures for mankind and the biosphere becomes clearer and more crucial with each passing day."[77] In reply, Skolimowski accuses deep ecologists of Stalinist dogmatism.[78]

Sessions' critique is problematic not only because of its us-versus-them style, but also because many of the views he condemns in allegedly anthropocentric humanists like Skolimowski are also found in the work of Theodore Roszak. Sessions reads Roszak selectively, omitting reference to his New Age side. Like Teilhardian scholar Conrad Bonifanzi, who says that earth is a psychosomatic entity, the psyche of which "is principally concentrated in human beings,"[79] Roszak asserts that human destiny "is tied to the need and the will of the Earth."[80] In this era of biospheric emergency, the Earth is sending instructions to us about what we must do: "*the planet thinks through us.*"[81] Affirming the view that humans are Gaia's central nervous system and a source of self-awareness capable of ensuring Gaia's own survival, Roszak asserts that humanity's is "the planet's risky experiment in self-conscious intelligence."[82] Having increasingly achieved "an interdependent world society that promises physical security for all and a world-cultural synthesis," we can see that "the planet's prime need is now to moderate our technological and organizational excesses so that all her endangered children might live."[83] If Roszak is right, "the cry of personal pain which [the countercultural] generation utters is the planet's own cry for rescue."[84] At times, counterculturalists may have resorted to human-centered vocabulary to express their suffering, for they could not yet see that their pain was not merely personal, but planetary.

In *The Unfinished Animal,* Roszak anticipates Skolimowski by introducing "the idea of destiny into the evolutionary process."[85] In the history of life, we discern "an ascending order of mindlike receptivity, a steady increase of the power to perceive, discriminate, and make meaningful use of the world roundabout." Even at the level of protein molecules capable of recognizing each other, there emerges "mindlike behavior which will later build into tropisms, instincts, simple intelligence, abstract intelligence, extrasensory powers. *What else is the universe about but the hierarchy of mind?*"[86]

The view that humankind has attained a higher capacity of awareness suggests that in some respects humans are more important than other creatures, a view regarded by deep ecologists as unjustifiably anthropocentric. Paul Shepard denies that "human consciousness is the cosmic pass toward and through which all life must make its way."[87] Like many New Agers, however, Roszak affirms that human beings are uniquely endowed to give voice to the complex processes that gave rise to us. Hence, he calls on the alchemical saying: "As above, so below." "Above" is the macrocosm, "the world of the heavenly spheres, the angelic hosts, and Dame Nature vast as all the planet Earth." "Below" is the microcosm, the human soul. Exponents of the great wisdom traditions knew that "two were in living dialogue. Understanding the universe was a matter of listening, having ears to hear the music of the spheres, the voice of the Earth. Wisdom meant connecting."[88] Since its beginning, Roszak says, the universe has been developing "finer orders of complexity," reaching

toward realms so subtle and complex that they can be fabricated only out of the delicate dynamics of the human imagination. *And what stands at the crest of the hierarchy holds a crowning position.* [Humankind] embodies the full potentiality of all that has gone before, realizing it, expressing it. It occupies the *frontier* of the cosmos.[89]

DEEP ECOLOGY AND NEW PARADIGM   Wary of anthropocentric New Agers like Fuller and Teilhard, deep ecologists have failed to acknowledge that in the 1980s, New Age began giving way to New Paradigm, whose leading figures include Roszak, Capra, and others linked with deep ecology. Skolimowski, too, may be better understood as a New Paradigmer than as a New Ager. Arising from New Age, New Paradigm moves toward deep ecological views, including its emphasis on pluralism and diversity. Charles Jencks says that what I am calling New Paradigm exhibits an "intense concern for pluralism" in the arts and elsewhere; the desire to reclaim certain traditional values, "but in a new key that fully recognizes the ruptures caused by modernity"; an affirmation of difference and otherness, especially in connection with feminism; "the re-enchantment of nature," as guided by recent scientific trends; and "the commitment to an ecological and ecumenical world view that now characterizes post-modern theology."[90] New Paradigmers and deep ecologists agree on the following propositions.[91]

We are in the midst of a global crisis that heralds a paradigm shift to a socially harmonious and ecological era. Like Capra and Roszak, New Paradigmers hold that the dualistic, atomistic, mechanistic, materialistic, patriarchal, militaristic, and nationalistic paradigm of modernity is being transformed by "the spiritual, human potential, feminist, and environmental movements," which are creating "the social and perceptual *context*" for a new politics.[92] Explanations vary regarding how this paradigm shift will occur. Deep ecologists and transpersonal psychologists speak of it in terms of maturation and/or self-realization, whereas some New Paradigmers appeal to chaos theory to explain how the new sociopolitical constellation will emerge.[93]

Personal transformation/evolution is necessary for cultural change. According to Hans-Jürgen Ruppert, New Paradigm's central belief is that social change follows from the evolution of consciousness. He cites Sri Aurobindo: "The circumstances in which man lives upon the earth are the results of the condition of his consciousness. To want to alter the circumstances, without altering consciousness, is an idle illusion."[94] Similarly, deep ecologists stress the internal relation between personal transformation and the development of an ecologically harmonious society.[95] Although acknowledging the potential charlatanism of the counterculture's experimentation with drugs, meditation, Eastern religions, esoteric studies, body work, yoga, holistic health, ecology, new age science, alternative psychotherapies, neoprimitivism and paganism, pop culture, and a host of related phenomena, Roszak nevertheless maintains that this psychic exploration "has been Western society's troubled passage through a crucial stage in the evolution of the human race." Having become so spiritually alienated, "it now becomes our task to reclaim the human potentialities we have denigrated and sacrificed along the way."[96]

The reenchantment of the world is consistent with "postmodern" science. Recalling a new version of romantic naturalism, New Paradigm emphasizes that self-realization occurs through the "dynamism and creative striving" characteristic of all life.[97] Deep ecology and New Paradigm alike seek "a synthesis . . . of old and new, traditional and foreign representations of the world for the expansion of consciousness."[98] Crucial to this synthesis are new cosmologies that depict the universe as a meaning-generating process, in which humankind has a role to play. For Roszak, reenchanting nature requires not only reawakening the "hidden wisdom" (gnosis) of the great spiritual traditions (tribal, Asian, Christian mystic), but also appropriating aspects of contemporary science.

There are problems involved in efforts to reenchant nature by combining science and religion. For one thing, such efforts tend to float into abstractive speculation that conceals the real power-interests that support contemporary scientific research.[99] For another, attempts to equate science to mystic revelation undercut efforts to make science more accessible to lay people. What happens instead is "a further empowerment of the scientist, allotted the task of pursuing reason's higher mysteries, released from any obligation to speak of them in an intelligible language."[100] Counteracting this danger, however, has been a flood of books written by scientists to inform lay people about scientific developments and to speculate about their broader cultural implications.

An ecological sensibility must be developed. Many deep ecologists would agree with Roszak that humankind must be liberated "from the death grip of the urban-industrial dominance. Nothing less than a revolution of the sensibilities will serve our purpose, whatever social revolutions we may also have to undertake."[101] Although emphasizing the particular and local, Roszak also maintains that the achievement of "transpersonal subjectivity" will require a "planetary consensus," a universal convergence of "great souls and teachings [that] arise from all corners of the planet."[102] Transcending the alienating condition of dualistic perception, ecological sensibility directly apprehends the interrelatedness of all things. Since humans are only a part of the living cosmic order, genuine self-realization involves the self-realization of all beings.

A relational type of self must emerge that is inextricably involved with the larger cosmic whole. By expanding the sense of self so as to affirm its internal relationships with all things, humankind will align itself with the terrestrial and cosmic process of which it is only a part. Doing so is necessary not only to avoid ecological disaster, but also for self-realization and social transformation. Like deep ecologist John Seed, who regards tropical rainforests as part of himself, New Paradigmer Peter Russell says:

[A]ll aspects of the world are just as much part of us as our bodies. To cut down the tropical rainforest for any short term goal, would seem to us as not any less crazy than to cut off our finger, simply because it hurts or somehow bothers us.[103]

Many deep ecologists and New Paradigmers acknowledge that the "human potential" movement helped lead to transpersonal psychology, which emphasizes humanity's capacity for developing a holistic, cosmic sense of self. Though wary of the anthropocentric aspects of humanistic psychology, Sessions maintains that deep ecology "is a spiritual or *human potential movement,*" which involves "the growth or increasing maturity of the self."[104] A mature self identifies not only with other humans, but with nonhuman individuals, species, and ecosystems.

Cosmic holism is consistent with holistic health. Maintaining that humanity must learn to work with nature, New Paradigm not only calls for ecologically sound modes of production, but also for holistic health practices (from autogenetic training and macrobiotic cooking, to rebirthing and dream therapy) and spiritual work (from martial arts and medicine wheels to consciousness expansion of all sorts.)[105] In many cases, sick bodies and perverted societies are supposedly manifestations of constricted, atomistic, dualistic, fearful consciousness. Polluting the body with drugs, alcohol, and white bread is the personal version of polluting the planet with nuclear waste, toxic chemicals, and pesticides.

Some critics charge that New Paradigm has a *therapeutic* message: that isolation and alienation can be overcome simply by identifying with the larger "cosmic unity" and becoming attuned to evolutionary processes.[106] In fact, however, New Paradigmers and deep ecologists emphasize the necessity of acting in many different arenas to effect the needed changes. Despite the benefits of taking better care of one's body, then, an obsession with personal health may be the flip side of the death-denying, fear-driven practices fueling the ecological crisis. Moreover, as Andrew Ross points out, New Paradigm criticizes the technological worldview, even while describing the healthy body as "an efficient, smoothly circulating system of energies, resonating, on a higher plane, with the natural frequencies of the global/astral body itself." Such a view of the body contrasts sharply with that of postmodern theory, which tends to describe the body as fractured, troubled, and disordered by the effects of socialization.[107] Because the well-oiled, but ahistorical New Paradigm body is "immune, and often strictly opposed, to any conception of 'nature' as a social construct," New Paradigm's concern about pollution and health threatens to "feed into a social philosophy saturated with the historical barbarism of the politics of quarantine, natural selection, and social apartheid."[108] New Paradigmers, in other words, must examine whether their search for eternal harmonies is driven by an aversion to the imperfections, limitations, and mortality characteristic of finite, historical beings.

The new gnosis or esoteric wisdom is available at first to only a few. The leaders of spiritual and transformational movements usually believe they are part of an elite vanguard endowed with sacred knowledge that will eventually influence the vast majority who remain in the grip of a dying paradigm. Capra remarks that the paradigm shift "is grasped in its full extent only by a small minority."[109] Noting that steps to higher consciousness have always been taken by a noble few, Roszak wonders why we have "no anthropology of this remarkable human constant—an anthropology which recognizes the visionary genius as the first world citizen, the prophet of a planetary culture we have yet to see born?"[110] Today, he says, we need new teachers who can remind us that people can *choose* to move to a higher order of understanding.[111]

It is important to think globally, act locally. New Paradigmers and deep ecologists agree that current practices may be triggering off changes that will drastically alter global ecosystems. Keeping this planetary view in mind, people must focus on healing individuals, society, and natural areas at the local level. The process of networking helps to reconcile global awareness with decentralized, bioregional action. That such networking usually requires electronic means does not mean that New Paradigmers have "sold out" to modern technology. Consider the contemporary Native American shaman, Black Elk, who says that Western science is often consistent with insights that he gains by very different methods.[112] Nevertheless, deep ecology and New Paradigmers agree that modernity's adoption of mechanistic materialism has been a major factor in human alienation and ecological problems.

The proximity between New Paradigm and deep ecology is evident in Willis Harman's book, *Global Mind Change: The New Age Revolution in the Way We Think* (1988).[113] President of the Institute of Noetic Sciences, Harman argues that contemporary ecological and social problems are symptoms of the materialistic metaphysics that emerged in connection with early modern science's paradigm shift: from the spiritual and participatory sensibility of medieval humanity to the materialistic, mechanistic, objectivistic, and dualistic world of modernity. Since the mechanistic paradigm gave rise to the three macroproblems of our age—widespread poverty, environmental degradation, and nuclear weapons—reforms made *within* that paradigm cannot solve those problems.[114] Only a paradigm shift involving a transformation of consciousness can save humanity and earth from destruction. Emphasizing that the universe is the manifestation of consciousness, mind, spirit, or Atman, Harman believes that transpersonal psychology is central to the new paradigm. Like deep ecologists, he stresses the "perennial wisdom," esoteric teachings, and *gnosis,* whose "deep intuition" reveals our interrelatedness with all phenomena.[115] According to Harman, the coming transformation will involve a "respiritualization" of Western society, "with emphasis on *self-realization,* transcendent meaning, and inner growth leading to wisdom and compassion."[116] The "gentle revolution" is being led by the ecology, peace, and feminist movements, which leave behind the belief system

in which the Earth exists to be exploited, "premodern" cultures are to be superseded, people with non-white skins are inferior, women have a subordinate role, nuclear weapons bring "security," profligate consumption is "good for the economy," and so on.[117]

Instead of being frantically concerned about achieving ever-greater levels of production and consumption, we must shift our focus to lifelong personal growth and expansion of consciousness. If the production-oriented paradigm arose in connection with a materialist worldview, the personal growth paradigm will emerge in connection with a spiritual worldview. Like deep ecologists, then, Harman regards ecological problems as a crisis of character and culture, a crisis stemming from human immaturity. Only when sufficient numbers of individuals develop a wider identification with all life, and thus a deeper awareness "awareness of the finiteness and multiple-interconnectedness of the planetary ecosystem," according to Harman, will large-scale social and economic changes begin to take place. Such awareness, promoted by deep ecology, involves a "subtle awareness of the oneness of all life, the interdependence of its multifold manifestations, and the irrepressibility of its tendencies toward evolution and transformation."[118] Personal transformation will replace gigantic centralized technology with resource- and energy-saving "appropriate technology," that is ecologically benign, labor intensive, and comprehensible by individuals and communities. This type of technology complements

a strong ecological ethic; *strong identification with nature,* fellow human beings, and future generations; a lifestyle characterized by voluntary frugality ("doing more with less"); appreciation of the simple life and simple virtues; and the kind of work that fosters these attitudes.[119]

Like deep ecologists, Harman maintains that appropriate technology and lifestyle change will help prevent modern Western industrial monoculture from becoming the inescapable destiny of all countries. The wave of the future, we are told, is "toward an ecology of diverse cultures—each with its own interpretation of human development, social goals, and ultimate meaning—and toward a world system that tends to support rather than diminish, thwart, and bias against this diversity."[120] Although suggesting that deep ecology gives the most direct spiritual expression to the envisioned paradigm shift, Harman notes that the Green movement in general manifests this shift. Rejecting the goal of endless technological and material growth at the expense of nature, he agrees with the Greens' emphasis on ecological holism, pacifism, feminism, human-scale technologies, "self-realization, transcendent meaning, and inner growth leading to wisdom and compassion."[121]

Recent polls suggest that about 10 percent of American people have been significantly influenced by New Paradigm ideals. Leftist critics point out, however, that this considerable following is disproportionately constituted by middle and upper-middle class white people, who retain modernity's optimism, even while questioning the political institutions and strategies long identified with Marxist progressivism. Are New Paradigmers right in saying that we are witnessing the birth of a new era that leaves behind the violent binary of capitalism versus communism? Or are they politically naive idealists who fail to see the social and ecological implications of a world run by multinational corporations?

If leftists question the political wisdom of New Paradigmers, transpersonal theorists like Ken Wilber question their insight into human existence. Affirming the harmonious, luminescent, joyful New Era, New Paradigmers often ignore the tenacity of the intertwined phenomena of death anxiety and evil. If New Paradigmers have not matured beyond the level of egoic consciousness, their desire to "save the world" is likely to be motivated by the same death-denying, survivalist fantasies that animated those modern revolutions that ended in violence and oppression.[122] To the extent that they insufficiently address death denial and evil, deep ecologists also risk advocating movements that will liberate neither human nor nonhuman beings.

Despite substantial and in some cases problematic similarities, New Paradigm and deep ecology differ in at least two respects. First, New Paradigm is more optimistic about the possibility that technological modernity's institutions can be transformed in socially progressive and ecologically sustainable manner. Second, New Paradigm is often more committed to the view, shared by the esoteric wings of many religious traditions, that "reality" is constituted by complex, interrelated levels, of which the spatiotemporal domain is only one. Using the rubric of the "perennial philosophy," deep ecology sometimes speaks affirmatively of nondualistic traditions. Yet deep ecologists also assert that the concept of "Great Chain of Being," according to which "reality" is constituted by a hierarchy of levels, has often been used to denigrate the organic level and simultaneously to elevate the status of humans, who are supposedly the only creatures inhabiting the "higher," transcendent levels. In emphasizing ecocentrism, deep ecology understandably resists the transcendentalism held responsible for arrogant anthropocentrism. But in affirming what sometimes seems to be a one-level universe, some deep ecologists not only contradict the perennial philosophy to which they often appeal, but also undermine transpersonal psychology's argument that attempts to dominate nature will end only when humankind evolves to a higher, more integrated level of consciousness. In the next chapter, we examine whether Arne Naess's view of human maturation is consistent with an evolutionary interpretation of the perennial philosophy's multiple-level view of reality.

Postmodern theorists would emphasize that the shared utopian aspirations of New Paradigmers and deep ecologists are easily seduced by modernity's totalizing logic of identity. But leftists warn that insofar as self-realization is defined primarily as personal transformation, and insofar as such transformation is linked with occult and irrational traditions, deep ecologists and New Paradigmers may be unwittingly aiding the neoconservative, even reactionary trends allegedly at work in the postmodern theory that deconstructs rational foundations and rejects a progressive reading of history. In a secular age that many people find alienating, violent, and increasingly pointless, we should scarcely be surprised at the widespread yearning for transformation, spirituality, transcendent meaning, and utopian social changes. Marxist literary critic Frederic Jameson emphasizes

the necessity of the reinvention of the Utopian vision in any contemporary politics; this lesson, which Marcuse first taught us, is part of the legacy of the sixties which must never be abandoned in any reevaluation of that period and of our relationship to it.[123]

Despite their critiques of modernity, New Paradigm and deep ecology—each in its own way—retain modernity's conviction that human progress, evolution, or maturation is possible. A commitment to progressive ideals is *not* necessary to generate dramatic social movements, however, as National Socialism and movements driven by fundamentalist religious beliefs make clear. Despite many drawbacks, fundamentalist movements at least have the virtue of emphasizing human moral frailty and the wiles of the self-worshiping ego. By way of contrast, some New Agers and New Paradigmers have rather naive views about the ease with which human depravity can be overcome in a "paradigm shift" that is supposedly just around the corner. Though deep ecologists criticize human violence, they have not examined in much detail the roots of human evil.

Arthur Mendel, arguing that the flip side of the counterculture's utopian aspirations is despondency, nihilism, and retreat into quests for personal salvation, suggests that the 1960s counterculture, like many millennial movements, shared with fascism certain aspects of the "politics of cultural despair."[124] People who are socially alienated and bereft of personal direction are often seduced into exchanging their personal responsibility for the salvation promised by an elite few who are allegedly attuned to the mysterious workings of immortal cosmic forces. In 1932, conservative revolutionary Oswald Spengler wrote that the return of esotericism signaled a decaying civilization: "Occultism and spiritualism, Indian philosophies, metaphysical brooding of Christian and pagan colors emerge once again. It is the mood of Rome at the time of Augustus."[125] For Spengler, occultism meant the mood of Munich at the time of Hitler. For modernist critics of New Age, New Paradigm, and deep ecology, occultism means the mood of Berkeley at the time of Reagan. The fact that Martin Heidegger's thought has certain parallels with deep ecology and has been crucial for much of postmodern theory, fuels the suspicion of modernity's defenders that deep ecology and postmodern theory are neoconservative, regressive, and reactionary. Deep ecologists would seem to be walking a tightrope across an abyss: slipping to the right may plunge them into an antimodernist ecofascism; slipping to the left may lead them to reinforce modernity's control obsession.

3 · DEEP ECOLOGY, HEIDEGGER, AND POSTMODERN THEORY

New Paradigm and deep ecology are usually ignored by postmodern theorists, who regard them as philistine and naive, even though these countercultural offshoots join postmodern theory in criticizing modernity's dark side: its control obsession, its logic of identity, its anthropocentric humanism, and its dualism. Unlike postmodern theory, however, New Paradigm and deep ecology hold that this dark side can either be discarded or transformed in a maturation process that will lead to an ecologically sound society. If New Paradigmers and deep ecologists retain elements of countercultural utopianism, however, many French postmodern theorists either never had such a vision, or lost it when the "days of May" in 1968 led not to social revolution, but to a reinforcement of capitalist modernity. Around this time, many French intellectuals began turning away from Marxism not only because party leaders had supported efforts to quell the revolution, but also because reports of the horrors of the Soviet Gulag could no longer be denied. Concluding that modernity led either to Marxist totalitarianism or to the global un-culture of American "businessism," French intellectuals became increasingly postmodern, turning for inspiration to Nietzsche's bitter critique of modernity, to George Bataille's celebration of irrational expenditure and sensual excess, and above all to Heidegger's antimodernist antihumanism.[1]

In 1962, structural anthropologist Claude Lévi-Strauss had encouraged this antihumanistic turn in France by arguing, against Jean-Paul Sartre, that there was no universal human history, no linear progress, and no cultures that were more "advanced" than others: the "savage mind" is just as complex as the "modern mind."[2] Condemning the Eurocentrism that had justified genocidal practices against non-Western peoples, he later criticized the anthropocentric humanism that justifies the extermination of thousands of species, each of which was as valuable as a person. Decrying the strutting arrogance of modern "man," Lévi-Strauss preferred the humility of tribal people, for whom "a well-ordered harmony does not begin with the self, but rather places the world before life, life before man, the respect for other beings before the love of self."[3] Lévi-Strauss insisted that his antihumanism was not misanthropy, but rather a critique of that "shameless humanism" that "makes man into the lord, into the absolute master of creation."[4] Much like a deep ecologist, he asserted not only that "care about mankind without a simultaneous solidarity-like caring for all other forms of life . . . [leads] mankind to self-oppression and self-exploitation,"[5] but also that "the rights which one can and should recognize for mankind are only a special case of those rights which we must grant to the creative force of life."[6]

Though adopting many of the antihumanist attitudes of Lévi-Strauss and Heidegger, postmodern theorists such as Foucault, Derrida, and Lyotard focused on human social and cultural affairs, thus minimizing Lévi-Strauss's and Heidegger's criticisms of modernity's assault on nature. In North American academic circles during the late 1970s, French postmodern theory began achieving a respectability never won by New Paradigm, deep ecology, or counterculturalism in general. Cross-fertilization has occurred between postmodern theory and counterculturalism, but they have often been wary of one other, postmodern theory fearing that New Paradigm and deep ecology are naively utopian, whereas the latter two accuse postmodern theory of anthropocentrism, ecological ignorance, and nihilism.

In the first section of this chapter, I show how some basic themes of postmodern theory impinge upon deep ecology. The second section draws some initial comparisons between deep ecology and Martin Heidegger, whose work is crucial to much of postmodern theory. In the third section, I outline the "ontological phenomenalism" of Heidegger, Naess, and Mahayana Buddhism. Finally, section four studies whether Derrida's deconstructive postmodern theory can be read as consistent with Naess and Buddhism's deconstruction of "reality."

POSTMODERN THEORY AND DEEP ECOLOGY   What I am calling postmodern theory is often associated with the "poststructuralism" of French theorists like Jacques Derrida, Michel Foucault, Jean-François Lyotard, and Gilles Deleuze. Such labels are always misleading. Indeed, Derrida nor Foucault refused to call themselves either postmodernists *or* poststructuralists. Despite important differences, mentioned below, I gather these writers under the term "postmodern theorists" because they offer such a relentless critique of the presuppositions of modernity. Most of these theorists, including the American neopragmatist Richard Rorty, adhere to many of the following positions.

Critique of representational epistemology: Truth does not consist of propositions that correctly "mirror" or "represent" an independent, preexisting reality. Instead, what passes for "objective" truth is a construction generated by power-interested elites. Although emphasizing that marginal social groups are oppressed by virtue of these supposedly universal and objective truths, postmodern theorists influenced by Nietzsche (such as Foucault) insist that no one is innocent; everyone (including the deep ecologist) is concerned with defining truth as a way of acquiring and retaining power. To counter the power elite's hegemonic grip on truth, postmodern theorists maintain that "truth" should result from negotiations in which as many voices as possible are heard.

Critique of representational concepts of language: Drawing on Saussure, deconstructive postmodern theorists such as Derrida maintain that words have no positive meaning, but rather gain meaning by how they differ from other words. Language, then, is not an instrumental medium referring to entities in the external world, but is instead a self-referring, indefinitely complex, open-ended, *differential system* of signifiers. Derrida says that everything is a vanishing moment in a linguistic play that always bears the "trace" of the other. Language does not mirror *the* world, but constructs *worlds* according to ever-shifting power perspectives. What we call objects or things are phenomena that show up *within* the charmed circle(s) of language. Language is not something we possess, but instead "we" are primarily functions of it. Without language, Heidegger said, things would not "be."

Hence, in claiming that its own language game "reflects" reality, science makes a bid for hegemony, which diminishes the status of alternative language-games, including literature and traditional narratives. In league with universalistic claims about the modern ego-subject, the totalizing claims of modern science have often helped to justify oppression and exclusion. Challenging the validity of all the ultimate truths, transcendental signifiers, or metaphysical master names, including Subject, History, Reason, Truth, Man, and Nature, and criticizing all "total systems," postmodern theorists are skeptical of ecosophies that trade in one type of "centrism" (anthropocentrism) for another (ecocentrism). Supposedly, all centrisms, like all ideologies promising "unity," operate according to the logic of identity, which effaces and at times sacrifices individuals for the good of the larger "whole." Although Foucault criticized the domineering "discursive regime" of modernity, he did not join Derrida in saying that there is nothing outside the text. For Foucault and Deleuze, Nietzsche's restless will to power works through language and institutions to shape the human body, which is power's primary site of contestation. Neither the body nor the will to power are "textual" phenomena.

Critique of foundational metaphysics: Postmodern theorists charge that the search for a metaphysical foundation or ground is not only confused (there is no origin, *arche,* or reason for things), but also ideological: political regimes gain legitimacy by virtue of metaphysical foundations dreamt up by ideologues. Denying that there are deep structures beneath "surface" phenomena, deconstructive postmodern theorists such as Foucault say that power is spread throughout the technological system. Overthrowing a certain class of people would not do away with the authoritarian tendencies that are reproduced in relations at every social level. Power is not to be understood merely negatively, as repression, but also positively, as productive of the very types of selves that we are.

Denying that there is a metaphysical ground for things, Derrida says that there is only the realm of appearances that unfold in the unpredictable and ultimately unjustifiable play of language. To the extent that deconstructive postmodern theory's emphasis on the linguistic play of appearances can be read as a type of aestheticism, and insofar as postmodern theory denies any deep structures to be revealed in the act of "ideological unmasking," leftist critics charge postmodern theory with being a reprise of the irrational, antimodernist aestheticism of early twentieth-century reactionaries, who affirmed the given social circumstances as the latest manifestation of the incomprehensible Will to Power. Postmodern theorists reply that they take an oppositional stance to modernity's domineering structures, though they insist that there is no neutral metaposition from which to grasp those structures *in toto*, nor is it possible simply to leap outside of them. Although global theorizing may be impossible, local resistance and action are not.

Since postmodern theory usually undermines the reality and agency of the subject, many critics ask: *who* will enact such resistance? Rainer Nägele contends that by replacing "the human agents and heroes of humanistic models of (his)tory with the dynamic of structural constellations," postmodern theory threatens to "become an ontological justification for the existing structural forces of the concrete power constellations."[7] Liberals criticize postmodern theory even more than do leftists, according to Nägele, for liberals need the ideology of the autonomous subject "to cover up the real destruction of subjectivity and autonomy in [contemporary] social praxis."[8]

Critique of the self-grounding, self-present, self-centered, patriarchal, anthropocentric subject: Many postmodern theorists argue that the ego-subject is not autonomous and self-grounding, but is rather a secondary effect of hidden processes (e.g., material, unconscious, vitalistic, power-interested, cultural, ontological, linguistic-grammatical). When postmodern theorists speak of "the end of man" or "antihumanism," they mean that the once autonomous, white, male, class-privileged European subject is a construct challenged by a myriad of alternatives.[9] The centered subject is splintered into a bewildering set of possible perspectives, several of which can coexist simultaneously within the same "person."[10] Following thinkers like Heidegger, Marx, and Freud, postmodern theorists conclude that the subject disappears into: (1) a set of social functions and discourses generated by an oppressive system; or (2) the play of signifiers that never gains grounding in a transcendental "signified"; or (3) an irreconcilable plethora of heterogeneous desires and impulses; or (4) haunting self-images born of aching desire for a lost paradisiacal unity; or (5) a reflexive registering of ever-changing electronic images: the simulacra of hyperreality. If the autonomous subject is a fiction constituted by self-concealing processes, there would seem to be no agency, purpose, or intention to human life.

Like Theodor Adorno, postmodern theorists assert that the self-grounding modern subject operates according to a totalizing logic of identity, which forces what is different (e.g., Third World people, women, and other nonelites) to conform to categories consistent with the allegedly universal principles of the subject. For deconstructive postmodern theorists, nothing is simply self-identical. Despite many differences, Heidegger and Adorno agreed that the modern subject's project of using technology to free itself from material constraints backfired, because modern technology reveals everything, *including* the subject, as raw material for enhancing the power of the technological system. In trying to "dominate" nature, the subject turns itself into another means for an irrational end. In view of the all-encompassing character of technological modernity, postmodern theorists see little chance of escaping its oppressive grip.

Critique of master narratives: Western grand narratives describe the historical process whereby the subject (whether autonomous ego or social collectivity) becomes master of its own destiny, often by colonizing other peoples and their lands in the name of universal "freedom." Believing that the myth of progress helped fuel totalitarianism, and chastened by the organized violence of our century, postmodern theorists doubt that humanity is undergoing an evolutionary transformation that will end the metaphysical dualism responsible for domination and hierarchy. Progressive critics argue, however, that if there is no *telos* or progress in history, one can no longer differentiate between "reactionary" and "progressive" views.

Deep ecologists have an ambivalent stance regarding the aforementioned attitudes. On the one hand, deep ecologists join postmodern theorists in criticizing anthropocentric humanism's master narrative, according to which progress entails dominating what rationality perceives as "other" and thus inferior. On the other hand, deep ecologists feel that postmodern theorists restrict the "other" to the human, thereby ignoring nonhuman nature. Further, deep ecologists join postmodern theorists in criticizing modernity for its dualism, including its tendency radically to differentiate or even to dissociate humankind and nature. Yet though seeking to overcome such dualisms, deep ecologists are wary of postmodernity's tendency to de-differentiate distinctions that deep ecologists may wish to retain. Consider, for instance, postmodern theory's tendency to de-differentiate or to negate modernity's distinction between high art and mass culture, the latter of which was a commercial enterprise that threatened the integrity of high art. Deep ecologists feel that postmodern theorists and postmodern artists want to extend this same de-differentiating tendency to the distinction between wild nature and modern technology, the former being an allegedly privileged domain that deep ecologists seek to protect from commercial onslaught. Some postmodern artists had hoped that by de-differentiating high art and mass culture, they could help to impede the reduction of everything to a commodity, but things did not turn out this way. In fact, the process of commodification has speeded up.

Though aware that some postmodern artists have taken up ecological themes, deep ecologists are afraid that much of postmodern art is helping to erase the distinction between wild nature and representation.[11] Critics note that postmodern art has increasingly become a self-reflexive media event, whose images circulate in the "political economy of the sign" (Baudrillard), to which there is no "outside." Hence, national parks are becoming "natural" Disneylands; beautiful landscapes portrayed on television somehow threaten to become more "real" than the place itself. For someone like Baudrillard, however, the "death of nature" as a transcendental signified, that is, as an independent realm that can resist being sucked into the "black hole" of electronic media, already began with the very concept of "ecology" to which deep ecologists seem so attached. Ecology is a scientific concept that, by offering a scientific scheme for interpreting complex environmental processes, constitutes an important step in what Heidegger meant by reducing the world to the status of a "picture" or "representation" for the technological human subject.

Most postmodern theorists, however, influenced by Heidegger's notion of the ontological difference between being and entities, insist that they are not promoting an indifferent de-differentiation, but rather genuine *difference*. They argue that it is modernity, despite its dualisms, that engages in a totalizing, destructive type of de-differentiating, namely, the "logic of identity," that forces everyone to conform to ostensibly universal categories. Modern humanism effaces cultural differences and marginalizes those people who do not conform to supposedly universal cultural categories that were in fact abstracted from white, property-owning, Western males. Deep ecologists agree with this critique of the logic of identity, but maintain that postmodern theorists usually forget that *nonhumans* as well as humans have been harmed by that logic. Yet postmodern theorists would reply that they understand quite well how modernity's logic of identity de-differentiated humankind and nature such that both were disclosed as raw material for modernity's aim of gaining total control over everything. These postmodern theorists fear that deep ecology's "ecocentrism" is not only contributing (though unwittingly) to a de-differentiation that effaces important differences between human and nonhuman, but is also promoting a totalizing worldview that reflects a problematic yearning for a lost origin or ground.

Of course, most deep ecologists deny that ecocentrism is simply another totalizing foundationalism that expresses their own interests, for example, their interest in hiking in untrammeled wilderness areas. Arne Naess, however, who celebrates conceptual and cultural pluralism, might be willing to concede that his Ecosophy T is only one power-perspective among others, for Ecosophy T does promote his own *conatus,* his own striving for self-realization. Nevertheless, he would add that for him self-realization cannot be restricted to his own personal satisfaction; instead, genuine self-realization requires the self-realization of all other beings in this interconnected world.

Naess's views on language and knowledge are sufficiently sophisticated to take into account postmodern theory's critique of representationalism, but many other deep ecologists ignore it. They take for granted that their assertions about humankind, animals, plants, the biosphere, wider identification, and Atman accurately correspond to or correctly disclose these phenomena. Because of a lack of critical reflexivity about the role played by language in shaping cultural experience and definition of "nature," the writings of some deep ecologists seem philosophically naive in comparison with the hypersophistication of postmodern theory. In reply, many deep ecologists say that deconstructive postmodern theory promotes a relativism inconsistent with the search for enduring truth, amounts to a linguistic idealism that recapitulates modernity's anthropocentrism, undermines claims about the intrinsic worth of life, and relativizes scientific assertions relied on by deep ecologists to justify their struggle to save wilderness and threatened species. Deep ecologists ask: if everything, including species, is a linguistic construct, on what basis are we to justify preserving species? Although it may be true that most texts involve a narrative structure, metaphors, tropes, and other devices associated with fiction, this does not mean that every text— including purportedly veridical texts by philosophers, historians, and scientists—can be regarded as instances of fiction. To be sure, finite beings have no access to absolute truth, and establishing finite truths is often a difficult, disputational, and politically charged process. Still, none of this prevents some historical, philosophical, or scientific texts from being more informative, illuminating, and "truthful" than others.

Some deep ecologists hesitate to grant the perspectival character of deep ecology, because they themselves were influenced by philosophers like Spinoza, who described God, or Nature, as a totally interrelated, rational whole. For example, although George Sessions concedes that modern science encourages people to exploit nature by disclosing it abstractly as lifeless stuff, he also says that modern science made possible a new cosmology, according to which humans are part of nature, not its lord and master. Spinoza believed that abstract scientific knowledge was a necessary stage in attaining the cosmic identification promoted by many deep ecologists.[12] For Sessions, then, modern science says something *true* about nature, even if science's quest for truth may have been seduced by humanistic ideologies. Following Nietzsche and Heidegger, however, postmodern theorists charge that modern science and modern metaphysicians, including Spinoza, were influenced from the start by the power-interests of the emerging modern subject. Sessions attempts to explain away Spinoza's instrumentalist view of nature by saying that the urbanite Spinoza never attained an adequate sense of "biological identity" with nature; hence, he conceived of it in terms of the formal systems of early modern physics.[13] But as we have seen, some commentators regard anthropocentrism an *essential* to Spinoza's thought.

Postmodern theorists suspect efforts to purge Spinoza's thought of its power-motivated aspect. In their view, no significant truth claims are wholly innocent of power-interests. By acknowledging the *perspectival* character of truth, competing groups may be more willing to enter into negotiated contests about how to weigh various assertions. Many deep ecologists, however, resist conceding that scientific ecology's claims—for example, that life is interrelated, or that rich species diversity is needed for healthy ecosystems—are perspectival, since such a concession would presumably undermine the authority of such claims, thereby weakening deep ecology's presumption that its views are based on "scientific truth." If the claims made by deep ecology's favorite ecologists are not uncontestably true, but instead are merely power-interested perspectives, there would seem to be nothing wrong with the practice whereby developers hire scientific experts, such as in connection with an Environmental Impact Statement, to justify the claim that the proposed project will cause minimal environmental damage. Environmentalists may hire experts of their own to rebut such testimony. In the process, truth seems reduced to competing assertions made by hired scientific guns of power-interested organizations.

Even friends of deep ecology maintain that scientific theories are constantly evolving and inevitably shaped by the ideologies and interests of the scientists who develop and test those theories. Recently, Brian Steverson has shown that contemporary ecologists contest one of the claims most favored by deep ecologists: that humans exist in ecosystems that are clearly "interrelated" with non-human ecosystems.[14] In fact, humans have increasingly segmented their own world from the domain of wild nature. Similarly, Donald Worster says that ecological science does not necessarily agree with deep ecology's claim that because "nature knows best," that is, because humans cannot understand the enormous complexity involved in sustaining the equilibrium of ecosystems, humans ought to drastically curtail their interventions in nature.[15] Hoping that their findings would "offer a pathway to a kind of moral enlightenment that we can call . . . 'conservation'," whose aim was to achieve "a lasting equilibrium with nature," early ecologists like Frederic Clements argued that natural landscapes gradually flow toward a stable "climax" stage, in which they take on the self-organizing, coherent traits of an organism.[16] He believed that scientists should help right the imbalances inflicted upon the land, thereby regaining "some approximation of nature's original health and stability."[17] In the post-World War II era, ecologists like Eugene Odum developed the popular view of the ecosystem as a community of organisms interacting with the material environment by virtue of complex energy flows. Tending toward the maximum diversity compatible with available energy, ecosystems evolve from an early stage in which organisms compete with each other, to a later stage—homeostasis—in which mutualism and symbiosis abound. Worster notes that Odum's notion of the "mature ecosystem" replaces Clement's idea of a landscape's "climax" stage. To maintain desirable ecosystem fragile balance and abundant diversity, Odum and deep ecologists recommend that humans interfere as little as possible in natural systems.

Beginning in the late 1970s, however, a few ecologists—whom we might describe as "postmodern"—began postulating that ecological succession has no direction, that there is no "progression" of any sort, that change is the only constant, and that nature never reaches a point of stability. Regarding a forest not as a self-regulating ecosystem, but rather as "an erratic, shifting mosaic of trees and other plants," these new ecologists "could see lots of individual species, each doing its thing, but they could locate no emergent collectivity, nor any strategy to achieve one."[18] As opposed to equilibrium, order, harmony, cooperation, system, and balance, the new ecologists began seeing disturbance, disorder, perturbation, rupture, competition, and heterogeneity—the same characterizations that postmodern theorists use to describe complex social processes, which totalizing modern metaphysicians wish to constrain within the limits of an all-embracing "system." Worster hypothesizes that this shift, from ecosystem to a landscape composed of constantly changing patches of living organisms, occurred in part because many new ecologists were trained in population biology; hence, they focused from the start on individuals, not on collectivities and their emergent properties.[19] To explain this new focus on individuals, Worster appeals to ideological factors, including a preference for entrepreneurial individualism and outright social Darwinism. Thomas Söderquist agrees that those whom I describe as the new postmodern ecologists

are individualists, abhorring the idea of large-scale ecosystem projects. Indeed, the transition from ecosystem ecology to evolutionary ecology seems to reflect the generational transition from the politically conscious generation of the 1960s to the "yuppie" generation of the 1980s.[20]

A final factor, the rise of chaos theory, also helps explain why a number of ecologists have moved away from the vocabulary of linear progression, regularity, and equilibrium, and toward the vocabulary of unpredictable fluctuations. According to Worster, although chaos theory shares John Muir's notion of interconnectedness, it undermines his conviction that ecosystems can be understood as grand systems of internal relationships that constitute, and thus are ontologically prior to, individual organisms.[21] In contending that most phenomena cannot be explained in terms of linear equations, chaos theory reflects postmodern theory's critique of the oppressively unifying logic of modern systems (including science) which marginalize hetereogeneity, spontaneity, and difference. Worster warns, however, that by undermining the notion of ecosystemic harmony and stability, and by emphasizing the fact of constant and unpredictable change, the idea of natural chaos legitimates two claims advanced by capitalist entrepreneurs. First, there are no stable ecosystems to disrupt; second, no one can predict the consequences of human interventions in the biosphere.[22] In the final chapter, we examine parallels between the creative chaos of market systems and the generative chaos of organic systems. Such parallels suggest that a market system may be a necessary but not sufficient condition for addressing contemporary ecological problems in an effective manner.

Ecofeminists Karen Warren and Jim Cheney have recently discussed a new approach to ecological science (unfortunately named "hierarchy theory"), according to which there are several different ways of understanding ecological phenomena, no one of which is privileged or "true."[23] Hence, the fact that we can interpret individual plants and animals as dependent functions of a whole ecosystem does *not* legitimate the conclusion that the latter is more real and/or valuable than the former. Hierarchy theory disagrees with ecological models that portray energy flows or nutrient cycles as the "really real," in comparison with individual organisms that are merely temporary constellations of such flows and cycles. By foregoing modernity's supposition that there is only one "truth," and by embracing postmodern theory's assertion that truth is perspectival and contestable, Warren and Cheney help to address deep ecology's problem of specifying which entities are more real and/or more valuable: individual organisms or systemic phenomena.

Postmodern theorists say that in purporting to speak for nature, deep ecologists are masking their own interests, for example, they want to preserve large tracts of wilderness in which they enjoy hiking. Even if deep ecologists are protecting wild nature for its own sake, however, this interest is *not* universally shared. There are political dangers involved in claiming that one's own views are true not only by virtue of unchallengeable scientific assertions, but also by virtue of an "ecological sensibility" arising from identifying more widely with nature than do benighted industrialists and tree-burning peasants. A tyrant rarely portrays himself as motivated by naked power-interests; rather, he depicts himself as being inspired by profound truths that are ignored by those responsible for the oppression against which he fights. Even though I regard the current rate of species-extinction as suicidal, tragic, and reprehensible, I know that the causes of this loss are complex. In struggling to preserve wild nature, I must enter into dialogue with multiple contestants with varying perspectives on what "preservation" means. Similarly, deep ecologists must be willing to take the risk of *contesting* Earth's future in cultural and political arenas populated by people with very different perspectives.

HEIDEGGER AND DEEP ECOLOGY   Given the fact that most French postmodern theorists have evinced such scant interest in ecological issues, direct comparisons between French postmodern theory and deep ecology would seem to have limited benefit. Moreover, the former regards the latter as naive and utopian, whereas the latter regards the former as anthropocentric and nihilistic. Comparisons between deep ecology and first-generation *German* postmodern theorists, especially

Nietzsche and Heidegger, who were influenced by a long tradition of nature romanticism, prove to be more interesting. Recently, for instance, Max Hallman has interpreted Nietzsche as a deep ecological thinker.[24] Reading Heidegger in the same vein, I once believed his thought would provide a way out of technological modernity's nihilistic disclosure of everything as raw material.[25] Today, because I see that his total critique of modernity was in many ways consistent with the critique advanced by Nazism, I am more cautious about abandoning the political institutions of modernity, though I remain critical of its dark side.

Critics use the potential Heidegger-deep ecology link as evidence that the latter may lean toward ecofascism. Such critics employ the following logic: Heidegger supported National Socialism; his thought is at least partly compatible with deep ecology; therefore, deep ecology must be compatible with National Socialism.[26] Although this logic of contamination is invalid, deep ecologists—as well as the postmodern theorists whose work Heidegger has so influenced—must take seriously the political drawbacks of his unrestrained attacks on modernity. Many deep ecologists now disown Heidegger not only because of his political problems, but also because they conclude that—despite his protests to the contrary—he remained trapped by the anthropocentrism common to modernity and postmodern theory. As we shall see, however, Naess retains an interest in Heidegger despite these problems.

In part because of my essays, Devall and Sessions once said that Heidegger made three contributions to deep ecology. First, he argued that the anthropocentric trend taken by philosophy since Plato "paved the way for the technocratic mentality which espouses domination over Nature." Second, he encouraged people to begin a kind of "meditative" thinking" that would "let things be," a notion with certain similarities to what Taoism calls *wu wei*. Third, he "called us to dwell authentically on this Earth, parallel to our [Devall and Sessions] call to dwell in our bioregion and to dwell with alertness to the natural processes."[27] For Heidegger, subjectivism, dualism, anthropocentrism, and the progressive view of history gave rise to the technological age, in which all things are disclosed as nothing but raw material for consumption. Forgetting that its highest calling is to "let things be," that is, to allow things to manifest themselves according to their own appropriate possibilities, modern humanity becomes reduced to the "clever animal" that dominates everything for the sake of power and security. To move beyond technological nihilism, Heidegger said that the West needs a new beginning as profound as the one initiated in ancient Greece.

Like Heidegger, many deep ecologists maintain that since modernity's attempt to dominate nature stems from a constricted understanding of what things *are*, only an ontological paradigm shift can generate new attitudes, practices, and institutions that exhibit respect and care for all beings. In Heidegger's view that authentic human *Dasein* let things be, deep ecologists discern similarities to their idea that human self-realization is bound up with letting other things realize their own potential. A difference between Heidegger and deep ecology concerns how this ontological shift is to come about. Rejecting Hegel's progressive views, Heidegger said that only an unpredictable turn in the "destiny of being" (*Seinsgeschick*) could reverse the West's long decline into anthropocentric nihilism. He believed that the "inner truth and greatness" of National Socialism lay in the possibility of initiating such a turn. By way of contrast, deep ecology's norm of self-realization may be read as broadly consistent with a "progressive" view of history, according to which humanity may have lost an earlier sense of connection with the living earth, but nevertheless may be gradually maturing or evolving in such a way as to realize a hidden potential for caring for all beings.

Granted, some deep ecologists resist my progressive reading of their work because the emancipatory goals of modernity seem so closely interwoven with the goal of conquering nature. After all, progressive ideologies uniformly denigrate the achievements of neolithic and tribal societies while overestimating a "progress" based on efforts to control domination nature. Similarly, postmodern theorists hold that progressive views of history are ideologies justifying Western colonialism. In my view, however, if deep ecology does not adhere to at least a critical version of historical maturation or evolution, deep ecology has no apparent basis for expecting a paradigm shift that will move Western culture toward ecocentrism. Appealing to chaos theory to account for such a shift is problematic because the outcome of chaotic "phase shifts" are unpredictable; hence, the new era might not turn out to be ecotopian after all.

For humankind to evolve in such a way as to move beyond militaristic, patriarchal cultures, a profound shift is needed: away from death denial and toward affirmation of personal and species mortality, limitation, finitude, and dependence. In my view, such a shift would require insight into an eternal domain that transcends, yet includes the phenomenal realm. Without such a shift, political movements will continue to be motivated by the personal and collective craving for immortality. Such movements will simply generate new oppressive social institutions, new nature-dominating projects. Deep ecology's emphasis on personal transformation is criticized by leftists, who say that such ideas neglect capitalism's role in shaping individual consciousness and in destroying ecosystems. But the left has never dealt effectively with the possibility that death denial has helped to encourage capital accumulation, authoritarianism, and hierarchy. Arguably, so long as people require immortality symbols, wealth, status, and violence will continue to be popular.

The dark side for modernity's totalizing, universalistic ideas of progress reflect a deep-seated drive for control: for an end to uncertainty, anxiety, and imperfection; for a return to the blissful unity attributed to the origin. For those coming to terms with personal and species mortality, progress would be redefined as *diverse* processes of personal and social evolution that take different shapes in different times and places. Moreover, progress would be understood as a *very* long-term affair, not something that can be completed in a few centuries. For many Western people, a more mature, less death-denying attitude would include: forsaking dissociative attitudes toward the body, woman, and nature; accepting mortality and limits (including limits to knowledge and certainty) as integral aspects of human existence; and integrating traditional wisdom about humanity's relation to nature, even while continuing to take seriously modern science's claims about the dynamic structure of things.

But how is this more mature attitude supposed to come about? Heidegger's deconstruction of the human subject and of teleological potency/act metaphysics undermined modernity's view of history as progressive human self-realization. Today, there is widespread speculation about a postmetaphysical teleology that may help to explain self-realization. Some deep ecologists, however, view self-realization as involving a sudden conversion experience. This view seems consistent with Heidegger's later notion that authenticity (*Eigentlichkeit*) occurs when one is suddenly appropriated (*vereignet*) by a shift in the destiny of being. If the "conversion" view proves more consistent with deep ecology than the progressive "maturation" view, Heidegger may more easily be read as a forerunner of deep ecology. Such a reading, however, may further the efforts of critics to describe deep ecology as irrationalist and also potentially ecofascist.

In the end, however, Heidegger's thought and deep ecology may be incompatible because they seem to have very different views of nature. Heidegger denied that humans are intelligent animals, whereas deep ecologists surely maintain that humans are complex animals that have arisen from the matrix of organic life. Strong antipathy toward such naturalism led Heidegger to criticize Nazi racism, which he regarded as a crude naturalism. (Students of National Socialism may well wonder how he could have regarded racism as an accidental feature of that movement!) As we discuss later on, Heidegger's nonnaturalistic views about human existence have important similarities to those developed by Arne Naess and Mahayana Buddhism. All three adhere to some version of what I call "ontological phenomenalism." Before turning to this issue, however, let us first examine those themes in Heidegger's thought which originally led me to see it as compatible with deep ecology.

For Heidegger, for something "to be" means for it *to be manifest* or *to be present*. Only because entities can manifest themselves and can thus be encountered *as entities,* can they subsequently be interpreted as objects in various domains: for example, in science, industry, and everyday life. Unlike animals, humans can encounter entities *as entities* because humans can apprehend the "ontological difference" between being and entities. "Being" does not name a superentity, a metaphysical ground, a primal source, or a divine creator. Radically other than any entity, being names the event of presencing (*Anwesen*) by which an entity presents, reveals, or shows itself. Human existence constitutes the temporal, historical, linguistic clearing, or absencing (*Abwesen*) in which the being (presencing, self-manifesting) of entities can occur. Without human existence, things could not be manifest and in this sense could not "be" at all. Early Heidegger sometimes spoke as if this clearing, this capacity for understanding *that* entities *are*, were a *human* capacity, but later, seeking to purge his thinking of anthropological residues, he argued that human existence occurs only *within* a larger clearing that transcends merely human concerns.

Because modern humanity's openness for being has become so constricted that things can only show themselves one-dimensionally as flexible raw material, modern humanity has become oblivious to its highest possibility, namely, to *let things be* by holding open the clearing in which they can reveal themselves. Like a deep ecologist, Heidegger argued that reforming existing institutions would only reinforce the destructive urges of the control-obsessed subject. Claiming that anthropocentric humanism *underestimates* humanity, he favored a "higher humanism" that lets things be, instead of disclosing them as instruments serving the power-interests of the human subject.[28] Like many deep ecologists, he said that the ethics needed to improve our treatment of nature cannot arise from the metaphysical framework of humanism, but only from a new *ethos,* a new way of understanding what humans and nonhumans *are*. In this sense, ontology proceeds ethics.

This idea has been criticized by Emmanuel Levinas, who says that *ontology* forces the Other to conform to the identity posited by the subject, whereas *ethics* demands that I conform or accede to the ethical demands of the Other. For Heidegger, ontology meant the study of humanity's openness for the self-manifesting of things, but at times

Levinas seems to define ontology in a way that corresponds to what Heidegger meant by *metaphysics*—an anthropocentric, subjectivistic ways of understanding things. Yet Levinas's concern with ethics and his mistrust for Heidegger's ontology is important when we recall the grim political consequences of Heidegger's belief that National Socialism was "a complete transformation of our German *Dasein*," a revolutionary ontological shift, which—renouncing the ethical limits of democratic modernity, Judaism, and Christianity—would establish a new ethos to save Germany from modernity. Nevertheless, it is worth noting that Heidegger's critique of dualistic thinking, anthropocentrism, and subjectivism, and his call for nondual openness for things, are shared by many mystical and esoteric proponents of leading religious traditions. Many of such traditions, however, have elaborate procedures to verify the spiritual attainments of followers and prospective priests. Although such procedures can make religious institutions rigidly conservative, those same procedures can also guard against a false enlightenment that can lead to ego-inflation and fanaticism. In 1933, had Heidegger been willing to submit his experience of ontological transformation to the scrutiny of those trained in the dangers of ego-inflation, perhaps he would have avoided his disastrous political engagement.

Early Heidegger's nondualism is apparent in his claim that people generally don't experience themselves as subjects standing apart from objects, but rather as always already engaged in tasks in the "world." Such holistic experience may be subsequently divided into "subjective" and "objective" aspects. Once separated, however, subject and object cannot be reunited, which is why Descartes could not explain how the subject can transcend its internal mental sphere and reach the external object. Heidegger defined human existence as the existential clearing in which the body, ego, feeling-states, memories, thoughts, tools, and natural things can all appear. Tending to conceal that it exists as this clearing, Dasein becomes absorbed in its dealings with entities. This falling into the world and away from one's own being stems from the fact that Dasein's being is inherently mortal and finite. Indeed, the clearing that lets things be is in effect no-thing at all, but finite, mortal nothingness or openness. Forgetting this openness lets Dasein work unself-consciously with the instruments of everyday life, but such everyday forgetting can be aggravated when the mood of anxiety (*Angst*) threatens to reveal Dasein's mortal nothingness. Fleeing from this disclosure, Dasein plunges into inauthenticity, which involves two related aspects. First, inauthentic Dasein conceives of itself as a stable, self-grounding subject, thus transforming Dasein's uncanny nothingness into a defendable thing: the ego-subject. To defend itself, the ego-subject sets out to control all entities. Second, since Dasein cannot succeed in turning itself into a fixed entity, inauthentic Dasein continues to experience a sense of existential lack or incompleteness. One way of overcoming this lack is to fill up the self by consuming ever more entities. Death-denying, inauthentic Dasein, then, seeks to protect and to complete itself by dominating other people and by devouring the planet. Though later Heidegger no longer emphasized the role played by death-denial in inauthenticity, he continued to suggest that being authentically human required insight into and affirmation of mortality. In connection with this suggestion, and in connection with the idea that death-denial plays a central role in humanity's mistreatment both of other humans and nature, I agree with Heidegger.

Later Heidegger said that modern Western humanity as a whole is in the grip of certain moods that disclose things in constricted ways. Descartes's quest for absolutely clear and certain truth arose from early modern humanity's mood of insecurity and uncertainty. The modern subject seeks absolute truth as a way of controlling nature and thus of avoiding death. Making itself the measure for all truth, reality, and value, the subject compels things to show themselves solely according to dictates of rationality: to be means to be a clear and distinct idea. Because mathematical physics is most capable of generating such ideas, only objects capable of being known by physics can really be said "to be." Objects are "representations," in that for them to be, they must be *re*-presented, that is, re-positioned by the subject in accordance with its own standards. The death-denying subject portrayed itself as a substance striving to actualize its potential (Leibniz). Although Hegel maintained that human striving furthers the Absolute's struggle to become self-conscious and thus free, Heidegger argued that such striving indicated that humanity had become reduced to the clever animal, the monstrous human-animal hybrid, Nietzsche's blond, power-craving beast. Since power can be sustained only by constantly increasing itself, the Will to Power amounts to the constant Will to *more* Power: the Will to Will. Heidegger concluded that "the securing of the highest and unconditioned self-unfolding of all human capacities to the unconditioned dominance over the whole Earth is the hidden thorn which drives modern man."[29] In this process, nature becomes nothing more than a gasoline station for fueling the drive toward infinite power.[30]

The power-driven subject either excludes or devours what differs from it, that is, what cannot be fitted into the categories determining the subject's identity: difference is reduced to identity. The one-dimensional, undifferentiated character of entities in technological modernity stems from humanity's obliviousness to difference as such: the *ontological difference* between being and entities. When difference and otherness is effaced, the distinction between subject and object vanishes, too. Hence, Heidegger asserted, entities now show themselves in such an impoverished way that they scarcely "are" at all. By way of contrast, authentic existence means becoming caretaker of entities and "shepherd of being." Caring involves freeing things so they can manifest themselves appropriately, thereby becoming what they already are. *Gelassenheit,* which refers to the condition of being freed from the compulsion to dominate, allows Dasein to reveal things according to their own contours, rather than forcing them to conform to categories imposed by the subject.[31]

For Heidegger, anthropocentric subject inserts itself and its vaunted rationality in the place of the Biblical God. One might think that agnostic versions of Darwinism would have undermined anthropocentric humanism, which—even in its secular form—was supported by the Biblical doctrines, but such humanism "adapted" itself to these new circumstances by becoming "naturalistic humanism." Such humanism, described by one critic as "the basis for a technological assault on nature without precedent in history," uses Darwin's doctrine of the struggle for survival to provide a "natural" justification for the human conquest of nature.[32] The idea that humanity is the source of all truth and value is strengthened by Darwinian concepts, which conceive of industrial modernity *values* as the "tools" needed by the clever animal to survive in a hostile world. Whereas the modern subject once saw industrial processes as means for its own power, the means-end relation has now been reversed: today, everything—including the "subject"—is disclosed as means for the ends of the technological system.

Heidegger said that Western history began when the ancient Greeks were appropriated as the ontological clearing.[33] They were almost shattered by the realization *that* things are, for in that moment they became ever more aware of their own mortality. Their task, whose accomplishment is revealed in their artistic achievements, was to provide limit and order for the overpowering surge of being. Gradually, being (*Anwesen*) gradually concealed itself, so that it became permanently presence (*Anwesenheit*), the metaphysical ground or foundation for other entities. This ground has been depicted as Plato's eternal forms, Aquinas's Supreme Being, Hegel's Absolute, and Nietzsche's Will to Power. Corresponding to the increasing self-effacement of being as presencing was the growing constriction of humanity's openness for being. The more being concealed itself, and the more humanity forgot its dependence on being, all the more aggressively did humanity assert its independence. Although Heidegger regarded modernity as an insurrection against the ontological order, the arch-humanist Marx called Prometheus his hero and portrayed history as the progressive unfolding of human potential. Later Marx considered nature the ground from which humanity evolved and as the material source needed for a human self-reproduction.[34]

By 1932, Heidegger concluded that Germany could be saved from Bolshevism only by Adolf Hitler, who knew the shortcomings of Enlightenment modernity, including capitalism, communism, democracy, liberalism, rationalism, commercialism, and cosmopolitanism; who appreciated the enduring relationship between a *Volk* and its soil; who understood the hardness, ruthlessness, and sacrifice required of a *Volk* resolved to make a new beginning out of the ashes of defeat. By submitting to Hitler's leadership, Germans would supposedly align themselves with the ontological shift needed to save the spirit of the West and to preserve nature from devastation. This shift was not to be understood as a "progressive" moment, but rather as tapping into the elemental ontological power that made possible the creation of a new world in which things could show themselves at least momentarily in their richness, splendor, and danger.

Heidegger supported the Nazi regime for years, never unequivocally apologized for such support, and never publicly expressed regret about the victims of Nazism. At least for a time, he approved of the harsh measures that the Nazis used to complete the "revolution." Mercy for the weak and concerns about human rights had to be abandoned as symptoms of a degenerate Christianity and modernity. Claiming that humanism animates all modern political ideologies, including liberal capitalism and communism, Heidegger finally concluded that Nazism, too, was a type of "humanism." Heidegger's method of "abstracting by essentializing," as Habermas has put it, ignores important differences among the above-mentioned political systems, including the fact that both liberalism and communism were manifestations of the emancipatory impulse of modernity, whereas National Socialism condemned modernity outright.[35] Moreover, the idea that Nazism was a type of humanism shocks those who define humanism as a doctrine promoting universal human rights, human autonomy, and individual worth. In accepting Heidegger's critique of humanism, many postmodern theorists have also accepted his postwar justification for his political actions. But the radical deconstruction of the humanistic subject, as well as the liberal traditions associated with it, leads to risky political terrain. Despite their critique of liberal humanism, however, most postmodern theorists oppose totalitarianism in all forms and indirectly embrace individualistic ideals that were foreign to Heidegger.[36]

Heidegger defined humanism as the degenerate outcome of Aristotle's definition of humans as rational animals. Anthropocentric humanism describes humans as clever animals who have the right to dominate the earth in their quest for security and power. Heidegger's critique of the idea that humans are animals put him at odds not only with most National Socialists, who were racist naturalists, but also with many deep ecologists, many of whom emphasize that humans must be understood as part of nature, not as transcendent masters of it. Attempts to understand humanity's relation to nature are faced with the difficulty of defining "nature." Heidegger's own views about nature changed.

Early on, he argued that we disclose things either as useful things or as scientific objects, but this instrumentalist ontology would seem inconsistent not only with his later critique of the technological domination of nature, but also with his youthful love for nature. Early Heidegger said that nature could only "be" insofar as it was disclosed within Dasein's historical world. Moreover, since humankind's mode of being is radically other than any other entity, he said that humankind cannot be conceived as part of nature, that is, as an animal life-form. In lectures from 1929–1930, he distinguished animal being from human being: humans exist within a fully articulated world, but animals live in a much more restricted world, since they lack language.[37] This distinction must be understood in its historical context as a protest against racist naturalism, which he regarded as a branch of anthropocentric humanism. Heidegger was trying to steer National Socialism toward an ontologically more appropriate account of human existence.

According to Heidegger, animals are not so much inferior to as they are *different from* humans.[38] In failing to note this distinction, modern humanists and Darwinists conceive of humankind as the clever animal, that is, as a monstrous, half-human, half-animal hybrid. Humanists portray as "natural" the clever animal's craving for pleasure, power, and control. But although the cravings of this hybrid may seem similar to the drives of animals, there is an important difference: animal drives are self-limiting, whereas the cravings of the clever animal lack such limits. The reason is simple: humans really desire being, but being has increasingly concealed itself. Hence, humankind's ontological desire has been diverted into a craving for *entities*. But consuming even an infinite amount of entities cannot slake the desire for being, which "is" not an entity. The monstrous animal-human hybrid claims that it is free, in having license to acquire ever greater wealth and power, but Heidegger said that striving for the merely "useful" is akin to slavery: the monstrous hybrid is "unbound in the sphere of compulsion."[39] The clever animal's unlimited cravings push things beyond their own proper limit. Disclosed according to technological modernity's one-dimensional framing (*Gestell*), things show themselves only as raw material.

By coming to understand itself as a clever animal, Western humankind could no longer see that whereas humans "die" (*sterben*), animals "perish" (*verenden*): "Mortals are they who can experience death as death. Animals cannot do so. But animals cannot speak either. The essential relation between death and language flashes up before us, but remains still unthought."[40] Regardless of the uncanny similarities between the animal and the human body, the gift of language means that "the human body is essentially other than an animal organism."[41] Despite ethological studies revealing the extraordinary parallels between primate and human behavior in the social and emotive domains, Heidegger's philosophical reasons for refusing to say that humans are part of a larger life-community *could* have a political point: defining humans as animals promotes racism and even concentration camps. Had Heidegger been willing to express regret about the millions of people killed in Nazi concentration camps, the political import of his critique of a naturalistic view of humankind might be more widely appreciated.

In contrast to Heidegger, Lévi-Strauss said that concentration camps result from a humanism that *denies* that humans are animals. Sounding like a deep ecologist, he says that since human rights "are only a special case of those rights which we must grant to the creative force of life," then "care about mankind without a simultaneous solidarity-like caring for all other forms of life . . . [leads] mankind to self-oppression and self-exploitation."[42] Racists apply in the human community the same radical distinction that they establish between humans and nonhuman animals; for racists, only *some* people are recognized as truly human. Replying, in effect, to Heidegger's call for a "higher" humanism, Lévi-Strauss asserts:

The respect of man before man cannot be grounded on a special dignity, which mankind ascribes to itself, for then one part of mankind can constantly assert that it possesses this dignity in higher measure than the others. Rather, one must go forth from a *principled humility:* If man respects all other forms of life, he protects himself from the danger of not respecting all human forms of life to the same extent.[43]

Elsewhere, however, Lévi-Strauss contends that modern societies are to primitive societies as viruses are to higher animals. Western scientific method is like a virus that invades other cultures and forces them to reproduce Western ways. Left unchecked, viruses destroy their hosts: "And we may well ask ourselves what will happen when our civilization has injected its formula into all other living civilizations and transformed them into its own image and, consequently, will no longer possess this mode of perpetuating itself."[44] The parallels between this view of Western civilization and the Nazi view of Jews and other "vermin" are disturbing, for the same reasons that the comparisons made by certain Earth First!ers between humanity (especially Western humanity) and a cancer on the planet are disturbing. By depicting humans as pests worthy of extermination, one may end up embracing the same crude metaphors (and unwittingly inviting similar practices) used by the Nazis. Given the complexity of the relation between human and nonhuman life, it seems just as inadequate to say that we are "simply animals" as it is to say that we are "radically other than animals."

Heidegger's student Hans Jonas criticized his mentor's denial that humans are animals. Noting that the Greeks defined the "animal" as any animated being, including gods, stars, and even the ensouled universe, Jonas concluded that what Heidegger really objected to was placing humans in *any* natural scale.[45] Though condemning the technological domination of nature, Heidegger was never a "biocentrist," but rather a gnostic, who viewed humans as aliens adrift in an indifferent or even hostile cosmos.[46] Since such cosmos could scarcely contain an entity for whom its own being makes a difference, Jonas concluded that "[Heidegger's] disruption between man and total reality is at the bottom of nihilism."[47] Anticipating deep ecology, Jonas remarks that "ontology as the ground of ethics was the original tenet of philosophy." Only by revising our concept of nature can there

result a principle of ethics which is ultimately grounded neither in the autonomy of the self nor in the needs of the community, but in an objective assignment by the nature of things (what theology used to call the *ordo creationis*)—such as could still be kept faith with by the last of a dying mankind in his final solitude. . . .
[Thus] only an ethics which is grounded in the breadth of being, not merely in the singularity and oddness of man, can have significance in the scheme of things.[48]

Despite such differences with Heidegger, Jonas joins him and Werner Marx in saying that only an ethics grounded in human finitude can lead to a nondomineering attitude toward nature.[49] But another of Heidegger's students, Karl Löwith, regarded his mentor's refusal to conceive of humans as animals as consistent with his refusal to take seriously Heraclitus' claim that humanity must conform itself to the cosmos. By defining Dasein as *essentially* different from all other entities (only Dasein "exists," whereas other entities merely "are"), Heidegger promoted a new version of Christian-Cartesian anthropocentrism. A number of deep ecologists influenced by Spinoza's stoicism share Löwith's suspicion that transcendental philosophy, including Heidegger's thought, denies a cosmic order to which humans are subordinated. Transcendental philosophy describes the cosmos either as a correlate of consciousness or as an entity that appears *within* the human clearing. For Löwith, however, no matter how consciously we may exist, "the world does not belong to us, however—we belong to it."[50]

George Sessions says that if Heidegger had begun with the cosmos and worked his way toward human beings, humans would have seemed less significant in his scheme. Yet by beginning with human Dasein, he disclosed nature as ancillary to human concerns.[51] Sessions says that this anthropocentric turn began when Socrates insisted that philosophy concern itself primarily with human affairs and was reinforced by Aristotle's suggestion that nature "has made all things for the sake of man." This view was popularized by Stoicism and later by Christianity, which depicted Creation as the backdrop for the drama of human salvation.[52] Self-assertive Renaissance men intensified this anthropocentrism. Later, Protestant reformers emphasized the nonsacred charter of nature, thus opening the way for a new burst of empirical inquiry and technological exploitation of nature. The triumph of scientific positivism culminated the drive to interpret all phenomena, including humans, as nothing more than quantifiable material events. That Sessions and Heidegger arrive at such similar conclusion about modernity indicates that both are critics of anthropocentric humanism, even though they seem to differ on the source for such humanism. Sessions says that humanism stems from arrogance in the face of nature. Later Heidegger said that humanism stems not so much from human arrogance, though this does play a role analogous to hubris in Greek tragedy, but rather from the fateful self-concealment of being.

Heidegger asserted that human self-assertion, combined with the eclipse of being, threatens the relation between being and human Dasein.[53] Loss of this relation would be even more dangerous than a nuclear war that might "bring about the complete annihilation of humanity and the destruction of the earth."[54] This controversial claim is comparable to the Christian teaching that it is better to forfeit the world than to lose one's soul by losing one's relation to God. Heidegger apparently thought along these lines: it is possible that after a nuclear war, life might once again emerge, but it is far less likely that there will ever again occur an ontological clearing through which such life could manifest itself. Further, since modernity's one-dimensional disclosure of entities virtually denies them any "being" at all, the loss of humanity's openness for being is already occurring.[55] Modernity's background mood is horror in the face of nihilism, which is consistent with the aim of providing material "happiness" for everyone by reducing nature to pure energy.[56] The unleashing of vast quantities of energy in nuclear war would be equivalent to modernity's slow-motion destruction of nature: unbounded destruction would equal limitless consumption. If humanity avoided nuclear war only to survive as contented clever animals, Heidegger believed we would exist in a state of ontological damnation: hell on earth, masquerading as material paradise. Deep ecologists might agree that a world of material human comfort purchased at the price of everything wild would not be a world worth living in, for in killing wild nature, people would be as good as dead. But most of them could not agree that the loss of humanity's relation to being would be worse than nuclear omnicide, for it is wrong to suppose that the lives of millions of extinct and unknown species are somehow lessened because they were never "disclosed" by humanity.

Later Heidegger became attracted to the view of nature found in the poetry of Hölderlin, who proclaimed "the coming god," the Dionysian divinity who would restore meaning and weight to a nature flattened by excessive rationalism and commercialism.[57] In the 1930s, Heidegger believed that his own thought and National Socialism were opening the way for this god. Years later, though chastened because he had supported a regime that contributed to modern nihilism, Heidegger still concluded that "only a god can save us."[58] Political activism reinforces the slide into nihilism, for politics manifests the subject's striving for control, from which the coming god was to free humankind. Similarly, deep ecologists say that reformism will only reinforce the status quo, unless people undergo a spiritual conversion. From Heidegger's viewpoint, however, the Deep Ecology Platform, ostensibly broad enough to be embraced by activists of many stripes, may itself be influenced by the modern control impulse criticized by deep ecologists. The DEP justifies mass movements, which, despite their noble aim of halting ecological destruction, may unwittingly trigger off events with the opposite effect, for example, the Wise-Use Movement's growing opposition to deep ecology. To avoid being seduced by their own version of self-righteous subjectivism, then, deep ecologists must be skeptical about whether they have in fact achieved nondualistic, ecological sensibility.[59]

Heidegger's perceived anthropocentrism, his concerns that the DEP manifests modernity's control-impulse, and the fact that some deep ecologists adhere to progressive views of history, indicate problems in attempts to read Heidegger as a forerunner of deep ecology. But Arne Naess sympathizes with Heidegger's view that humankind is the site through which entities show themselves: "Man may be the measure of all things in the sense that only a human being has a measuring *rod*, but what he measures he may find to be greater than himself and his survival."[60] Since our "measuring rod" is language, we fulfill ourselves when we responsibly and joyfully "speak" the world anew. With Heidegger, then, Naess calls for a "more lofty image" of human maturity, in which human interests can be harmonized with deep ecological norms. It is a "sorry underestimation" of humanity's potential to think that humanity is "destined to be the scourge of the earth." An "eradicable part" of humankind's "evolutionary potential" involves being "*the conscious joyful appreciator of this planet as an even greater whole of its immense richness.*"[61] Apart from the reference to "evolutionary potential," which is reminiscent of Hegel's progressive reading of history, Heidegger could agree with much of this. He once said that insofar as man is an entity,

he belongs to the totality of being—just like the stone, the tree, or the eagle. To "belong" here still means to be in the order of being. But man's distinctive feature lies in this, that he, as the entity who thinks, is open to being, face to face with being; thus man remains referred to being and so answerable to it.[62]

Suggesting that human existence lets things manifest themselves in a way not otherwise possible, Naess cites the following remarks made by T. L. S. Sprigge, who thinks "in the spirit of Heidegger." Sprigge encourages us

> to think of the point of our consciousness as being that it supplies a home in which objects can enter into actuality, so that we as consciousness are to be thought of as existing for the sake of the objects which need us in order to exist rather than its being the objects which exist for our sake.[63]

HEIDEGGER, NAESS, AND ONTOLOGICAL PHENOMENALISM Just as Ecosophy T was influenced in part by the nondualisms of Mahayana Buddhism and Advaita Vedanta, so Heidegger had a long interest in Western mysticism, as well as in Buddhism and Taoism. This shared interest in nondualism brings deep ecology into proximity with two themes in Heidegger's thought. The first theme, which I call "ontological phenomenalism," says that for something "to be" means for it to be present or manifest. The second theme says that human existence is authentic when increasingly open for the presencing of things. To those who fear that ontological phenomenalism brings Naess too close to Heidegger's antinaturalism, Naess replies that a tough-minded materialist ecology does *not* guarantee that one will arrive at a position consistent with ecological sensibility. For instance, some ecologists say that organisms and ecosystems are constituted by interrelated energy flows. Yet calculations of such flows may be used either by environmental groups to justify preserving a forest, or by timber companies to justify logging it. Though scientific assertions may provoke *prudential* concerns about poisoning our own nest, they provide no *immediate* guideline either for metaphysics or for moral behavior, nor do they invariably promote a wider identification with other living things. As we saw earlier, Spinoza's rationalistic anti-anthropocentrism is consistent both with an instrumental view of animals and with a deep ecological attitude. Conservation ecologists like Michael Soulé do seek to draw normative conclusions from their disciplines, but many scientists feel constrained to separate their academic research ("fact") from morality, politics, and their own original love for living nature.[64] Denying the ultimate validity of the fact-value dichotomy, Holmes Rolston III contends that after studying the amazing complexity of organisms and ecosystems, many people are moved to make positive evaluations about the intrinsic worth of both.[65] Nevertheless, awe in the face of nature's complexity is sometimes matched by wonder regarding humankind's ability both to *understand* such complexity and to *control* it for human ends.

According to ontological phenomenalism, prior to dividing experience into knowing subjects and complex objects, manifesting occurs, that is, phenomena arise. There is no *Ding an sich,* no previously existing, independent object that stands "behind" those phenomena. Providing causal explanations for phenomena has some validity, but such explanations always come after the fact and are products of a cognizing subject that has separated itself out from the phenomenal manifold. Emphasizing that presencing occurs because *phenomena are self-luminous,* later Heidegger said that humans are not the "lookers," but are *looked upon* by self-appearing phenomena. Not only is the ego-subject simply another event within the self-luminous field of appearances, but human openness itself occurs *within* a more original clearing. The visual horizon on which objects appear is not produced by the subject; instead, the "horizon is but the side facing us on an openness which surrounds us; an openness which is filled with views of the [self-showing, self-luminous] appearances of what to our re-presenting are objects."[66] The self-luminosity of things and the openness in which such luminosity occurs are not separate from one another; they constitute aspects of the same event.

Similarly, Naess says that the subject-object distinction is not primary. Further, he denies that there are primary qualities, essences, substances, or even "things," if by the latter we mean solid, unchanging, isolated material objects. Things are useful constructs for dealing with constantly changing, internally related phenomena, which constitute "experience." If interrelated phenomena lack substance, essence, or self-existence, as suggested by the Buddhist formula *sarvam dharmam nihsvabhavam,* there is no ultimate ontological gap between self and not-self, humanity and nature.[67] "People" and "environment," then, result from projecting abstract interpretative schemata (including scientific explanations) upon "concrete contents," that is, upon the incessant play of phenomena.[68] Following gestalt psychology, Naess contends that experience is holistic; individual "things" are experienced in terms of a complex, layered fabric of experience.[69] Reasoning vainly attempts to ground the flux of phenomena, but a deeper insight reveals that ego and other, self and object are gestalts whose contents are constituted by an infinite number of self-arising, differentiating, concrete phenomena. Existing in a fully awakened way means being simultaneously: (1) those concrete contents; (2) the organizing gestalt; (3) the awareness of the contents/gestalt; *and* (4) the nothingness or openness in which they all (including consciousness) manifest themselves. Awakening means shattering all dualisms, thereby revealing that all phenomena are interrelated. Awareness of one's insubstantiality elicits a sense of *identification* with phenomena that were once regarded as not-self or other. Naess asserts:

Gestalts bind the I and the not-I together in a whole. Joy becomes, not *my* joy, but *something joyful* of which the I and something else are interdependent, non-isolatable fragments. "The birch laughed/with the light easy laughter of all birches . . ." This gestalt is a creation which may only incompletely be divided to given an I which projects laughter into a non-laughing birch tree.[70]

The assumption that the gestalt-like character of spontaneous experience is merely subjective, when compared with the objective view that abstracts from such experience, is inherited from early modern science, which conceived of nature as composed of invisible, externally related atoms, the primary or objective properties of which are quantifiable: motion, mass, and extension. In contrast, sensory properties—color, smell, touch, taste—are secondary properties that do not characterize the object itself, but are merely subjective sensations triggered off when sense organs interact in predictable ways with primary qualities. Having stripped from things the sensory qualities that we experience spontaneously, the modern subject could look upon nature as a mere resource. For this objective viewpoint "every passionate appeal that reveals deep feelings, empathy, and keen identification with natural phenomena must be ruled out as irrelevant."[71] Applied consistently, such objectivism conceives of humans as complex physical structures, lacking any meaning or purpose, since the universe itself is valueless.

Naess says that maturity requires un-learning this objectivating attitude and re-learning how to experience phenomena holistically.[72] Even immature, fragmentary experience, however, involves gestalts. If a forester discloses trees solely in terms of the subordinate gestalt of "board feet of lumber," he or she has to block out the super-ordinate gestalt of the forest. The inability to take seriously such superordinate gestalts stems from the primacy of fragmentary and abstract experience. Although abstract structures belong to reality, they are not identifiable with it. A thing is a thing *in relation to* something else, just as a quality (warm, red, noisy) is a quality *in relation to* other qualities. Hence, "there are no completely separable objects."[73] Keeping in mind Heraclitus' view that "everything flows,"

we must abandon fixed, solid points, retaining the relatively straight-forward, persistent relations of interdependence. "Objective descriptions of nature" offered us by physics ought to be regarded not as descriptions of nature, but as descriptions of certain conditions of interdependence and thereby can be universal, common for all cultures.[74]

Like a postmodern theorist, Naess denies that there is a preexisting reality "mirrored" by mind. Scientific objects are relational phenomena that show up recurrently in connection with performing certain procedures. Since a thing is a conjunction of relations in a *relational field* to which the perceiver also belongs, we would be advised to say, "Object A is warm in relation to hand B," rather than saying "Object A is warm." Phenomenal contents are constituted by the internal relationships between a perceiver involved in the world and a perceived that is not radically independent of the perceiver; hence, there are *not* two, internal self and external object. Since experience is a nondualistic, interwoven fabric of self-luminous phenomena, Naess identifies *"the world with the set of contents, not with structures."*[75] The conceptual structures with which we interpret the world, then, are *not* the phenomena. We must not confuse map with territory.

In suggesting that organisms are temporary phenomenal gestalts lacking selfhood, substance, and essence, Naess verges on nominalism, as did Heidegger in deconstructing the metaphysical doctrine of essence. Heidegger linked Plato's doctrine of essence to a subjectivistic view that culminated in modern technology. Allegedly, Plato gave a central role to the knower's correct view of *eidos* (form, essence). Centuries later, Descartes asserted that for something "to be" means for it to be a clear and distinct idea, that is, representable by the rational subject. As essence was reduced to ideas quantifiable by mathematical physics, nature became an image projected in accordance with the power-interests of the subject. Hence, the internal structure of natural phenomena, such as the human genetic structure, is now studied so that it can be altered by the subject.

In view of this deconstruction of essence, however, what basis is their for Heidegger's objection to treating animals and plants as machines?[76] If what things "are" is defined by the historical epoch in which they appear, on what basis can one criticize the *technological* disclosure of being as flexible raw material? Though later Heidegger proposed that it is now virtually *impossible* to treat things other than as raw material, early Heidegger can be read as suggesting a basis for a nonessentialistic, nonsubjectivistic view of the internal constitution of things. Early Heidegger had two different senses of "the being of entities." The first is the *aletheia*-logical sense of being, according to which being names the truth, disclosedness, or manifestness of an entity. Here, being belongs to Dasein's understanding: no Dasein, no being. The second sense of being is *ousia*-logical, referring both to the ontological constitution of a thing, that is, to its "what," and to its persistence, that is, to its "that it is." Heidegger said that "entities *are*, quite independently of the experience by which they are disclosed."[77] William F. Vallicella argues that by ascribing to both these senses of being, early Heidegger tended toward an "*idealism of Being but a realism of beings*."[78] Later Heidegger, discovering the incompatibility of these two senses of being, tended to eliminate the *ousia*-logical sense.[79] The "realistic," *ousia*-logical sense of being is presupposed in his analysis of the being of the entity called human Dasein. In disclosing that Dasein's being is care, Heidegger believed himself to be saying something true about that entity's ontological structure. Likewise, in his study of animal being in 1929–1930, he distinguished between the inherent (one is tempted to say "essential") ontological structure (being) of animals and that of human Dasein. Later Heidegger concluded that the *ousia*-logical sense of being was an aspect of metaphysical foundationalism. Focusing on the radically historical character of the *aletheia*-logical sense of being as presencing, he stopped analyzing the ontological constitution of entities, including human Dasein.

Assuming that entities have an ontological structure that constrains what we can say about and do with them, early Heidegger adhered to what Hubert Dreyfus calls a "hermeneutical realism" in regard to science.[80] Science examines things by de-worlding them, that is, by stripping from them all "projected" attributes, such as beauty, purpose, and religious power. In Heidegger's view, more basic than the *ontical* question "What caused X" is the *ontological* question "How is it possible that X is manifest?" Nevertheless, science's abstract, de-worlded analysis of entities can say something transculturally "true" about them. Adopting scientific methods, people from many different cultures can arrive at similar conclusions about the structure of entities. Contrary to his later view that modern science was motivated from the start by power-interests, early Heidegger said that all "scientific" (*wissenschaftlich*, rigorous) knowledge has no interest in technical application, but instead freely binds itself to the task of disclosing the entity under investigation.[81] Science lets an entity be, in the sense of letting it manifest (*aletheia*-

logical sense of being) its own inherent structure (*ousia*-logical sense of being). Arguing that Heidegger resisted radical scientific pluralism, Dreyfus maintains that Aristotle and Newton's use of incommensurate vocabulary to explain motion does not mean there is no basis for preferring one vocabulary over the other. Instead, Newton's vocabulary discloses something true about motion, in light of questions important to mathematical physics; Aristotle's vocabulary also discloses something true, but in light of very different questions.

As noted earlier, people disagree about whether science can disclose that nature has inherent worth. Hence, the issue of whether Heidegger's thought can help deep ecology may hinge on whether the inherent worth of nature can be discerned in phenomena *not* disclosed by science. Heidegger often unfavorably compared modernity's disclosure of being (e.g., treating forests as a source for cellulose) to the early Greek disclosure. Late in his career, however, forsaking such apparent nostalgia, he concluded that there are no privileged epochs in which human Dasein was somehow closer to nature or more in tune with being. Instead, every historical era has its own characteristic unconcealment and concealment, truth and obscurity. Lacking a God's-eye perspective from which to assess the validity of a historical epoch's disclosure of being, we have no grounds for preferring the Greek or the medieval worlds to the technological world; we can only say that they are *different* from one another. The "destiny of being" names the unpredictable "granting" of these alternative world-formative disclosures, which take place *through* human Dasein, but are *not* human achievements. The task of thinking is not to evaluate how entities are revealed in any given epoch, but rather to ponder the self-concealing play of being that "gives" each temporary, finite, perspectival disclosure of being.

For Heidegger, the only possible kind of "resistance" seems to be the discovery of the finite, historical character of technological modernity's understanding of being. This discovery helps prepare for the possible advent of an alternative, posttechnological disclosure of what things are. But having forsaken any metaposition (including a progressive reading of history) from which to evaluate different historical epochs, Heidegger was in a position only to say that the new disclosure of being would be *different* than, not an *improvement* over, the present one. Since the new world's cultural vocabulary would be incommensurate with the vocabularies of previous epochs, it could be assessed only according to its own internal norms, which may well be incompatible with deep ecology's ecocentrism.

Nevertheless, even in some of Heidegger's later writings one can find suggestions that entities have an internal dimension that resists being fully disclosed in any historical epoch. Though focusing on the *aletheia*-logical aspect of being, then, later Heidegger did not entirely lose interest in finding a nonessentialistic vocabulary for the *ousia*-logical aspect of living phenomena. This vocabulary is discernible in his notion of nature as *physis*, which means neither the totality nor the ground of entities, but rather the self-articulating event of presencing. Presencing has a twofold sense. On the one hand, it refers (*ousia*-logically) to the self-guiding emergence of living beings—the sprouting of a seed, the birth of an animal. On the other hand, it refers (*aletheia*-logically) to the self-manifestness of entities in a historical human world. There is a physical, force-like, material, spontaneous, rhythmic dimension to the first that is missing from the second. But Michel Haar asks:

How to affirm that physis is "being itself" if it presents with regard to being [understood *aletheia*-logically] at least a double difference: repetitive [nonhistorical] production, [and] "substantial" density of that which conceals itself? In a word, is it not necessary to recognize in *physis* an element irreducible to any historicality, a dimension always *nonepochal?*[82]

Later Heidegger distinguished between these two senses of physis, self-emergence and self-disclosure, by differentiating between earth and world. Earth does not merely refer to what conceals itself, in contrast to what manifests itself in the historical world. Earth names the self-concealing power, *physis*, which generates the things that can thrust themselves into and thus appear within an historical world.

Though including aspects of what was traditionally known as *essence,* earth differs from essence in being inherently mysterious, resistant to being fully disclosed in any human world. World names the historical clearing through which earth can be partially disclosed in various ways. No historical world is ever self-transparent; a world always involves ambiguity, concealment, and uncertainty. Earth and world contend with one another. Earth strives to prevent itself from being disclosed; *physis,* Heraclitus said, loves to hide itself. World, however, strives to disclose what is hidden. A world sustains itself only so long as this striving is characterized by limit and balance. Because the technological world tries to compel earth to reveal all its secrets, Heidegger called it a "world night," an "un-world."[83]

At times, he hoped that modernity would give way to a new epoch or world that establishes the differences necessary for things to show themselves appropriately.[84] This world, founded by the poet, "grants to things their presence. Things bear world. World grants things."[85] World names the hidden unity, *Ereignis,* of earth and sky, gods and mortals, gathered together through the thing named by the poet. World is not constituted by a transcendental subject, nor by the temporal ecstases of human Dasein, but instead is gathered together by the things shining forth within it.[86] The new world would involve the "fourfold" (*Geviert*) of earth and sky, gods and mortals. Mortals fulfill themselves by participating in a dance through which all constituents fourfold bear and allow each other to become manifest. Each is as an element in the "event of appropriation" (*Ereignis*) which lets each constituent come into its own.

Interpreting Hölderlin's poetry, Heidegger spoke of *physis* as older than historical times and vaster than the cosmos.[87] Comprising both the presencing of entities and the historical clearing through which such presencing can occur, nature involves holy chaos and the "primal rift." Reminiscent of the ontological difference, this holy rift conceals itself, while simultaneously granting the open realm, prior to space and time, in which poetry can let things manifest themselves. Poetry embodies nature as ontological difference, thereby granting to things their own self-defining outline. Without the poet, humanity could not encounter things, for they would be held back in nature's self-concealing holy wildness. This holy wildness is yet governed by "the law" that

preserves the earth in the sufficiency of the emerging and perishing of all things in the allotted sphere of the possible which everything follows, and yet nothing knows. The birch tree never oversteps its possibility. The colony of bees dwells in its possibility.[88]

Here, Heidegger sounds like Lao-tzu, who suggested that things spontaneously coordinate themselves with each other, forming an ever-changing, yet intricately patterned world by gathering themselves together in a play of opposition. *Tao* itself does nothing, but by virtue of it the pattern of things consistently reestablishes itself. The self-concealing Tao names "a great hidden stream which moves all things along and makes way for everything. All is way."[89] An enlightened man of Tao lives according to patterns that lie far beyond his ken and will; by the time "truth and justice" come on the scene, society is far removed from the Tao. The self-assertive, arrogant man rises up against the earth's hidden law, but in so doing he pushes things out beyond the limit and measure that define their own possibility. Hence, they become "impossible," non-things, mere stuff: chickens or pigs in factory farms, DNA in a genetic engineering laboratory, hospital freezers full of dead fetuses stockpiled for spare parts and tissue. While the agribusiness operator exploits and ruins the earth to extract a more profitable yield, the peasant "does not challenge the soil of the field. In the sowing of the grain [the peasant] places the seed in the keeping of the forces of growth and watches over its increase."[90]

Heidegger affirmed, however, that humans disrupt natural orders and rhythms. In 1935, describing the violent world-founding activity of the early Greeks, he noted that for Sophocles human existence is uncanny (*unheimlich*), in that humans leave home (*Heim*) and venture into physis. Greek Dasein was fated to be the "breach" through which the overpowering power of physis was delimited, so that specific entities could appear. Appropriated by *physis*, Dasein—"the violent one"—captured living things, snatching them out of their own extraordinary internal rhythms and limits, and forcing them into pens and under the yoke.[91] The violent process of world-formation is itself a dimension of *physis*, which names something other than the domain of matter and energy. By 1940, however, Heidegger was saying that human existence is authentic only when Dasein is granted "releasement" (*Gelassenheit*) from the will to power, thereby becoming able to let things be appropriately. Letting be has at least three aspects. First, it means not unduly interfering with things. Second, it means taking care of things, in the sense of making it possible for them to fulfill their potential. Third, letting be involves not just the ontical work of tending to things, but also the *ontological* work of keeping open the clearing through which they can appear.[92] This disclosive sense of letting be lies beyond the distinction between activity and passivity, if activity means imposing one's will, and if passivity means standing around.

Regarding Heidegger's negative evaluation of the allegedly all-embracing era of technological modernity, one may ask the following. Since Heidegger himself was born into and thus shaped by modernity's understanding of being, how could he conclude that the technological disclosure of things is constricted or inconsistent with the possibilities of things? Moreover, how could his yearning for an ontologically richer, posttechnological world be squared with his contention that there are no privileged epochs? Is not the technological age simply *one* way of disclosing things, and the fourfold another? If the "law of the earth" conceals itself, how can we know whether our world fails to conform with it? Further, if *physis* appropriates Dasein as the site through which to gather and disclose itself, is not technological modernity, too, consistent with *physis*? Heidegger could read modernity as the most constricted mode of disclosure only by viewing Western history as decline and fall from a nobler origin. Eventually abandoning this view, he could say only that technological modernity excluded the ancient Greek disclosure of being, but ancient Greece excluded the technological disclosure. I would add that ancient Greece also excluded modernity's egalitarian commitments. Given Heidegger's claim that each epoch is governed by a principal mode of disclosure, he was not able to say that a world could be ontologically double-coded: technological, on the one hand, and fourfold-like, on the other. Problems like this make it difficult to read Heidegger as a forerunner of deep ecology.

In view of these issues, we may wonder whether Naess's onto-logical phenomenalism undermines his own contention that all life deserves respect. Stressing the Buddhist rather than the Heideggerean aspect of Naess's phenomenalism may assist the latter's deep eco-logical concerns. Mahayana Buddhism says that even though indi-viduals are temporary phenomenal gestalts, lacking essence and sub-stance, they deserve proper treatment insofar as they are sentient. The Bodhisattva vows to liberate *all* sentient beings before he himself attains nirvana. Though Hinayana Buddhism restricts sentience to humans and to some animals, Mahayana Buddhism suggests that sentience cannot be thus restricted, since all things are interrelated.

For Mahayana Buddhism, humanity is a special instance of the luminosity characteristic of all phenomena.[93] In humanity, lumi-nosity becomes self-aware. Being awakened means apprehending everything, including the self, as temporary phenomenal constella-tions. As deep ecologist Joanna Macy suggests, someone awakened to the emptiness and the interrelation among all phenomena spon-taneously identifies with them and seeks to alleviate their suffering.[94] Like early Heidegger, Buddhism suggests that human life is char-acterized by dissatisfaction borne of a sense of ontological lack. Seeking to overcome this lack, one conceives of oneself as a sub-stantial ego-subject, which then defends itself against threats posed by the "external" world. Moving beyond this defensive view of self requires experiencing self as emptiness, as the openness in which each phenomenon appears as interrelated with all others. Here, one may recall Heidegger's fourfold and Spinoza's intuition that each thing manifests the whole.[95] Naess's ideal of self-realization *may* be read as Buddhist *satori,* that is, as a sudden recovery of original emptiness.

Neither predictable nor gradual, such recovery cannot be squared either with Spinoza's developmental process of gaining wisdom, or with a progressive reading of history. In fact, many Buddhists agree with Heidegger that, if anything, humankind has *declined* dramatically in the past 2500 years. Some Buddhist scholars, however, say that Buddhism's traditional ahistoricism must be rethought in light of its encounter with Western progressive historicism. Others assert that the "not-thinking" involved in Zen's nondualism can all too easily involve a simpleminded refusal to think, which can encourage passivity in the face of redressable injustice and misery. This passivity may be a major problem for Heidegger's "thinking," which can be read as an ontological aestheticism with little concern about concrete suffering.[96]

Although Naess finds Buddhism appealing because of its claim that awakening spontaneously leads to compassionate treatment of *all* phenomena, Buddhism's denial of essence and substance still poses problems. As noted earlier, ecologists once promoted the ideas (and ideals) of ecosystemic integrity and identity, summarized in the ideas of "climax forests" and "stable ecosystems." Today, some ecologists say that since organic processes involve incessant change, there are no "stable" ecosystems, no "climax" forests, and no "natural balance." Those who deny stability would seem more in tune with ontological phenomenalism than are those who insist on stability. Many Buddhists would warn that efforts to alleviate suffering must not be confused with frantic attempts to preserve the illusory identity of spatiotemporal phenomena, for such efforts may reflect the very yearning for permanence that is responsible for suffering. Naess says as much when he observes that although ecosystem and organism are useful abstract concepts, they are not to be confused with concrete experiential contents.

In view of the influence of Buddhism and Vedanta on Naess, I interpret him as saying that spatiotemporal phenomena do not constitute the only experiential "level." By Atman, Naess has in mind an eternal, nondual, unutterable "source," a level of consciousness, as it were, that generates, embraces, and yet transcends all phenomena. Insofar as all living phenomena participate in Atman, they are inherently valuable manifestations of what lies beyond all possible experience. But insofar as all phenomena are also finite and transient, they are not of absolute worth. The demise of finite phenomena justifies lamentation, but will not be a source of devastating grief for those who have identified with eternal Atman. Those who have attained such identification, however, spontaneously care for and seek to alleviate the suffering of all finite phenomena.

Critics charge that concern about the suffering of sentient beings is paradoxical, if there are no selves or substances to begin with! Naess might reply in two ways. Calling on Spinoza, Naess would say that for a fully enlightened person, God/Nature manifests itself in each individual thing. The ingression of the eternal in the finite is a paradox only for those who have not experienced firsthand the multilayered character of "reality." Calling on Mahayana Buddhism, he would say that suffering accompanies the illusion of separate identity. Compassion is called for until that illusion and its accompanying suffering are dissolved. Since the illusion of personal identity is so powerful, even more so than the illusion that the world is composed of discrete substances, some Mahayana Buddhists maintain that only a Boddhisattva can dissolve such illusions, thereby ending the manifold suffering of all phenomena.

Some environmental philosophers are not as sanguine as Naess is about the ecological relevance of Asian religions. Despite concern for suffering, Buddhist scriptures do not make recognizably "ecological" recommendations. Moreover, Hinayana's restriction of sentience to humans and some higher animals suggests that nothing else deserves compassion. Further, some types of Vedanta cast dispersions on the phenomenal domain and depict it as a distraction that hinders reunion with Atman. Holmes Rolston III criticizes Asian nondualisms not only because they seem to devalue individual, species-level, and systemic empirical phenomena that many Westerners want to validate, but also because they make inspirational recommendations—such as, "show compassion for all beings"—which provide little concrete guidance for adjudicating complex ecological disputes.[97]

Noting that the same criticism can be leveled at Heidegger's phrase "let things be," some social ecologists charge that by endorsing Asian nondualisms, deep ecologists support quietism, authoritarianism, dogmatism, and antidemocratic attitudes. Many contemporary American Buddhists, however, attempt to combine the ideal of compassion with democratic, egalitarian, and ecological ideals.

Recently, naturalist Ty Cashman has complained that ontological phenomenalism, subjective idealism, occultism, and spiritualism all became popular in connection with the counterculture's hope that Asian religions and quantum theory would provide an alternative to modern nihilism: "The '80s were a period of detaching from reality (sometimes conveniently defining 'reality' subjectively) and a dissolving of the individual's natural connection with the concrete world of responsibility, action and result."[98] Maintaining that humanity's capacity for perceiving and acting results from eons of evolution, Cashman says that quantum idealists overemphasize the role of human perception in "constituting" quantum phenomena. Some of the paradoxes of quantum theory arise because we have not evolved in a way that enables us to perceive events at the atomic and subatomic levels. Cashman also criticizes Humberto Maturana's solipstistic "neuro-idealism" for denying "the autonomous existence of an environment in relation to which more perfectly adapted nervous systems could have evolved through natural selection."[99]

Finally, Cashman argues that "Buddho-idealism" is most common among those who become stuck at the second of what Zen master Seigen regarded as the three stages of enlightenment: First, he thought mountains are mountains and rivers were rivers; but then, he saw that mountains were no longer mountains and rivers no longer rivers; finally, he returned to ordinary life and lived in peace, at which point mountains once again became mountains, and rivers became rivers. Those who reach stage two, and who draw ontological conclusions from it, can end up endorsing objective idealism or ontological phenomenalism, according to which all entities (including the perceiver) are nothing but an interdependent realm of phenomena. This conclusion fails to see in the *third* stage mountains are once again mountains, that is, one acts in a world of "solid" entities, not mere perceptual "phenomena." One must make the crucial distinction between perception and action:

We can never perceive the world directly, but our actions always affect the world directly. The actions of our bodies *directly* move, disturb, change, refashion parts of the world. Yet, our perceptions and cognitions are only internally-generated *maps* of the world which are organized by the central nervous system from the ways that sound waves, light waves, and tactile pressures impinge upon the parts of our bodies.[100]

In stage two, one directly apprehends that experience is constituted not by solid objects, but rather by images arising through complex neural processes, which meditation can partly deconstruct. Since in stage three the enlightened Buddhist realizes that he or she cannot walk on rivers or swim through mountains, Cashman maintains that Buddhism ends up largely in agreement with the view of evolutionary naturalist realism, according to which "action is in *direct* contact with the independently existing natural world, even though cognition is only in indirect relationship with it."[101] When we dive into the river, which involves our whole organism, not merely our cognitive faculties, we are "directly outside," in contact with the real things: mountains and rivers.

Cashman's evolutionary naturalism appeals to those deep ecologists who fear that ontological phenomenalism verges on subjective idealism. In speaking of the whole organism as capable of establishing *direct* contact with what is "outside," that is, the environment in which the human organism evolved, Cashman adheres to an organically grounded realism, according to which one can directly encounter the reality transcending cognitive processes, including language and thought. Yet such realism would seem to be denied not only by ontological phenomenalists, but also by deconstructive postmodern theorists, for whom all experience is linguistically mediated, or—more emphatically—that all is text. Derrida's postmodern theory shares Heidegger's deconstruction of essence and identity, but also seeks to purge Heidegger's thought of residual metaphysical commitments, in particular his yearning for the ontological origin.

DERRIDA'S DECONSTRUCTIVE POSTMODERNISM AND DEEP ECOLOGY　According to Derrida, there is no origin, ground, or foundation. Everything is a "text," that is, an endlessly differentiating play of signifiers. Being human means existing *within* this linguistic play, which can never achieve identity or closure with its referent. Lack of closure, and thus lack of a stable "self," gives rise to insecurity and fear. From Heidegger, Derrida took the notion that the history of metaphysics posits a unified, stable, transcendental referent (e.g., essence) to ground the play of language, knowledge, and experience. But Heidegger's longing for the ontological primal that initiated the history of being parallels the metaphysician's misguided search for the transcendental signified that grounds reference. Those deep ecologists who hope to make "nature" the transcendental signified engage in the same quest for security and stability. The supposedly self-identical, essentialist foundations of metaphysical systems support political movements that try to force what is different to conform to "universal" norms. Pulling the rug out from under Western theo-anthropo-ethno-ego-phallo-logo-centrism, Derrida argues that Lévi-Strauss's structuralism is such a centrism, which shares Heidegger and Rousseau's nostalgia for the "origin" of myth and culture.

> Turned towards the lost or impossible presence of the absent origin,
> [Lévi-Strauss's] structuralist thematic of broken immediacy is there-
> fore the saddened, *negative*, nostalgic, guilty, Rousseauistic side of
> the thinking of play whose other side would be the Nietzschean
> *affirmation*, that is the joyous affirmation of the play of the world
> and the innocence of becoming, the affirmation of a world of signs
> without fault, without truth, and without origin which is offered to
> an active interpretation. *This affirmation then determines the noncenter
> otherwise than as the loss of center.* And it plays without security.[10]

Deep ecologists agree with Derrida's deconstruction of anthropocentrism, however, they resist his deconstruction of nature, wilderness, and ecosphere, and they regard ecocentrism as a desirable alternative to anthropocentrism. For Derrida, however, ecological problems cannot be solved by turning the ecosystem into yet another metaphysical absolute, since doing so is motivated by the same control-impulse that animates all centrisms, including those responsible for social oppression. He argues that we never encounter nature either in itself or as a whole; instead, nature is a social phenomenon, whose meaning is always contested within particular, local discourses. Succumbing to the impossible dream of unity and closure with the origin (Nature, God), people have generated crusades and political systems that have wreaked havoc for centuries. For Derrida, however, there was no blissfully innocent age in which the Greeks dwelt closer to being (Heidegger) or hunter-gatherers lived in great harmony with nature (deep ecologists). Many a tribe has its tale of a Golden Age when the ancestors spoke with animals and ate only fruit, but the fact is that language irrevocably splits human from world, word from object, desire from desired. The challenge is to live playfully and affirmatively, minus nostalgia and regrets, without a center that allegedly transcends the ceaseless play of language.

Derrida deconstructs metaphysical systems by showing that they work as binary oppositions. In every case, the alleged self-presence and self-identity of the privileged pole (e.g., man or reason) are achieved at the expense of and are thus inextricably bound up with the marginalized pole (e.g., woman or feeling).[103] Although metaphysics explains difference in terms of a prior unity, Derrida maintains that identity arises from *différance* (spelled with an "a," unlike the usual French word, "différence"), by an irreducible play that

makes possible the relatively unitary and atomic structures that are called names, the chains of substitutions of names in which, for example, the nominal effect *différance* is itself *enmeshed*, carried off, reinscribed, just as a false entry or a false exit is still part of the game, a function of the system.[104]

Derrida's *différance* derives in part from Heidegger's idea of the ontological difference, and in part from Saussure's notion that language functions differentially; that is, no term has intrinsic meaning, for all terms acquire meaning only by their *differentiation* from all the other terms in a language. Since any living language is continually shifting and changing, the meaning of terms (as well as their reference) is constantly deferred, put off. Like Derrida, Umberto Eco insists that "there is no Being that speaks. There is a language that speaks Being. . . . Language comes first. . . . Being is only an effect of meaning. Meaning is an effect of cultures. The cultural universe is a labyrinth."[105] Since nothing guarantees that ideas correspond to the order of things, life involves conjectures that are to be evaluated, corrected, and rejected. There is no closure in this process of differentiating (*différance*, as difference and differal), whose "trace" undermines all efforts to establish a fixed center or determinate meaning for any sign or word. Derrida asserts that "there is no presence before and outside semiological difference," that is, there is nothing outside the text.[106] By text, he means not merely the contents of printed pages, but practically everything. A text arises along with "a trace, a differential referral of one trace to another." The idea of a limitless text

presupposes that in no instance can one fix something outside of the sphere of the differential referrals, that would be something real, a presence, or an absence, something which itself would not be marked through the textual *différance*.[107]

Claiming that "*reality is a text* in this new sense," Derrida defines the text as an "openness without limits to the differential referral."[108] Denying that this view is a linguistic idealism, he follows Heidegger in maintaining that things show up only within the play of language. The complex economy of texts, generated by the indeterminate play of *différance* that escapes human control, gives rise to such metaphysical binaries as subject and object, human and nature, reason and emotion, male and female. Though the metaphysical quest for a stable ground can never be overcome, we can become aware of its weakness, namely, that the identity of the privileged pole is never self-sufficient and stable, but always bound up with its other. In disclosing the instability of power structures, deconstruction opens space for those who are marginalized because they are perceived as other than the dominant pole. Influenced by the Jewish philosopher, Emmanuel Levinas, who has sharply criticized Heidegger's lack of ethical concern, Derrida focuses on oppressed *humans*. Only infrequently has he expressed concern about exploited nonhumans.

Derrida's view that everything is an endlessly self-differentiating text may call to mind contemporary scientific claims about the interrelatedness of all things.[109] Such resemblances are misguided, of course, if interrelated physical events are not what Derrida means by "textual" interrelatedness.[110] Recently, David Loy has suggested that Derrida's claims about textuality resemble Mahayana Buddhism's principle of *pratitya samutpada,* mutually interdependent coproduction.[111] A metaphor for this doctrine is the jewel net of the god Indra. Representing the entire phenomenal domain, this net is composed of an infinite number of extraordinary jewels, each of which mirrors all the other jewels. The jewel net "symbolizes a cosmos in which there is an infinitely repeated interrelationship among all the members of the cosmos. This relationship is said to be one of simultaneous mutual identity and mutual inter-causality."[112] Paralleling Derrida's claim that language involves a process of deferral without beginning or end, the jewel net cosmos has no origin, no foundation, and no teleology. Because Buddhism has no myth of a time of plenitude before humans fell into consciousness and history, Buddhism "harbors no dream of returning to any such pure origin."[113] In addition to lacking Biblical eschatology and a progressive view of history, Buddhist cosmology also lacks Greek foundationalism. The Buddhist cosmos is not a totality of material particles governed by causal laws, but is rather a self-apprehending, self-originating, self-maintaining, playful, meaningless, aesthetic spectacle. Humans cannot appreciate this play, however, because they crave solidity, certainty, and thus an end to the circulation of phenomena.

Despite parallels between Buddhism and Derrida, Loy says that the latter's deconstruction cannot lead to liberation, because it is too concerned with deconstructing identity, but does not sufficiently deconstruct *difference.* Though agreeing that the lack of a transcendental signified makes language "a general circulation of signs," Loy seeks an alternative to the view that "because language cannot point outside itself, we must remain forever inscribed in its sign-circulation."[114] If philosophy can only "reinscribe" oppressive binary systems, Derrida's "sole solution is to disseminate wildly, in the hope of avoiding any fixation into a system that will subvert his insight."[115] Far from leading to the release promised by awakening from dualism, dissemination amounts to a textual "bad infinity" of difference.[116] Agreeing that ordinarily phenomena manifest themselves according to linguistic concepts and norms, Buddhism postulates the possibility of an *extralinguistic* encounter with phenomena, that is, the possibility of stepping outside the linguistic "cosmic egg" that shapes experience. Whereas Derrida's *différance* undermines the self-identity of textual meaning, Buddhism's *pratitya samutpada* undermines the self-identity of individual entities and thus also undermines causality. Hence, translating *pratitya samutpada* by "interdependent coproduction" is misleading, for "reality" is not composed of material entities interacting causally, but is rather a dreamlike realm of appearances—except that there is no solid "reality" to contrast with it.[117] For Buddhism, the linguistic process of naming perceptions gives rise to the apparently solid phenomena. Since suffering stems from trying to turn ourselves into fixed, stable things, *nirvana* would follow from the cessation of naming-activity.

Since [the objective, everyday] world is as differential, as full of traces, as the textual discourse Derrida works on, the Buddhist response is to use those differences/deferrals to deconstruct that objectified world, including ourselves, since we sub-jects are the first to be ob-jectified.[118]

If we cease naming perceptions, and thus stop trying to turn them (and ourselves) into fixed objects, we emerge into the sheer presencing of constantly shifting, self-luminous phenomena. Here, "there is no security and also no need for security, because everything that can be lost has been, including oneself. Especially oneself."[119] Since there is no longer any distinction between emptiness and form, "self" is "everything," though of course there is no "self" and no "things." Toying with language because existing outside of it, the Zen master has compassion for all sentient beings, especially those bewitched by language. Since for Derrida there is no "outside" to language, however, deep ecologists suspect him of promoting a linguistic idealism that lacks compassion, whereas others claim he undermines important social and political causes.[120]

Despite differences, deep ecologists and Derrida alike have been described as reactionary irrationalists for decentering the triumphalistic historicism and instrumental rationality of the Western subject. Commenting on Kant, Derrida deconstructs the binary dualism of Enlightenment, rationality versus irrational mystification. Kant criticized mystagogues who, professing to have a privileged mystical illumination that dispensed with the need for rational analysis, supported the aristocratic order, whereas he praised rational-critical philosophers sided with progressive, democratic forces. Derrida affirms that we cannot renounce the Enlightenment's "enigmatic desire for vigilance, for the lucid vigil, for elucidation, for critique and truth."[121] But he also warns that Enlightenment *lumière* and mystagogue alike seek an ultimate truth that will bring about the "end" of history, by achieving its hidden goal. Having himself once spoken provocatively of the "end of man," Derrida now warns of the dangers involved in apocalyptic calls for the end of the subject, consciousness, history, class struggle, God, the West, or literature. Hence, like Foucault, he asks what such visionaries wish to produce: "In view of what immediate or adjourned benefit? To seduce or subjugate whom, intimidate or make whom come?"[122] Today, Derrida asserts, everyone is both *Aufklärer* (enlightenment philosopher) and mystagogue to someone else.

Kant would have regarded deep ecology as a mystagogy purporting to gain absolute truth not by rational inquiry, but by way of mystical intuition. In fact, however, deep ecologists usually avoid the term "mysticism," because they wish to avoid such problematic associations. Hence, they point out that the way to Spinoza's nondual intuition runs through scientific rationality. They also share Kant's vision of an increasingly harmonious future in which humans realize their potential, though unlike Kant deep ecologists call for the self-realization of *all* beings. Whereas such progressivism may be used to defend deep ecology against charges of being reactionary, Derrida cautions that progressive movements are dangerous, since adherents may become so persuaded by their vision that they may wish to impose it on others. Many proponents of deconstruction, however, have been accused precisely of attempting to *impose* their methodology on people and institutions.

Jürgen Habermas disagrees with Derrida about many things, but he would agree that deep ecology's "intuition" is a type of mystagogy, in which the subject purportedly discerns timeless, absolute truth. Moreover, he would add that deep ecology's idea of "wider identification" involves an individual (difference) becoming absorbed into the absolute (identity). To avoid such problems, he recommends viewing modernity's emancipation project not as the self-realization of the subject, but rather as a dialectical process that intertwines critical reason with intersubjective, discursive human consciousness. Habermas maintains that two alternative paths have also been followed in coping with the dilemmas posed by modernity. Right-wing Hegelians yield "uncritically to the rampaging dynamism of social modernity" by trivializing modernity's historical, developmental consciousness and by reducing critical reason to mere understanding and purposive (scientific-technical) rationality.[123] Young conservatives, including postmodern theorists inspired by Nietzsche, take dialectical criticism to excess by radicalizing modernity's historical sensibility (history becomes an unintelligible, directionless sequence of *epistemés*); by unmasking "reason as [nothing but] purposive rationality, as a form of depersonalized exercise of power"; and by appealing to an avant-garde aestheticism incompatible with critical reason.[124] Habermas suspects deep ecology of falling into the same camp as such postmodernists.

Although not rejecting rational critique, Derrida insists that the Enlightenment's emancipatory project is tainted by the same control impulse animating the very eschatological mystagogy that progressive rationality purports to unmask. For Derrida, something like "freedom" would seem possible only in forsaking the security promised by either pole of binaries such as rationalism versus irrationalism, reason versus faith, modernity versus antimodernity. Instead, one should inhabit the "difference" generating those poles. Critics say that such inhabitation deprives one of a standpoint from which to make any positive political recommendation. Supporters say that this radical negativity, far from reflecting nihilism, is tied to Jewish negative theology, according to which efforts to gain ultimate truth (identity between signifier and signified) amount to idolatry and blasphemy.

For nondualists like Meister Eckhart and Sankara, the *via negativa* involves leaping out of the illusion-producing conceptual oppositions of language and into the silence associated with eternal, nondual consciousness (absolute Nothingness). In view of his warning that negative theology often ends up affirming a superessential Divine, Derrida may be read as suggesting that the Divine lacks unified self-presence and always involves rupture, split, and division within itself, a fact that allows language and questioning to arise. If there is no extralinguistic intuition of the Divine, could a stirring of God's insistent questioning be discerned in silence?[125] Although Sankara seeks to avoid the trap of language by transcending it in order to intuit Divine (non)-presence, Derrida avoids the trap "by staying within language but on the middle path between the pairs of opposites."[126] Because any attempt to speak "the real" leads to one pole of the binary, he feels that the best (and most challenging) alternative is to live in the uncertainty involved in deconstructing and thus in constantly swinging *between* the binaries. If Harold Coward is right, there is a teleology involved in Derrida's deconstruction. Since we ourselves are the texts being deconstructed, "deconstruction is the process of becoming self-aware, of *self-realization*."[127] Such self-realization, however, is *not* consistent with deep ecology's self-realization, which involves an aspect of maturation or evolution.

Deep ecology is influenced not only by Mahayana Buddhism, but also by Sankara's Advaita Vedanta, which emphasizes "self" in a way that seems foreign to Mahayana Buddhism, later Heidegger, and Derrida. Naess argues that individual organisms deserve concern because they are inherently worthy manifestations of Atman (Vedanta) or God/Nature (Spinoza). According to Naess, by identifying with the Atman in others, the boundaries of self expand. By virtue of wider identification, care for others "flows naturally," for "protection of free Nature is felt and conceived as protection of ourselves."[128] Deep ecology asks not only for the "narrow ego of the small child" to grow into "*the comprehensive structure of a self that comprises all human beings,*" as well as all life forms.[129] That with which one identifies in others is not their phenomenal array, but rather the Atman within them.[130] Warning against "strong mystical traditions" that call for "the dissolution of individual selves into a nondiversified supreme whole," however, Naess emphasizes *both* the relative reality of individuals *and* their internal relationships with other phenomena.[131] Still, his notion of Atman and his view of the self as "a juncture in a relational system without determined boundaries in space and time"[132] are not easily reconciled with traditional Western notions of selfhood and individuality.

Advaita Vedanta's nondualism seems to differ radically from Mahayana Buddhism's. For the former, dualism vanishes when one realizes that all phenomena are manifestations of Atman; Self absorbs not-self. For the latter, dualism vanishes when one realizes that all phenomena lack self (*anatma*) and are empty (*sunya*); not-self absorbs self. For Advaita Vedanta, Mahayana Buddhism amounts to nihilism, whereas for Mahayana Buddhism, Advaita Vedanta mistakenly clings to a Self.[133] Though Buddhism wonders how Atman can in any sense "be" since it lacks any conceivable attribute, and though Vedanta wonders how phenomena can "arise" out of absolute nothingness, in practice these positions may amount to the "same." Brahman/Atman is so absolutely other than appearances ("the veil of Maya") that it cannot be described in terms of any conceptual categories suitable for describing phenomena. The difference is primarily one of emphasis on a distinction, Self versus non-self, which eventually became so minimal that it practically vanished. Experientially, in the moment of liberation, Atman verges on *sunyata.*[134]

Naess was drawn more to Vedanta than to Buddhism in part because Vedanta's Atman seemed more compatible with the idea of self-realization. Gandhi helped to shape Naess's conviction that social action, *karma yoga,* is an integral path to such self-realization. Like Gandhi, Naess not only holds that enlightened people working in concert can improve social circumstances, but also that *all* beings should benefit from such progress. Although criticizing a linear model of history, Naess's idea of self-realization may be read as generally consistent with the Western progressivism that results from secularizing Christian eschatology.[135] Such a reading leads Roderick Nash to argue that deep ecology expands modernity's emancipatory project by recognizing the rights of all sentient beings.[136]

In light of postmodern theory's claim that grand narratives of progress achieve domineering aims by "normalizing" the other, and in view of John Rodman's analogous critique of moral extensionism, however, Thomas Birch argues that the liberal mission of "granting rights to [wild] nature requires bringing nature into our human system of legal and moral rights, and this is still a (homocentric) system of hierarchy and domination."[137] Instead of "locking up" wilderness, and thus turning it into well-managed "preserves" within the repressive system of global empire, Birch recommends transgressing boundaries, cultivating "wildness" and spontaneity everywhere, and resisting the homogenizing and enslaving trends of modernity. Sharing Birch's criticisms about the domineering tendencies of modernity, but concerned about the political dangers of uncritical antimodernism, I encourage deep ecology—like New Paradigm—to conceive of itself as a movement that seeks to transform modernity's emancipatory impulse in light of an insight missing from progressive ideologies: that humankind is dependent on and related to the organic, phenomenal, and historical realms as well as to an eternal, extrahistorical, transphenomenal domain.

By recommending that deep ecology adopt this self-understanding, I seek to defend it from charges that it is reactionary and prone to ecofascism, charges that were fueled in part by my attempts to portray Heidegger as a forerunner of deep ecology. Yet by suggesting that deep ecology affirms what transcends all phenomena, I may not only meet resistance from some deep ecologists, but I might also provide fuel for those social ecologists who regard talk of the transcendent as an instance of the irrational, "magical" thinking that invites authoritarianism. As we shall see, however, not all social ecologists agree with this attitude toward the transcendent; moreover, some ecofeminists reject what they regard as *mascullinist* efforts to portray the non-rational as dark or evil.

In addition to the reasons I have described above, I now hesitate to describe Heidegger as a forerunner of deep ecology because what he means by the transcendent (the self-concealing absencing that "gives" understanding of being that shapes historical epochs) differs from what Naess seems to mean by Atman, the nondual, generative consciousness described in various ways by the esoteric wings of world religions. Tending to be a "private religion" in which the divine plays a secondary role to being, Heidegger's thought has an interesting, but problematic relationship to mystical religious traditions. Nevertheless, Heidegger's emphasis on the uniqueness of human existence is consistent with many religious traditions, which hold that humanity stands between the eternal and the finite, the hidden and the phenomenal. Gifted with language, humans inevitably have a mediated experience of themselves, nature, and the divine. Such a gift, which may not be available to other terrestrial organisms, brings with it great opportunities and responsibilities. Some deep ecologists fear that emphasizing this linguistic gift privileges humankind in a way that invites anthropocentrism, but Naess agrees with Heidegger in searching for a nonsubjectivistic, non-anthropocentric way of describing humanity's capacity to disclose, to bear witness to, and to help generate phenomena.

Social ecologist Murray Bookchin also contends that humankind has evolved so as to give "voice" to nature. Yet he views deep ecology as a regressive movement inclined toward ecofascism. In the following chapter, after examining the contention that deep ecology has affinities with the nature-worshipping side of National Socialism, we consider whether Bookchin's progressive-evolutionary account of history provides a satisfactory alternative to deep ecology. As we shall see, his evolutionary views are in many ways consistent with the claims made by Ken Wilber, the leading transpersonal theorist. Since Arne Naess and Warwick Fox agree that Ecosophy T is consistent with transpersonal psychology, studying Wilber's transpersonal view of human evolution may be a way of mediating the dispute between deep ecology and social ecology.

Most radical ecologists may be considered "social" ecologists insofar as they discern a link between ecological problems and hierarchical, patriarchal, authoritarian, militaristic social structures. Emphasizing this link, the U.S. Green movement and Green parties bring together the peace movement, the social justice movement, and the ecology movement. The peace movement works not only against nuclear weapons, arguably the most ecologically dangerous inventions, but also against the ideology of militarism or "warism" so closely wedded to nationalism. Militarism, whose macho posturing is described in Helen Caldicott's, *Missile Envy,* not only leads to wars, but also generates secrecy and state control, distorts economies, causes enormous pollution, and strips resources from already desperate people, especially in Third World countries. The social justice movement emphasizes that militarism, First World arms merchandising, and racism contribute to the grinding poverty of Third World countries. Moreover, Third World elites often control vast amounts of arable land, which are used to grow export crops bound for the First World. Meanwhile, deprived of decent farmland, the indigenous population is forced to eke out an existence by living and working (if jobs are available) in heavily polluted cities; by farming marginal land, thereby causing erosion; or by slash and burn agriculture that not only destroys wildlife habitat, but also deprives the planet of vegetation needed to produce oxygen and to absorb the carbon dioxide generated in vast quantities by First World countries.

Increasingly, even mainstream politicians and economists are beginning to agree with the Greens that there is a link between militarism, social injustice, and ecological problems. Reviewing the debates at the United Nations Earth Summit held in Brazil in June 1992, however, one sees much disagreement about how to deal with these links, which often concern policies that guarantee First World status and wealth. Deep ecologists have much in common with those Greens who argue that a basic alteration in consciousness is necessary for enduring structural changes. Although appreciating Green views about the link among peace, social justice, and ecological problems, however, most deep ecologists believe that special attention must be paid to issues such as ozone depletion, the greenhouse effect, and species-extinction due to loss of wilderness habitat.

The U.S. Green movement has nowhere near the political influence of its German counterpart, but has all the conflicts familiar to those who have worked in radical politics. Often at the center of these conflicts has been social ecology, a component of the U.S. Green movement, led by Murray Bookchin and his colleagues, who also call themselves Left-Greens. Their aggressive debating tactics have been criticized by other Greens and radical ecologists. Though social ecology is but one wing of the Green movement, though there are other approaches to social ecology apart from Bookchin's, and though his work is not strikingly original (it is indebted to the organicist social views of Lewis Mumford, among others[1]), I focus on his writings because he has so forcefully articulated a progressive radical ecology that draws on neo-Hegelian doctrines similar to those that inspire the work of the transpersonal psychologist, Ken Wilber. Deep ecology, the reader will recall, has much in common with transpersonal ecology. This conceptual proximity of Bookchin, transpersonal psychology, and deep ecology helps to offset Bookchin's sometimes unduly harsh critique of the "reactionary" aspects of deep ecology.

Despite their sometimes heated debates, deep ecology and social ecology have much in common. Deep ecology's idea of self-realization, influenced by Spinoza, is in some ways similar to Bookchin's view, influenced by Hegel, that the universe is gradually realizing its capacity for greater diversity and freedom. Despite Warwick Fox's suspicion that scenarios about the "evolution" of consciousness risk being anthropocentric, some deep ecologists say that wider identification involves human maturation or evolution. The idea that humankind is evolving is also shared by many New Paradigmers, who appeal to contemporary scientific ideas about the self-organizing universe to explain how such progressive evolutionary change occurs. Postmodern theorists argue, however, that the teleological worldviews at work, *mutatis mutandi,* in New Paradigm theory, deep ecology, and social ecology have ties with the modernity that produced totalitarian regimes and ecological disaster. Offshoots of the counterculture's utopian impulse, social ecology and deep ecology agree on the following points: humans are part of nature; nature is self-generative, novelty-seeking, and inherently valuable; nature is too complex ever to be controlled by human intelligence; wilderness areas, lightly inhabited by humans, are needed to sustain a rich diversity of nonhuman life; a new ecological sensibility and spirituality is required to save the planet; modern economic systems are socially hierarchical and ecologically destructive; needed are decentralized, nonhierarchical, pluralistic, ecologically sustainable, bioregionally federated communities.

The most distinctive feature of Bookchin's social ecology is its claim that mistreatment of nature is a consequence of authoritarian, hierarchical social structures. Hence, he contends, liberating humankind from the ancient plague of social hierarchy will contribute to the flourishing of humanity and nature alike. Contending that the Enlightenment's emancipatory vision must itself be "enlightened," for example, purged of its mechanistic and dualistic views of nature, Bookchin charges that deep ecology's critique of anthropocentrism fails to see that it is not humankind in general, but rather specific social groups that are responsible for poisoning and pillaging nature. For Bookchin, deep ecology adheres to the same reactionary, antihumanistic, and irrational assumptions that presaged National Socialism and that are discernible in the work of Heidegger and contemporary postmodern theorists.

Largely sharing social ecology's critique of capitalism and state socialism, deep ecologists agree that critically analyzing, resisting, and providing alternatives to existing economic structures are crucial for protecting wilderness. Yet although conceding that Bookchin's work is a useful bridge between left-anarchism and radical ecology, deep ecologists see Bookchin as akin to anthropocentric New Agers, who want to seize the tiller of planet earth. Positing that "second" nature (culture) develops out of "first" nature, Bookchin argues that humans are destined to continue terrestrial evolution by creating yet a "free nature" that reconciles first and second nature. Deep ecologists believe that by "free nature" Bookchin does *not* mean areas of nature restricted to relatively nonintrusive human use, but rather a planet pacified by humankind.

SOCIAL HIERARCHY AND ECOLOGICAL DESTRUCTION   In *Our Synthetic Environment* (1963), a critique of the devastating ecological consequences of capitalism's replacement of the natural with the artificial, Bookchin helped initiate the ecological side of the counterculture.[2] In 1965, arguing that "the harmonization of nature and man" requires a radical transformation of society, he said that nature's complex interrelationships cancel out "all human pretensions to mastery over the planet."[3] Conceiving of the planet as "a lump of minerals," instead of as "a complex web of life," capitalism relies on colossal technical "gimmicks" to simplify and homogenize life on earth, thereby "undoing the work of organic evolution" and leading to biospheric breakdown.[4] Capitalism is "the absolute incarnation of social evil," because of its competitiveness, its egoism, its commitment to endless growth, and its arrogant view that humans can remake the natural world.[5] Like deep ecologists, Bookchin distinguishes between "ecological sensibility" and a "superficial environmentalism" that hopes to reform capitalism.[6] If current trends go unchecked, we are told, the future offers two grim scenarios: either nature will take "revenge" on our profligate behavior, or capitalists will replace faltering biological systems with synthetic substitutes. Echoing Ernst Jünger's nightmarish vision of the future ruled by "the gestalt of the worker," he foresees the appalling possibility that "huge industrial installations will supplant natural processes" in "a nightmarish totalitarian society."[7]

In *Post-Scarcity Anarchism* (1971), Bookchin argues that the same technological means leading to "ecological extinction" could also eliminate material scarcity in an ecologically sound manner. Though appreciating Marx's critique of commodity fetishism, Bookchin abandons Marxism, in part because Marx uncritically accepted the old justification for repression: namely, that only a hierarchical society such as capitalism could overcome material scarcity. Viewing humans as "producers" and as "economic resources" in the "struggle to overcome scarcity," Marx could only see nature as a natural resource.[8] Bookchin says that instead of worrying about scarcity, we should begin with the idea of nature's abundance. Further, instead of trying to control everything, we should encourage the "natural spontaneity" that generates the diversity needed for a healthy planet. Bookchin sees increasing diversity as a sign of healthy organic and social evolution. Through social evolution, the hierarchical, abstract, exploitative, and competitive social relations of capitalism will give way to open, nonalienated, creative, social relationships in organic communities, guided by the principles of usufruct, complementary, and the irreducible minimum.[9] Bookchin suggests that ecological problems may be the new "general interest" that transforms people from many different classes and groups into citizens, united in a genuine *movement of the people* that recaptures the democratic ideals of the French Revolution. Restoring the ideals of civic virtue and responsibility is possible only in face-to-face communities that eliminate hierarchical institutions.[10] Since people would be drawn to different communities based on shared concerns and interests, affiliation would replace coercion.

Bookchin's own combination of participatory economics and politics, "libertarian municipalism," "*politicizes* the economy and *dissolves* it into the civic domain," so that economic policy is formulated by the whole community, in face-to-face democratic meetings, along the lines of the New England town meeting. By making the economy "a truly *political* economy: the economy of the *polis* or the commune," the people divest the economy of "an identity that can become privatized into a self-serving enterprise."[11] Although largely self-sufficient, municipalities would enter into voluntary, co-operative political and economic confederations, based on the principle of mutual assistance. Many Greens, criticizing Bookchin for promoting what they regard as municipal socialism, prefer decentralized market economies as an alternative to monopoly capitalism. As we see later, other critics maintain that the face-to-face requirement of his municipalism undermines the possibility of trade, transportation, and communication among confederated municipalities.

Arguing that homogeneity and simplification are regressive, whereas spontaneity and diversity are progressive, Bookchin maintains that both humanity and nature must be *released* from repression and control, so that they may realize their hidden potential of maximum social and ecological diversity.[12] Bookchin often criticizes deep ecologists and many ecofeminists for favoring dangerously "irrational" practices and attitudes, but he himself encourages exploring sensuous, artistic domains that are surely nonrational. Favoring the counterculture's celebration of sensuousness, tribalism, anarchist social arrangements, alternative modes of consciousness, and affirmation of nature, for instance, Bookchin once said that countercultural youth were alienated from their creative capacities and from natural cycles, all of which "were familiar and comprehensible, and evoked in [preindustrial] men a sense of religious awe, of oneness with nature, and, more pragmatically, a sense of respectful dependence."[13] Tribal rituals in which dancers imitate animals "form a communal and choral unity with nature, a unity that edges into the intimate intercourse of sexuality, birth, and the interchange of blood."[14] In rituals designed to validate the "citizenship" of nonhumans, tribal peoples regard nature as kin and as an active participant in the life of the tribe.[15]

Because primal people viewed the human as part of the nonhuman, and because they experienced nature a fecund source of life, not a stingy mistress to be seduced and conquered by "Faustian man," Bookchin asserts that they had no need either for social hierarchy or for mistreatment of nature.[16] In early societies, organic facts such as sex differences and age served not as an excuse for hierarchy, but for complementary social roles that made nonhierarchical organic society possible. Projecting this nonhierarchical attitude onto the natural world, primal peoples considered themselves as only a filament of the larger fabric of life. Hence, they used magic and ritual to persuade nonhuman beings to cooperate in ways designed to mutually enhance each other's well-being. Bookchin maintains that the attitude of primal peoples toward the nonhuman was neither biocentric nor ecocentric, nor even anthropocentric. Their only sense of "centricity" was toward their own communities.[17]

Here, I would like to make two remarks. First, I can easily see why deep ecologists would protest that Bookchin ascribes to them, unjustly, the desire to appropriate only the most regressive and dangerous aspects of tribal traditions, whereas he portrays himself as capable of exploring and appropriating only the positive and beneficial aspects of those traditions. Second, no one knows for sure what Pleistocene people believed, though some radical ecologists claim to discern in contemporary tribal peoples traits mirroring practices and attitudes of people 20,000 years ago, as if today's tribal peoples are somehow "primitive throwbacks" who have not undergone cultural evolution. It is not difficult to discern the unspoken ethnocentrism in such attitudes. Some Native Americans charge radical ecologists with practicing a new form of colonialism: instead of taking land, white theorists misappropriate Native American sagas, legends, and insights. By romanticizing the distant past, these new colonists ignore the real social and ecological problems faced by contemporary Native Americans.

Bookchin's attempts to trace the origins of hierarchy are not always consistent. In *The Ecology of Freedom,* he argues that hierarchy initially took the form of a tribal gerontocracy, in which old men had authority over young men.[18] The elevated social status of old men over young men really became a problem when some elderly men took on shamanistic and later priestly roles, which provided magical and religious grounds for having dominion over young men.

Bookchin suggests that gerontocracy gradually led to the domination of women by men. At times, however, he seems to agree with the ecofeminist view that patriarchal domination of women precedes all other hierarchies:

Even before man embarks on his conquest of man—of class by class—patriarchal morality obliges him to affirm his conquest of woman. *The subjugation of her nature and its absorption into the nexus of patriarchal morality forms the archetypal act of domination that ultimately gives rise to man's imagery of a subjugated nature.*[19]

Bookchin notes that in the "shadowy period of transition," when the Neolithic passed into Bronze Age and Iron Age civilizations, "strongly patriarchal invaders were to overwhelm settled, often matricentric, cultures."[20] Some years later, however, he sharply criticized ecofeminists for arguing that patriarchal invaders displaced matricentral cultures, for this theory does not explain how the invading tribes themselves had become patriarchal.[21] Yet such ecofeminists are doing no more than what he himself did in *The Ecology of Freedom:* to demonstrate first, that matricentral societies existed before patriarchal ones, and second, that in a particular part of the world—Asia Minor—those societies were displaced by invading patriarchal tribes. Many ecofeminists maintain that matricentric civilizations gave way to patriarchy when men began identifying themselves with mind, spirit, immortality, and culture while simultaneously projecting body, feelings, death, and nature onto women. In dissociating themselves from and trying to control everything that reminded them of their mortality, patriarchal men also initiated attempts to dominate nature. Bookchin grants that survival issues motivated the development of gerontocracy: the elderly created social and religious institutions to help compensate for their own physical weakness.[22] Far more than Bookchin, many ecofeminists emphasize death denial's role in the formation of patriarchal society. For this reason, in my view, some types of ecofeminism provide a better account of the origins of hierarchy.[23]

After power-hungry elites invented social hierarchy, Bookchin says, they began projecting it onto nature. Hence, the increasing exploitation of humans by other humans led to efforts to "dominate" nature. This claim, central to social ecology, is contentious. Some theorists assert that objectification of nature precedes social hierarchy. Social ecologist John Clark argues, however, that a dialectical view never looks simplistically for "which came first": domination of humanity or objectification of nature.[24] Bookchin insists that "no ecological society, however communal or benign in its ideals, can ever remove the 'goal' of dominating the natural world until it has radically eliminated the domination of human by human."[25] Against this claim, Warwick Fox has argued that eliminating social hierarchy would not necessarily eliminate the domination of nature, for one can imagine a relatively nonhierarchical society in which people collectively decided that they would treat nature *instrumentally*.[26] Clark replies that Fox fails to see that because we are part of nature, our interactions with it are continuous with our interactions with one another, and vice versa. Social ecology seeks to reveal "the complex interaction between these various realms of interaction *within* nature." If ecological consciousness transforms society, this will require

that humanity think and act as "nature rendered self-conscious." This means that we think as self-conscious energy, self-conscious life, self-conscious animal, self-conscious earth. As we do this, as we reform ourselves into true members of the "earth household," we begin to abjure our quest for domination of one another and for conquest of nature.[27]

According to Bookchin, human culture elaborates nature's own "cooperative and associative tendencies,"[28] which are necessary for the realization of human freedom. Yet ethics cannot be directly derived from nature; nature's cooperative unity-in-diversity provides the model for nonhierarchical, tolerant, mutualistic social relations. Preliterate societies established complementary and mutual relations with nature, for they saw that their own good lay in promoting nature's thrust toward diversity. Unlike modern societies, which regard nature as a resource to be objectified and appropriated by human labor, preliterate peoples had kinship relations with nature. Bookchin calls for reestablishing such kinship relations, though at a more advanced, self-conscious level of social development. To replace the "tyranny" of subject over object, he envisions the "synchronicity" of craftsperson and material. Suggesting that authentic "producing" involves drawing out the potential in the material at hand, he shares one sense of Heidegger's notion of "letting things be."[29] Inspired in part by Charles Fourier, Bookchin's utopian future involves free, nonhierarchical, mutualistic, sensually liberated societies, which would give "voice" to nature in the form of science and philosophy, music and dance, narrative and drama, sculpture and painting, manufacture and horticulture.[30]

Initially hoping that the counterculture would bring the changed psyche and sensibility needed to give rise to free nature, he later attributed the failure of the counterculture not only to structural economic trends that undermined abundance and promoted economic insecurity, but also to the fact that counterculturalists had not explicitly adopted a rhetoric still important to many Americans: the communal rhetoric of those radical Puritans who prohibited clerical hierarchy and who prized "face-to-face" popular assemblies or town meetings as instruments of self-government.[31]

Bookchin recognizes the profound political and ecological implications of attempts to define humanity's relation to nonhuman nature. Those who portray humanity as the lord of nature help to justify practices that lead to ecological disaster. Those who portray humankind as a parasite help to justify reactionary ideologies that require humans to submit to "nature's laws."[32] Although humans are part of nature, they have developed social categories—such as domination and hierarchy—that are inapplicable to the natural world. Hence, Bookchin concludes, it is misleading to speak straightforwardly of the "domination" of nature. Indeed, deep ecology's claim that humans should "submit to nature's laws" is a mirror image of the technological imperative saying that nature must submit to human laws.[33] In attempting to conceive of humanity's relation with nature, one must employ categories other than domination and submission.

If domination is a *social* category misleadingly projected onto nature, however, what terms *can* be used to criticize practices that kill nonhuman organisms, or treat them as machines in laboratories and factory farms? Are domination, coercion, and competition exclusively social (i.e., human) phenomena? Why can't "domination" be used to describe *any* process that negates the ontological possibilities of a living being? Posing such questions, deep ecologists charge that Bookchin makes human domination of nature vanish by waving a conceptual magic wand. Bookchin willingly says that cooperation and mutual aid are not merely social, but natural phenomena, for this view supports his contention that hierarchy and competition are exclusively social phenomena, which can be readily discarded by people who cultivate their natural cooperative proclivities. Bookchin sees human competition as an eliminable function of greed, which arises because of artificial scarcity imposed by hierarchy. Obviously, however, nature can be read as involving competition as well as cooperation.

Bookchin's analysis of the relation between humankind and nature is influenced in part by the competition between the views of Georgy Lukács and Theodor Adorno. Guided by the materialist view that nature is the organic substrate of and raw material for human society, Lukács distinguished social theory from any theory of nature. Yet he defined the social so broadly that it virtually swallows nature, which can no longer have independent ontological status. For Lukács, speaking of nature as something that can be encountered outside social praxis is an instance of contemplative bourgeois consciousness that reifies nature, thereby concealing the *social* origins of the world in which we actually live. As Steven Vogel argues, Lukács regarded the merely natural as what is *not yet* transformed into a human product by the revolutionary human subject.[34] Vogel goes on to say that even wilderness areas exist today only by virtue of complex social decision-making procedures. From this viewpoint, human practice will actualize its hidden (currently alienated) potential when nature as an independent realm is finally abolished.

John Ely counters, however, that Lukács's Promethean stance, which conceives of emancipation as "coincident with the expansion of the forces of production brought about by capitalism," and which views nature solely as a social category, "makes it virtually impossible to generate a conception of the embeddedness of human beings in their ecological context."[35] By fetishizing society, Marxists reduce nature to a social construct, thereby encouraging postmodern theory's relativism "in which actuality in whatever form is dissolved into a floating sea of signifiers capable of endless permutations of 'constructions'."[36] According to Ely, Lukács joined Lenin in denying to nature any ethical or subjective dimension, conceiving of it instead solely as raw material for human progress. Clearly, such anthropocentric Marxism cannot enter into serious dialogue with radical ecology.

Anticipating postmodern theory, Adorno believed that Lukács was overly influenced by Hegel's logic of domination, in which Reason (working through historical human agents) negates nature's otherness, thereby transforming it into mere raw material.[37] Today, so Adorno maintained, the subject must recognize the object's difference, its *irreducible otherness,* instead of arrogantly forcing it to conform to the subject's identitarian schemes. To replace Hegel's positive dialectic, which achieved reconciliation between subject and object only at the expense of the object, Adorno proposed that reconciliation take place by way of a "negative" dialectic. Instead of seeking the universal, infinite, and identical, philosophers should "literally seek to immerse ourselves in things that are heterogeneous to [totalizing reason], without placing those things in prefabricated categories."[38] Hence, much like the later Heidegger, Adorno insisted that nature involves an aspect of difference that cannot be assimilated to scientific rationality or any other social category. Vogel argues, however, that Adorno sought to make nature's otherness (analogous to Heidegger's "earth") so impenetrable to totalizing rationality that he ended by making it inaccessible to virtually any experience. Hence, he left us with no criteria for understanding what it is about nature that we are supposed to respect and protect.

Bookchin hopes to avoid such problems by negating the radical otherness of nature. Like Ernst Bloch, he asserts that all natural phenomena are characterized by a subjectivity that is always striving toward greater freedom and awareness. Unlike Hegel, however, he affirms that human consciousness has evolved from earlier organic life. Respect for nature follows from respect for the subjectivity that permeates both ourselves and all other things. Maintaining that the cosmos is self-like in being characterized by a measure of inwardness, Bookchin acknowledges the basic intuition of deep ecology, that there is no ultimate cosmological divide between the human and the nonhuman. This intuition is grounded in profound "empathy and identification" with the subjectivity and striving that characterize all things.[39] He adds, however, that by speaking of the "rights" of nature, deep ecologists mistakenly project social categories onto nature. To be sure, humanity and nature are not to be *dissociated,* but they must be thoughtfully *differentiated.* It is humanity's unique capacity "to think conceptually and feel a deep empathy for the world of life, that makes it possible for humanity in an ecological society to reverse the devastation it has inflicted on the biosphere."[40] Not unlike Heidegger, Bookchin believes that if humans are merely clever animals, there is no basis for objecting to modernity's (absurd) project of gaining total security by conquering nature.

Recognition of universal subjectivity once provided the basis for the pre-Socratic belief that in some sense the universe has "a moral character *irrespective of human purposes.*"[41] To articulate his idea of a self-organizing, nonhierarchical cosmos, Bookchin combines three ancient concepts: Heraclitus's view that the rational cosmic order (*logos*) is "pregnant, fecund, and immanently self-elaborating;" the Pythagorean notions of *arche* (grounding form) and *krasis* (equilibrium); and the idea of *isonomia,* which affirms the equality of all cosmic elements.[42] *Isonomia* affirms that genuine equilibrium is not "the mechanical equipoise of contrasting powers," but rather something like cosmic justice.[43] Though citing Cornford's notion that

Greek political ideals led them to see the cosmos as a *polis,* Bookchin apparently wants to say something stronger: that insight into cosmic justice (the natural order of things) shaped Greek political consciousness. But such a view would seem to run counter to his notion that sociopolitical categories cannot apply to nature.

According to Bookchin, by replacing the pre-Socratic ideal of the self-regulating cosmos with the notion that "inferior matter is governed hierarchically by static, eternal, transcendental mind (*nous*)," Plato and Aristotle undermined a view that lent cosmic grounding to social democracy and equality. In early modern times, philosophers restricted natural law to human society.[44] Curiously, this human-centered turn took place precisely when early modern scientists (including Descartes) were rescuing Pythagorean doctrines about the cosmos being an intelligible whole.

Bookchin maintains that for millennia the social pendulum swung back and forth from centralized, hierarchical societies to relatively decentralized, nonhierarchical ones. But in early modern times, Western culture started becoming an egotistical, greedy, and competitive society, which supposedly contrasts with medieval society, its hierarchical structure notwithstanding, as well as with communal sensibility and ecological rootedness of most preliterate societies.[45] Despite the gains of modern science and the emancipatory political aims of the Enlightenment, recent Western history has been largely hierarchical. Bookchin argues that modernity's history of hierarchy, domination, and destruction of nature could have been avoided if during the "watershed" fourteenth and fifteenth centuries, Western society had chosen the alternative of decentralized, nonhierarchical, ecologically grounded communities.

The rise of capitalism was reflected by the philosophical turn toward subjectivism. According to Bookchin, Kant was even more important than Descartes in effecting the radical subjectivistic turn. Ruling that efforts to discover the objective order of things was impossible for finite intelligence, Kant transformed the natural world into a subjectively ordered succession of representations. Although scorning Kant's doctrine of things in themselves, Hegel ended up in much the same place: "After the toil of Spirit, object and subject finally come to rest in Mind—in knowledge as self-knowing in all its totality."[46]

Bookchin's critique of subjectivism parallels deep ecology's critique of anthropocentrism. Both criticize Plato's subjectivistic turn, and both admire Spinoza's attempt to restore (with scientific grounding) the ancient view of the cosmos as a self-ordering, objective, rational system pervaded by a nonhuman-centered cosmic justice. Asserting that "human intervention into nature is inherently inevitable," however, Bookchin uses humanity's (apparently) unique ability to conceptualize justice as the basis for the more contentious claim that "an ecological view definitely involves *human stewardship of the planet.*"[47] Humanity, we are told, "has been *constituted* to intervene actively, consciously, and purposively into 'first nature' with *unparalleled effectiveness and alter it on a planetary scale.*"[48] In such intervention, "nature can act upon itself rationally, defined mainly by coordinates created by nature's potential for freedom and conceptual thought."[49] Bookchin argues that nature *invites* us, as an aspect of itself, to intervene in its own development.

The question is: what does "intervention" involve? Robyn Eckersley argues that in saying that humanity is obligated to help realize "first nature's potentiality to achieve mind and truth," and in asserting that humanity has the right to control the planet by creating a more diverse and complex ecosphere, Bookchin adheres to anthropocentric humanism.[50] Replying that efforts to control the planet are both arrogant and foolish,[51] Bookchin rejects "natural engineering" and decries a "strutting arrogance" toward nonhuman life.[52] As an example of an intervention designed by an ecological society to promote organic diversity, he suggests a "very *prudent, nonexploitative,* and *ecologically guided* enterprise" of turning the Canadian barrens into "an area supporting a rich variety of biota."[53]

Recently, Arne Naess has argued that because deep ecologists "wish to protect the richness and diversity of life whether decreases in richness and diversity are caused by humans or not," it would be appropriate to restore the biodiversity destroyed by the Mount St.

Helens' eruption in 1980.[54] At first glance, restoring the Canadian barrens and the area around Mount St. Helens seem quite similar. Naess, however, differentiates between them.[55] In part for reasons of scale (the damage at Mount St. Helens was great, but nowhere near the size of the Canadian barrens), and because of the eruption's recent occurrence, he suggests that Mount St. Helens would be a legitimate site for "restoration ecology," defined as the attempt to restore land to the condition it was in before being harmed by human or natural events. The arctic Canadian barrens would not be a legitimate site for restoration, however, in part because they are not as "barren" as some might think: ecological communities have evolved there over thousands of years. Many deep ecologists suspect that Bookchin wants not to *restore* land, but rather to *improve* it in terms consistent with his scheme to pacify nature.

Bookchin charges that "deep ecology tends to see nature not as a development but as a scenic view in which human beings—granted certain 'unique' traits—are fixtures in a virginal habitat rather than products of a complex evolution."[56] Some deep ecologists are in fact influenced by ecological ideals emphasizing stability and balance, an example of which is the climax forest. As we have seen, however, some ecologists insist that change is more characteristic of ecological processes than stability. Yet deep ecologists argue that human practices are altering the ecosphere far more rapidly than most natural changes, apart from natural calamities. Conceding the difficulties involved in establishing wilderness in the face of rapid human population growth, deep ecologists maintain that protecting wild nature is needed primarily because wild species and ecosystems are inherently valuable.

Although Bookchin also favors protecting wilderness, he fears that deep ecologists wish to establish a wilderness versus humanity dualism. He insists that humankind "embodies nature's thrust toward self-reflexivity. To write an active human presence out of nature would be as unnatural as a rain forest that lacks monkeys and ants."[57] But deep ecologists also affirm that wilderness is needed for the self-realization of humanity as a creative, self-reflexive species.[58] Following Maurice Merleau-Ponty, deep ecologist David Abrams has eloquently argued that human language is a complex version of the myriad of "voices" that have emerged in countless other species. Since language is one way in which corporeal beings "commune" with one another, humans can also commune with nonhumans by listening to their voices.[59] Here, as elsewhere, there would seem to be common ground between deep ecology and social ecology.

Deep ecologists fear, however, that in describing humanity as the "voice" of nature which helps other beings realize their potential for self-consciousness, Bookchin elevates humans above other beings, thereby justifying human control of nature. According to deep ecologists, nonhuman species do not need our help to realize their potential; rather, they need only to be allowed to pursue their own evolutionary destinies with minimal interference. Bookchin insists, however, that "humanity as it *now* exists [especially in its capitalist mode] is not the *voice* of nature rendered self-conscious."[60] Denying that he wants nature to bow to human control, he accuses deep ecologists of wanting humanity to bow to nature's laws, allegedly in a way that has certain similarities with the perverted "naturalism" of National Socialism. Beginning around 1987, he began a series of vituperative attacks on deep ecology, and on what he took to be its activist wing, Earth First!, for fostering ecofascist ideas. The fierceness of his critique suggests that Bookchin may have projected his own theory's "shadow" onto deep ecology, as a way of deflecting criticism from leftists who suspect that he himself overemphasizes nature at the expense of history. Even if such projection is a factor, however, he raises some important issues about the political dangers of radical ecology in general.

BOOKCHIN, DEEP ECOLOGY, AND ECOFASCISM   Bookchin's campaign against deep ecology, an "Eco-la-la" that amounts to a "'black hole' of half-digested, ill-formed, and half-baked ideas,"[61] took some people by surprise, in part because Devall and Sessions had approvingly cited Bookchin's work. Since then, Bookchin has also attacked social ecologists who do not adhere to his own views, as well as ecofeminists who favor Goddess spirituality. Critics charge that his militant style (and that of certain of his associates) exhibits a domineering, win-at-all-costs tendency connected with a masculinist concern to gain status by annihilating opposition and by enforcing ideological hierarchy. Defending his "stylistic militancy,"[62] Bookchin calls his critics misguided spiritualists who "shrivel from activism into quietism and from social organization into privatistic encounter groups."[63] (Surely Bookchin cannot have in mind Earth First!, the highly activist organization that he often associates with deep ecology, in order to besmirch the latter!) Allegedly gripped by a "therapeutic" orientation, these critics believe that the *manner* of presenting ideas is more important than their content: "The moral outrage that once stirred the human spirit over the ages in the thundering words of the Hebrew prophets is denounced as evidence of 'aggressiveness,' 'dogmatism,' 'divisiveness,' and 'male behavior'."[64] Bookchin's confrontational style stems in part from his Marxist origins, which led him to view the political world as composed of opposing factions that meet in frontal conflict: this is the political concretization of the dialectic. One critic charges that Bookchin's attempt to force complex situations into "the conceptual boxes of two clashing opposites" reinforces dualistic thinking and encourages violent acts of "negating the thesis." In the name of "progressive development," left-wing politicians often "focus on creating and inflating conflict, searching for contradictions in positions espoused by peers, and verbally attacking other people with great intensity."[65] Bookchin's pugnacious and at times abusive rhetoric has undermined his standing among radical ecologists.

Bookchin justifies his harsh criticism of deep ecology in part because, in interviewing Dave Foreman in the mid-1980s, Bill Devall did not challenge the following remarks:

When I tell people how the worst thing we could do in Ethiopia is to give aid—the best thing would be to just let nature seek its own balance, to let the people there just starve . . . they think this is monstrous. But the alternative is that you go in and save these half-dead children who never will have a whole life. Their development will be stunted. And what's going to happen in ten year's time is that twice as many people will suffer and die.

Likewise, letting the USA be an overflow valve for problems in Latin America is not solving a thing. It's just putting more pressure on resources in the USA. It is just causing more destruction of our wilderness, more poisoning of water and air, and it isn't helping the problems of Latin America.[66]

Not only Bookchin, but deep ecologists were upset by such remarks, which smack of racism and of a triage mentality that conveniently ignores that starvation in Third World countries often results not from "nature seeking its own balance," but from colonial policies and superpower disputes.[67] Because the Devall-Foreman interview was originally published in an obscure journal, many deep ecologists were at first unaware of the interview, but soon dissociated themselves from the ideas mentioned above. More unseemly grist for Bookchin's mill was provided, however, by the *Earth First! Journal*, which has printed misanthropic views, including the contention (made under pseudonyms like "Miss Ann Thropy") that the AIDS plague is a blessing, since it will reduce human population, thus alleviating pressure on Mother Earth. The fact that deep ecology theorists have often supported the sometimes courageous (if controversial) efforts by Earth First!ers to protect old-growth forests and other wilderness areas from being clear-cut or otherwise damaged is no excuse not to distinguish between the writings of deep ecology theorists and rhetorical excesses of a few Earth First! activists. Recently, even Bookchin has made this distinction.[68]

Bookchin's attacks on deep ecology's "misanthropy" have led some deep ecologists to counterattack with complaints about social ecology's "anthropocentrism." From a defensive posture, people no longer attend to what is valuable in their opponent's views; instead, they parody and distort them. In such a poisonous context, people who attempt a fair-minded discussion of "enemy" views risk being labeled traitors, fellow-travelers, or dupes. Only genuine dialogue can be fruitful, whereas statements made from undisguised contempt only harden positions that could benefit from thoughtful criticism. As someone who has learned from Bookchin's writings, I wish that his initial critique of deep ecology had been more measured.

In his recent dialogue with Earth First!er Dave Foreman, Bookchin shows his capacity for *constructive* critique.[69] Moreover, he has supported Earth First! activism and criticized the federal government's campaign to convict Foreman on a conspiracy charge. Other social ecologists have written constructive criticisms of deep ecology.[70] And Bill Devall has remarked that

I consider myself a social ecologist. I have studied the social and economic reasons for our current dilemma. . . . I find great strength in arguments that identify imperialism and growth of state power as a cause for our problems. . . . I also agree with those who study political economy and who argue that the logic of capitalism leads to environmental degradation.[71]

Still, some deep ecologists share Bookchin's view that "there are differences within the ecological movement . . . that are utterly at odds with each other to a point where their divergences are more important than their so-called 'common goal.'"[72] Criticizing deep ecology as a wilderness cult, Bookchin claims that it separates the ecology movement from the struggle by women, gays, the poor, and oppressed Third World people for social and economic equality.[73] Although himself attracted by the same counterculture's interest in tribalism, Bookchin fears that deep ecology's interest in Paleolithic consciousness reflects reactionary political views, consistent with a "politics of cultural despair."[74] Further, he argues that New Paradigm's and deep ecology's claim that personal transformation will usher in a new epoch exhibits the same political quietism and failure of nerve found in Western gnosticism and Asian religions. Bookchin calls *not* for self-realization achieved by union with the Absolute, but rather for social justice achieved by communal action that reconciles the social and natural domains.

Agreeing with the contention made by Bookchin and other Greens that environmental well-being cannot be achieved at the expense of social justice, some Third World authors argue that deep ecology seeks to impose wilderness preservation plans on impoverished Third World countries. Ramachandra Guha says that such plans, which allegedly force countries to save tigers while depriving poor people of farmland, amount to Western chauvinism disguised as ecological enlightenment.[75] Criticizing deep ecologists for turning Asians and tribal peoples into the nature-mystical Other to technocentric-rationalistic Western man, Guha praises Greens who focus on achieving human and ecological well-being by dismantling Western militarism and consumerism. Deep ecologists reply that Guha does not take into account the needs of nonhuman species, which are vanishing because a growing human population destroys habitat. Further, without the possibility of experiencing wild nature, people would have fewer chances to identify with nonhuman life and thus fewer opportunities to develop a deep ecological attitude.[76] In a reply to Guha, deep ecologist David M. Johns points out that many Third World people—women in particular—are leading movements to protect wildlife habitat and tropical forests, for such people see that they are part of a larger ecological whole being undermined by industrialization, social injustice, and overpopulation.[77] John's fine essay reveals that deep ecology can be reconciled with the social justice concerns of Greens and Left-Greens.

Discounting the possibility of such reconciliation, however, Bookchin prefers to read deep ecology's ecocentrism as an atavastic attitude resembling National Socialism's perverted nature mysticism. Citing Devall and Sessions' claim that "certain outlooks on politics and public policy flow naturally from this [deep ecological] consciousness,"[78] he concludes that their favorable reference to Malthus's problematic views on population and "carrying capacity" indicate just what sorts of policies might "flow" from deep ecology.[79] Though the quotation does not do justice to Devall and Sessions's views, Bookchin is right to warn of the political dangers associated with a resurgent Malthusianism. Moreover, some Earth First!ers have voiced offensive views about human population. Dave Foreman has even stated that humans "are a cancer on nature."[80] While rightly condemning such remarks, Bookchin himself recently restated a view he advanced years ago, that "man could be described as a highly destructive parasite who threatens to destroy his host—the natural world—and eventually himself."[81] Though condemning Thomas Berry's claim that humans are "the most pernicious mode of earthly being,"[82] Bookchin himself has described humans as "a curse on natural evolution."[83] Such charged rhetoric is dangerous no matter who employs it.

Bookchin is right that deep ecologists need to inform themselves of the dangers of movements that demand that society reorganize itself according to "nature's laws." But nature mysticism is *not* necessarily authoritarian. After all, many Native American tribes—celebrated by Bookchin himself—had nature mystical tendencies, yet were nonauthoritarian. The obvious example is German National Socialism, which was guided in part by what Robert Pois calls a "religion of nature."[84] Critics often trace this twisted, reactionary religion back to early German romanticism and idealism, from which Bookchin's own views stem. But as Manfred Frank has argued, German romanticism did not set out in this dark direction.[85] Originally, romanticism was broadly democratic and hoped that the synthesizing power of art could restore legitimacy, harmony, and meaning to a society undermined by analytic rationality, abstract market forces, and industrial technology. Schelling, Hölderlin, Novalis, and others regarded Dionysus as "the coming God," the divine presence needed to resacralize and rejuvenate society. Even Jürgen Habermas comments favorably on this movement:

The new mythology was supposed to restore a lost solidarity but not reject the emancipation that the separation from the primordial mythical forces also brought about for the individual as individuated in the presence of the One God. In Romanticism, the recourse to Dionysius was supposed to open up only that dimension of public freedom in which Christian promises were to be fulfilled in a this-worldly manner, so that the principle of subjectivity—deepened and at the same time authoritatively brought to dominance by the Reformation and the Enlightenment—could lose its narrowness.[86]

According to Frank, the idea of the freely acting self was fundamental to romanticism. Hence, romantics asked "how must *nature* be arranged and 'provided' to correspond to this idea, or more correctly: to manifest this idea."[87] The answer was that since a free humanity could not be part of a merely mechanical cosmos, nature itself must be conceived as rational, purposive, teleological, and in some measure free.[88] Likewise, Bookchin argues that only an incipiently subjective nature could generate a free and purposive humankind. Indeed, he has called for "a quasi-animistic respiritization of phenomena."[89] (Presumably, of course, *his* "quasi-animism" is purged of all the regressive aspects that supposedly haunt the nature mystical leanings of misguided deep ecologists.) The romanticists' efforts to forge a new mythology, one that would be compatible with reason while providing the unifying basis for a radical people's democracy, were promoted by the young Wagner, by early nineteenth-century French socialists and anarchists, including Charles Fourier, and later by French surrealists.[90]

Unfortunately, beginning in the second half of the nineteenth century, visions of a transformed humanity dwelling in harmony with purposive nature began to be used in support of reactionary and racist doctrines. The older Wagner, Nietzsche, Lagarde, Langbehn, van der Bruck, Spengler, Schuler, Klages, George, Heidegger, Benn, and others proclaimed that Enlightenment progress had led to nihilism and decline. In the 1920s, long before French postmodern theorists picked up the term, Ludwig Klages railed against "logocentrism" and joined Alfred Schuler and Stefan George in saying that a battle raged between the cosmic principles of life and death. Conservative revolutionaries called for a "new god" to save humanity from big cities, science, democracy, socialism, capitalism, and industrial technology (for Klages, "The airplane was Wotan's downfall"), which were manifestations of the nihilistic death-force ("Moloch," often identified with the Jews) destroying humanity-nature harmony.[91] Denying that "man" could either conquer or comprehend nature, conservative revolutionaries "enticed [people] to retreat into a rural nostalgia," rather than to face the problems of modernity.[92] Irrationalist, nature-centered, antidemocratic, frequently racist, *völkisch* movements helped pave the way for Nazism, which called for "purifying" German blood and soil.

Recently, Raymond Dominick has shown that pre-1933 Germany had a nature conservation (*Naturschutz*) movement with some parallels to contemporary radical ecology. In support for its efforts to protect nature, the *Naturschutz* movement appealed to scientific ecology, public health, Eastern religions, empathy for nonhuman life, and respect for Creation. Far more crucial in the rise of Nazism than either empathy for nonhuman life or nature mysticism, however, were the *Führer* principle, xenophobic nationalism, male chauvinism, militarism, statism, anti-Semitism, and Social Darwinism. Important for both movements was the conviction that land shapes national character, but Dominick notes that neither racism nor territorial expansionism, both of which were *central* to Hitler's movement, had "any intrinsic connection with Nature conservation."[93] Nevertheless, both the *Naturschutz* movement and National Socialism affirmed the importance of national regeneration, blood and soil, the peasantry, greater Germany, antimodernism, antimaterialism, *Volksgemeinschaft,* and anticommunism.[94] Because of such problematic ideological links between these two movements, a whole generation had to pass in Germany before the Greens could emerge as a political force during the 1970s. The task for deep ecologists is to make clear that one can feel a strong identification with and concern for nonhuman life, *without* thereby being drawn to authoritarian and misanthropic attitudes.

Nazism was a complex and contradictory movement, which combined tribalism and modern technology, nature worship and high modernist art. Hence, attempts to assign it to an ideological pigeonhole are problematic.[95] Nevertheless, Robert Pois's attempt to describe Nazism as a religion of nature repays study, because it reveals some disturbing parallels between Nazi rhetoric and the claims made by some deep ecologists. I wish to emphasize, however, that such parallels do not prove that deep ecology is fascistic, any more than that nature mystical native peoples were fascistic.[96] Describing religions as technologies designed to overcome the risk of death, Pois argues that Judaism and Christianity do not serve this purpose very well, since they emphasize the gap between an eternal God and a mortal humanity, thereby requiring people to lead morally responsible lives in a historical world that lies between the transcendent and the natural domains. George Steiner argues that pogroms and the Shoah were

desperate endeavor[s] by Christianity and by its pagan-parodistic offshoots such as Nazism, to silence once and for all the curse of the ideal inherent in the Mosaic covenant with God, in the more-than-human humaneness of Isaiah, in the teachings of Jesus the Jew. Eradicate the Jew and you will have eradicated from within the Christian west an unendurable remembrance of moral and social failure.[97]

Cut off from the "wholly Other" Divine, adherents of Judaism and Christianity were simultaneously alienated from nature, over which they were granted dominion. Seeking to eradicate these allegedly degenerate, other-worldly, life-denying, nature-degrading religions, whose secularized variants were Marxism and liberalism, National Socialism promoted a scientifically grounded *Volksreligion,* which proclaimed the sacredness of nature, and which celebrated "man's" immanent unity with the "mysteries of the blood." Living according to nature's laws meant, in effect, living outside of a history that was perceived as alienating, demanding, and inconsistent with racial purity.[98] Alfred Rosenberg was attracted to the mystic Meister Eckhart (also favored by Heidegger) because he differentiated between the transcendent God of history and the true God who dwells "within."[99] Other leading Nazis, including Himmler, were attracted by some Asian religions, evidently because they promised eternity within one's own breast.[100]

As chief priest of this religion of nature, Hitler denounced the evils of modernity (including liberal democracy, capitalism, and communism), proclaimed the need for renewed contact with elemental forces, and stressed the importance of restoring folk-customs, traditions, and attitudes. His organicist totalitarianism appealed to many people who were made anxious by the social atomism of liberal capitalism and who were ready to sacrifice their own "selfish" interests to Hitler's tribalistic "blood and soil" *Gemeinschaft.* Pois notes that this ideal of community grounded in nature echoes a theme found in more than one version of bourgeois ideology: "the overcoming of alienation, not through some hideous form of class war, *but rather through a revolution of consciousness,* the result of which would be a new sense of rootedness and belonging."[101]

Unfortunately, the Nazis believed that achieving this wholesome "natural" community required the exclusion (later, the elimination) of certain "unnatural" human groups. Nazi leaders regarded themselves as an elite vanguard of a "higher" humanity that would manifest the creative life-impulse of divine nature. By rooting humankind in immortal nature, National Socialism overcame spirit-matter dualism and simultaneously offered people a way of overcoming death.[102] Nazi death-denial is visible in Nazi contrasts between their life-affirming movement and life-alien Judaism and Christianity.[103] If their movement was rooted in life, the Nazis had to deny that nature contains death. Hence, Ernst Kriek proclaimed that "there is no inorganic nature, there is no dead mechanical earth. The great mother has been won back to life."[104] He also attacked man's "hubris and guilt" for trying to "master" nature, for such an attempt could only destroy life's "natural foundations."[105] Hitler proclaimed that men "owe their higher existence . . . to the knowledge and ruthless application of Nature's stern and rigid laws."[106] Rejecting anthropocentrism, another Nazi author argued that "man is a link in the chain of living nature just as any other organism."[107] One such law indicated that superior races could lose their potency by mingling with racially inferior and degenerate races. Though rejecting Jewish-Christian transcendentalism in favor of naturalistic immanentism consistent with modern science, the Nazis nevertheless believed in

a variety of what one could call "natural mysteries" and *in the emergence of a new age, one to be ushered in by some sort of "great world transformation" whose precise character eluded scientific observation and measurement.* There was soon to be a *turning point* in history, a belief which Rauschning saw as constituting the cornerstone of Hitler's "biological mysticism."[108]

Despite practicing their own murderous version of Social Darwinism, the Nazis were suspicious of Darwin's evolutionary theory.[109] Supposedly, Aryans had developed from their own noble blood line, uncontaminated by the unnatural poisons running in the veins of Jews and other such "vermin". Many National Socialists concluded that since history does not involve progress, humans could be saved only by identifying with the life-giving, conflict-ridden forces of nature. Adhering to the idea that life is justified only as an aesthetic phenomenon, the Nazis sought to produce a "higher race" of creators, capable of the "hard" things required of all great artists.[110]

Pois warns that today people are still tempted to flee from the responsibilities imposed by being historical agents and to seek instead an extrahistorical, "natural" way of life. The hope that a total paradigm change could bring about a "future primitive" humanity living in a reenchanted nature is undeniably appealing to many people, when faced with "the rape of planet Earth that has occurred as the most significant result of predatory capitalism."[111] In an implicit critique of many aspects of New Age, Pois adds that "nature worship, varieties of occultism, psychedelic religiosity, [and] adherence to perverted forms of Eastern mysticism" are either implicitly or explicitly antihumanistic and reactionary.[112] Given deep ecology's proximity to nature mysticism, Tim Lukes says that "deep ecologists must demonstrate why their philosophy would not conclude in a similarly deformed fusion of modernity with premodernity."[113] Leftists like Lukes are not alone in suspecting deep ecology of being ecofascist. Asserting that "we will not allow our right to own property and use nature's resources for the benefit of mankind to be stripped from us by a bunch of ecofascists," libertarian Ron Arnold describes radical ecology "the new paganism."[114] By ecofascism, Arnold means a society that appeals to higher "natural" laws to demand the sacrifice of individuals and their property for the larger social good.

Christopher Manes might be the kind of deep ecologist that Arnold has in mind. Agreeing that deep ecologists are "deeply primitive activists opposed to industrial civilization," Manes says that many radical ecologists see themselves as "future primitives," "as part of a tribe rather than a political movement, as a resurgence of the primal culture that has been quiescent since the Neolithic."[115] For Manes, modern technology is only an expression of the *real* problem: civilization itself and its false ideals of "progress."[116] Even Manes admits that his utopian vision of a future-primitive humanity, living materially simple lives in various bioregions, is "unrealistic."[117] Apparently more realistic is the view that Earth can be saved only by radical political change. In connection with the claim that technological elites might use ecological problems as an excuse to consolidate their power, Manes cites Heilbroner's fear that in the future perhaps only an authoritarian regime may be able to help humanity escape catastrophe.[118]

In view of approaching "ecological scarcity," Manes apparently concludes that eco-activists should put into effect authoritarian measures of their own before the technological elites do so. To avoid ecological destruction and even "extinction as a civilization," we must be willing to abandon "the individualistic basis of society, the concept of inalienable rights, the purely self-defining pursuit of happiness, liberty as maximum freedom of action, and laissez-faire itself."[119] Given Manes's preference for a hunter-gatherer lifestyle and his condemnation of modern civilization, one is puzzled when he now says he considers the latter worth saving. More disturbing is his tendency to condemn modernity wholesale, thereby ignoring its emphasis on human rights.[120] Speaking in favor of the Nazi "revolution" that would supposedly save Western civilization, Heidegger was silent while thousands of German socialists, communists, liberals, and other "un-German" types were rounded up into concentration camps near Freiburg. After the War, he refused to comment on the murder of millions of Jews and other people. During difficult times, he apparently concluded, difficult things have to be done. If Manes's radical views prevail during a time of ecological scarcity, would the ecologically unenlightened be jailed, so that the earth could recover from the "human cancer" now afflicting it?

Despite the fact that deep ecology calls for a spiritual transformation involving wider identification with nature, I do not believe that deep ecology necessarily entails fascism, any more than did early German romanticism. Nevertheless, deep ecologists must study the eventual fate of such romanticism. Deep ecologists would be unlikely to favor a mass-cultural totalitarianism like National Socialism, however, since they shun centralized collectivism and prefer a type of anarchism that they discern in many Native American tribes. Believing that the Nazis appealed to "natural law" only to justify dominating nature and supposedly inferior races, deep ecologists adhere to the norm of self-realization for all beings, emphasize social pluralism and ecological diversity, and endorse Gandhi's nonviolent approach to social change—views that are hardly consistent with fascism. George Sessions explicitly rejects attempts to compare deep ecology with Nazism.[121] Since Arne Naess played a role in the Norwegian resistance against Nazi occupation, his encouragement of wider identification with nonhuman beings is informed by awareness of the dangers posed by reactionary tribalism.[122]

Warwick Fox argues that criticizing arrogant anthropocentrism does *not* mean that deep ecology is misanthropic or antihumanistic.[123] Bookchin contends, however, that ecological destruction stems not from a vague "anthropocentrism," but from specific social relations (e.g., multinational capitalism) that let *some* humans dominate *other* humans and misuse nature.[124] Naess agrees with Bookchin's critique of oppressive elites and class structure. But Fox warns that overcoming social hierarchy would *not* necessarily end humanity's domineering treatment of nature. An egalitarian society may still agree to exploit nature for human ends, without recognizing nature's inherent worth. Fox argues that elite groups generally use anthropocentric arguments ("Our goal is to promote human progress") to justify their own social and economic power. Hence, challenging anthropocentrism is the most basic form of ideological unmasking.[125] Needed are nonanthropocentric movements calling simultaneously for an end to social hierarchy and to attempts to dominate nature.

Far from calling on individuals to sacrifice themselves to a larger whole, deep ecologists say that "individual biological organisms [including humans] should be free to follow their diverse individual and evolutionary paths to the extent that this does not involve seriously damaging the autopoietic (self-organizing) functioning of their own ecosystem or the ecosphere."[126] Questions remain, however. Who will decide what counts as "serious" damage? Who will assign blame for causing it? And who will determine what changes must take place to correct it? Deep ecologists hope that conservation biologists, working in close cooperation with local, national, and international groups, would help to answer such questions. Clearly, because the issues involved here are central to the future of planet Earth, they must be contested in an arena in which many different voices are allowed to be heard.

Bookchin fears that deep ecology's appeal to conservation biology reveals a tendency to conceive of humans primarily as animal organisms, in a way that ignores the fact that humans are also historical agents. If biologists say that humans are too populous, Bookchin suspects deep ecologists might support dire measures to curb population growth in order to "save nature," thereby substituting population control for social justice.[127] Deep ecologists have become increasingly sensitive to these criticisms. They now acknowledge that hunger and ecologically destructive agriculture often stem not from Third World "overpopulation," but rather from First World political and economic policies. Further, since large families are often an economic advantage and a form of social security, they admit that Third World birth rates may decline only when women receive better education and economic opportunities, as well as more respect from their husbands, for whom many children is a mark of virility. Since many of the world's rainforests fall not to commercial loggers, but to poor people desperate to make a living, the remaining rainforests will soon vanish unless Third World poverty is addressed.

Although acknowledging the complex socioeconomic origins of population and poverty, and although affirming that humans live in a historical as well as a natural world, deep ecologists assert that we must not forget that humans are animals whose population growth is destroying what remains of wild nature. Paul and Anne Ehrlich emphasize the negative ecological results of the "Green Revolution" and related attempts to deal with human population growth by globalizing modern agricultural methods.[128] Insisting that their concern about overpopulation does not reflect a desire to control Third World women, but rather a wish to save wild nature, deep ecologists urge that human population be stabilized and reduced on a *voluntary* basis, in connection with education, ecologically sustainable economic development, and the evolution of attitudes consistent with the self-realization of all beings. The goal of reducing current human population to one or two billion people may take a thousand years, if achieved by noncoercive methods.

Though deep ecologists are not ecofascist, I can imagine how—in the context of a perceived ecological and economic emergency—ideas drawn from their writings could be used to support neofascist programs.[129] Today, reactionary politicians still condemn the "overpopulation" of inferior races, decry racial "mongrelization," and criticize industrial pollution for contaminating the soil that nourishes the "blood" of the people. Though rejecting such racist views, deep ecologists—like Rousseau before them—often appeal to "nature" as a standard by which to criticize modern society. By comparison with some deep ecologists, many social ecologists are more conscious of the political dangers of nature-worshipping tribalism. Nevertheless, despite criticizing the reactionary dangers of tribalism, Bookchin himself has said that tribal demands "are regressive only in the sense that they go back *temporally* to pre-hierarchical forms of freedom.

They are profoundly progressive in the sense that they go back *structurally* to *non*-hierarchical forms of freedom."[130] He apparently supports his own version of a postmodern primitivism that reconciles individual with community, and community with nature.[131] Recently, in a passage reminiscent of what Heidegger and deep ecologists mean by "dwelling," Bookchin defines "home" as

a treasured place enhanced by tradition, the imprint of the past, long-gone generations to which we still belong, a personal remembrance of our origins and our individual development, the palpable stuff from which we have formed our biography, a loyalty to the land and community that surrounds it, a dedication to the preservation of its uniqueness and meaning for us. All of these sentiments have yet to be incorporated into the splendid work of the bioregionalists, who call for a sense of regionality in terms of watersheds and the flora and fauna with which we share a given area.[132]

Recognizing the use to which Nazis put the idea of organic "rootedness" in the soil, Bookchin emphasizes that his anarchistic municipalities should be based on elective social ties, not on blood kinship. But one can readily imagine how bioregions could become jingoistic and expansionistic rather than tolerant communities open to the challenges posed by the "differences" of their neighbors. Bookchin insists that because people in ecomunicipalities would no longer be greedy, "one liberated community will not try to dominate another because it has a potential monopoly of copper."[133] But Bookchin provides little convincing evidence that greed and competition will vanish in ecocommunities. Hence, there is good reason to believe that such communities would probably have the same chance of leading to wars and ecofascism as deep ecological communities.

The fact that social ecology itself shares with deep ecology the risk of inadvertently promoting an intolerant tribalism helps explain the furious character of Bookchin's critique of deep ecology. (Of course, *most* political movements risk promoting intolerance toward those who oppose them. This problem is hardly restricted to radical ecology movements.) In condemning deep ecology's proximity to National Socialism's version of nature-worship, Bookchin must also confront the fact that Nazis also called on the German romanticism to which he himself is so indebted. Arguably, Bookchin's social ecology shares with deep ecology a factor that played a role in the success of Nazism's death denial. Many Nazis solved the problem of death by denying it. Like many deep ecologists, Bookchin virtually ignores personal mortality and discounts death in nature. Defining humanity as immanent within nature, and rejecting both Hegel's Absolute and a transcendent Divine, he conceives of nature as a rational, evolving life-force, with which he identifies and for which he speaks. In identifying with immortal nature, does Bookchin hope to triumph over personal mortality?

The same question could be asked of those deep ecologists who favor the poetry of Robinson Jeffers. Jeffers sought to triumph over death by climbing into "the tower beyond tragedy," that is, by identifying with the allegedly eternal cosmos. Sympathetic with fascist aestheticism, he saw life as a beautiful, but temporary man-ifestation of profligate natural processes. Why worry about losing one's own life, or even the whole earth, if one can identify with the immortal cosmic Whole? Why not simply *apprehend* and *affirm* that the cosmic spectacle, both in its creative and self-destructive phases, is a manifestation of cosmic will? Of course, deep ecologists would deny as vigorously as Bookchin that their views have anything in common with National Socialism, but the potential link between death denial and authoritarianism, hierarchy, and fascism is worth pursuing.

I have suggested that deep ecology might defend itself against the charge of being ecofascist by highlighting its own version of a progressive historical narrative, so the next chapter begins by exam-ining some progressive cosmic narratives. But even if deep ecologists do promote such a narrative, so long as they do not address and integrate adequately the issue of death anxiety, their talk of wider identification may be contaminated by the widely shared desire to surrender one's separate-self sense and to be absorbed in a larger Whole. Despite certain nontrivial differences, Bookchin's social ecology is faced with the same risk, so long as it fails to deal adequately with the issue of death denial. In the next chapter, we examine the work of transpersonal psychologist Ken Wilber, whose developmental historical narrative is largely consistent both with the narrative favored by Bookchin, and with deep ecology's vision of human maturation. In addition to helping mediate the dispute between deep ecology and social ecology, Wilber's work has the virtue of identifying death anxiety as the central factor in humankind's long history of warfare, social violence, and assaults on nature. As we see in still later chapters, many ecofeminists agree that a major shortcoming of social ecology and deep ecology, and an indication of their latent masculinist bias, is their failure to examine the death-denying roots of man's domination of woman and nature.

Some deep ecologists agree with New Paradigmers that humankind may be evolving toward a nondualistic ecological sensibility. Given that modernity's anthropocentric narratives of progress have justified attempts to dominate nature, however, deep ecologists call for a *non*anthropocentric, evolutionary narrative to explain the possibility of a shift to ecological sensibility. Although in recent decades the Big Bang hypothesis has encouraged a number of narratives about cosmic and human evolution, some narratives agree with deep ecology's call for an evolving humankind to let nature be, whereas other narratives summon an evolving humankind to conquer the universe. The future of planet Earth will be decided, in part, by the contest among these competing narratives.

According to the Big Bang hypothesis, the universe—along with space and time—emerged in a gigantic, incredibly hot explosion about 20 billion years ago. As the heat from this explosion cooled off, hydrogen atoms began to form; gravitational attraction gathered them first into gaseous clouds and then into first-generation stars. Intense heat and pressure within these stars created the heavy elements that would later prove necessary for carbon-based forms of life. After billions of years, these stars collapsed and exploded, spewing out their heavy elements, which gradually coagulated into planets like our own. After billions of years, early life forms emerged. Gradually, organic evolution led to the rise of conscious and self-conscious life, including humankind. Literally made of stardust, humans may be understood as matter-energy in the process of understanding itself. A number of cosmologists now argue that the emergence of self-conscious life (though not in its specifically human form) may be *inevitable* in a universe that has a tendency to generate order and complexity.

For New Paradigmers, as well as for many radical ecologists, this narrative of cosmic evolution has the potential of restoring meaning to human life. Far from being a cosmic accident, life on earth may be a moment in the stupendous cosmic saga of self-generation and self-discovery. New cosmic narrators with friendly attitudes toward radical ecology suggest that humanity's most inspiring possibility is to participate in and to bear witness to this ongoing event of cosmic self-creation. A few centuries ago, modern science undermined meaning-bestowing cosmologies and depicted humankind as a freakish alien in a clockwork, but absurd universe. Hence, modern humankind tends to conceive of itself as a clever animal whose only aim is to forestall death at the expense of nature. Contemporary science, however, is providing rational grounds for humans to conceive of themselves not only as kin to all life, but also as members of a meaningful cosmos in which they have a significant, if still incompletely defined role to play. Suggesting that there has been a progressive evolution of human consciousness, some new cosmic narrators argue that growing awareness of our evolutionary kinship with the rest of life on earth may lead to a shift in human self-understanding that would avert catastrophe by giving rise to an era of social and ecological harmony.

This progressive-evolutionary vision is not universally shared, however. Consider that tribal cosmic narratives often described humankind not as evolving toward some higher level, but rather as declining from an originally blissful, nondualistic condition. Similarly, the Greco-Roman tradition depicted humankind's decline from the

Golden Age, on down through the Silver, Bronze, and Iron ages. Likewise, the Hindu tradition speaks of a stepwise decline from the extraordinary epoch (*yuga*) of Krita down to the most degenerate stage, Kali. Mahayana Buddhism says that humankind has long been falling away from the Dharma. Christians and Jews also maintain that humans fell from Paradise. Seeds for Western culture's progressive vision are found in the conviction, shared by Judaism and Christianity, that God promised to humanity a New Covenant that would eventually heal society and renew creation. Christian liturgy speaks of Adam and Eve's "happy sin," which introduced human freedom and thus the possibility of redemption. In medieval times, Roman Catholics emphasized that by committing good works, Christians could contribute to their own salvation. In leading the Protestant Reformation, Luther and Calvin denied the efficacy of good works and insisted instead that only the faith inspired by God's grace could bring salvation. In the face of such debates, Francis Bacon argued that although only God could heal humanity's moral fault suffered in the fall, humankind's own diligent efforts to understand creation through science could win back a measure of rightful control over creation. Eighteenth-century narratives about the *moral* evolution of consciousness and society culminated in Hegel's vision of humankind as the organ through which the Absolute achieves self-consciousness and freedom. Marx and Engels praised Darwin's evolutionary theory for achieving in the realm of nature what they sought to achieve in the realm of society. Similarly, Herbert Spencer and a host of others affirmed the possibility that humanity would evolve into a higher, less greedy, less violent species. The horrors of the twentieth century have convinced many that there is no evidence for such evolution. Many Christians in particular believe that these horrors reflect God's judgment on an arrogant, blind, sinful humankind that confuses technological power with salvation. I do not dismiss this view lightly. New Paradigmers and many radical ecologists, however, have renewed the hope that humankind is capable of entering into a new era, though perhaps not without extra-human assistance.

In the first section of this chapter, we see that some contemporary cosmic narratives are generally aligned with deep ecology and social ecology, whereas other such narratives affirm modernity's impulse to control the universe. In the second part, we see that Ken Wilber's cosmic narrative mediates between Bookchin's neo-Hegelian views and deep ecology's transpersonal views.[1] Wilber emphasizes that death anxiety plays a crucial role not only in efforts to dominate nature, but also in the evolutionary process that will lead humankind to establish a nondualistic attitude toward nature. In section three, we compare and contrast Wilber's narrative with the views of deep ecology, social ecology, and postmodern theory. Finally, we focus on postmodern theory's critique of the idea of the evolution of consciousness.

RADICAL ECOLOGY AND NEW COSMIC NARRATIVES In *Should Trees Have Standing?*, Christopher Stone called for a "new myth" to guide our treatment of the nonhuman world.[2] Years later, however, influenced by postmodern pluralism, he concluded that a variety of moral standpoints are needed to deal adequately with ecological issues.[3] Objecting to such moral pluralism, J. Baird Callicott maintains that contemporary science, including evolutionary theory, provides the basis for a *univocal* ecological worldview.[4] Though Arne Naess would probably support Stone's pluralism, Murray Bookchin would tend to agree with Callicott. Influenced by Hegel, Bookchin has developed a grand narrative of the cosmic trend toward differentiation, freedom, and self-consciousness.

Like other counterculturalists, Bookchin believes that ecological problems stem in part from the prevalence of analytic rationality, which emphasizes a rigid concept of identity, efficient causality (to the neglect of final cause), fixity and radical independence of phenomena, mechanical interaction, and stratification.[5] But Bookchin criticizes Fritjof Capra's attempt to replace analytic rationality with an eclectic "spiritual mechanism," which forces systems theory and cybernetics into an unhappy marriage with Eastern religions.[6] He feels that because such religions lack a "developmental" cosmology, and because they emphasize unity at the expense of difference, they are too consistent with repressive regimes.[7] He envisions the "respiritization" of nature not as deep ecologists supposedly do, that is, as a mystical whole that annihilates all distinctions into a featureless cosmic mush, but rather as a Hegelian *unity in difference*.[8] Like many deep ecologists, Bookchin agrees with Morris Berman that cybernetics can justify a mechanistic-reductionistic holism in which individuals become transient functions of processes that transcend them.[9] Above all, however, what Bookchin misses in systems theory, cybernetics, and Asian religions is the idea that matter-energy has the potential to generate order and differentiation.[10]

Though inspired by Hegel's view that humans are the cutting edge of nature's tendency "to press itself toward the level of thought and conscious self-direction,"[11] Bookchin holds that *all* of nature is self-organizing and evolving. Hegel rejected the idea that species evolve successively, such that more highly developed animal organisms arise from lower ones.[12] Instead, he regarded species as either eternal or as phenomenal manifestations of dialectical movements within spirit. In any event, species are not consequences of merely physical processes. Genuine evolution occurs not in nature, which he described as "petrified spirit," but only in history, where spirit is completely mobile and capable of full self-realization. Infusing Hegel's thought with modern evolutionary theory, Bookchin refuses to describe nature as a "self-degradation" of the Absolute Idea, but rather as a self-generating, self-organizing, graded continuum that includes humanity and its cultural achievements. Bookchin even suggests that ecosystems may manifest a "cerebral subjectivity" similar to that of humankind.[13] Transforming Hegel's vision that social evolution will heal the rift between spirit and nature, Bookchin maintains that this dialectical healing process does not terminate in the Absolute.[14] He looks for first nature and second nature (culture) to be synthesized as "free nature" (not to be confused with deep ecology's "free nature"—large expanses of land relatively free from human intrusion). Having reached the stage of conceptual thought, free nature would "thoughtfully" deal with conflict and compulsion. Moreover, in free nature

neither first nature nor second would lose its specificity and integrity. Humanity, far from diminishing the integrity of nature, would add the dimension of freedom, reason, and ethics to first nature and raise evolution to a level of self-reflexivity that has always been latent in the very emergence of the natural world.[15]

Bookchin's cosmic narrative reminds some deep ecologists of Skolimowski's assertion that humankind is evolving as the crowning glory of nature. Warwick Fox, for example, doubts that evolution is a progressive process, or that it culminates in the human species. Like Stephen Jay Gould, he criticizes the traditional iconography of evolutionary development—a tree (or a cone, or a ladder) with one main trunk and various ascending segments: invertebrates (including branches of insects, sponges, and so on), vertebrates (with branches of reptiles, fish, amphibia), and mammals (with branches of ungulates, cetaceans, and so on). At the top of this tree stands "man," the "crown of creation" or the "goal of evolution." By contrast, biologists Robert Whitaker and Lynn Margulis depict evolution as a bush with many diverging branches, or as a hand with four fingers and a thumb, representing the five families of life: monera (bacteria), protocista (water-dwelling microbes), plants, fungi, and animals. Such iconography more accurately represents the equal status of these five families, each of which will continue to evolve, unless prevented from doing so by external forces.[16]

To support his contention that life is *not* ascending a ladder toward ever-increasing diversity, complexity, and excellence, Gould analyzes the significance of 570 million-year-old fossils (from the start of the Cambrian), discovered at the turn of the century in Canada's Burgess Shale.[17] Charles Doolittle Walcott initially interpreted the ancient creatures to be less advanced members of surviving phyla, but other scientists have recently concluded that some of the creatures belonged to *extinct* phyla. Though biological diversity has increased *within* species belonging to extant phyla (e.g., vertebrates, mollusks, etc.), Gould argues that the loss of phyla at the start of the Cambrian means that life has become *less,* not more diverse. Further, far from being the culminating phase that is "implicit in all that came before," humanity is but one little twig at the end of a particular branch of a bush that has a manifold (not a unified) "trunk." Suggesting that we are "only an afterthought, a cosmic accident, just one bauble on the Christmas tree of evolution," Gould claims that "our continued allegiance to the manifestly false iconographics of ladder and cone" is "a desperate finger in the dike of cosmically justified hope and arrogance."[18] The sequence of events that led up to humans is so *contingent,* so fraught with accidents and freak events, in Gould's view, that if we were to "replay" evolution, there is virtually no chance that humans would again appear.

Insisting that the universe is both coherent and meaningful, Bookchin replies that the Burgess Shale "provides us with extraordinary evidence of the fecundity of nature, not with evidence against directionality in evolution toward greater subjectivity."[19] Eric Lerner agrees that over time "there has been an irregular but unmistakable tendency toward adaptability to a greater range of environments, culminating in human adaptation to virtually any environment."[20] Also contesting Gould's reading of the Burgess Shale fossils is Jeffrey Levinton, who asserts that "modern animals do represent progress beyond or improvement on their ancient forebears."[21] Biologist John Maynard Smith concedes that if the Cambrian began all over again, it would be "enormously unlikely" that beings just like humans would evolve, but he gives better odds that in the course of terrestrial evolution *some* type of self-conscious, tool-using organism *would* have evolved.[22]

I would add that odds favoring the emergence of life and self-conscious life *somewhere* in the universe become much greater if we look beyond earth and consider that among the countless trillions of stars, many are likely to have planets with conditions favoring life-formation. Consider that among the thousands of eggs laid by a frog, conditions are such that only a few survive to adulthood. Perhaps something analogous holds for the many planets in the incomprehensibly vast cosmos: on some of them, despite improbable events and difficulties, life will somehow begin and flourish. Contemporary cosmologist Paul Davies would argue, however, that the emergence of life and self-conscious life depends not merely on there being a sufficiently vast number of life-hospitable planets on which to play a kind of cosmic roulette, but also on the fact that matter-energy has an inherent tendency toward self-organization, such that it "will inevitably be led along the road of increasing complexity toward life. In the same vein, the existence of intelligence and conscious beings [may also be] regarded as part of a natural progression that is somehow built into the laws."[23] Although Gould himself concedes that there is a "directionality" or "trend" to evolution, he warns against reading social ideas about progress into the history of a species: "A trend is a positive sorting of certain kinds of species, *not the gradual transformation of a continuous population*."[24] If Gould is right, of course, New Paradigm's and radical ecology's speculation about the "evolution" of consciousness has no scientific basis. Siding with those who discern a developmental trend in cosmic history, I analyze later on Ken Wilber's transpersonal doctrine of what is involved in such "development." Far from seeking to bring closure to the definition of evolutionary "development," I believe it is crucial that this concept be contested by everyone with a stake in the future of planet Earth.

J. Baird Callicott has argued that even if evolutionary theory proves inadequate to explain human development, we can explain such development by appealing to the fact that humans are self-conscious agents who help to shape their own cultural histories, thereby generating *social* evolution. Hence, there may be long-term positive directional trends in cultural evolution that are analogous to long-term positive trends in the selection of species. In *The Universe Story*, regarded favorably by some deep ecologists, Thomas Berry and Brian Swimme sound like Bookchin in suggesting that the cosmos' own tendency to generate increasing order and complexity underlies evolutionary trends in nature and human culture.[25] By discovering that the universe is a historical or a "time-developmental event," Berry and Swimme comment, we now know that "we inhabit a single, multiform, creative, energy event. . . . *After fifteen billion years of its development, the drama of being has thundered into human awareness*."[26] The discovery that we are part of a larger evolutionary event is an enormous "mutation" within the Earth-human order, an event signaling that humanity is undergoing "the single greatest transformation of consciousness to take place since the human species emerged."[27] Humanity will either commit itself to furthering this transformation, or else will resign itself to destroying life on Earth. Central to the new paradigm are: recognition that humanity emerges from and is thus part of the rest of life; affirmation that life is a self-organizing web that we must cease controlling mechanically; acknowledgment that the Earth community is itself sacred; realization that morality must be attuned to the "languages" of the larger Earth community; recognition that we must encourage the flourishing of all life, human and nonhuman. The narrator of Swimme's book, *The Universe is a Green Dragon*, comments that we are always faced with the following cosmic responsibility:

to shape and discharge [the original cosmic] fire in a manner worthy of its numinous origins. We cherish it by developing conscience in our use of it: Are we tending this fire; revering it? Are we creating something beautiful of our planetary home? This is the central fire of your self, the central fire of the entire cosmos: it must not be wasted on trivialities or revenge, resentment or despair. We have the power to *forge* cosmic fire. What can compare with such a destiny?[28]

Some deep ecologists might blanche at Swimme's assertion that humans forge a "cosmic fire," for such assertions have been used to justify cosmos-conquering anthropocentrism. In saying humanity has the obligation and opportunity both to celebrate and to participate in the glory of cosmic evolution, Berry and Swimme do in fact echo themes found—*mutatis mutandi*—in Bookchin and Skolimowski. But their alleged anthropocentrism is open to question, since they assert that humanity must be allowed to fulfill its own potential, but *in ecologically harmonious ways*. Moreover, Naess himself acknowledges humanity's special creative and conceptual gifts. By appreciating the glories of the cosmos, he tells us, humans fulfill their own evolutionary potential of bringing greater "joy" to the universe.[29] Naess, Bookchin, and Skolimowski would all agree with

Heidegger that humanity's disclosive capacity is not a human possession to be used despotically, but is rather a gift that entails special responsibilities.[30]

Many deep ecologists and social ecologists thus seem to agree both that there are evolutionary trends in nature and human history and that there is a link between human self-realization and the realization of other life-forms. Bookchin would seem to agree with deep ecology that we become fully human by *identifying* with the self-evolving cosmos, instead of merely with our narrow egos. Despite other conflicts, deep ecologists and social ecologists seem to agree that human morality can be grounded in "the breadth of being itself" (Hans Jonas). I, too, am attracted to narratives that say that the self-organizing universes generate value and purpose, along with organisms and ecosystems. Warwick Fox has asserted, however, that a morality grounded in narratives about "cosmic purpose" is contentious.[31] Not only can one never demonstrate that one's narrative is true, one can never be sure that narratives grounded in a contemporary science will be interpreted in ways consistent with radical ecology. Fox's assertion is important, as we see momentarily, but it cuts two ways. He himself appeals to scientific findings to support his call for a new iconography to replace the idea of the tree or ladder of life. Levinton, however, in his reexamination of the Burgess Shale fossils, concludes that an "evolutionary tree" model *can* still be used to map the Cambrian echinoderms![32]

The fact is that cosmic narrators interpret scientific theories, which are already colored by the political views of those who conceived those theories, in ways that support their own political, ethical, and spiritual outlooks. Consider two recent cosmic narratives, *The Life Era: Cosmic Selection and Conscious Evolution*,[33] by astrophysicist Eric Chaisson, and *The Big Bang Never Happened*,[34] by another scientist, Eric Lerner. In important respects, Chaisson's cosmic narrative tells much the same story as that of Berry and Swimme: in the eons following the Big Bang, the universe generated increasingly complex phenomena, including human beings. Chaisson denies that "humans are the pinnacle of cosmic evolution," for many planets are capable of evolving intelligent life.[35] If on the *cosmic* scale humans are a "mediocrity," however, on the *terrestrial* scale they remain the pinnacle of evolution.[36] Hence, Chaisson speculates that evolving cosmic-technological "man" will acquire mastery over the planet, solar system, and eventually the whole universe! This is a far cry from Berry and Swimme's vision of humanity's evolutionary future, despite the fact that they call on the same basic narrative as Chaisson to explain cosmic evolution up to the present time.

Eric Lerner speculates about humanity's progressive future in a way similar to Chaisson, though his own cosmic narrative *denies* that the Big Bang ever occurred! According to Lerner, Big Bang theory is in a state of crisis that will eventually lead cosmology to a Kuhnian paradigm shift.[37] As anomalies counting against the Big Bang hypothesis have mounted, supporters have posited farfetched *ad hoc* hypotheses—ranging from black holes and "dark matter" to neutron decay and cosmic strings—to defend it.[38] Siding with Nobel laureate Hannes Alvèn, Lerner asserts that the universe is virtually eternal, or at least *two trillion* years old. Lerner believes that only a truly openended, evolutionary cosmic narrative can enable humanity to shake off its contemporary pessimism and nihilism. Cosmologies describing the universe as created and finite tend to support pessimistic and authoritarian regimes. The implicitly religious dimension of the Big Bang hypothesis was reinforced when Pope Pius XII compared the idea of increasing entropy (presupposed by many interpretations of the Big Bang cosmos) to the biblical notion that all things will end in the Last Judgment. Lerner finds it curious that the idea of a dying universe "provides a common meeting ground for one type of Christian faith and a pessimistic existentialism that rejects all religion."[39]

Praising Ilya Prigogine for demonstrating both the irreversibility of time (change happens), and that universe generates order out of chaos, Lerner claims that "evolution has not been a random, aimless process—the biosphere has progressed away from equilibrium by the objective measure of energy flow, at an accelerating pace, in the process of transforming the environment on earth."[40] Rejecting the "either/or" of accidental evolution or creation-bydesign, Lerner maintains that contemporary science can explain the tendency of matter-energy to generate increasingly complex structures, including self-conscious organisms that study the cosmos. Prigogine's evolutionary cosmology views humanity "as the most advanced expression of the infinite history of the material universe." As members of an open-ended and infinite universe, our "capabilities are infinite, human creative potential is infinite, because in a real way we contain infinity within us."[41] Apparently, humanity could eventually gain control of the earth, solar system, and beyond.

Bookchin has little sympathy for such cosmic-conquering scenarios, but he would agree with Lerner that if despair triumphs because of a gloomy cosmology, the resulting social decay "can be transformed into the unbridled evil of fascism, as Spengler's fashionable pessimism of the twenties paved the way for Hitler's vision of a *Götterdämmerung* where only the strongest and most ruthless would prevail."[42] Like Bookchin, Lerner calls for reason in the face of irrationalism, and also for "a radical transformation of politics" that rejects bureaucratic planning and autocratic capitalism in favor of democratic-socialist control of industry and workplace.[43] Yet Bookchin would disagree with Lerner's assertion that

it is impossible for an evolving system to stop growing—*it must grow or die.* To achieve the higher level of complexity needed to advance or even to survive, society needs more individuals, just as the biosphere must continually generate more species. A more technological society needs *a greater division of labor,* and thus, inevitably, more people.[44]

Not only is the idea of an increasing division of labor difficult to reconcile with Bookchin's notion of decentralized bioregional communities held together by the social glue of "affinity," but the idea that society must grow or die is central to the capitalist dogma Lerner seems to reject. But Lerner also claims that the most rapidly evolving societies are the "unstable" ones that "encourage innovation," by letting free individuals "make changes in the mode of production and thus in the society as a whole."[45] Even Bookchin asserts that "in nature, balance and harmony are achieved by ever-changing differentiation, by *ever-expanding* diversity."[46] But it would seem that only the *market* system promotes such rapid change and diversification. In the final chapter, we examine in more detail the question of whether the self-organizing character of market economies is consistent with progressive cosmic narratives, especially those that appeal to chaos theory.

Social ecology and deep ecology seem to agree that "progress" does not involve gaining technological control over nature, but instead involves the process of self-realization on the part of human and nonhuman beings. Intrigued by nonanthropocentric cosmic narratives, many deep ecologists remain suspicious of narratives that continue to portray humans as the "cutting edge" of terrestrial evolution. In the next section, I examine Ken Wilber's cosmic narrative, which sides with social ecology's contention that humans have a crucial role to play in cosmic evolution, and which sides with deep ecology's transpersonal view of the cosmos as constituted by entities striving for self-realization.

KEN WILBER'S TRANSPERSONAL VIEW OF HUMAN EVOLUTION   Ken Wilber is widely regarded as the leading theorist in the growing field of transpersonal psychology, though his work has not yet figured much in the controversies of radical ecology. By virtue of several remarkable books synthesizing esoteric traditions with Western psychology and social theory, Wilber has gained a reputation among people ranging from New Paradigmers to contemporary physicists. Transpersonal psychologists like Wilber differ from humanistic psychologists in maintaining that the human psyche is only one manifestation of a "cosmic consciousness" that animates and manifests itself in all phenomena. Like deep ecologists, Wilber adheres to the perennial philosophy, which affirms a nondualistic Absolute, the "Nature of all natures." According to this view, Wilber remarks,

Nature is not something set apart from mountains, eagles, rivers, and people, but something that, as it were, runs through the fibers of each and all. In the same way, the Absolute—as the Nature of all natures—is not something set apart from all things and events. The Absolute is not Other, but, so to speak, is sewn through the fabric of all that is.[47]

Wilber's cosmic narrative relates a twofold process: first, in involution, the Absolute forgets itself by emptying itself (Big Bang) into space-time and matter-energy; second, in evolution, the Absolute remembers itself in the a long evolutionary process, which generates self-consciousness life—such as humans and possibly other terrestrial and nonterrestrial organisms—to serve as the medium for the process of re-membering.[48] The view that physical nature is a manifestation of mind has gained acceptance among scientists not satisfied with the antiteleological, materialistic views of orthodox science. Nobel laureate George Wald maintains that the material cosmos

is actually an *avatar,* the materialization of primal consciousness. In that case there is no waiting for consciousness to arise. It is there *always,* at the beginning as at the end. What we wait for in the evolution of life is only the culminating *avatar,* the emergence of self-conscious *bodies* that can articulate consciousness, that can give it a voice, a culture, literature and art, and science.[49]

Arguing that humanity's cultural achievements are moments in humanity's historical struggle to awaken to its original oneness with the Absolute, Wilber's narrative is indebted to Hegel's progressive narrative, which was in turn inspired by Christianity's providential view of history.[50] In a controversial move, Wilber imports ideas about the evolution of consciousness into Asian religions, including Buddhism and Vedanta, claiming to find evidence for such ideas in the fact that there are stages in the process of attaining enlightenment.[51] Agreeing with many (though not all) aspects of Bookchin's neo-Hegelian views regarding cosmic evolution, Wilber also shares deep ecology's conviction that because social conditions are the outward expression of subjective attitudes, personal transformation is needed to generate the nondualistic, transpersonal level of consciousness consistent with an ecologically sound society.

For Wilber, nondualistic experience reveals the Divine not as external Other, but rather as the all-embracing, nondual, generative awareness, with which humans are always unified, even though we usually experience ourselves as separate from it. Wilber says that when a person remembers this original oneness with the Absolute, he or she is freed from "the chains of alienation and separate-self existence."[52] Although a few advanced individuals have attained such awareness, the rest of humanity remains at an earlier stage of awareness. A person's most profound need is to be reunited with the Absolute. Nondualists like Wilber recognize that the vocabulary of "unity" and "oneness" must be used with great caution, since the concept of oneness presupposes what is *other* than oneness. Instead of speaking of the attainment of unity, then, nondualists prefer to speak of "enlightenment" as seeing through the illusion of separateness. According to Wilber, such insight can occur by virtue of an evolutionary development involving the loss of the separate sense of self. To lose one's self, however, one must first develop one; to become nobody, one must first be somebody.

Existing as an apparently separate ego involves defensiveness, fear, and death anxiety. Some people make the mistake of attempting to alleviate the pain of separate selfhood by regressing to a pre-egoic, collective stage of consciousness. Wilber describes this move as the "pre-trans-fallacy." Instead of evolving toward a higher, more integrated, *transpersonal* consciousness, some deluded people seek a return to *prepersonal* consciousness. On the individual level, committing the pre-trans-fallacy often leads to destructive personal relationships; on the social level, committing this fallacy often contributes to the success of authoritarian regimes. As we have seen, National Socialism offered an escape from the pain, responsibility, and death anxiety of individual existence. By identifying with *Führer* and *Volk*, one achieves blood-union with the immortal life-force of the cosmos. Morris Berman argues that National Socialism was one of several Western social movements inspired by the craving to "ascend" to an ecstatic plane that overcomes the complications and contradictions of ordinary existence.[53] Since such "ascent" is often recommended by esoteric traditions, one can understand Bookchin's contention that National Socialism reveals the dangers posed by such traditions. Wilber, however, would describe National Socialism as a perverted type of esotericism. Genuine ascent involves movement to a higher stage consciousness that integrates all previous stages. Such ascent is made possible by puncturing the ego's illusions about separateness and immortality. By way of contrast, National Socialism called for people to surrender their egos to a mass movement purportedly aligned with immortal life-forces. The ecstasy involved in such surrender stemmed not from authentic ascent to a more integrated, transpersonal level of awareness, but rather from *descent* to prepersonal awareness. The tendency of National Socialists to exhibit dissociative attitudes toward their own bodies and emotions, as well as toward allegedly "parasitical," subhuman others, reveals not the integration that accompanies the move to transpersonal awareness, but rather the dissociation that accompanies death denial.

The Bible says that the separate-self sense dawned when Adam and Eve tasted forbidden fruit from the tree of the knowledge of Good and Evil. Rejecting the customary view that this event signified a fall in human history, Wilber argues that it initiated humanity's journey "up" from Eden, and thus was a crucial step in the long evolutionary journey back home to the Absolute. Adam and Eve's blissful unity with the Absolute was unmediated and unconscious, signifying the infantile era preceding the painful moment when the gap opens between self and other, and when people became aware of their mortality. The subsequent history of humankind involves the dialectical process in which consciousness both desires to regain oneness with Atman, but simultaneously resists doing so, because it requires the death of the separate-self sense. For the ordinary ego, such a sacrifice means simply being personally annihilated without transcendence. Desiring real unity and transcendence, but terrified of its cost, people usually seek transcendence in "symbolic substitutes" such as money, fame, power, sex, knowledge, drugs, and food. These unsatisfying substitutes are only finite tokens of eternal, nondual awareness. Regaining such awareness involves surrendering the separate-sense of self, but since such surrender is experienced as death, separate individuals prefer to offer "substitute sacrifices" in hopes of avoiding death. Hence, the long-standing popularity of warfare. Correctly intuiting that at the most profound level they participate in Atman consciousness, individuals go astray by "Atman projects" that attempt to turn the mortal ego into eternal Atman.[54]

According to Wilber, the separate self involves both a positive drive, Eros, and a negative drive, Thanatos. The former involves two related aspects, subjective and objective. The subjective aspect involves fashioning a mighty ego-subject that can resist death; the objective aspect involves constructing and acquiring cultural artifacts that provide symbols of the self's power, strength, and thus immortality. Eros names the positive force, the "ontological hunger," that draws the self back toward Atman. Since the separate self resists surrender itself, however, Eros is diverted into impossible attempts to make the separate self immortal. Thanatos names the force that negates all such attempts to establish boundaries separating individual self from Atman.[55] Although people deny death and flee from everything threatening the separate self, the anxiety-provoking work of Thanatos brings a vague dissatisfaction (*dukkha*) to the separate-self sense. As the "death instinct," Thanatos calls not for literal suicide, but for deconstructing the separate, defended, illusory self that prevents people from regaining transcendent awareness: Atman. Transcending to a higher level of consciousness cannot occur until a person has exhausted all possibilities for sustaining the separate self at the existing level. Working in tandem with boundary-dissolving Thanatos, Atman acts as a spiritual magnet (Eros) to draw people along the journey home, despite the fact that terrified egos resist every step of the way.[56]

Hegel sometimes said that his own philosophy constituted "the end of history," for his philosophy gave voice to absolute awareness and thus to the self-actualization of God as manifest in history. At other times, Hegel suggested that still to come was the planetary sociopolitical realization of such awareness. Though transforming Hegel's thought into a kind of humanism, Marx agreed with his mentor that humankind was on the verge of realizing its full potential. The worldwide communist revolution, always about to occur, would eventually give way to a postcommunist new age of complete human self-realization. New Paradigmers inherit from Marxism as well as from liberal progressivism the view that radical social transformation is just around the corner. Wilber cautions, however, that many more centuries of human evolution will be needed before a significant number of people achieve higher, post-egoic levels of awareness. Moreover, he asserts that even then most people will remain in the delusional, death-denying level of egoic consciousness.

Relying on the work of Jean Gebser, Wilber maintains that there are eight levels of human consciousness. Contemporary adults have usually reached level four, mental-egoic consciousness. The first three levels through which contemporary individuals pass during the maturation process recapitulate three earlier levels of human consciousness: (1) the *uroboric* level corresponding to unself-conscious ancient humanity; (2) the *magical-typhonic* level of dimly self-conscious pre-agricultural tribes; (3) and the *mythic-membership* level attained by increasingly self-conscious, but still group-identified people living in the cities of ancient Egypt, Babylonia, and China. These three levels of consciousness correspond to the infancy, early childhood, and adolescence of contemporary people. Like Hegel, Wilber says that earlier levels are not simply left behind, but instead are *aufgehoben:* canceled and preserved in later levels. Unfortunately, people trying to consolidate mental-egoic (level four) consciousness often fear falling back into earlier levels. Hence, they repress and even dissociate themselves from those earlier levels, which are often identified with the infantile, bodily, emotional, female, and natural realms. Such dissociation, which is encouraged by viewing nature as the source of infirmity, limitation, and death, helps to explain why Western society strives to control nature and everything associated with it, including the female.

Wilber argues that growing self-consciousness brings with it growing levels of death anxiety. People at level two use magic to ward off death, while performing rituals to acquire mana, power, or life. Carl Becker argues that primitive man "set up the whole cosmos in a way that allowed him to expand symbolically and to enjoy the highest . . .

pleasure: he could blow the self-feeling of a mere organismic creature all the way up to the stars."[57] Self-inflation does *not* mean attaining nondual Atman awareness, for self-inflation means attempting to reunite with Atman *without* the necessary step of surrendering the separate sense of self. For Wilber, if self-inflation is what deep ecologists mean by wider identification, they are committing the pre-trans-fallacy, which encourages people to regress to an earlier level of consciousness.

Critics complain that Wilber views the consciousness of tribal peoples as inferior to that of "civilized" people, but he does not deny that living tribal peoples have evolved in ways parallel with other civilizations. Upon contact with Europeans, then, Native Americans had already achieved their own version of level-four consciousness. Contemporary tribal peoples have something to teach Western people, Wilber would say, but *not* because tribal people are noble savages frozen in time. Prehistoric people in some very distant past may have existed in blissful harmony with nature; hence, the abundance of myths recounting a golden era when the elders lived at peace and did not kill animals for food. But tribal myths also recount the fall out of this blissful condition into self-conscious awareness of one's own fragility, dependence, mortality, and separateness. Every society regards regression to an unmediated, holistic, infantile level as an unacceptable way to cope with the anxiety provoked by the condition of separateness.

Wilber contends that at level three consciousness, mythic-membership, Great Mother worship emerged as a way of coping with ever-increasing individuation and death-anxiety. Citing Louise Kaplan, he explains the Great Mother in terms of early childhood development, when one gradually differentiates oneself from one's mother, who in the process takes on different aspects: good provider and angry punisher.[58] Experiencing the original maternal matrix as "everything," people tend to conceive of nature—the background from which things emerge—as female. Nature becomes the Great Mother, as the now bountiful, now withholding body that gives rise to, encompasses, and destroys everything. In a controversial interpretation, Wilber argues that blood sacrifice is the key feature of

Great Mother societies. Noting that menstrual blood stops flowing in association with human pregnancy, but not yet fully understanding other facts about reproduction, mythic-membership people concluded that blood was a crucial ingredient in the production of new life. Depending on the Great Mother to provide for a bountiful harvest, mythic-membership people engaged in blood sacrifice to provide Her generative side with life-giving substance and to propitiate Her devouring side. A symbolic substitute for one's own death, blood sacrifice was part of the Atman project of mythic-membership societies. Wilber distinguishes sharply between the Great Mother and the Great Goddess. Those who worship the former hope that sacrifice of another will spare their own separate selves from death, whereas those who worship the latter know that authentic Atman consciousness demands sacrificing the separate sense of self, *without* dissociating oneself from nature, corporeality, or emotions. In mythic-membership societies, murder and warfare became rampant as the separate-self sense grew stronger. Still today, people hope that by murdering the enemy, they will rid the world of mortality and evil, which have been projected onto the enemy. Although wishing to sacrifice oneself, "one arranges the *substitute* sacrifice of actually killing somebody else, thus acting on, and appeasing, the terrifying confrontation with death and Thanatos."[59]

Around 2500 B.C., Egyptian kings began manifesting the first stage of the mental-ego characteristic of level four consciousness. Wilber maintains that the Egyptian king, the first mental ego, was almost literally mad, since he conceived of himself as the visible, but immortal sun god. Complicit in the king's Atman project were his people, who identified with his immortality as a way of protecting themselves, just as followers do in contemporary mass movements. Gradually, the capacity for "solar," mental-egoic consciousness spread. Unfortunately, for a number of reasons associated with the rise of patriarchy, such consciousness was increasingly restricted to men.

Many feminists contest Wilber's claim that everyone must pass through and consolidate mental-egoic consciousness before moving to the next level, which finally begins the long process of reintegrating body, feeling, woman, and nature. In suggesting that achieving mental-egoic consciousness is a necessary condition for human evolution, Wilber would seem to be repeating the old patriarchal story. He agrees, however, that it was *not* necessary that the evolution of consciousness took a patriarchal, dissociative turn. Such evolution *could* have more effectively integrated the mental-feminine *and* the mental-masculine. A combination of natural tendencies and unnatural inclinations explain why the history of consciousness took its lamentable patriarchal turn.

First, according to Wilber, male and female bodies *tend* to be innately "wired" to sex-stereotypical behavior, although socialization and growing self-awareness can transcend these biological differences. Long ago, however, the emotive-intuitive strengths of women may have put them at a disadvantage in developing the logical-rational mentality associated with egoic consciousness. Second, men often associated women with the natural powers of childbirth and menstruation, whereas men gradually reserved for themselves the realm of culture. Since the mental-egoic level was more easily reached by those with access to cultural activities, the patriarchal dualism of nature versus culture, female versus male, favored the psychological-spiritual development of men at the expense of women. Although affirming that the Great Mother era had to be superseded, Wilber emphasizes that brutally *dissociating* the Great Mother was *not* a necessary stage in consciousness evolution. Because mental-egoic consciousness has dissociated itself from and repressed the body, feeling, woman, and nature, that is, from everything reminding the ego of its finitude, mortality, and dependence, such consciousness— especially in its Western mode—is flawed.[60] Contrary to Freud and Adorno, Wilber maintains that personhood does not have to be built on such dissociation and repression, since the person is a manifestation of the *ascent* of consciousness, a "natural unfoldment of higher potentiality,"[61] rather than a taming of "unruly" animal instincts.

Maintaining that women as well as men should be encouraged to consolidate level four consciousness, so as to make possible the envisioned evolutionary shift to level five, Wilber admits that if Enlightenment "fathers" had extended the rights of personhood to *all* peoples, women as well as men, slaves as well as free, the evolution of consciousness would have proceeded more smoothly. Hence, he encourages measures like the following to insure the full personhood of women: improving their economic well-being, granting them equal access to educational opportunities, ending patriarchy, and insuring political liberty for all people. But for Wilber, egoic personhood is not the final goal; even if all persons had equal rights, they remain egos—stricken with dissatisfaction, greed, aversion, delusion, and death anxiety.

The patriarchal ego's concern with power is reflected in the fact that monotheistic religions, such as Judaism, Christianity, and Islam, tend to portray God as a titanic patriarch who demands obedience and who stands radically apart from corrupt, changing material creation. For the esoteric wings of these monotheisms, however, the divine surrenders itself to and empties itself into creation, even while simultaneously transcending all phenomenal displays. Nondual experience reveals this divine not as a tyrannical male person, but rather as all-enveloping, generative awareness. God became male, however, because of the unfortunate fact that the heroic male ego attained the treasure of separate egoic consciousness by *dissociating* itself from the bodily and emotional domains. Having thus burst out of confinement in the female world-soul, the patriarchal ego was now ready to vanquish goddesses, mother nature, and everything female.[62] According to Wilber, today's ecological crisis stems from the fact that in moving to level four consciousness, patriarchal men did not simply *differentiate* the mental ego from the bodily-emotional realm of the Great Mother, but *dissociated* themselves from that realm. Because of such dissociation, particularly heightened in the West, there was

no longer respect for Nature, but a technological assault on Nature. The ego structure, in order to rise arrogantly above creation, had to suppress and repress the Great Mother, mythologically, psychologically, and sociologically. . . . It is one thing to gain a freedom from the fluctuations of nature, emotions, instincts, and environment—it is quite another to alienate them, In short the Western ego did not just gain its freedom from the Great Mother; *it severed its deep interconnectedness with her.*[63]

The patriarchal ego divinizes reason, because it seems eternal in comparison with mortal flesh. In recoiling from death, the ego must also shrink back from life. Egoic dissociation represses the entire human organism. Ecstasy is rejected in favor of control; sensuality becomes reduced to genital sexuality. Women, the body, emotions, and nature are all constant reminders of what has been dissociated. They represent the unruly, unpredictable, boundary-less Other, which always threatens to invade the patriarchal ego's well-defended psychic space. The dissociated ego cuts itself off both from nature (its cosmic origin) and from the Divine (its ontological ground and goal). The European witchhunts occurred as Western "man" was making the transition to the final stage of mental-egoic consciousness, in which "man" attempts to turn himself into God and the planet into a technological Paradise.[64] Having severed itself from body and nature, however, the ego initiated

a premeditated assault upon nature, regardless of the *historical* consequences of such activity, because history and nature were no longer integrated in a mutually dependent fashion. Likewise, the ego failed, almost from the start, to comprehend that an attack upon nature was already *an attack upon its own body* . . . , so that the whole project was, in the deepest and truest sense, finally suicidal.[65]

Like Wilber and a number of ecofeminists, Morris Berman concludes that the logical outcome of dissociating the animal/natural/ female Other is nuclear holocaust, "a scientific vision of utopia, in which the world is finally expunged of the messy, organic, and unpredictable by being wiped out—'purified.'" In one blow, man will destroy "any vestige of wild, disorganized Other *entirely,* so that the Self [mental-egoic ego] now reigns supreme in a pure, dead, and totally predictable world."[66] In reply to those who contend that the brutality of the twentieth century makes the idea of consciousness evolution, not to mention Atman, seem absurd, Wilber says that such intense violence is in fact consistent with the paranoid stage of advanced, patriarchal, mental-egoic consciousness. Though contending that Atman's journey back to itself cannot fail, Wilber concedes that humankind may well destroy itself before attaining the next level of consciousness. Hence, the evolution of consciousness is probably occurring elsewhere in the universe.

As we have seen, Wilber explains the origins of domination and hierarchy in terms of predictable reactions to death anxiety. Unable to find true transcendence, emerging egos "are reduced to stealing what immortality symbols and tokens of transcendence as we may from our fellow human beings."[67] Wealth and property, that which is "proper to" (owned by) me, constitute basic immortal symbols. Social hierarchy and exploitative systems are manifestations of anxiety-ridden egos who, seeking to guarantee their own immortality, dominate others and seize property. Social revolutions usually fail because the revolutionaries have not come to terms with death anxiety; hence, they establish new hierarchies that serve as immortality symbols. For mental-egoic consciousness, the ultimate property is egoic personhood. Treating personhood as if it were absolute, modern people engage in idolatry. Wilber maintains that until people surrender the property they call personality and awaken to the transpersonal, "time, guilt, murder, property, and persons will always remain synonymous."[68] Though denying that modern personhood is the pinnacle of human evolution, then, Wilber favors Enlightenment modernity's emancipating project. Freeing dualistic, mental-egoic persons is a stage along the way to *nondualistic* Atman consciousness.

Insofar as he affirms both a ground and a direction to history, Wilber disagrees with postmodern theory. He agrees with it in at least two respects, however. First, he affirms that dualistic, foundationalist metaphysical claims are illusions designed to enhance the power and privilege of the patriarchal ego. Second, he agrees that utopian hopes for a rapid transformation of humankind are dangerous. Even if humanity avoids destroying itself, the next stage of awareness will not come to fruition for centuries. Attaining mental-egoic personhood is only a moment in the lengthy evolution of consciousness; lying ahead are levels five through eight! Wilber calls these next four levels *Nirmanakaya, Sambhogakaya, Dharmakaya,* and *Svabhavikakaya,* details of which cannot be discussed here. Suffice it to say that each level involves increasingly integrated, increasingly nondualistic consciousness, eventually ending up in complete identity of universe and void, manifest and unmanifest.

Wilber believes that so long as mental-egoic awareness prevails, reform environmentalism will be the order of the day, for the ego is concerned above all with its own survival. If modern economic practices threaten to undermine the biological conditions necessary for human life, the ego can be expected to take measures to change those practices. Even if the ego concedes that nonhuman beings have inherent worth, however, its primary motivation for caring for those beings would be primarily self-interested and prudential. A genuinely ecological sensibility would occur only with a shift to level five consciousness. Since a necessary condition for such a shift is the consolidation of level four consciousness on a global scale, Wilber believes that the real task facing humankind is for everyone to become a responsible person, whose rights are recognized and guaranteed by governments everywhere. In effect, he promotes worldwide liberal democratic humanism.

Recognizing the extent to which most Western men are gripped by patriarchal versions of mental-egoic consciousness, Wilber anticipates that women will be the new heros showing the way to level five consciousness, *Nirmanakaya.* Such consciousness will be

centauric (which means mind and body united not dissociated), whole-bodied, mentally androgynous, psychic, intuitive *and* rational, male *and* female—and the lead in this new development most easily can come *from* the female, since our society is *already* masculine-adapted.[69]

Level five people sound much like the evolving humanity envisioned by New Paradigmers and by many radical ecologists. Citing

Erik Erikson, Wilber even uses the term "widening identity" to describe the process whereby people overcome old divisions.[70] At level five, people "*will see the same Consciousness in each and every soul, indeed, in all creation, and will start to act correspondingly.*"[71] Intuiting Atman in all things makes possible the wider identification that leads to compassion for all beings. Wilber remarks that dissociation from nature prevents the mental-egoic ego from seeing "that an attack upon nature was already an attack upon its own body . . . , so that the whole project was . . . suicidal." So deeply rooted was the patriarchal mental ego's prejudice against body and nature, that "the ecological interdependence of human body and natural environment . . . became obvious" only in this century."[72]

Despite the ecological implications of Wilber's work, however, deep ecologists give it mixed reviews. On the one hand, they approve its critique of the dissociative attitudes that justify the domination of nature; further, they share his commitment to the nondualism of the perennial philosophy. On the other hand, they argue that since *Up From Eden* approves the concept of the Great Chain of Being, which puts humans near the top of the cosmic heap, with other species further down, Wilber's thought is anthropocentric. Bill Devall has asserted that the idea of developmental stages of human consciousness stems from New Age Eurocentrism and anthropocentrism.[73] Opposed to linear teleology, the hubris of which is great enough to have awed even Auguste Comte, Devall prefers a cyclical or flowing sense of time.[74] Many deep ecologists are attracted to the seasonal cycles of the hunter-gatherer lifestyle, celebrated in myth, lore, and popular culture.[75] Despite some advantages, a cyclical view of time can be made consistent with the political aestheticism of fascism. Notwithstanding the antimodernist attitude of some deep ecology literature, I have emphasized those aspects of it that can be given a progressive reading. To the extent that deep ecologists, like New Paradigmers, promote an alternative to modernity, they accept modernity's basic premise that people do not have to accept the given social circumstances.

Although elevating humanity, Wilber also decenters it in two ways. First, he suggests that nonhumans on other planets (possibly even on

Earth) are undergoing an evolution of consciousness that parallels what is taking place in humankind. Second, he insists that humankind is not really "above" anything; rather humankind is the medium through which the Absolute plays out a drama surpassing the ego's understanding. Being authentically human means surrendering attempts to make the ego immortal and abandoning the craving for the hierarchal status that justifies domination and control. In nondual awareness, affirmation and appreciation of all aspects of creation arise spontaneously. I agree with Wilber that such appreciation includes acknowledging that humankind, and other self-conscious forms of life, introduce a remarkable difference into the evolutionary process. To Christopher Manes's assertion that "in the observation of nature there exists not one scrap of evidence that humans are superior to or even more interesting than, say, lichen,"[76] Wilber would reply that such "observation" is both constricted and out of touch with the "perennial philosophy" supposedly affirmed by deep ecology.

Wilber sees some positive aspects to deep ecology, but warns that its yearning for wider identification with nature may involve a regressive longing desire for *reunification* with nature, that is, a desire to return to the womb, instead of continuing the demanding voyage to higher consciousness. Consider the following passage from the poet Robinson Jeffers, which speaks of what many deep ecologists seem to mean by wider identification:

I believe that the universe is one being, all its parts are different expressions of the same energy, and they are all in communication with each other, influencing each other, therefore parts of one organic whole. (This is physics, I believe, as well as religion.) The parts change and pass, or die, people and races and rocks and stars; none of them seems to me important in itself, but only the whole. This whole is in all its parts so beautiful, and is felt by me to be so intensely in earnest, that I am compelled to love it, and to think of it as divine. It seems to me that this whole alone is worthy of the deeper sort of love; and that there is peace, freedom, I might say a kind of salvation, in turning one's affections outward toward this one God, rather than inwards on one's self, or on humanity, or on human imaginations and abstractions—the world of spirits.[77]

Elsewhere, Jeffers remarked that Orestes, the hero of his celebrated poem, "The Tower Beyond Tragedy," identified himself with the "divine nature of things," that is, the organic whole that constitutes all things: "This perception is his tower beyond the reach of tragedy; because, whatever may happen, the great organism will remain forever immortal and immortally beautiful."[78] Sessions comments that Jeffers' poem expresses the "spiritual quest for freedom in the *whole* of Nature/God."[79] Wilber approves of surrendering the ego to unite with the Divine, but he would ask whether Jeffers's surrender involves *prepersonal* regression to earlier union with the Great Mother, or *transpersonal* progression to higher unity with the Great Goddess. Mounting "the tower beyond tragedy," that is, identifying with the allegedly eternal cosmos, Orestes hopes to escape the mortal's tragic fate. If Big Bang cosmology has validity, however, the universe is *not* eternal. Since eternity lies completely *outside* of time, Wilber warns against identifying with any spatiotemporal phenomenon, including the whole of the vast and beautiful cosmos. Atman includes the phenomenal domain, but also transcends it. Wilber's view, with which I have considerable sympathy, and which *may* be discerned in Naess's ontological phenomenalism, amounts to *panentheism,* which holds that all phenomena are manifestations of Atman, but do not exhaust it.

Some deep ecologists read Jeffers' poetry not as panentheism, but rather as pantheism, according to which the Divine is equivalent with nature. Such a reading tends to align Jeffers with Spinoza, who himself influenced Hegel. But the panentheist Hegel criticized Spinoza's pantheistic Substance (God/Nature) for lacking an adequate conception of the transcendent subjectivity manifesting itself spatially (in nature) and temporally (in history). For Hegel, as for Wilber, genuine freedom involves transcending natural necessity in the process of attaining absolute consciousness. Wilber regards pantheism as dangerous because it defines freedom as affirmation of natural necessity and as reabsorption of the individual into the cosmic whole. Such a view is not only psychologically regressive and spiritually misguided, since Atman transcends phenomenal nature, but is disturbingly consistent with aspects of fascist ideology, to which Jeffers was in fact attracted.

Sessions would reply that deep ecology calls for the self-realization of *individual* beings, not for their surrender to a totalizing whole. In 1978, he said that "from Nietzsche, and Buddha, and perhaps Spinoza, came [Jeffers's] preoccupation with the importance of the individual, and individual spiritual human freedom."[80] But these reassuring lines are preceded by the following remarks:

[Jeffers saw] the need for a transvaluation of Christian morals, the need for man to rise above his everyday state, and to develop a re-spect for more traditional Greek *aristocratic values.* Nietzsche, to-gether with Spengler, raised doubts in his mind about the reality of human progress, and implanted the idea of a Greek cyclical concep-tion of time and "eternal recurrence."

According to Nietzsche and Spengler, the elite few know that people are subject to fate, that history lacks any purpose, and that the cosmic spectacle is simply a manifestation of the will to power. In aligning oneself with the restless will to power, Nietzsche suggested, an individual could turn his own life into a self-creating work of art. Hence, his view of genuine individuation involved not the self-realization of the bourgeois ego, but rather identification with the higher will at work in the world. Crucial for this vision of self-creation are aesthetic considerations, not moral ones. National Socialism has been described as "national aestheticism" to emphasize its goal of transforming state, people, and land into a total work of art grounded upon a self-glorifying myth of national immortality.[81] This myth appealed to many Germans gripped by death anxiety and "ontological hysteria."[82] Though this "Wilberian" reading is *not* the only possible way to read Jeffers, it is a reading that deep ecologists must confront.

If Wilber warns that the tragic human split will take many cen-turies to heal, he does posit that such healing is possible, at least for some. Postmodern theorists suggest, however, that fissure, negativity, and incompleteness can never be overcome, since they are necessary for self-consciousness. Following Jacques Lacan, Slavoj Žižek remarks that culture amounts to an effort to channel and "*cultivate* this traumatic kernel, this radical antagonism through which man cuts his umbilical cord with nature, with animal homeostasis." The source of totalitarianism, mass murders, and holocausts is precisely the attempt to overcome this tension "*in the name of man as harmonious being, of a New Man without antagonistic tension.*"[83] But since there is no regaining of the lost balance, people can only accept their fissured condition: "all other solutions—the illusion of a possible return to nature, the idea of a total socialization of nature—are a direct path to totalitarianism."[84]

Wilber would not agree that we are left with one of two choices: either to remain stuck in fissured ego-consciousness, or else to deal with death anxiety by dismantling the ego, thereby undergoing psychic regression that ends in personal and social catastrophe. The problem is *not* the yearning to end dualism, but rather seeking to do so *inappropriately.* According to Wilber, the fissure originated not in the dawn of self-consciousness, but far earlier when the Absolute emptied itself into matter-energy. If the Origin is not matter-energy, but the divine, separation cannot be healed by regressing to an infantile level ("return to nature") in which one seeks to be reabsorbed in the womb. Only evolving toward a higher unity with Atman will gradually cure the fissure. Totalitarianism is one manifestation of attempts to substitute merely *symbolic* wholeness for *real* wholeness. The urge to dominate is intrinsic to mental egoic consciousness. In dominating others, we feel ourselves to be higher, more valuable, and thus better protected against death. Similarly, in dominating nature (including our own bodies), we reinforce the dissociative attitude sustaining the illusion that the mental-ego is eternal and thus superior to the mortal body.

WILBER AND SOCIAL ECOLOGY   Bookchin and Wilber both regard humanity as participating in a teleological process bringing matter-energy to self-consciousness; both see the ecological crisis as the symptom of problems involved in this process; and both are neo-Hegelian. But there are important differences in their appropriation of Hegel. For openers, Wilber would argue that by discarding Hegel's Absolute, the eternal metaphysical ground and goal of human striving, Bookchin makes it impossible to understand human history. For Hegel, the Absolute's desire for self-actualization manifests itself in human agents who, in striving to actualize their own personal potential, inadvertently contribute to fulfilling the Absolute's goal. Hegel would say that without an Absolute that gives rise to and that also acts as a "lure" for cosmic evolution, Bookchin's view of cosmic evolution risks becoming a "bad infinity," that is, continual expansion of differentiation without an adequate internal concept.

As we have seen, Wilber explains human history as a developmental process driven by two powerful factors: Eros, the Absolute's desire to regain unity and self-consciousness; and Thanatos, the death anxiety that undermines existing Atman projects and forces people to forge ever-greater defenses against mortality. Death-denying Atman projects constitute the evolutionary stages of human history. Bookchin cannot offer an adequate account of human history, particularly the rise of hierarchy and domination, not only because he eliminates the Absolute, but also because he virtually ignores mortality and death anxiety. Wilber argues that the craving for power, authority, and status arose as increasingly conscious selves needed death-denying Atman projects to play out on their fellow humans:

The rage at being only a finite creature was soon turned into rage at other finite creatures, so that today the world is split into several large and heavily armed camps of finite creatures, glutted in overkill, bent upon mutual destruction.[85]

Suggesting that scarcity is the impulse behind oppression, Bookchin writes that the domineering bourgeois ego results from capitalist social relations, whose accumulation-obsession conceals the natural abundance that flows in nonhierarchical societies:

Humanity is afflicted not because it has eaten of the fruit of the tree of knowledge but because it has eaten of the bitter fruit of scarcity. Scarcity is not the penalty of sin but rather its cause. Given a level of abundance that removes this bitter fruit, individuals have no need to dominate, manipulate, or empower themselves at the expense of others.[86]

We are told that gerontocracy, allegedly the first form of hierarchy, arose because elders "were more vulnerable to abandonment in periods of material want than any other part of the population."[87] It is left to the reader to observe that abandonment meant death. Wilber insists that nonhierarchical societies became hierarchical in direct proportion to the emergence of a greater sense of personal separateness and thus a stronger dose of death anxiety. Though egalitarian societies remain an attractive ideal, attempts to establish them have generally failed, because people generally want to accumulate more immortality symbols (including status, wealth, power, and education) than others. Hence, material abundance, equitable distribution of wealth, and equal access to educational opportunities will not in themselves end the craving for status and hierarchy; instead, they may provide new opportunities for competition among anxiety-ridden egos. Wilber wholeheartedly agrees, however, that poverty is *not* conducive to self-realization or to consciousness evolution. A relatively egalitarian society would provide more people with the opportunity of consolidating themselves at the mental-egoic level, thereby setting the stage for a possible shift to level five consciousness.

Bookchin observes that the obsession with accumulation is widespread, but not universal. For instance, some Native American societies condemned stinginess and encouraged wealth to flow through the community by the potlatch, in which a man displayed his generosity by giving away his wealth, sometimes to the point of beggaring himself. One could argue, however, that the generosity of the "big man" is linked to his own complex Atman project: a generous man is socially superior to, more special, and thus better defended against death than other people. Further, the fact that gift societies made stinginess the cardinal sin indicates just how strong the temptation was to accumulate wealth. Of course, many Native American societies had more important immortality symbols than material wealth. Men often hunted the spiritual "power" that women already possessed insofar as they could create children, themselves a symbol of parental immortality.

In Wilber's view, by failing to see that hierarchy results from growing self-awareness and death anxiety, Bookchin abandons the basis for Hegel's progressive view of history. Despite affirming that civilization has become differentiated enough to give rise to the ideal of the autonomous individual, Bookchin tends to view history as an oscillation between scarcity and abundance, hierarchy and egalitarianism, though hierarchy has won out in the past few centuries. Wilber says that capitalism was generated by increasingly anxious Renaissance egos, who emerged after the middle ages when death anxiety was to some extent assuaged by the Church's promises of personal immortality.[88] The breakdown of the organic medieval worldview displaced the earth from its central (if inferior) position, and thrust "man" into the vastness of isomorphic space. Emboldened by scientific rationality, and dissociated from nature below and God above, modern man undertook the greatest Atman projects of all time, including global industrialization and planetary war. Unlike Bookchin, then, who tends to see capitalism as a social structure that generates greedy, self-regarding egos, Wilber suggests that because mental egoity helped to generate capitalism, ending capitalism will not end the mental ego's striving for power, status, and wealth.

On this issue, I tend to side with Wilber and with ecofeminists like Susan Griffin and Mary Daly, who argue that death denial motivates the violent history of patriarchy, including its capitalist phase. Similarly, Joel Kovel, often associated with social ecology, asserts that "the march of Egoic civilization can be measured in its increasingly widespread denial of death and fear of death."[89] Only by coming to terms with mortality and finitude will men abandon their obsession with controlling everything, ranging from women to weather. But *how* can this rage against finitude be overcome? Wilber's answer: only by evolving to higher, more integrated levels of awareness will people experience that at the deepest level they are *already* eternal, that the Divine manifests in and through all phenomena, but is not identical with any of them, including the body and mental ego. Thus assured that there is nothing to fear, humans—women and men alike—can increasingly shed their defensiveness and their need for control.

For Wilber, individuation and autonomy are only temporary stages to be sublated (*aufgehoben*) on the way to higher consciousness, but for Bookchin, autonomous individuals pursuing personal and collective goals in nonhierarchical communities seem to be the aim of human maturity. Although Bookchin praises interdependent communities and criticizes the isolated bourgeois ego, critics charge that his reliance on Aristotle's idea of substance reinforces a masculinist concept of individuality that is inconsistent with ecological thinking. Following Aristotle, Bookchin maintains that "until [living things] are what they have been constituted to become, they exist in a dynamic tension."[90] An individual organism is free only when it can ripen "into the fullness of its being."[91] In view of the link among freedom, autonomy, and individuality, Bookchin warns that the idea of interconnectedness "should not replace the entelechial processes that are involved in differentiation and the realization of potentiality."[92] Entelechial development involves the dialectical process of "self-formation through the self-realization of potentiality."[93] In this process of development and differentiation, Janet Biehl asserts, organisms actively maintain "their identity until, barring any accident, they fulfill their potentialities."[94] The striving of nonhuman organisms to maintain their identity in the process of realizing their potential is strengthened in autonomous individuals striving to realize their potential. Bookchin insists, however, that self-realization does *not* mean the triumph of the isolated bourgeois ego, but rather the fulfillment of individual possibilities in the context of mutually supportive, face-to-face, ecologically sound communities.

As we have seen, some ecologists say that insofar as everything is internally related, an organism cannot be understood as an individual actualizing its potential. According to J. Baird Callicott, an organism not only cannot be conceived apart from its ecological niche, but is a function of it.[95] Explicitly rejecting Aristotle's views, Callicott argues that "relations are 'prior' to the things related, and the systemic wholes woven from these relations are 'prior' to their component parts."[96] Callicott distinguishes his "holism" from Asian religions that claim that the phenomenal world is "one" because all things are a manifestation of Brahman. Instead,

nature is a *structured, differentiated* whole. The multiplicity of particles and living organisms, at either level of organization, retain, ultimately, their peculiar, if ephemeral, characters and identities. But
they are systemically integrated and mutually defining. The whole
revealed by ecology and quantum theory are unified, not blankly
unitary; they are one more as organisms are one, than one as an in-
divisible, homogeneous, quality-less substance is one.[97]

If this ecological doctrine of internal relations is valid, we cannot adequately conceive of ourselves as "independent," "self-
actualizing" substances, for we cannot clearly say where "I" end and
the rest of "reality"—natural or social—begins. In comparison with
this idea, Bookchin's notion that substances "self-form" and "self-
realize" themselves may seem atomistic. Although criticizing the
bourgeois ego's tendency to guard "individual inwardness from a
threatening, invasive otherness,"[98] elsewhere Bookchin complains
that "myths" about the interrelationship of all things will reduce the
personality to a "vegetative state."[99] Hence, he condemns Nazism for
seducing insecure bourgeois egos to surrender their individual per-
sonalities, freedom, and responsibility to a movement emphasizing
the "interconnectedness" of all things.[100] Bookchin rightly warns of
the dangers posed by political movements calling for the effacement
of individual autonomy in favor of a higher social will. Moreover,
adhering to the idea of interconnectedness no more guarantees
ecologically appropriate political behavior than does adhering to Big
Bang cosmology guarantee views consistent with radical ecology.
Bookchin's defense of autonomy is made problematic, however, by
his tendency to depict it as the *ultimate* goal of evolutionary development, when it may be no more than a crucial stage along the way
to a more integrated level of Atman consciousness. Like Freud,
however, Bookchin fears that the yearning for higher unity will lead

to regression to an infantile state lacking in autonomy, for allegedly there is no Divine with which to identify.

As noted above, those who describe Bookchin's thought as "un-ecological" argue that his dependence on a neo-Aristotelian doctrine of organic substance is inconsistent with scientific ecology's emphasis on interconnectedness. But in an earlier chapter, we saw that many contemporary ecologists now favor an individualistic rather than a systemic model to describe ecological phenomena. Alan Wittbecker explains that such ecologists hold that relationships are *not* prior to individual organisms; rather, an organism and its relationships arise together. All phenomena in the complex matter-energy field have relatively equal status; hence, there is no point in reducing an or-ganism to the totality of "prior" relationships. Similarly, "a specimen is more than the sum of its species' relationships to an environment; it is an *intentional being* that, with other members of the species, can create niches, as well as adapt to them."[101] Attempting to conceive of organisms primarily as "dissipative structures," temporary phe-nomena dependent on a continual influx of energy, assumes that "energy is a more fundamental reality than discrete entities."[102]

Wittbecker argues that Callicott neglects Koestler's idea that there are various levels of wholes, or "holons," each of which has unique traits not reducible to those of the ever-more inclusive holons within which it itself may be included. Wholes engage in an enormously complex "dance" both with higher- and lower-level holons; hence, holons (such as organisms) are neither radically independent nor slavishly dependent. Some molecular biologists, formerly staunch reductionists who argued that cells replicated themselves strictly in accord with the "directives" of DNA, now acknowledge that DNA, RNA, cells, organism, and environmental conditions all play a role in cell replication. Hence, "wholes are mutually defining, but also self-defining or self-making. The ontology of any living system is the history of the maintenance of its identity through continuous self-making, or autopoiesis."[103]

All this may be consistent with a *charitable* reading of Bookchin's views about organic substances. Bookchin may at times exhibit a masculinist control obsession, a fact that leads ecofeminist critics to argue that his emphasis on individual substance and autonomy is "contaminated" by patriarchal attitudes. Bookchin does praise autonomy, which he says is developed in "civilization" rather than in preliterate societies, where personal uniqueness was tempered by the larger social context. He adds that civilization has unfortunately too often associated will, freedom, and autonomy with mastery over others. As an alternative, he recommends Schiller's ideal of authentic individuality as "the expression of joy, play, and fulfillment of the esthetic sensibility," an ideal manifest in the great artists of the Italian Renaissance, whose free imagination produced extraordinary beauty. Like Nietzsche, Bookchin even suggests that we consider a "highly individuated life as an art."[104]

Bookchin not only seems naive about those Renaissance artists, whose lust for personal power and wealth is legendary, but also about the nature of the autonomous, rational, "individual." Wilber would agree with those ecofeminists who say that the control-drive is *essential* to the death-denying, patriarchal ego. To be sure, Bookchin would distinguish between his ideal individual and the power-craving bourgeois ego. Further, Nietzsche's great individual can be read as giving up the heroic will, surrendering death-denying pretensions, abandoning the identitarian mental ego in favor of a plurality of conflicting selves. By saying "yes" to mortality and limitation, by affirming and loving fate, the great individual moves beyond individualism to a nobler, self-effacing type of creativity.[105]

THE "EVOLUTION" OF CONSCIOUSNESS?   Wilber's neo-Hegelian grand narrative makes his thought an even bigger target for the critical barbs of postmodern theorists than Bookchin's narrative, which at least denies the Absolute and a necessitarian teleology. Richard Rorty would argue that by adopting an absolute standpoint purporting to know humanity's predetermined destination, Wilber denies humanity's mortality and contingency, and thus his own as well.[106] In contrast with Rorty's "lonely provincialism," which affirms that "we are just the historical moment that we are, *not* the representatives of something ahistorical" (e.g., stages along the Absolute's way toward self-realization), Wilber prefers the "metaphysical comfort" provided by the thought that "our community cannot wholly die."[107] For Rorty,

the notion of human nature as an inner structure which leads all members of the species to converge to the same point, to recognize the same theories, virtues, and works of art as worthy of honor, assures us that even if the Persians had won, the arts and sciences of the Greeks would sooner or later have appeared elsewhere.[108]

Wilber would say that Rorty makes the same mistake made by Ernest Becker, who acknowledged that craving for immortality symbols is motivated by the yearning to repudiate death.[109] But having denied that there is Atman, Becker interpreted hunger for the eternal as "man's capacity to delude himself in the face of terror, a position which overlooks the age-old wisdom that fear produces superstition, not religion."[110] Hence, he assumes that the vast majority of people, who have always believed that life has a transcendent meaning, have been deluded cowards. Becker joins Rorty in holding that the task of liberal democracies is not to re-enchant the world, but to "de-divinize it."[111] Rorty's view contrasts markedly with that of his pragmatist predecessor, Charles S. Peirce, who remarked that one day

man will see God's wisdom and mercy, not only in every event in his own life, but in that of the gorilla, the lion, the fish, the polyp, the tree, the crystal, the grain of dust, the atom. He will see that each one of these has an inward existence of its own for which God loves it, and that He has given to it a nature of endless perfectibility. He will see the folly of saying that nature was created for his use.[112]

Rorty does not extend to nature his appeal for solidarity to one's own community and for toleration of different ones. For him, values are linked to *human* interests, for example, in how those things can promote communal well-being, stimulate our curiosity, or prove aesthetically pleasing. Since all value is a human construct, animals, plants, and biomes have no intrinsic worth.[113] Just as he denies an objective basis for value, he insists that Western narratives are power-interested yarns that have justified liberal democracy, as well as colonial wars and imperialism.[114] There is no extrahistorical Archimedian standpoint from which to generate a totalizing metadiscourse to explain the meaning of local discourses and related events.[115]

In response to Rorty and other postmodern theorists, Wilber and Bookchin might recall Sartre's critique of Foucault's "magic lantern" view of history, according to which writing history means merely providing a description of various discursive regimes, without *explaining* why one is replaced by another, or why one may be *better* than the other. Foucault's archeology is like a positivistic historical geology describing unintentionally deposited sediments: history is one damned thing after the next. This descriptive attitude resembles Dilthey's historicism in holding that each epoch is as valid as any other, and thus in disallowing any critical stance capable of contrasting "is" and "ought." Foucault went beyond Dilthey, however, in making no claim to *understand* different discursive regimes. This renunciation of understanding makes Foucault's historical method "genealogical." As Manfred Frank explains, just as Darwin rejected Lamarcke's idea that species develop as the result of (goal-oriented) adaptive activity that produces meaningful and inheritable changes, so Foucault rejected the teleological paradigm in the human sciences. Following Nietzsche, Foucault held that the modern subject's teleology is a function of an epistemic regime that is itself merely a temporary configuration of power, a fissure in the order of things, a mere fold in knowledge that will soon vanish.[116]

Man has not arisen from the animal realm through some secretive (Herderian or Hegelian) "resolve of nature to freedom," but instead on the basis of genetic mutations and selective mechanisms, which offer the best chances for survival to the organism constantly adapting to its environment.[117]

Although Bookchin acknowledges that there is no *linear* human progress, postmodern theorists regard his dialectical naturalism as a variation of Hegel's view that history begins with a primal unity that differentiates itself and gradually moves toward reconciliation in a higher, mediated unity-in-difference. Many postmodern theorists insist, however, that history is characterized by rupture and dislocation, not by dialectical development. Dialectical views allegedly involve a nostalgia for lost origins and a yearning for a utopian future. As Martin Jay explains, for Derrida

the metanarrative of a process of original unity progressively articulating itself into a series of increasingly autonomous and internally homogeneous subsystems is far less compelling than an antinarrative of heterogeneous but interpenetrating movements that flow in no discernible historical or evolutionary direction.[118]

Bookchin's humanism suggests that there are essential human traits, such as generosity, kindness, creativity, and the yearning for freedom and autonomy, which have been "repressed" by hierarchical social structures. Postmodern theorists, however, deny that there are any "essential" traits to be repressed. Moreover, not only do postmodern theorists question the idea that people can free themselves from their own epoch's oppressive discursive formation, they also maintain that such emancipatory ideologies are used to colonize non-Westerners in the name of "freeing" them from practices that do not coincide with Western values. Bookchin's dream of decentered ecological communities then, can be read as nineteenth-century anarchism tainted by the utopianism that led to totalizing regimes in the twentieth century.

Although Bookchin condemns postmodern theory as the same kind of nihilistic relativism that helped lead to Nazism, Wilber regards postmodern theory as a predictable response of intellectuals faced with the demise of the immortality symbols of mental-egoic consciousness: purposive history, subjective selfhood, unending material progress, and the conquest of nature that promised to vanquish death itself. Though able to see through these symbols, postmodern theorists have not made the transition to level five consciousness.

Hence, the gap between their personal behavior, which continues to be self-assertive and self-interested, and their theories about the death of the authorial "subject." Furthermore, the fact that postmodern theory generally exhibits little concern about nonhuman beings and tends at times to portray nature as a human construct indicates that the dissociative and anthropocentric tendencies of level four consciousness persist in postmodern theory, despite its rhetoric about affirming "difference." As we shall see later on, however, some radical ecologists influenced by postmodern theory have attempted to overcome these shortcomings by criticizing attempts to "colonize" nature by denying its otherness.

Wilber would agree with postmodern theory that there is nothing absolute about modernity's scientific truths or its political ideologies, for these are the constructs of finite, control-obsessed mental-egoic consciousness posturing as godlike intelligence. Wilber would also agree that these constructs have often been useful for enhancing the power interests of privileged groups. But in contrast with most postmodern theorists, Wilber would also insist that the emergence of modernity's emancipatory political ideals, such as the universal rights of persons, represents an important step in protecting and consolidating mental-egoic consciousness, which—despite its significant limitations—represents an advance over collective, prepersonal modes of consciousness. Because postmodern theorists renounce a developmental interpretation of history, they see little redemptive value in modernity that would help to compensate for its dark side. Seemingly gripped by the spirit of resentment, some postmodern theorists seem to revel in dismantling the foundational structures of mental-egoic consciousness and society, without envisioning a constructive alternative to them.

Wilber would maintain, however, that it is dangerous blithely to expose the "groundlessness" of mental-egoic consciousness and its institutions at a time when these have not been sufficiently consolidated. Terrified by the loss of the relative stability provided by the institutional and personal immortality symbols associated with mental-egoic consciousness, some people might flee into a "community" promising health and wholeness, on the one hand, and an end to the conflict, uncertainty, and corruption of democratic society, on the other. The twentieth century has revealed just how tempting and horrifying such communities can be. Hence, whereas Wilber would agree in principle with much of postmodern theory's critique of the modernity's foundationalist metaphysics, he would also say that not everyone is capable of enduring such a deconstruction, for example, a deconstruction of the person defined as ego-subject. Postmodern theory, then, like counterculturalism, is an ambiguous phenomenon that *may* signal the dawn of a postmodern or post mental-egoic era, but may also signal the failure of Western humankind to bear up under the strains imposed by mental-egoic consciousness. Understandably, postmodern theorists might wonder whether Wilber really wants them, like the guardians in Plato's *Republic,* to tell ordinary people "noble lies," for example, that the founding myths of Western society retain their validity, so as to guarantee the continuing smooth functioning of society. Further, postmodern theorists would ask how Wilber can be so certain of the validity of his interpretation of nature, history, humankind, and the divine, especially at a time when doubts about "universal" and "objective" truths have been expressed from so many different angles.

To these objections, Wilber might reply that he appeals to traditions that are either completely ignored or underestimated by postmodern theorists. Furthermore, he would concede that in important respects his account of history is itself a construction, but a useful one that encourages the development of a kind of consciousness that would no longer need such a construction. In effect, the ladder provided by the perennial philosophy's progressive metaphysics would be kicked away by those who arrive at nondual awareness. Insofar as such awareness dwells in eternity, and insofar as eternity has nothing to do with "time" and "history," nondual awareness cannot be understood in terms of a "progressive development." Indeed, such awareness encounters phenomena in terms of play, not purpose.

Here one may discern certain echoes of the Nietzscheanism that helped to inspire so much of postmodern theory. Yet Wilber would insist that one cannot arrive at nondual, playful awareness by leaping over the developmental stages that lead up to it, even if not "producing" it. Many centuries must pass before nondual awareness is possible for more than a few. In the meantime, one may become enamored of Nietzsche's ideas or of nondual mysticism, but such infatuation is *not* evidence that one has really moved beyond mental-egoic consciousness. Indeed, great crimes against humankind have been committed by many a "fearless leader," who proclaims that he is endowed with "higher" consciousness, but who in fact is a mental-egoic megalomanic whose empire is a symbol designed to conceal his mortality. Effective consolidation of mental-egoic consciousness in the form of democratic institutions would mean that such leaders could no longer arise, because people would no longer surrender their personal responsibility to some charismatic figure promising to relieve them of anxiety. For Wilber, level five consciousness, which is the first step toward fully integrated and nondual awareness, would involve a different type of person, whose relational, intuitive, cooperative sensibilities are far better developed than the typically hyperrationalist, masculinist, competitive, atomistic mental-ego. If sufficient numbers of people are ready and able to make the transition to this more integrated level of consciousness, which resembles the postpatriarchal sensibility described favorably by many feminists, postmodern theory's critique of the foundational pillars of patriarchal modernity is timely. If, on the other hand, most people are still struggling to be level four persons, committed to such modern ideals as democratic principles and human rights, then deconstructing those ideals is a risky business, since it may lead to a political vacuum that regressive forces would be all too happy to fill.

Martin Jay defends modernity's emancipatory impulse against those "who counsel a leap into the postmodern dark." He warns that postmodern theory risks dissolving all social structures into "a night of endless *différance* in which all cows are piebald, which is as deceptive as the old idealist trick of turning them all black."[119] Similarly, Frederic Jameson cautions that a de-centered, fragmented, postmodern subject does not automatically give rise to more satisfactory sociopolitical arrangements. Such a "subject" loses its capacity for affect, no longer feels alienated (for there is no "self" to be alienated), exists superficially (there are no longer any historical or psychic "depths," only surfaces), becomes politically inactive (there are no public goals to be achieved), and exhibits a free-floating euphoria.[120] According to Jameson, postmodern culture constitutes "the internal and superstructural expression of a whole new wave of American military and economic domination throughout the world; in this sense, as throughout class history, the underside of culture is blood, torture, death and horror."[121] Late capitalism has not only emptied language of its capacity to refer and has thus made it merely self-referential, but has generated an enormously complex proliferation of social, technical, and cultural codes that amount to

a field of stylistic and discursive heterogeneity without a norm. Faceless masters continue to inflect the economic strategies which constrain our existences, but no longer need to impose their speech (or are henceforth unable to); and the postliteracy of the late capitalist world reflects, not only the absence of any great collective project, but also the unavailability of the older national language itself.[122]

For Jameson, postmodernity's heterogeneity, fragmentation, depthlessness, and lack of historical awareness reflect the splintering of society into isolated, de-centered subjects incapable of theorizing either the historical origins or the systemic nature of late capitalism.[123] Similarly, Bookchin condemns postmodernism as a "veritable campaign . . . to discard the past, to dilute our knowledge of history, to mystify the origins of our problems, to foster dememorization and the loss of our most enlightened ideals."[124] Jameson maintains that the breakdown of the signifying chain abandons the fragmented subject to the overpowerful and meaningless present, thereby giving rise to symptoms reminiscent of schizophrenia. By completely rejecting the concept of the whole, without discriminating between its useful and problematic types, postmodern theorists renounce the tools needed to criticize the historical origins of their own circumstances. Terry Eagleton maintains that truth is not dead simply because postmodern theory has discredited a particular representational epistemology; nor has the subject vanished simply because "certain traditional ideologies of the subject" have disintegrated.[125]

Similarly, although Adorno voiced suspicion about the destructive potential of totalizing narratives, and although he promoted heterogeneity and nonidentity as a last-ditch "great refusal" against the all-embracing positivism of monopoly capitalism, he nevertheless insisted that

discontinuity and universal history have to be thought together. To cross out universal history as a remnant of metaphysical superstition would confirm mere facticity as the only thing to be recognized and accepted. . . . Universal history has to be considered and negated.[126]

Commenting on Jameson's work, Steven Best defends the need for a systematic analysis of the complex relationships involved in capitalism. Without such analysis, postmodern theory's notion of the "play of difference" seems pointless: "Within the very narrow conditions of human possibilities provided by a homogenizing global capitalism, the 'infinite play of difference' celebrated by poststructuralists becomes a more naive and utopian notion than anything to be found in the Marxist tradition."[127] Taking into account the dangers of totalizing narratives, linear views of history, the centered subject, and false metaphysical closures, on the one hand, and nihilistic, anarchistic, incoherent pluralism, on the other, Jameson seeks a narrative that affirms progress while simultaneously acknowledging contingency and openness. Such a narrative is not merely an ideological reflex of a given discursive regime, but an alternative to it. Best remarks that although it is appropriate to deconstruct repressive wholes, postmodern theorists

fail to see how repressive and crippling the opposite approach of valorizing difference, plurality, fragmentation, and agonistics can be. The flip side of the tyranny of the whole is the dictatorship of the fragments. . . . Without some positive and normative concept of totality [and universality] to counter-balance the poststructuralist/postmodern emphasis on difference and discontinuity, we are abandoned

to the seriality of pluralist individualism and the supremacy of competitive values over communal life.[128]

Clearly, I prefer to avoid succumbing to the temptation of a simple
either/or: either totalizing, essentializing rationality, or differentiating, fragmenting discursive play.[129] Postmodern theory is certainly
justified in criticizing totalizing ideologies that justify centralized
regimes that crush opposition. In celebrating difference, postmodern
theory not only forgoes modernity's control obsession, but also
recognizes that creative alternatives can best arise out of a pluralistic
free play, without a controlling center. Critics charge, however, that
a positive "pluralist individualism" is not the only possible outcome
of deconstructing the subject and dismantling universal social and
political norms. Moreover, skepticism about the "metaphysics of
presence" prevents postmodern theorists from making any *positive*
contribution to contemporary political discourse, except ironically,
in "quotation marks."[130] Thomas McCarthy argues that Derrida's
"constant reminders of the groundlessness of all our basic schemes"
are "the reaction . . . of a disappointed metaphysician still under the
sway of its arch-opposition: all or nothing."[131] Foucault, too, feared
that any positive recommendation would simply reinforce the "normalizing" regime of modernity. Moreover, by rejecting the idea that
there is any human essence, he deprived himself of a basis for
criticizing "repressive" practices, despite the fact that he worked
actively for causes such as penal reform. Derrida and Foucault share
Heidegger's pessimistic diagnosis of modernity. According to that
diagnosis, even a pragmatic effort (undertaken without recourse to
eternal foundations) to reconstruct democratic ideals will simply
reinforce the system of domination. Yet mere condemnation of the
violence associated with the "march of the universal through history"
will not suffice to renovate social and political life. McCarthy warns
that

it is sheer romanticism to suppose that uprooting and destabilizing
universalist structures will of itself lead to letting the other be in
respect and freedom rather than to intolerant and aggressive particu-

larism, a war of all against all in which the fittest survive and the most powerful dominate.[132]

Bookchin and Wilber would agree with McCarthy that deconstructing such "prosaic" modes as reason, truth, and justice without simultaneously offering a viable alternative may not only deprive marginalized and oppressed people of a crucial recourse, but may also lead to what Derrida once called, in another context, a "monstrous mutation."[133] Even if Derrida's anarchy is "responsible," argues McCarthy, "we know from experience that devaluation of these [prosaic democratic political] modes opens a space, or rather creates a vacuum that can be filled in quite different ways—for instance, by a call for submission to some indeterminate authority."[134] Questions like the following face democratic progressives: Can existing democratic norms be transformed in a way that does not ultimately undermine the creative interplay of individuals? Can such creative interplay be encouraged without a fairly comprehensive, normative critique of the large-scale socioeconomic forces that undermine that interplay? Can attempts to challenge those forces succeed without simply reinstalling new hierarchies? Can ecologically sustainable and socially beneficial socioeconomic arrangements arise from the partially chaotic interplay characteristic of market systems? We address some of these questions in the final chapter.

Despite exploring the possibility of a generally progressive reading of history, I am also sympathetic to the claim that the triumphalistic, progressive ideologies of modernity have done at least as much harm as good. Global militarism, social oppression, and heedless destruction of wild nature scarcely seem like evidence of "progress." Hence, some deep ecologists and postmodern theorists would agree that progressive evolutionism is an anthropocentric conceit that justifies tyranny.[135] To avoid the idea of developmental stages of consciousness, some deep ecologists suggest a shift to ecological sensibility would be sudden and incommensurate with what has gone before, much like Zen *satori*. More often, however, deep ecologists speak of self-realization as a process of maturation. Like many New Paradigmers, deep ecologists suggest that humanity is entering a new stage of human evolution, in which people will recognize that their own self-realization is bound up with the self-realization of the rest of life on Earth. In speaking in this way, deep ecologists part company with Heidegger, who criticized progressive narratives of Western history.

Roderick Nash argues that deep ecology's vocabulary of rights and its ideal of self-realization expand modernity's emancipatory ideal to include nature.[136] Robyn Eckersley says that the norm of wider identification is the ideal of "emancipation writ large."[137] Deep ecology's reading of Spinoza has inevitably been influenced by Hegel's effort to link emancipatory political goals to an evolutionary view of history. Hegel's Absolute Subject may be read as Spinoza's Substance historically unfolding its potential for self-consciousness. Although deep ecologists criticize Hegel's anthropocentrism,[138] Naess claims that humanity has the potential to expand its awareness so as to contribute to the well-being of all life. Ecosophy T *"says yes to the fullest self-realization of man."*[139] More recently, Sessions has also suggested that humanity is evolving into a more compassionate, life-affirming species. According to this viewpoint, humanity is now in the stage of late adolescence: lusting for control, totally self-centered, denying its own finitude and mortality, and wasteful of resources. Humanity's maturation process is not linear, but involves a "loop back" to reintegrate the lost wisdom of primal peoples. Such reintegration is a far cry from hunter-gatherer consciousness of twenty thousand years ago. Sessions concedes that

there is cultural development as well as individual development. It is not as if [human history] has been for naught. It will be if we do in the species. . . . There has been progress, now we have this winnowing process we have to do. Paul Shepard asks if we can face that the primal peoples were more human than we are. In some ways they were, but not in all ways.[140]

Acknowledging that modern humanity surpasses the self-reflexivity of ancient tribal peoples, Sessions concludes that Thomas Berry may be right in maintaining that

we are the species that can understand the overall outlines of the cosmological and biological evolutionary process. Our theoretical

science can be used to appreciate and understand the world and produce ecologically benign technology, or we can erroneously try to
dominate the planet with it. Our self-reflexivity has made us aware
of the ecological crisis, so that we can correct ourselves. It can help
us to take a larger, more objective cosmic and ecological perspective.[141]

Although agreeing with Bookchin that cosmic evolution has led
to "greater subjectivity, consciousness, [and] self-reflexivity . . . ,"
deep ecologists maintain that he draws the following problematic
conclusion: humanity's greater consciousness justifies human intervention in the evolutionary development of everything less conscious.[142] Bookchin's view that it is "the *responsibility* of the most
conscious of life-forms—humanity—to be the 'voice' of a mute
nature"[143] resembles Heidegger's idea that human existence is the
clearing through which entities can manifest themselves. This proximity, despite important political differences between Bookchin and
Heidegger, confirms the suspicion of many deep ecologists that
Heidegger's thought is anthropocentric.

To defend deep ecology against charges of being ecofascist, I have
read it as adhering to a progressive view of human history, one that
emphasizes compassion and development of nondual awareness,
though not all deep ecologists would share this reading. Moreover,
those who do have not carefully explained how human maturation—
the shift to an ecological sensibility—is possible. Many ecofeminists
charge that progressive views of history are accounts of the rise to
power of the masculine ego. Some ecofeminists read deep ecology's
ideal of wider identification as grounded in a masculinist concept of
self which seeks to obliterate difference by reducing everything
"other" to "same." But if ecofeminists conclude that progressive,
"maturational" views of history are all tainted by patriarchy, and if
they insist that there is no human "essence" being actualized through
history, is there any reason to hope that humankind will develop a
more satisfactory relationship with the nonhuman world? Can
ecofeminism develop a postpatriarchal "progressive" view of history?

Of the three branches of radical ecology under consideration in this
essay, ecofeminism is the most complex. During the past decade, it
has become increasingly sophisticated and self-critical. Providing a
balanced evaluation of it is challenging not only because of its scope
and refinement, but also because I probably think in light of certain
masculinist presuppositions that are difficult for me to discern, despite my best efforts. At times, this problem seemed so daunting that
I considered omitting ecofeminism from this volume. By failing to
consider ecofeminism, however, I could have been read as suggesting
that it is less important than deep ecology or social ecology. In fact,
however, I believe that ecofeminism offers some of the most important explanations of humanity's current social and ecological
problems. Moreover, ecofeminism provides insightful criticisms of
postmodern theory, modernity, deep ecology, and social ecology.
Having chosen to discuss ecofeminism, I ask for the reader's generosity when my analysis goes astray; further, I ask for understanding
about omitting important issues because of lack of space.

In what follows, I focus on a particular approach to ecofeminism,
which I call *cultural* ecofeminism. Such ecofeminism shares many of
postmodern theory's criticisms of modernity's domination of na-

ture, dualism, the self-grounding subject, and patriarchal attitudes, but nevertheless rejects postmodern theory's pessimism, indifference, and deconstruction of the category and even the body of "woman." Holding that deep-seated cultural attitudes—philosophical, religious, and psychological—have shaped gender in ways that gave rise to patriarchal, nature-fearing, militaristic, hierarchical politicoeconomic systems, calling for a cultural and spiritual revolution that will transform human society, and affirming that women and men can act to bring about a better future, cultural ecofeminism is aligned with many aspects of New Paradigm and deep ecology. An important task for cultural ecofeminism is to reconcile a progressive and even utopian vision of the future with criticism of patriarchal modernity's idea of progress.

The first section of this chapter briefly surveys contemporary feminism, indicates how it has been shaped by changes in attitudes toward "difference," and shows how it has been influenced by postmodern theory. The second section examines two different approaches to cultural ecofeminism. And the last section explores some criticisms of cultural ecofeminism.

FEMINISM AND THE QUESTION OF DIFFERENCE   Agnes Heller speaks for many women in saying that feminism is not only "the most decisive social revolution of modernity" but also "a watershed in all hitherto existing cultures."[1] I believe that transforming gender relationships, and changing the institutions that arose from and are reinforced by those relationships, would have an enormous impact on the future of humanity and the planet. Since emancipating women and transforming patriarchal institutions would also free men from the constraints imposed upon them by patriarchy, I regard feminism as a human emancipation movement.

The current wave of American feminism, which can be regarded as a dimension of the counterculture, emerged when the Civil Rights Movement was reaching its peak in the mid-1960s. Looking to existing political ideologies, such as Marxism and liberalism, to guide the struggle for liberation, feminism was rent by disputes from the beginning.[2] Liberal feminists, for example, demanded that the "equal rights" promised under the American constitution be extended to women, so that women receive equal access to institutions and equal pay for their work. Criticizing the social atomism at work in liberal feminism, Marxist feminists argued that it was not enough that individual women be allowed to compete on equal terms in an intrinsically domineering, exploitative, class-bound, alienating, and patriarchal economic system. Real emancipation requires that the system be radically altered to eliminate structural sources of exploitation. Although sharing some of the assumptions of Marxist feminism, socialist feminism argues that some certain elements of oppression, such as racism and sexism, will not be eliminated by changing ownership of the means of production. Only a nonhierarchical, nonauthoritarian society will end all forms of oppression. Despite some exceptions, these three types of feminism have generally supported modernity's instrumental attitude toward nature. When liberal, Marxist, or socialist feminism addresses ecological issues at all, it adopts the reform environmentalist view that a healthy society requires wise and equitable use of natural resources.[3]

In its early stages, a fourth kind of feminism, radical feminism, agreed with the premise that the liberation of women demanded the control of nature. Radical feminists argued both that the oppression of women has been justified on the basis of a supposedly natural biological-reproductive role and that patriarchy is prior to all other forms of oppression, including that based on private property. Hence, as Alison Jaggar explains, the radical feminist

reverses the emphasis of the classical Marxist feminist by explaining the development of class society in terms of the biological family rather than explaining the development of the family in terms of class society. She believes that the battles against capitalism and against racism are both subsidiary to the more fundamental struggle against sexism.[4]

According to Shulamith Firestone, since patriarchy is grounded on woman's biological constitution, the oppression of women can be ended in part by making reproduction an artificial process.[5] Her "revolutionary ecological project" would replace the natural balance with an artificial one, "thus realizing the original goal of empirical science: total mastery of nature."[6] Despite early radical feminism's dim view of reproduction and childrearing, a later branch of radical feminism celebrates the female body and calls for a feminist culture that differs from and is superior to masculinist culture. This type of radical feminism emerged in connection with a shift in feminism regarding the issue of difference.

In the 1960s and early 1970s, most feminists insisted that apart from certain biological features, women were not essentially different from men. In fact, men kept women socially dependent by claiming that their allegedly weak biological constitution "naturally" or "essentially" made them suited for housework and raising children, but not for doing a "man's job." Feminists argued that the differences between women and men were primarily a function of culture (which determines gender) not biology (which determines sex). After having taken positions in the patriarchal public world, however, many women found that they did not like the identities they were expected to adopt in it. Some feminists began arguing that women shouldn't overemphasize their similarities with men for the sake of conforming to male-defined roles, since such patriarchal roles are profoundly disturbed to begin with. Instead, women should discover what is positive about how they are *different* from men.

Some feminists began to reevaluate the biological factors that had been condemned by many other feminists as an excuse to portray women as inferior to men. Praising the female body in all its fecundity, complexity, and mystery, these new feminists concluded that women are not only different from men, but in some ways better. Agreeing with radical feminism that patriarchy is the basis for all forms of oppression, these feminists are called "cultural" feminists because they urge women to found a female counterculture to replace the misogynist, hierarchical, domineering, violent, militaristic, death-denying culture of patriarchy. One type of cultural feminism is described as "nature" feminism, for it maintains that women's embodiment, including the capacity for childbirth, makes them intrinsically more relational, gentle, nurturing, creative, life-affirming, and connected with nature.[7] Although other feminists fought against the idea that "anatomy is destiny," then, many nature feminists *affirmed* the female body and the female values denigrated by patriarchy.

A number of cultural feminists, however, emphasize the distinction between sex and gender. Although conceding that some sexual differences between women and men are biologically based, they insist that gender differences are a function of *acculturation* and social coding. Seeking to avoid biological determinism, they urge women to challenge the cultural categories that have been defined by men who assumed that their experience was *universally valid*. Supposedly universal norms are often functions of particular historical, social, class-based, racial, and masculinist circumstances, which exclude consideration of the experience of women. For cultural feminists, the alternative values developed by women over the centuries constitutes a "different voice" that needs to be heeded, for as victims of patriarchy, women can be more critical of oppressive structures to which men are often blind. Virginia Held remarks that if women and men can reveal "the aspects of 'mankind' that have been obscured and misrepresented by taking the 'human' to be the masculine, virtually all existing knowledge may be turned on its head."[8] Despite disagreements, most cultural feminists agree in promoting a culture that valorizes the relational, other-oriented, nurturing traits that traditionally have been most highly developed in women.

Other feminists, however, criticize cultural feminism precisely for valorizing attitudes and tendencies that were developed by women while living in the gender-ghetto to which patriarchy confined them.[9] In addition to allegedly reaffirming stereotypical views about women, and simply reversing the binary dualism between women and men (this time with women "on top"), cultural feminists are said to have raised unreasonable expectations about women's behavior, by portraying women as essentially kinder, more life-affirming, relational, and concerned about others.[10] In short, some types of cultural feminism go astray by making *essentialist* claims about women. Such essentialism is found both in the claim that gender differences are biologically grounded and in the claim made by white, middle-class, educated Western women that *their* experience is representative of the experience of *all* women. Women from minority groups and the Third World, asserting that their experience was different, have charged that middle-class feminists are blind to oppression based upon race, class, and ethnicity. Although sexism is hurtful, racism and poverty also have appalling consequences for women and men alike. Third World women also note that middle-class Western feminists generally participate in a consumer culture involving technological and economic exploitation of poor people in faraway lands. Nancy Fraser and Linda Nicholson explain that many feminists originally sought the "metaphysical comfort" and political advantages associated with a universal conception of woman. But growing emphasis on "difference," especially when abetted by postmodern theory, began to fragment the very concept of women and introduced other "differences"—such as race, ethnicity, age, and sexual orientation—that had to be factored into "complexly constructed conceptions of social identity."[11] Such revisionary criticisms have undermined the old dualism of men-as-oppressors and women-as-oppressed. Women, too, can be the oppressors. Further, some feminists argue that patriarchy is not *the* source of all oppression, but is instead linked in complex ways with all other forms of oppression.[12]

Ecofeminism has evolved in conjunction with the development of feminism at large. An example of this evolution can be seen by comparing two essays by ecofeminist, Ariel Kay Salleh. In the first, "Deeper than Deep Ecology: The Ecofeminist Connection" (1984), she argued that despite their laudable ideals, male deep ecologists are unaware of their masculinist bias; hence, they fail to take into account patriarchy's role both in the destruction of nature and in the oppression of woman. Women are in a better position to lead the radical ecology movement, because biological factors (menstrual cycle, nursing infants, etc.) "ground women's consciousness in the knowledge of being coterminous with Nature." The lived experience of women could provide the basis "for the alternative consciousness which the deep ecologist is trying to formulate and introduce as an abstract ethical construct. Women already, to borrow Devall's turn of phrase, 'flow with the system of nature.'"[13]

Although defending here a viewpoint largely consistent with the radical, cultural, or nature feminism developed in the 1970s by Mary Daly, Susan Griffin, and Adrienne Rich, five years later Salleh seems to have retreated from the view that it is women's *biological* constitution that gives them an advantage in the ecology movement. In "Stirrings of a New Renaissance" (1989), she writes:

Ecofeminists . . . argue that by constructing feminine experience in this way [i.e., as closer to nature], patriarchy placed women in a privileged nurturant relation to other living things. Hence the value of feminine insights in a time of eco-catastrophe. *It's not that women are actually closer to nature than men, clearly we all live in continuity with gaia.* But throughout history, men have chosen to set themselves apart, usually "over and above" nature and women.[14]

Now we are told that it is the socially constructed victimized status of women that better enables them to see how patriarchy exploits other living beings. In an essay published in 1992, Salleh denies that she *ever* adhered to biological essentialism, according to which women are "closer" to nature than men.[15] That so many people (including a number of ecofeminists) read her 1984 essay as adhering to a kind of essentialism suggests otherwise, or at least that she did not make herself clear. Even granting that Salleh is right in this matter, I believe that a significant shift *did* occur among several ecofeminists from biological essentialism to cultural constructivism.[16] This shift corresponds to others that feminists made in light of self-criticism, criticism by minority and Third World women, and criticism from postmodern theory. Yet this emphasis on difference threatens to undermine the very identity of "woman."

Feminists influenced by postmodern theory emphasize that the concept of invariant identity is linked with the idea that there is one truth about the world. Supposedly, "true" statements simply mirror a pre-given, self-identical reality. Concealing the fact that knowledge involves interpretation, such an epistemology privileges *one* truth, while marginalizing alternative interpretations of the world. Donna Haraway says that feminism often adopts this problematic epistemology: "The feminist dream of a common language, like all dreams for a perfectly true language, of perfectly faithful naming of experience, is a totalizing and imperialist one."[17] Feminist taxonomies—socialist, Marxist, radical, cultural—lead to efforts to "police deviation from official women's experience."[18] American feminists, however, "forced kicking and screaming" to discover "the non-innocence of the category 'woman'," must learn to hear the "disorderly polyphony" arising from black, yellow, brown, and Third World women. One cannot develop an all-inclusive position that takes into account the multitudinous variations of class, gender, race, and ethnicity. Haraway also argues that white feminists must abandon the idea that the standpoint of the oppressed is somehow innocent.[19]

The search for such a "full" and total position is the search for the fetishized perfect subject of oppositional history, sometimes appearing in a feminist theory as *the essentialized Third World Woman.* . . . Subjugation is not grounds for an ontology.[20]

Haraway insists that the partial, perspectival character of knowledge does not mean that large-scale accounts of social phenomena are fallacious, but simply that they are neither timelessly true nor universally valid. One must factor into any theoretical account one's own concrete situatedness and interests. As we see later, some ecofeminists reply that postmodern theory promotes skepticism and nominalism by so narrowing the scope of the validity of truth claims, that assertions are true only for the particular de-centered subject who makes them. Further, postmodern theory not only questions the agency of both masculine and feminine "subject," but also deconstructs the very category of gender. If there is no "essential" content to anything, everything is ultimately "undecidable," including the concept "woman." How can a liberation movement proceed, however, if there is no agreed upon class to liberate?

CULTURAL ECOFEMINISM   In feminizing the ecology movement, and in ecologizing the feminist movement, cultural ecofeminists argue that patriarchy is responsible both for oppressing women and destroying nature. Cultural ecofeminists take two somewhat different approaches to criticizing patriarchy and to envisioning the ecofeminist culture that should supplant patriarchy. One approach emphasizes philosophical (metaphysical, epistemological, political) factors, whereas the other emphasizes spiritual factors. These distinctions make no claim to comprehensiveness, but are simply expository devices to assist discussion of an enormous volume of material.

Arguing that masculinist philosophical categories play a crucial role both in oppressing women and in dominating nature, cultural ecofeminists see such categories at work in moral extensionism, which seeks to extend rights to nonhuman beings. Although appreciating the desire to include nonhuman within the moral community, cultural feminists agree with other critics who maintain that the concept of "rights" presupposes the validity of a masculinist view of self, other, and nature.[21] Natural rights doctrine is: *androcentric* because its conception of persons is based on a masculinist experience that excludes (and implicitly negates) female experience; *hierarchical* because it gives precedence to male experience, and also because it portrays humans as radically more important than anything else[22]; *dualistic* because of its distinction between human (rational, intrinsically valuable, rights-possessing) and nonhuman (nonrational, instrumental, lacking in rights); *atomistic* because it portrays humans as isolated social units; and *abstract* because conflicts about rights are settled by rationalistic, impersonal debates that ignore both the feelings and the particular needs/traits of the individuals involved. Founders of modern natural rights doctrines were men who presupposed that their experience of the world was universal. According to Naomi Scheman,

the view of a separate, autonomous, sharply individuated self embedded in liberal political and economic ideology and in the individualist philosophies of mind can be seen as a defensive reification of the process of ego development in males raised by women in a patriarchal society.[23]

Hobbes most forcibly articulated the idea of the person as an isolated ego competing for scarce resources. A version of this idea was reinforced by Darwin's evolutionary doctrine, which reflects the competitive social relations of nineteenth-century English capitalism.[24] Many contemporary ethologists argue, however, that the "state of nature" is neither so bellicose nor as male-dominated as Hobbes and Darwin would have had us believe.[25] So long as people conceive of themselves as isolated egos, only externally related to other people and to nature, they inevitably tend to see life in terms of scarcity and competition. When people conceive of themselves as internally related to others and to nature, however, they tend to see life in terms of bounty, not scarcity, and in terms of cooperation, not aggressive competition.

Though atomistic and competitive views may not disclose ultimate truths about human "nature," they may say something valid about the experience of men raised in patriarchy. Naomi Scheman contends that males can adhere to a social doctrine emphasizing social atomism and competition because *women at home* knit together the social fabric on which the competing males depend.[26] In a controversial theory, Nancy Chodorow argues that male and female identities are shaped by differential relationships with the primary caretaker, who is almost always female.[27] This differential relationship leads men to conceive of themselves as self-contained egos with only temporary, external relations to others, whereas women learn to conceive of themselves as primarily related to others. Although a boy initially identifies himself with his mother, he later discovers that he is sexually differentiated from her. In search of his own sexual identity, he withdraws from his mother, but experiences this process as abandonment. Profoundly angered and grieved by this perceived abandonment, he subsequently fears, mistrusts, and even hates all women, upon whom he projects his primal relationship with his mother. Moreover, given the usual lack of a strong, positive father figure, the boy tends to define himself as *not female*. Seeking to control both the woman within (internalized mother image) and the woman without, he blocks his feelings, which overwhelmed him during the trauma of separation, and defines himself as separate from others; he fears intimate relationships, since his most important one ended in loss and pain. Further, because "mother" was originally identified with all of reality, boys and girls alike tend to regard as female the undifferentiated natural background against which individual entities stand out. Hence, for boys and men, Mother Nature appears as a threatening, unpredictable force over which a man must gain control. The domination of nature, then, can be understood in terms of the same psychological mechanisms that lead to the oppression of women.

Because girls continue to identify with their mothers for a longer time than do boys, many women apparently experience themselves not as radically separate, self-contained egos, but rather as a network of personal relationships that constitute the "self." Cultural ecofeminists often argue that early modern scientists projected their own masculinist sense of social isolation upon the world, "discovering" that it is composed of "atoms." Ecofeminists often argue that contemporary science affirms that reality is interconnected and internally related, a view that is more consistent with the female relational sense of self.[28] If a relationship is removed, the thing constituted in part by that relationship is changed. The male ideal of the "lone wolf" apparently does not appeal to most women, who conceive of themselves as essentially related to others.[29] But if men often have difficulty in relating to others, women often have difficulty in assuming their own identity. According to some feminists, the solution to many of these gender-identity problems would involve changes in childrearing practices, so that men would become as involved as women now are in caring for infants and small children.

Carol Gilligan has postulated that the differing male and female senses of self lead to differences in moral perception and moral decision making.[30] Hence, the male preoccupation with "rights" can be related to the male's sense that there need to be certain rules protecting isolated egos competing with other egos for scarce resources. Disputes arising among conflicting egos are to be adjudicated according to rational discourse guided by universal norms, which discount particular circumstances. Prizing analytic rationality above all else, the isolated masculinist ego regards feeling and emotion as biased by particular circumstances and thus incapable of providing guidance when it comes to a matter of justice. According to many feminists, however, feeling and mood have crucial roles to play in assessing moral issues and in guiding social interaction. Moreover, the purely prudential and self-interested calculations at work in the exploitation of nature can go forward only so long as one does not allow oneself to *feel* the consequences that those calculations have for life on Earth. One way to block such feelings is to conceive of oneself as essentially disconnected from nature: a pure intellect hovering on the face of the planet. Another way may be to expand one's sense of self so as to embrace the entire cosmos, but in such a way as to become detached from particular relationships. As we shall see, many cultural ecofeminists charge that this is the path taken by deep ecologists, a charge that we examine in the next chapter.

Some feminists have questioned the validity of object relations theory, the basis for claims about relational versus separate self-sense. Object relations theory is said to be problematic because it: (1) tends to universalize childrearing practices that are in fact historically situated; (2) underestimates the extent to which later experience can shape one's sense of self; (3) reinforces traditional views that women are relational, men are selfish; women are caretakers, men are competitive, and so on; (4) fails to recognize that Hume and other male Scottish and English moralists were reared in the social atomism of the eighteenth century, but nevertheless developed moral philosophies emphasizing feeling and personal relationship, not reason and abstract rules. Carole Pateman says that women wrongly conclude that "since 'justice' is the work of men and an aspect of the domination of women, women should reject it totally and remake their lives on the basis of love, sentiment, and personal relations."[31] The liberal concept of rights, justice, and the individual help guide the dialectic that goes on "between the particular or personal and the universal or political."[32] Gilligan herself has suggested that a morality of compassion based on a sense of relatedness is in some ways complementary with the morality of justice based on a sense of separateness.[33] By overemphasizing interrelatedness, feminists risk leaving no categories for conceiving of themselves as individuals. Jane Flax notes that "women, in part because of their own history as daughters, have problems with differentiation and the development of a true self and reciprocal relations."[34]

Regarding the attempt to connect female relational experience with contemporary scientific views about the interrelatedness of nature, ecofeminist Marti Kheel observes that overemphasizing internal relatedness can lead to an environmental totalitarianism, which sacrifices individuals for the sake of the larger whole. Although individuals may not be radically separate, and thus may be better described as interrelated "knots" in the cosmic fabric, *these knots are intrinsically important:*

A vision of nature that perceives value both in the individual and in the whole of which it is a part is a vision that entails a reclaiming of the word *holism* from those for whom it signifies a new form of hierarchy (namely, a valuing of the whole over the individual). Such a vision asks us to abandon the dualistic way of thinking that sees value as inherently exclusive (i.e., they believe that the value of the whole cannot also be the value of the individual).[35]

Anthropologist Peggy Reeves Sanday offers an environmentally based account of why men have come to view themselves as essentially cultural, nonnatural, immortal, and transcendent while regarding women as essentially natural, noncultural, mortal, and body-bound.[36] Contesting Sherry Ortner's claims that "women are universally assigned to the low ground of nature and men to the high ground of culture," Sanday argues that different environmental conditions produce differing solutions to the question of how women and men are related to nature and culture.[37] She arrived at her conclusions by examining the creation myths of many nonindustrial societies. Such myths provide accounts of the source of cosmic power and of the relationship between the people and nature: "This relationship, and its projection into the sacred and secular realms holds the key for understanding sexual identities and corresponding roles."[38]

Since people living in nonindustrial societies apparently believe that everything is enmeshed in complex webs of power and that appropriate access to this power is necessary for survival, the status of women and men is determined largely by which sex is apparently more in touch with these powers. Sanday finds some societies where women have more power, others in which men have more power, and still others in which power is about equally shared (in about half of the societies she studied, men had more power). People living in environments with predictable climatic conditions and stable food supplies (primarily plants) regard themselves as in a protective, internal partnership with these powers. Such societies, having an "inner orientation" to power, often develop creation myths in which a female power (usually associated with water or earth) gives birth to the world. Because women's reproductive capacities seem to link them directly with this cosmic power, women are given higher status and are assigned central roles in religious rituals. In such societies, the sexes mingle, there is group decision making, men spend a lot of time with infants and children, and male domination of women is unusual.

In the case of people living in harsher and less predictable environments, such as nomadic tribes hunting large animals, a different situation obtains. Since the environment is considered more dangerous, such people no longer regard cosmic power as being in partnership with or internal to the society. Such a society takes on an "external orientation," concerned with making contact with the power that controls things. Since males are the hunters, and since success in hunting depends on their having sufficient power to be worthy of killing an animal, the major issue is the male's relationship to power. Hence, the society's creation myth usually recounts that a male god (often associated with the sky) created the world. In such societies, the sexes are separated, men spend much less time with children, and women are portrayed as inferior to men. Under these circumstances, a dismissive, contemptuous, domineering attitude toward women arises on the part of men.

Carolyn Merchant agrees that the view of nature as threatening, wild, and uncontrollable sometimes gives way to an alternative vision of nature as a bounteous, generous, life-giving mother.[39] Patriarchal attitudes do not prevail constantly, then, but fluctuate because of complex factors. Accounts of social life in the European Middle Ages suggest that people, men and women alike, had a "relational" sense of self akin to what cultural feminists often describe as the "feminine" self. In "The Cartesian Masculinization of Thought," Susan Bordo cites approvingly Owen Barfield's contention that medieval humans did not experience "consciousness" as somehow isolated inside their bodies and thus cut off from the larger world. In light of the doctrine of the internal relation between macrocosm and microcosm, medieval man felt "each different part of him being united to a different part of it by some invisible thread. In his relation to his environment, the man of the middle ages was rather less like an island, rather more like an embryo."[40]

According to Merchant, with the coming of modernity, however, the view that mother nature is caring and bountiful was eclipsed by the view that nature is a fearsome, wild woman who must be controlled by knowing her (Francis Bacon).[41] According to Bordo, the process in which European people moved from the comfortable "cosmic unity" of the medieval world to the humanity-nature dualism of the modern world may have entailed at the cultural level anxieties similar to those experienced by children as they separate from their mothers. Descartes's thought offers an excellent example of the difficulties faced by someone trying to sustain this emerging sense of isolated selfhood, radically disconnected from the "external" world. Descartes is so anxious that he posits "God to sustain both his existence and his inner life from moment to moment, to provide a reassurance of permanence and connection, between self and world."[42] Regarding the inability to distinguish clearly between self and world a sign of immaturity, he sundered his rational ego from his body, which originated in woman and nature. Revoking his own childhood and asserting that mind-body dualism is a means of control, not a source of anxiety, Descartes enacted a highly abstract "father of himself" fantasy. He depicted sense experience as illusory; cut off passionate attachments; and replaced the female flesh of the world with the spiritual father God as the source of creativity. The mind-body dualism that guarantees the "objectivity" of science "also turns the formerly female earth into inert *res extensa:* dead, mechanically interacting matter."[43]

According to Bordo, it was no accident that the great witchcraft trials raged between 1550 and 1650 when Europe was making the transition to a mechanistic worldview.[44] This gynophobic era was "obsessed with the untamed power of female generativity and a dedication to bringing it under forceful cultural control."[45] Not only did reproduction come to be regarded as a process that required male supervision, but also (following Aristotle) men asserted that the female body was simply an incubator for the male seed. Bordo attributes such ideas to the fact that, after the sense of cosmic unity was lost, isolated, disconnected, alienated men experienced both nature and woman as radically other: fearsome, devouring, uncontrollable, and unpredictable. By "taming" the threatening other with reason and technology, "man" would feel increasingly secure, despite his lonely condition. In a world run by such desperate, power-craving men, an ecological crisis would seem an inevitable consequence.

Although taking into account the metaphysical, psychological, and epistemological factors that shape gender-identity, some cultural ecofeminists emphasize spiritual factors that might lead beyond patriarchy. The term "spiritual" is somewhat misleading, for it is often understood as referring to the otherworldly, disembodied domain favored by patriarchal theologians. For many cultural ecofeminists, however, "spiritual" concerns involve the sacred dimensions of the *corporeal* domain, including the female *body*. To avoid the mistake of simply valorizing the bodily pole of mind-body dualism, however, some cultural ecofeminists have explored the idea of panentheism, according to which the divine includes, but is not reducible to the body; but this issue remains contested.

Some cultural ecofeminists, such as Mary Daly, Susan Griffin, and Elizabeth Dodson Gray, suggest that the female body is essentially (perhaps biologically) more in tune with nature than is the male body. Gray asserts that the perception of men is limited because they lack the bodily experiences of women. Men alone cannot lead the way to an ecological society "because the male's is simply a much diminished experience of the body, of natural processes, and of future generations."[46] Although many cultural ecofeminists avoid a simplistic sexual/organic essentialism, most of them praise the female body for its reproductive powers and for its "soft boundaries" that enable a felt attunement to the world. Like all cultural feminists, cultural ecofeminists argue that Western socioeconomic structures are both legitimated by and in an important sense the expressions of "the central assumptions of Western religion and philosophy."[47] Unless these core assumptions of culture are challenged and transformed, changes at the institutional level will not be sufficient to end either the oppression of women or the domination of nature. One of these core assumptions is that the female body is inferior to the male body. Males adhered to this assumption as a protective reaction to the powerful mysteries of the female body. Since this contemptuous attitude has also been internalized by most women, a major aspect of cultural ecofeminism involves affirming female corporeality and encouraging in women a sense of their connection with the Earthbody from which all life comes. Many cultural ecofeminists avoid using the term "Mother Earth," however, not only because it reinforces problematic stereotypes, but also because it involves projecting human categories onto nature, thereby preventing nature from showing itself to us in its *own* terms.[48]

Cultural ecofeminists often maintain that men gradually began defining the male as truly human, while portraying the female as being only partly human, since she was so closely identified with "merely" natural processes (e.g., birth, lactation, menstrual cycles, etc.). Contempt for the female body may manifest male envy about her reproductive power.[49] Such envy, when combined with the discovery by men of their role in pregnancy, culminated in Aristotle's reduction of the female to the nourisher of the male "seed." Marilyn French suggests that man's experience of creating something with so little personal involvement may have led him to conceive of God as a transcendent, nonnatural, "male" source of power. As opposed to the Goddess who had emphasized pleasure, affiliation, mutual caring, and harmony between nature and humanity, the masculine God emphasized power, hierarchy, independence, and dualism between nature and man. The transcendent, male power-god symbolizes the rise of man's worship of power. According to French, "patriarchy is an ideology founded on the assumption that man is distinct from the animal and superior to it. The basis for this superiority is man's contact with a higher power/knowledge called god, reason, or control."[50] Man seeks to divest himself of whatever he considers other than and thus beneath reason: animality, femininity, emotions, even mortality. Above all, he seeks to become independent of nature. By creating an entirely artificial world, that is wholly under his control, "man himself would have eradicated or concealed his basic bodily and emotional bonds to nature."[51]

In her remarkable book, *Woman and Nature* (1978), Susan Griffin argues that patriarchal man's terror in the face of his own mortality leads him to establish such a radical dualism between his eternal essence—soul, mind, culture—and his inessential mortal aspect—flesh, blood, bone, feelings, sex, children, nature. He must control everything organic and spontaneous, including the wild animal, the wildness in his woman, and the wildness within himself. The wild sexual desires aroused in him by woman, for example, threaten to dissolve the rigid ego-boundaries he has forged to protect himself from being "absorbed" by the all-devouring female: "He faces annihilation in her, he says. He is losing himself to her, he says. Now, he must conquer her wildness, he says, he must tame her before she drives him wild, he says."[52] He puts woman in a domestic cage that resembles a zoo, a place where she can be observed and appreciated, now that her wildness has been contained. Because women have represented both nature-within (feelings, intuition, all that is other to linear rationality) and nature-without (childbearing, lactation, caring for the organic needs of other humans), they have borne the brunt of the patriarchal denial of and attack upon everything merely organic, fleshly, imperfect, material, and mortal. Man's subjugation of nature (land, timber, animals, wind, matter in general) parallels his subjugation of woman. Deprived of control of their own bodies, dispossessed of the language necessary to experience and to define their own existence, women live in a state of alienation and deremption.

Griffin contrasts the abstract, linear rationality of the patriarchal ego with the long-repressed female mode of awareness: particularizing, narrational, meaning-giving, and celebratory of passion, feeling, intuition, embodiment, and life itself. As opposed to the patriarchal vision of reality as a perfectly clear and ordered realm, running according to eternal laws, Griffin depicts a feminine reality constituted by chaos, movement, change, difference, interpenetration, all of which are expressive of an inner generative/creative power. The "roaring inside" woman names this turbulent, dynamic source of the web of life, this wildness that threatens all merely logical and technological achievements, as well as the fixed male ego. The masculinist drive to name, to know, betrays what cannot be named: "Behind naming, beneath words, is something else. An existence named unnamed and unnameable."[53] Instead of controlling, the emerging woman learns to let things be; she surrenders to the hidden movements that can never be brought to the surface, but without which there would be no life, no meaning, no joy. To patriarchal consciousness, all this seems merely dark, confused, and irrational: the stuff of witches, millions of whom were so horribly persecuted at the dawn of the modern age. According to Griffin, women must once more enter into the dream-world, surrender themselves to the unconscious movements and apparently inchoate unfoldings essential to all life, growth, and creativity. Affirming their own bodies, their sexuality, their disorderly desire, their capacity for pleasure, they must learn to affirm their kinship between the processes/domains of the Earth with the processes/domains of the female body.[54]

Not unlike Griffin, Rosemary Radford Ruether maintains that mechanical control of nature is only the latest stage in a body-denying drive for immortality that also fuels military arms races.[55] Projecting death and evil onto the enemy, man deludes himself by thinking that by killing the enemy, he will eradicate mortality and wickedness.[56] Paradoxically, man's effort to deny death by controlling everything seems to hasten the death of all things. Ruether argues that

it is not extreme to see this [self-destructive] denoument as inherent in the fundamental patriarchal revolution of consciousness that sought to deny that the spiritual component of humanity was a dimension of the maternal matrix of being. . . . Fundamentally, this is rooted in an effort to deny one's mortality, to identify with a transcendent divine sphere beyond the matrix of coming-to-be-and-passing-away.[57]

Assuming that the behavior of many males in patriarchal society is largely shaped by death denial, I often wonder whether women in patriarchy confront their mortality any more successfully and with fewer damaging ecological consequences. The obsession that many American women exhibit regarding the condition of their bodies, specifically with regard to their weight and appearance, suggests that such women have their own fears and resentments about age and death. The Western world's extraordinary "consumerist" mentality is supported in part by women who are fixated not only on improving their wardrobes and cosmetics, but also on somehow filling up the internal "void" experienced by so many people in materialistic societies. To be sure, female preoccupation with physical appearance is greatly influenced by the male gaze, but the situation is probably more complex than this. Men are themselves influenced by and seek the approval of the female gaze, particularly of those females whom men consider attractive. Arguably, so many modern Western men have been obsessed with acquiring wealth and power because these often prove effective in gaining the interest of women whom those men consider desirable.[58] Perhaps by attempting, with markedly little success, to fulfill sexual-romantic fantasies, men and women alike are concealing more disturbing issues about personal identity, life purpose, and mortality.

In the light of these and other considerations, some cultural ecofeminists do not assign to male death anxiety such a central role in the origin and maintenance of patriarchy. Taking into account Sanday's argument that ecological factors shape a culture's basic attitudes toward nature, life, and death, Riane Eisler and Charlene Spretnak emphasize that there is no historical necessity that males develop a high level of death anxiety. Indeed, Spretnak has suggested to me that by stressing death anxiety, some cultural ecofeminists may indirectly support Ken Wilber's linear conception of historical development, which makes problematic assumptions both about Goddess spirituality and native cultures. Wilber, of course, maintains that death-anxiety inevitably accompanies heightened self-consciousness and individuation. Though men may have attained such consciousness first, he believes that they did so primarily because of certain accidental biological features. Patriarchal "man" quickly learned to use such features to justify his attempts to subordinate women.

Citing archaeological findings by Marija Gimbutas and others, Eisler and Spretnak offer an account of early humanity that differs from Wilber's. Several thousand years ago, in Neolithic "Old Europe" (especially southeast Europe), people lived in unfortified agricultural settlements in which the burial patterns indicate egalitarian gender relations and the art reflects both the metaphor of the goddess and a profound sense of interrelatedness with nature.[59] Starting around 4500 B.C., nomadic pastoralists from the Eurasian steppes moved into Old Europe, establishing a patriarchal-chieftan social system (reflected by radically different burial patterns), a warrior cult, and a sky god.[60] Nuclear weapons are said to be the ultimate heritage of the social changes wrought by an otherworldly God associated with masculine power over nature and woman. According to many cultural ecofeminists, we must retrieve what was lost in the Goddess religions: the sense that there is a sacred dimension *immanent* in nature. Starhawk, for example, maintains that

spirit, sacred, Goddess, God—whatever you want to call it—is not found outside the world somewhere—it's in the world: it *is* the world, and it is us. Our goal is not to get off the wheel of birth nor to be saved from something. Our deepest experiences are experiences of connection with the Earth and with the world.[61]

Similarly, Eisler calls on women and men alike to "reaffirm our ancient covenant, our sacred bond with our Mother, the Goddess of nature and spirituality."[62] Spretnak notes that since no one knows what ancient Goddess rituals involved, contemporary rituals are creative attempts by women to transform the lived body, so that it becomes truly rooted in the living Earthbody, thereby disclosing that their own bodies are manifestations of and participants in cosmic creativeness. Paula Gunn Allen maintains that we have much to learn from tribal societies about healing ourselves (and the earth) by reintegrating mind and body, thought and feeling, human and earth, male and female.[63]

Goddess spirituality holds that the divine is both immanent (as "creativity in the universe, or ultimate mystery") and transcendent (as "the sacred whole, or the infinite complexity of the universe").[64] Although resisting the temptation to romanticize the past, or naively to call for a "return" to primitive ways, many of which were extremely demanding on women, Spretnak emphasizes that reconnecting with the feminine cosmic dimension can help empower modern women lacking in a sense of self-worth. Patricia Jagentowicz Mills, however, argues that such pronature feminism ignores nature's dark side and also forgets that appeals to let "nature take its course" tend to leave "the politics of abortion in limbo at best and, at worst, undermines those feminist arguments about the necessity for reproductive freedom based on the transformation of nature for human ends."[65] Allegedly, the "abstract pronature stance" of ecofeminists such as Starhawk and Ynestra King depoliticizes feminism, making it into a "handmaid of the ecology movement."[66] There is no guarantee that "freeing" nature from oppression will have a positive political outcome. After all, one could also argue that Nazism promised to free man's animalistic-natural instincts, allegedly long repressed by an urban-industrial society run by "unnatural" Jews. Influenced by Horkheimer and Adorno, Mills maintains that talk about reconciling humanity and nature must be tempered by recognition of the political dangers of such a project. Many cultural ecofeminists regard this critique as unfair and misinformed. In *States of Grace*, for example, Spretnak calls not only on the Goddess tradition, but also on Buddhism, Native American societies, and the social justice tradition of Judaism, Christianity, and Islam to support her contention that major socioeconomic and political changes must accompany changes in our attitudes toward nature and toward existing gender roles.[67]

CULTURAL ECOFEMINISM'S CRITIQUE OF POSTMODERN THEORY   In light of their claim that the "wisdom of the body" can reconnect alienated women and men alike to the Earthbody, we should not be surprised by how sharply many cultural ecofeminists criticize postmodern theory. Their criticisms often mirror those advanced by feminists like Seyla Benhabib. She voices the concerns of many progressive feminists who want to appropriate aspects of postmodern theory, without buying it wholesale, since they believe that postmodern theory and feminism are not always compatible. Benhabib argues that postmodern theory goes astray by affirming the deaths of the subject, history, and metaphysics. When feminists like Judith Butler follow postmodern theory's celebration of the death of the subject-as-agent (there is no "doer" behind the deeds), they unnecessarily undermine the possibility that particular people can act intentionally to alter their concrete circumstances.[68] Benhabib's "situated subjectivity" acknowledges the role played by social and linguistic structures in constituting and gendering the self, but also insists that subjects have some capacity for acting according to their own deliberations.[69] Lacking such a capacity, feminists would have to abandon aspirations for making a better future.

Benhabib agrees that we should retire patriarchal grand narratives that justify imperialism and oppression, but insists that recovering one's history can be a crucial aspect of the process whereby previously marginalized groups can gain a sense of their current situated identities and future possibilities.[70] Concerned with the reported death of metaphysics and critical philosophy, Benhabib maintains that without the capacity for rising above merely parochial perspectives to offer more general knowledge claims and criticisms of prevailing institutions and attitudes, feminism cannot successfully further its emancipatory aims. "Little narratives" that may be helpful in particular circumstances are of no use in addressing wider concerns that affect many locales. The point is to initiate critical inquiry that admits its historical situatedness and interests but nevertheless seeks a position from which to make legitimate assessments of large-scale social structures. That achieving such a position would be difficult is no argument against the importance of making the attempt.[71]

The most sustained ecofeminist critique of postmodern theory has been offered by Charlene Spretnak, according to whom deconstructive postmodernism (largely equivalent to my postmodern theory) is simply the latest in a long series of moves by male philosophers to disempower women. She deconstructs Derrida's deconstruction, describing it as profoundly slanted by his masculinist presuppositions, which he cannot evade by simply deconstructing the whole notion of gender! Spretnak is surprised that so many feminists have adopted *tout court* the premises of such white, Western, male, postmodern theorists. It is true that these theorists criticize modernity's domineering attitude, its centered subject, its exclusion of otherness, its marginalization of nonmale voices, its reliance on analytic rationality, and so on, in a way that seems to coincide with cultural feminisms's own critique. Moreover, since many feminist theorists belong to literature departments, they are thus predisposed toward the view that "textuality" is crucial to experience. Hence, their interest in Derrida's claims is understandable. Like many other cultural feminists, Spretnak agrees with postmodern theory's deconstruction of "natural" female traits that justify subordinate, passive, or inferior roles for women and other oppressed parties. Although conceding that in an important sense what we mean by nature is always culturally coded, she refuses to accept postmodern theory's claim that "there is *nothing but* cultural construction in human experience."[72] She also resists postmodern theory's attack on essence, since this makes it very difficult to speak of common features of oppressed women and men. Postmodern theory maintains that supposedly fixed, permanently present essences are social constructions, but does not offer a politically effective alternative for conceiving of collective phenomena.

Cultural ecofeminists also argue that patriarchal men, including many modern philosophers, try to protect the autonomy of the masculine ego from the "elemental power of the female body," desire, and emotions, which constitute the threatening "others" to "the man of reason."[73] Hence, Spretnak argues that although early Foucault developed insightful analyses of the oppressive regimes of modernity, his later writings reveal a typically masculinist, neo-Stoic retreat into an atomistic aesthetic of self-creation, characterized by emotional detachment and lack of significant relationship with others.[74] He seemed to regard *all* relationships as inherently oppressive. Thus, postmodern theory is the latest version of a longstanding effort by men to construct disembodied abstractions in order to negate the elemental power of the female body. The assertions of postmodern theory protect men from such power by declaring them

null and void on the grounds that *anything* associated with the female (or anything else) is merely a cultural invention! Any mention of the elemental capabilities of woman can be dismissed as merely a "valorizing narrative"! Since such concepts as "woman," "man," "nature," and "body" are regarded as nothing more than the cultural projections of a particular time and place, their "presence," or substantive validity, is "erased" by seeing through and deconstructing their cobbled nature.[75]

For Spretnak, Derrida's rejection of origins is a typically Cartesian denial that humans are organic creatures who individually emerge from a mother's womb and who as a species have evolved over millions of years upon a planet that gave birth to life far more than a billion years ago. For the anxiety-ridden male ego, perhaps the best way to deny his mortality-ridden natural origins is "by shrinking the awesome creativity of the unfolding universe into the realm of human invention. Nothing matters, or is even real, except the projects of human society."[76] But what of Derrida's critique of the centered subject, the denial that there is any self-present ego to be defended? Spretnak replies that "deconstructionist men are *nominally* willing to sacrifice identity because they experience their own, in patriarchal culture, as reactive and insecure, continually projected in opposition to nature and the female. Since it is all a house of cards, why not knock it down?"[77] Though some ecofeminists laud Derrida's attempt to shake up the metaphysical categories that legitimate authoritarian and patriarchal institutions, they expect him to offer a more constructive vision of the future. Like Foucault, however, he hesitates to do so, not only because of the undecideability of all concepts, but also because he apparently fears that he will somehow reproduce existing power structures.

Derrida's totalizing view of Western history is borrowed from Heidegger, with an important exception: he generally ignores Heidegger's discussion of the domination of *nature*. Derrida and Heidegger's dark vision of Western history is uncomfortably consistent with the National Socialist view that the Enlightenment was the final stage in the decline of the West.[78] But attacking Enlightenment notions of reason, liberty, and progress as *nothing but* ideological justifications for the Will to Power, especially when combined with deconstructions of the categories needed to provide a critique of existing power structures, risks promoting reactionary attitudes to current circumstances. This is the burden of Manfred Frank and Jürgen Habermas's critique of French poststructuralism. The latter in particular maintains that Heidegger's global critique of Western history should be contested. Postmodern theorists cannot dismiss alternative views of history by claiming that they adhere to ideas of "progress," or "reality," or "human agency," which postmodern theory has supposedly deconstructed. Such an argument begs the question and refuses to open postmodern theory's views to an external critique.

Criticisms of postmodern theory can also be used against cultural ecofeminism's suggestion that Western history has been in decline since the locus of the sacred was moved from Earth Goddess to sky god. Marxist, socialist, and liberal feminists, insisting that there is a progressive trend in Western history, maintain that modern feminism arose only because women insisted that Western culture live up to its emancipatory ideals. The very idea of liberating women, an idea notably absent from non-Western cultures, is a quintessential theme of those who would *expand* the emancipatory goals of the European Enlightenment. The criticism that cultural ecofeminism is incompatible with these goals has been promoted by Janet Biehl.

THE CONFLICT BETWEEN CULTURAL AND LEFT-GREEN ECOFEMINISM   One branch of the contested area of social ecofeminism is Left-Green ecofeminism, the major proponent of which is Janet Biehl, who is indebted not only to Murray Bookchin's social ecology, but also—unfortunately—to his combative style. Left-Green ecofeminism contends that only the elimination of capitalism, state socialism, and other hierarchical institutions can end the oppression of all people, including women, and can halt the senseless destruction of the natural world. Disputing cultural ecofeminism's claim that patriarchy is the original form of domination, Left-Green ecofeminists maintain that overcoming patriarchy would not automatically end racism, classism, or other forms of oppression. Since the latter are functions of social hierarchy, the most urgent task is to end *all* forms of hierarchy, including patriarchy. Ending social domination, we are told, would also halt the wasteful and destructive treatment of nature, since that practice is rooted in social domination. Just as people should work together to eliminate social structures blocking human self-realization, so people should encourage the realization of the possibilities of nonhuman nature. Biehl charges, however, that because most ecofeminists conceive of "'nature' [either] as a social construction, or as an effusive undifferentiated 'oneness'," they cannot conceive of nonhuman beings as having potentialities of their own.[79] Her statement implies, falsely, that most ecofeminists lack a metaphysical scheme (such as Bookchin's dialectical naturalism) that even *accounts for* nonhuman individuals.

Regarding as naive and regressive the idea that women are closer to nature, Left-Green ecofeminists also criticize the claim that creating a new feminist culture would end social oppression and the destruction of nature. As materialists, they deny that cultural changes—such as changes in mythic attitudes or religious beliefs—can effect basic alterations in economic and social structures. They level the same charge at cultural ecofeminism that Marxist and socialist feminism leveled at cultural feminism in general: dropping the critique of capitalism from the feminist agenda removes its revolutionary potential. Capitalism constructs and oppresses women in part by prohibiting them from actualizing their full human potential, in part by colonizing areas of life that were once semiautonomous and private, such as childrearing and reproduction. Even worse than cultural ecofeminism's invidious comparisons between "masculinist" values, on the one hand, and "feminist" values, on the other, is the tendency to lump "men" into an undifferentiated group who consciously set out to oppress women. Biehl argues that many types of oppression afflict men as well as women. Moreover, "if the oppression of women is primary, the prototype of all domination, then presumably men become capitalists and statists for the ultimate purpose of dominating women."[80] In fact, however, in capitalism some men tend to dominate other people not so much for the sake of oppressing women, but to gain wealth and power.[81]

In some respects, Karen J. Warren's "transformative" feminism comes close to Left-Green ecofeminism.[82] Warren argues that the oppression of women is linked to three other central types of oppression: racism, class exploitation, and ecological destruction. Although sympathetic with the aims of cultural ecofeminism, she is concerned about its essentialist tendency, as well as about its tendency simply to reverse an old dualism by making women somehow superior to men. Although rejecting cultural feminism's attempt to make patriarchy the key to all other sorts of oppression, she seems to adopt cultural feminism's contention that oppressive institutions are manifestations of *oppressive conceptual frameworks* utilizing the "logic of domination."[83] This logic has three features: (1) up-down (hierarchical) thinking; (2) value-dualisms, in which one pair of the duality is regarded as inferior (e.g., male versus female, mind versus body, culture versus nature, thought versus emotion); and (3) a substantive value claim, which justifies why the allegedly superior pole should be permitted to dominate the inferior pole.[84] Though hierarchical judgments, for example, A is better than B, may have their own legitimacy, they can be abused if appropriated into an oppressive conceptual framework. For then the hierarchical judgment "Humans are more intelligent than dogs" is linked to a substantive value claim, "the more intelligent has the right to do as it wishes with the less intelligent." With this link, the justification has been established for humans to dominate dogs. Unless the logic of domination, the foundation for *all* oppressive conceptual frameworks, is revealed and uprooted, attempts to end the oppression of women will inevitably come up short, for the "logic" needed to support a fresh wave of oppressive patriarchal practices is still in place. Despite similarities between social and transformational ecofeminism, a social ecofeminist like Janet Biehl would probably maintain that the notion of oppressive conceptual frameworks is too idealistic, for it offers a cultural instead of a materialist explanation for the rise of oppressive structures.

In "The Politics of Myth," Biehl at first acknowledges that women's spirituality can be an important factor in personal and social transformation, but then protests vigorously against alleged efforts to incorporate into "the core of the political agenda and practice" the need to provide for "members' spiritual needs."[85] Viewing spirituality as a personal matter, she claims that its intrusion into politics risks turning a political movement into a religious congregation requiring people to adopt certain religious beliefs. At this point, she attacks Goddess spirituality, suggesting that its leading representatives—despite their own plausible claims to the contrary—are "priestesses" of a dogmatic religion that wants to dictate the political direction of ecofeminism. Biehl also maintains that the invasion of matricentric cultures by sky-god worshipping warriors does not explain the *development* of hierarchy, but only points out its regrettable imposition on a nonhierarchical culture. Curiously, however, as we saw in an earlier chapter, Bookchin himself refers to this invasion as a specific instance of how patriarchy was imposed. Biehl also argues that since "both the Chinese and the Aztecs developed patriarchy, centralized states, warfare, and male deities with no help at all from 'Indo-European' invaders" there is "no pattern of correspondence between goddess worship and high social and political status for women. In fact, in many cases goddess worship corresponds more properly to low status for women."[86]

Biehl's critique gains some support from Huey-li Li's recent cross-cultural critique of cultural ecofeminism's contention that patriarchy is grounded on the binary dualism that identifies women with nature, body, and emotion, and men with transcendent reason, spirit, and divinity. Acording to Huey-li Li, it is entirely possible that women had *already* been assigned inferior status before this binary conceptual scheme arose.[87] Moreover, the alleged universality of the nature-woman identification is belied by the fact that no such identification obtains in Chinese culture. Taoism, for example, regards nature as an *impersonal,* generative cosmic function. The oppression of women in China occurred despite the fact that Chinese culture exhibits not a dualistic view of nature, but rather a holistic, organic view that reveres nature.[88] Although condemning patriarchy, then, Huey-li Li argues that there is no reason to assume that it is either the original or the most important form of social oppression.

Starhawk and Carol P. Christ come under attack by Biehl for claiming that ecofeminist myths can either explain or change social reality. But Biehl reserves her strongest attack for Charlene Spretnak, allegedly "a veritable religious determinist," who maintains that patriarchal religion is the basis for our ecological crisis. Biehl insists that such "Goddess worshippers" promote a mythic escape from real social and ecological problems. Though inviting, myths are politically dangerous, for they work on an irrational level that is not subject to critical scrutiny. For this reason, myths are often utilized to prop up authoritarian regimes. Goddess priestesses ask people

to model the new society on an era of ignorance and superstition, of parochialism and irrationality. . . . Goddess worshippers in turn close their eyes, pray to the goddess, and leap into a mythopoeic unknown, fraught with major social dangers.[89]

Biehl regards as "the rankest historical idealism" the idea that myth, including the sex of deities being worshipped, shapes culture.[90] She maintains that the cyclical temporality of Goddess religions undermines the progressive view of history introduced by Judaism and Christianity.[91] Following Feuerbach, she describes deities as fictitious entities bearing projected human attributes. Following Marx, she says that the socioeconomic base cannot be transformed by changes in the cultural superstructure, such as the rise of a new religion or myth: "Reality is not determined by myths, and capitalism and the nation-state do not obey the homilies of Sunday school teachers."[92]

Ecofeminists attacked by Biehl accuse her of distorting their views, introducing quotes out of context, and of using bullying tactics aimed at gaining control by ending discussion.[93] Denying that she is a priestess imposing a new religious orthodoxy, Spretnak notes that her essay, *The Spiritual Dimension of Green Politics,* though condemned by Biehl, does not even *mention* the Goddess, but instead calls for the "greening" of mainstream religion, including the potentially progressive views of Judaism and Christianity.[94] Her discussion of ancient Goddess-oriented societies does not purport to be a complete account of the origins of hierarchy, but rather seeks to counter the patriarchal dimension of mainstream religion by indicating that at one time people lived in an ecologically and socially harmonious society that honored a female symbol for creativity in the cosmos. Spretnak argues that because Biehl is an "Enlightenment fundamentalist" for whom religion is "strictly illusory," she "strongly equates religion with a party line of orthodoxy" and thus regards its introduction into politics as an intrusion.[95]

Of course, Enlightenment theorists made an important point in insisting on the separation of politics and religion: religious fanatics in charge of state power can cause terrible violence. Spretnak argues, however, that there is a difference between spirituality and dogmatic religion: the former has often served as a motivation for progressive political change. Further, altering the political orientation of many American women and men will not be accomplished by condemning religion as such, which remains an important factor in American self-understanding. Spretnak rightly argues, then, that it is wiser to transform existing religious attitudes than to debunk spiritual concerns. Objecting to the charge that she regards spiritual transformation as *the* way to achieve social and political change, she insists that most cultural ecofeminists acknowledge that *changes in spiritual orientation must be accompanied by specific political interventions and transformations.*[96] Such transformations include the decentralizing of economic power via community-based economics; strengthening grassroots democracy; ending the destructive dynamics of militarism; halting exploitation of the Third and Fourth Worlds by multinational corporations; transforming society in accordance with ecological wisdom and principles of nonviolence; and ending the "structural violence" that keeps people in poverty. Spretnak maintains that

the criticism by [Left-Green] ecofeminists that philosophical pieces on ecofeminism (which they disparagingly call "cultural" pieces, their code word for apolitical—but our term for an analysis that is deeper and more comprehensive than one based in economism and that *includes* economics) are ruining the movement by making it too ethereal and apolitical ignore (perhaps innocently, but usually on purpose) the fact that many, many ecofeminists work in the Green political movement, addressing economic, international, social, and other issues.[97]

In 1984, Spretnak helped formulate the American Green Movement's ten "key values," among which are grassroots democracy, social justice, nonviolence, decentralization, community-based economics, ecological wisdom, respect for diversity, personal and global responsibility, feminist values, and future focus. These values, which for Spretnak are *potentially* the political expression of the philosophy of ecofeminism, are also central to Left-Green ecofeminism—except that Left-Greens call for a type of "socialism," whereas the majority of Greens, including Spretnak, call for postcorporate, community-based, market economics. Many ecofeminists involved in the U.S. Green Movement charge that Left-Greens mimic the Stalinist political practices of the Marxists of whom they are supposedly so critical. Such practices are said to include vicious *ad hominem* and sexist attacks in political meetings and "hatchet job" broadsides aimed at those refusing to toe the Left-Green party line.[98]

Biehl maintains that the essentialism of many cultural ecofeminists leads them to rely on "feminine" intuition, associative thinking, and irrationality, which renders their work ineffective and politically dangerous, since it seems to undermine autonomy. Diana Fuss, however, argues that the essentialism versus constructivism debate must be understood within the larger context of identity politics within gender and cultural studies today.[99] Deconstructing this binary opposition, Fuss shows that essentialism and constructivism presuppose one another. Ignoring this internal relationship, Left-Green ecofeminists use the charge of essentialism as a club with which to attack opponents for being reactionary and politically ineffective, all the while wrapping themselves in the mantle of rationality and progressive ideals. Elizabeth Carlassare opposes such tactics. While studying with one of Biehl's colleagues at the Institute of Social Ecology in Vermont, Carlassare at first was persuaded of the validity of Left-Green attacks on essentialism. Later, however, encounters with Fuss and other feminists convinced Carlassare that the power interests motivating Left-Green criticism of essentialism often concealed the oppositional and constructivist dimension of "essentialist" writers like Susan Griffin and Mary Daly. Although conceding the importance of constructivist views about gender, Carlassare charges that by condemning essentialism and its nonrationalist discursive style, Biehl and Left-Green ecologists have sought "to marginalize spiritualist and poetic voices within ecofeminism, voices that do not employ traditional hegemonic discursive practices in their resistive strategies."[100] (Other ecofeminists at the Institute for Social Ecology, however, dispute these charges.) By not seriously entertaining many different feminist voices, Biehl risks the very consequence she fears from essentialism: "erasure of difference through domination."[101] Constructivist ecofeminism, then, must become self-critical enough to recognize that since it does not contain the whole truth, it must be open to alternative perspectives, unless it wishes simply to reinscribe the hierarchical attitudes against which it struggles. As Fuss maintains,

in and of itself, essentialism is neither good nor bad, progressive nor reactionary, beneficial nor dangerous. The question we should be asking is not "is this text essentialist (and therefore 'bad')?" but rather, "if this text is essentialist, what motivates its deployment?" . . . [E]ssentialism can be deployed effectively in the service of both idealist and materialist, progressive and reactionary, mythologizing and resistive discourses.[102]

Attempting to mediate the dispute between cultural and Left-Green ecofeminism, an attempt that has earned her Biehl's scorn, Ynestra King describes ecofeminist spirituality as a nondogmatic movement affirming women as "embodied, earth-bound living beings who should celebrate their connection to the rest of life."[103] This movement has inspired some women to participate in political protests designed to change the suicidal course of patriarchal civilization. King sides with cultural ecofeminists, and against Marxist base/superstructure theorists, in arguing that "no revolution in human history has succeeded without a strong cultural foundation and a utopian vision."[104] Despite acknowledging that cultural feminism is an "appropriate response to the need for mystery and attention to personal alienation in an overly rationalized world," she concludes that by itself it does not offer a satisfactory dialectical view of history. Hence, cultural feminism "is a necessary but not sufficient condition for ecofeminism."[105]

Many cultural ecofeminists, insisting that they are *not* interested solely in renewing a sense of mystery but also in transforming socioeconomic institutions, contend that cultural phenomena and economic factors interact with each other in a complex dialectic. In fact, one might ask, if it is the material/economic base that governs cultural phenomena, why should one be so concerned about the return of mythic beliefs, which seem to have no place in contemporary technological civilization? Moreover, does not the culture industry readily transform the most subversive countercultural myth into a mediocre commodity? To buttress her contention that cultural feminism's emphasis on myth and religion is dangerous, Biehl could argue that the politics of nature-myths were deeply involved in Nazism. Supposedly, Nazi ideology functioned as an irrationalist ideological screen to conceal what was *really* going on: a violent phase in big capitalism desperately struggling to survive the Great Depression. Though not discounting such socioeconomic factors, cultural ecofeminists emphasize cultural factors to account for the rise of fascism. Western males are raised to fear and to hate women, including the female dimensions of themselves, their own bodies, and their feelings. Hence, according to Spretnak,

when patriarchal man's deep-seated fears of the elemental power of the female, his own body, and his emotions are indulged, however, by a supposedly strong leader calling for even more intensely patriarchal social structures, fascism can result.[106]

Spretnak's argument is bolstered by Klaus Theweleit's salient study, *Male Fantasies,* which shows that the literature, recruiting posters, and journals of proto-Nazi *Freikorps* officers were filled with violent pornography and male fantasies about "staying hard" (remaining potent and thus maintaining rigid ego boundaries) in the face of the Bolshevik "red tide" (the devouring female) threatening to engulf them. Since desire threatens the rigid control required to protect oneself against invasion, the Freikorp man took perverse enjoyment in killing desire and also in turning everything spontaneous and unpredictable into something lifeless, restrained, and monumental. For Spretnak, fascism amounts to a particularly perverse form of the patriarchal urge to gain security by dominating everything female, and by controlling natural processes.

Foucault also disagreed with the neo-Marxist view that "Nazism was the power of the great industrialists carried on under a different form," because for him power is distributed throughout society.[107] Power is not merely external brute force oppressing hapless victims, but has a "productive" dimension in social practices that mold the human body into a certain kind of social operator. In this process, no one is simply victimized or oppressed: resistance is possible, but motivated by the individual's *own* desire for power. The apparently puritanical, repressive aspect of National Socialism masked its own peculiar way of eroticizing power. Foucault explained that

because Nazism never gave people any material advantages, it never handed out anything but power. You still have to ask why it was, if this regime was nothing but a bloody dictatorship, that on May 3rd, 1945, there were still Germans who fought to the last drop of blood; whether these people didn't have some form of emotional attachment to power.[108]

If Theweleit and Spretnak are right, Nazism's emphasis on power was attractive to men socialized to fear that their own desires were female, and that the female (as well as other "others," such as blacks and Jews) represented everything inferior, deadly, corrupting, and mortal. Nazism offered to such men a sadistic expression of their otherwise repressed erotic desires.[109] Yet Nazi mythology also took hold in part because Weimar Germany lacked the symbolic or mythic status that bestows legitimacy. Artists have long warned that a totally "enlightened" society, proposing to do without the synthesizing power of symbol and myth, ends up being fragmented and without direction. Every viable society seems to require a sustaining myth, symbol, or inspiring narrative, such as modernity's myth of progress. No society can succeed by defining social roles solely as functional units of a rationally ordered economic system.[110] Paula Gunn Allen rightly argues that myths should not be equated with naive beliefs contradicted by scientific rationality, but rather as imaginative narratives with the capacity for orienting and inspiring behavior.[111] So opposed is Biehl to the reactionary aspect of some myths, however, that she seems to discount this positive, culture-formative dimension of other myths.

Spretnak reports that her own search for a new form of spirituality, and hence for a new mythic dimension for human life, began when she recognized "with a low level of horror, that *there is no inner life in modern, technological society.*"[112] The mindless consumerism of the "advanced" societies may be explained in part as a desperate effort by people to fill a spiritual vacuum with endless material goods. Although acknowledging the role played by economic factors in shaping beliefs and attitudes, I share cultural ecofeminism's view that altered consciousness and attitudes can transform institutions. Surely socioeconomic factors were involved in the rise of Christianity, for example, but the power of its vision—that every person, Jew and Gentile, slave and free, were born equal before a loving God whose son died to redeem all sins—had far more to do with its capacity to inspire people. In many respects, I agree with those who say the world reflects the state of individuals: if they are driven by greed, aversion, and delusion, then social and political structures reflect this fact. Those structures surely help to reinforce such negative personal traits, but it is going too far to say that they are simply *produced* by them. Marx himself acknowledged the problem of a wholly materialist explanation of consciousness when, in his theses on Feuerbach, he asked: who will educate the educators?

Unless democratically minded activists address the loss of meaning felt by people living in a confusing, destructive, and mythically bankrupt world, then it is possible that activists with a far different orientation will step in. Many cultural ecofeminists share aspects of the goal of early romantic poets: to overcome social fragmentation and alienation by developing a new myth that is compatible with reason. Political activists who ignore this spiritual yearning in favor of secular rationalism fail to see that societies founded on such rationalism often lack legitimacy precisely because they do not satisfy the meaning-seeking aspect of human experience. By failing to address this yearning, progressives let reactionary ideologues do so. Manfred Frank asks:

May one leave it to Alfred Rosenberg and his like-minded comrades to recognize the mythical longing of 20th century Europeans as the loss of a "highest value" for the whole society? No doubt his talk of the "bourgeois and Marxist Germany which has become myth-less" interpreted the legitimation crisis of the Weimar Republic better, viz., more successfully, than the narrow Puritanism of the so-called bourgeois parties, but also than (as Bloch says) the "sectarian enlightened" of the communists, who indeed changed the world, but predictably did not want to interpret it in the moment of its highest need.[113]

Even Habermas recognizes that legitimacy, the central problem of modern democratic societies, cannot be won simply by holding free elections and achieving greater technological successes. Many radical ecologists insist that basic social changes can occur only if people adopt a different narrative about who they are and what their future might be. The re-emerging Goddess narrative may be one such narrative. For Spretnak, the Goddess is no supernatural entity, but rather the metaphorical expression of a way of reconnecting with her own corporeal being and the Earthbody, the being of the larger world. Like David Michael Levin, she holds that feeling, breathing, sensing, intuiting, and gesturing are not only complementary to analytical and dialectical reasoning, but provide the "opening" within which a person may begin to disassemble the internalized attitudes and behavioral codes which lock him or her into an oppressive society.[114] Hence, the "spiritual/personal" would seem to involve the "political."

Because of the disaster that ensued from the mythic narrative of Nazi Germany, cultural ecofeminists must address fears that their mythic narratives will not lead down a similar path. As I hope to have shown, however, the great majority of radical ecologists do not call for a renunciation of reason, or for a simplistic revival of tribal culture, as if this could ever be accomplished. They *do* call for reason to be reintegrated with other aspects of human experience, including a sense of relationship with the nonhuman world. In reply to those claiming that ecofeminists are reactionaries summoning a return of "mythic" attitudes, many ecofeminists would reply that they are merely challenging modernity's *own* myth of human control of nature. The question is whether that myth will yield to new myths consistent with ecological and spiritual insights, some of which are drawn from the experience of premodern peoples. Modernity's myth of the triumph of human rationality has been so destructive not only because of its dissociative tendencies (nature, body, feelings, and female are "irrational" and thus inferior), but also because it has been linked to *nationalism,* which transfers to the national level Hobbes's competitive, fear-driven, social atomism. It has been remarked more than once that the hyper-rational state generated by the French Revolution, under the pretense of establishing "universal" reason in the social domain, led to Napoleon's attempt to conquer Europe. Thus, France's imperial ambitions cloaked themselves in the garb of universal reason and human emancipation. Subsequently, this pattern has been repeated in many countries.

At the end of the previous chapter, I asked whether ecofeminism can develop a postpatriarchal narrative or narratives that share elements of modernity's emancipatory and progressive narrative. My answer is this: the fact that ecofeminists criticize the patriarchal and hegemonic aspects of that narrative does *not* mean that ecofeminists have no interest either in human emancipation or in improving the material circumstances of people. In fact, as counterculturalists believing that the world can change for the better, ecofeminists of various stripes are developing "progressive" narratives that often emphasize two things. First, much social and ecological healing would follow if people both recognized and tended to the complex *interrelationships* that constitute personal, social, and nonhuman phenomena. Second, people from the elite strata of "developed" countries must heed the voices of marginalized people at home, of tribal peoples, and of Third World peoples. Learning to listen is difficult for those who think that their own views about freedom, progress, humankind, and nature are always more "advanced" than those of less "privileged" peoples. Only in listening to the voice of someone who does not share one's own perspective can one discover its *limitations*.

Though underscoring the importance of listening to nonelite and non-Western voices, the best ecofeminist literature does not engage in gratuitous "Enlightenment bashing." Acknowledging that Western European modernity articulated emancipatory messages that continue to inspire non-Europeans, this literature nevertheless urges Western European societies to examine the inadequacies of those messages, including the extent to which they contribute to ecological destruction, social homogenization, and cultural imperialism. Many ecofeminists warn that modernity's emancipatory ideologies tend to universalize the preferred features and attitudes of European "man," thereby excluding or oppressing those who do not conform to those features and attitudes. Hence, instead of defining in advance what constitutes freedom, emancipation, progress, and ecological well-being, many ecofeminists prefer to allow these concepts to be defined gradually and continuously in the process of intracultural and cross-cultural dialogues, negotiations, and contestations. For many ecofeminists, entering into such a complex conversation would itself be a sign of enormous progress. Other features of genuine "progress" would include: celebrating embodied awareness, perhaps especially that of marginalized women, without simultaneously negating the value of analytical rationality; abandoning modernity's assumption that technological "development" is both inevitable and always positive; emphasizing living more in the here and now, though not forgetting the importance of planning for the future; disavowing the Western European definition of universal "man"; addressing the economic disparities that not only let millions live in luxury while billions are on the verge of starvation, but that also encourage socially and ecologically destructive practices in Third World countries.

For many ecofeminists, then, "progress" would not be a linear affair with Western "man" out front. Yet this is how many of them view Ken Wilber's transpersonal evolutionary theory, even though he agrees that a sign of a more integrated awareness is the capacity to celebrate diversity and to affirm phenomena—body, emotions, female, nature—dissociated in patriarchal modernity. Despite some disagreements, Wilber would agree with ecofeminism that unless important social and political changes occur not only in respect to how the First World treats the Third World, but also in how Third World governments treat their own people (especially women), the social and ecological consequences may be so dire that they will undermine the possibility of any subsequent human "improvement," however this may be defined.

Human progress, according to some ecofeminists, is to be viewed as akin to a long quilting party with many different people contributing patches to the ever-evolving quilt of humankind, or as akin to a conversation in which many voices contribute to insights that could not have been generated by any particular person. In such conversations, conflict will be inevitable, despite good intentions. Hence, a major issue is how to minimize its destructive effects, so that conversations can continue despite disagreements. Accentuating ideals such as respect and care, compassion and justice for everyone may be helpful in providing a context for successfully negotiating disputes. Some of these ideals were central to the emancipatory ideologies of European modernity and were often secularized versions of earlier religious attitudes, for example, that every person is precious in the eyes of God. Despite the fact that many European modernists tended to respect and to seek justice for only white, elite, male humans, I believe that the best of European modernity's ideals—participatory democratic government, respect for the dignity of *all* persons (not just members of privileged groups), justice for all regardless of particular circumstances—can help provide one crucial aspect of the contextual framework needed to foster intercultural dialogue. Lack of mutual respect and care encourages the dehumanization of those with whom one disagrees. Hence, the *ideal* that every human being deserves respect, care, and justice would seem to be a necessary, though not a sufficient ingredient for insuring the success of ecofeminism's vision of multicultural progress.

Precisely how one defines "human being" is open to debate, but the definition needs to be rather abstract, for if it becomes too concrete, some people will inevitably be left out. The dangers posed by a resurgence of racism and jingoistic nationalism seem to offset the dangers of homogenization posed by the ideal of an abstract "humanity" which every human somehow shares. Such an ideal does not *necessarily* lead to a dull uniformity; indeed, by emphasizing the inherent worth of all humans, this ideal can undermine the justification often used by colonizing powers: that they are "improving" the lot of allegedly inferior people and cultures.[115] There is no denying the fact, however, that encouraging people to treat each other with respect, justice, and compassion is not a "neutral" position. It is indebted to Christianity and to Western European modernity. Since I support this position, I would be loathe to negotiate it away, even though I believe that it could be incorporated by other cultures in ways that pay due respect to local customs, traditions, and attitudes.

It is worth noting that at the recent World Conference on Human Rights in Vienna, representatives of countries such as China, Burma, Yemen, Syria, Iran, and Libya insisted that supposedly transcultural "human rights" are in fact Western political and religious values that First World countries wish to impose on the Third World.[116] In the light of how poorly most women and men are treated in these countries, their criticism of "human rights" is little more than a ruse to cloak and to justify their own antidemocratic and oppressive practices. In my view, the issue is not universal human rights versus local customs, but rather whether intercultural dialogue can succeed by borrowing certain "universal" human ideals from the West, while simultaneously exploring how experience in other cultures can help to transform, strengthen, and enrich those ideals.

Many ecofeminists and deep ecologists agree about a number of important issues, including the idea that intercultural dialogue can contribute to solving many social and ecological problems. There have been sharp disagreements as well, however. As we shall see in the next chapter, one of those disagreements concerns the extent to which deep ecology's ideal of self-realization reflects not a universally valid possibility, but instead an ideal consistent with a white, Western, masculinist sense of "self."

Despite having much in common with deep ecology, a number of ecofeminists maintain that deep ecologists, most of whom are white males, are unaware of the extent to which masculinist bias colors deep ecology theory. In her 1984 critique of deep ecology, Ariel Salleh criticizes Arne Naess for omitting patriarchy's role in subjugating women and for failing to see that women's experience could provide an immediate "'living' social basis for the alternative consciousness which the deep ecologist is trying to formulate and introduce as an abstract ethical construct."[1] His admirable goal of promoting diversity of and symbiosis with other life forms and other cultures is undermined by the fact that he ignores the parallel between exploiting nature and treating women as commodities.[2] Salleh also maintains that Naess's appeal to instrumental factors—such as "exponential growth of technical skill and intervention"—for solutions to the ecological crisis, means that deep ecology "collapse[s] back into the shallow ecology paradigm and its human chauvinist ontology."[3] Moreover, his writing style is "highly academic and positivized," "dressed up in the jargon of current science-dominated [masculinist] standards of acceptability."[4] Women's "separate reality" could be "a legitimate source of alternative values" needed to replace technocratic attitudes and to help implement Naess's principles of local autonomy and decentralization.[5] But decentralization cannot occur until men recognize the extent to which they are gripped by a control obsession. Deep ecologists talk in one breath about "letting things be," while in the next breath they call for controlling the human birthrate and for zoning entire bioregions. Because the "ideological pollution" of patriarchy estranges men from their own "androgynous natural unity," the spiritual quest undertaken by deep ecologists is inevitably flawed by ego and will. Salleh concludes that the deep ecologists' abstract search for self-realization may be

sabotaged by the ancient compulsion to fabricate perfectibility. Men's ungrounded restless search for the alienated Other part of themselves has led to a society where not life itself, but "change," bigger and better, whiter than white, has become the consumptive end. . . . But the deep ecology movement will not truly happen until men are brave enough to rediscover and to love the woman inside themselves. And we women, too, have to be allowed to love what we are, if we are to make a better world.[6]

Most ecofeminists share Salleh's general position: that deep ecologists do not comprehend that their own views bear traces of the very same attitudes that have led to the ecological crisis. In the first section of this chapter, I examine cultural ecofeminism's critique of deep ecology. Section two critically examines that critique. And the last section presents a Buddhist proposal that seeks to adjudicate the dispute between deep ecology and cultural ecofeminism.

THE DEEP ECOLOGY-ECOFEMINISM DEBATE   Attempting to mediate the growing conflict between deep ecology and ecofeminism, I wrote an essay in 1987 which showed that both schools of thought agreed to the following claim: that the ecological crisis stems in part from modernity's atomistic, hierarchical, dualistic, and abstract conceptual scheme.[7] Distinguishing between deep ecology and ecofeminism, I argued that the former regarded *anthropocentrism* (human-centeredness) as the real root of the ecological crisis, whereas ecofeminism regarded it as *androcentrism* (male-centeredness). Though critical of Salleh's apparent essentialism, I acknowledged the validity of some of her complaints about deep ecology, including the fact that deep ecologists sometimes engaged in insensitive discussions about the human population problem.

In the light of recent criticism by Salleh, I now recognize that what I formerly called "ecofeminism" in fact approximates *cultural* ecofeminism.[8] Cultural ecofeminism maintains that patriarchy, as the original form of oppression, gives rise not only to the domination of women, but also to the exploitation of nonhuman forms of life. Despite its merits, cultural ecofeminism has come in for criticism. For one thing, essentialist versions of such feminism have been criticized by social ecofeminists and by nonessentialist cultural ecofeminists, both for wrongly identifying women with nature and for reinstituting a binary dualism between women and men, this time with men at the inferior pole.[9] Moreover, Karen J. Warren has observed that racism and classism may figure in the white, middle-class feminist's attempt to portray her own "female experience" as universal. Some cultural ecofeminists abandoned essentialist feminism upon discovering that "ideological pollution" is not restricted to the writings of males.

Although Warwick Fox and Janet Biehl disagree about many things, they do agree in rejecting cultural ecofeminism's contention that androcentrism or patriarchy is the source of the ecological crisis. For Biehl, social hierarchy is the key to all forms of domination; for Fox, anthropocentric ideology is a central factor in all forms of domination.[10] However, Biehl argues that by emphasizing anthropocentrism as the key factor in domination, Fox conceals the fact that it is not humankind in general, but rather particular groups of humans (often ruling-class males) who dominate other humans and nonhumans alike. In reply to Biehl, Fox distinguishes between anthropocentrism as the "*general* dominant assumption of human self-importance in the larger scheme of things," on the one hand, and the "higher order" aspect of anthropocentrism, on the other. The latter plays a crucial role as a legitimating ideology for *all* ruling classes. Ruling classes justify their status by saying that they are somehow more human than, and thus superior to, those over whom they rule. Whatever contributes to the well-being of the ruling class is said to further "human interests" in general. At the ideological level, anthropocentrism justifies social as well as ecological hierarchy: what is more human can dominate what is less human, whether that lesser party happens to be a male slave, a female, an animal, or a forest. Against Biehl, Fox asserts that one can imagine a socially egalitarian society that regards nonhuman beings as raw material to be exploited equitably for realizing the potential of *all* human beings. Against cultural ecofeminists, Fox argues that one can imagine a nonpatriarchal society in which humans treat nonhuman beings solely instrumentally.

Fox maintains that oppressed humans assert that they deserve respect and equal treatment because they are *fully human,* thereby reinforcing the very anthropocentrism used by the oppressor. Oppressed groups would better serve their own interests and those of the ecosphere by saying, "We are living beings and, like all other living beings, worthy of respect and equal treatment!" Hence, for Fox, deep ecology is not primarily concerned with pointing out which particular groups have been responsible for social domination and ecological destruction,

but rather with the task of sweeping the rug out from under the feet of those social actors by exposing the most fundamental kind of *legitimation* that they have habitually employed in justifying their position.[11]

Huey-li Li generally agrees with Fox's contention that some cultural ecofeminists engage in "scapegoating" by appealing to an essentialist view of men and women: aggressive men promote nature-exploiting capitalism, whereas women have an inherent love for nature.[12] She maintains that since many women share with men the desire for material comfort, women have a measure of complicity in originating and maintaining capitalism. Hence, "it is untenable to assume that an egalitarian relationship between men and women or an elimination of sexual differentiation can preclude the establishment of exploitative economic institutions or limit commercial expansion."[13] Like Karen J. Warren, Huey-li Li emphasizes that sexism has complex connections with *other* forms of oppression, including racism, classism, and the exploitation of nature. Fox, of course, singles out higher-order anthropocentrism as the principal justification for most types of oppression.

Fox's critical analysis of the ideological role of such anthropocentrism lets him counter social ecology's contention that deep ecology has no analysis of social power relations. For Fox, unless social revolutionaries undermine anthropocentrism, a more egalitarian society might still exploit nature for humankind's common good. Were oppressed groups (including women) to trade in an anthropocentric stance for an ecocentric one, they would simultaneously undermine the ideology legitimating the oppression of some humans by others, *and* the oppression of nonhuman beings by whichever human group happens to have gained social power. In exposing and defeating the anthropocentric ideology at work in patriarchy (men are more human then women; hence, men may oppress women), ecofeminists would promote an egalitarian world that would have room neither for patriarchy nor for the human domination of nonhuman nature.

Warren's notion of the logic of domination resembles what Fox means by anthropocentric ideology.[14] In both cases, one group of humans concludes that it can dominate another group, because the latter is allegedly inferior or less human. Rejecting essentialism, Warren indicates that there is only a historical, not a *logical* basis for linking patriarchy with destruction of nature. In his critique of anthropocentric ideology, however, Fox claims to reveal such a logical connection between patriarchy and destruction of nature. Further, he argues that because his critique of anthropocentric ideology undermines the basis for patriarchy (and other hierarchies), deep ecology cannot be accused of being androcentric, as some cultural ecofeminists have charged. In view of all this, Fox wonders why Warren doesn't simply call herself a deep ecologist, though one who emphasizes how anthropocentric ideology has particularly afflicted women and nature.

Warren resists this suggestion, however. Along with Salleh and other ecofeminists, she argues that because of the social roles women are called on to play, they bear a disproportionate burden of the damage caused by ecologically destructive practices.[15] For instance, if women in a Third World country are responsible for gathering wood for the cooking and heating, and if the forest on which they have long depended is felled to make way for economic "development," they will have to forage far longer and with dwindling success to acquire fuel, a life necessity. Moreover, women who eat pesticide-contaminated food and water may pass on those poisons to infants during breastfeeding. Thus, ecological issues are often related to women's issues *not* because women are "essentially" closer to nature or superior to men, but because women's social roles are often made more demanding by shortsighted, destructive practices masquerading as economic development.

Some deep ecologists believe that the issues mentioned above are primarily concerned with how humans (often women and children) are affected by various agricultural or industrial practices. Laudable in themselves, such concerns do not promote or justify a larger concern for preserving wild nature *for its own sake,* and not simply because a forest is useful for firewood, or because an exotic species might contain a substance that might cure a certain kind of cancer.[16] George Sessions asserts that some ecofeminists and social ecologists are so focused on social concerns that they tend to underplay the inherent worth of the *natural* world that sustains all life.[17] Yet a leading Third World ecofeminist like Vandana Shiva has called on deep ecology as well as ecofeminism to help theorize her activism.[18] Moreover, ecofeminists could argue that deep ecology does not sufficiently appreciate that nature is not merely "out there" in a beautiful landscape or a polluted aquifer, but in our living bodies.

Arguably, perhaps the most profound aspect of our alienation from "nature" is being alienated from our bodies. In "advanced" societies, women and men alike display highly problematic attitudes toward their bodies, but women in particular suffer from distorted body images. Defining themselves largely in terms of the patriarchal gaze, many women diet constantly, desperately attempting to force their bodies to conform to the ideal of thinness. Curiously, however, most men are not attracted to the "thin" image internalized by women. Hence, this image would seem to be a distorted projection of what some women take to be the expectations of the masculine gaze. Even in "normal" women, constant concern about looking good helps to generate the rampant consumerism of "developed" societies. Anorexia, a disease afflicting thousands of young women, shows the extent to which some women will go to become truly "thin." What many an anorexic woman hopes to achieve by fasting is not merely thinness, however, nor personal control, but rather *the total disappearance of her body.* As disembodied consciousness, she could not only "be" without being objectified by the male gaze, but she could also rid herself of her body, regarding which she has internalized negative evaluations.

In my view, patriarchy plays an important, but not an exhaustive role in the body-despising attitudes that play a role not only in anorexia, but in the lives of "normal" women. Women and men alike confront the existential problem of mortality.[19] Raised in traditional social roles, women are taught to think that beauty will make them desirable and special, thus well-defended against mortality. As bodily beauty and "attractiveness" fade, women are met with an uncomfortable reminder of their mortal condition, just as men meet such a reminder in the diminution of their own youthful vigor. Raised in traditional masculine social roles, however, older men can usually continue to engage in the wealth-producing and/or status-seeking activities that help to deny mortality and finitude. In patriarchal society, moreover, men defend themselves against recognizing their mortality by projecting their own corporeality onto women. For a time, at least, magical thinking may convince a man that if he can avoid taking part in the origin of life—childbirth, lactation, child-care—perhaps he can also avoid taking part in the end of life—sickness, old age, and death.

When Salleh says that men need to love the woman inside of themselves, she means that they should integrate the feminine dimension ordinarily projected upon real women and nature, both of which many men feel they must seduce and dominate. In view of feminist self-criticism and postmodern theory, however, we can no longer speak with confidence about the traits of *the* "feminine," for there are many different, sometimes even incompatible ways of being female. Indeed, for many feminists, the idea of dividing humans into two basic gender categories replicates the crucial dualism on which patriarchy rests.

Setting aside these concerns for the moment, we note that Salleh does *not* say that women should love the "man" inside themselves, only that women be "allowed to love what we are." Salleh apparently believes either that women do not project their "masculine" aspect upon real men; or else that masculine traits are so negative that she cannot believe that women might need to integrate them. But psychological projection is a *human* phenomenon, not merely a male one. That which is projected becomes distorted in the one carrying the projection. In projecting their feminine side onto women, men promote a negative self-image in women, not least because no woman can ever live up to the heightened expectations of a patriarchal "gaze," which is subsequently reinforced by women's own expectations. The "fear of success" reported by many highly competent women suggests not only that they fear that success (self-confidence, interdependent autonomy, and competence in shaping one's world) may sever important relationships, but also that success is something forbidden to women. What if it were the case that women tended to project these generally admirable qualities onto men? If so, we would expect that women would help to promote a problematic self-image on the part of the men who are carrying those projections. Are Western, middle-class, white men so success-hungry and control-obsessed because they are governed by the distorted projections of women? Is it possible that many women project their own violent attitudes, aggressiveness, selfishness, greed, hostility, desire for control, and death anxiety onto men? In view of the well-documented and widespread instances of institutional and personal violence directed at women in patriarchal societies, I do *not* wish to overstate this point. Nevertheless, if saner and less destructive social relationships are to arise, men and women alike will need to become aware of and to retract their projections.

Women suffer in many different ways in patriarchal society, but so do men. A highly overdetermined phenomenon, patriarchy cannot be explained solely in terms of the desire of men to dominate women. Male and female roles arise through complex historical processes that elude any easy explanation. Extraterrestrials studying human life would probably conclude that the similarities between women and men far outweigh the differences. The differences are not insignificant, of course, because many people—women and men alike—suffer from playing out those differences. Nevertheless, we ought not to overemphasize them to the neglect of what all have in common, in particular the given of self-conscious mortality.

Even if patriarchy is but one example of several historical forms of oppression, however, patriarchy has been one of the most important and enduring forms. Moreover, at least in patriarchal Western societies, women have long been identified with nature, so that regarding one as inferior helps to reinforce the notion that the other is inferior. Hence, although Karen Warren might grant the centrality of anthropocentric ideology, she emphasizes—in a way that deep ecology does not—how this complex ideology has been put into practice historically. Fox could be more sensitive to such historical factors, as well as to the practical issues of our own day.[20] Although Fox may be right that there is no *essential* connection between the domination of woman and the exploitation of nature, there are good reasons for emphasizing the *historical* connection. Perhaps Warren and Fox could find more common ground by agreeing that anthropocentric ideology (logic of domination) and androcentrism *both* play important roles in ecological destruction and social oppression.[21]

Many deep ecologists have heeded ecofeminist criticism. Bill Devall remarked that he finds "great cogency in the argument by feminists that patriarchy and androcentrism have contributed to the crisis of character and culture that we call the environmental crisis. I feel that I am a victim of patriarchy."[22] Despite a growing interest on the part of some deep ecologists in cultural ecofeminism, many ecofeminists continue to note in deep ecology not only an "abstract" concern with wild nature, but an unexamined masculinist voice. Jim Cheney argues that even though male deep ecologists generally criticize sexism, their views may be so (unconsciously) structured by patriarchal attitudes that they inevitably express and reinforce such attitudes. Minority and Third World women leveled a similar charge against white cultural feminists: their supposedly universal conception of woman revealed class and racial bias. Chastened by such charges, ecofeminists understandably expect deep ecologists to submit themselves to the same painful self-scrutiny and self-criticism. Renate Hof has observed that in feminism "the supposedly outside-perspective of women becomes problematized, one's own participation in the role of victim becomes discussed. On the side of *deep ecology*, such a self-critical reflection is not to be found."[23]

According to Jim Cheney, many ecofeminists are attracted to deep ecology because its relational, holistic, total-field image leads to "an ethical stance emphasizing interdependence, relationship, and concern for the community in which we are imbedded as opposed to an ethical stance which emphasizes individual rights, independence, and the moral hierarchy implied in the rights view."[24] Despite initial appearances, however, deep ecology is supposedly incompatible with ecofeminism, because deep ecology's holism promotes a "masculine sense of the self" that contrasts with the self defined by women's web-like relations.[25] To clarify the difference between these two types of self, Cheney (following Lewis Hyde) contrasts the "gift economies" of tribal societies, in which the self-sense is grounded in relations established in giving and getting gifts, with the "market economies" of modern societies, in which preexisting atomistic selves enter into relations only subsequently for acquiring and exchanging goods. An ethics of justice and rights is characteristic of market economies, involving individual competition for scarce resources, whereas an ethics of care and compassion is characteristic of gift/exchange economies, in which individuals are relational knots in the social fabric. In modern societies, women usually take over what is left of the "giving" role in gift/exchange societies. But efforts by modern women to sustain relationships by caring for others often ends pathologically in self-sacrifice, especially when women are dealing with the atomistically defined male self, "which acts as a sponge, absorbing the gift of the other, turning it into capital."[26] The atomistic male is, in effect, a vampire feeding on female energy.

Incapable of entering into the reciprocal give and take of genuine relationship, the atomistic male can perceive women and nature only in one of two ways: either as threatening Others that need to be controlled, or else as aspects of the self that need to be assimilated into himself. Even if a male does try to overcome his isolation, he tends to fuse with or to absorb the beings from which he feels alienated. Sucking everything into himself, the megalomaniacal male cancels out the Other.[27] According to Cheney, this regressive yearning for fusion or absorption "is a move toward health from a norm (an atomism) which is itself a pathological move toward health which, however, carries the sickness of atomism with it."[28] By maintaining that "I am the rain forest, and the rain forest is me," then, the deep ecologist inadvertently engages in "self-aggrandizement on a grand scale," for he conceives of himself as part of an organism, not as a member of a differentiated community.[29]

Cheney sees a "masculinist soul" motivating deep ecology's notion that, because the human organism stands in a delicately interpenetrating relationship with the rest of the world, ego-ism should be transformed into eco-ism. Allegedly, this recommendation depends too much on the ideal of male-bonding, in which the sense of individual self is suppressed for the good of the whole. Deep ecology, then, fails to differentiate between human organisms as parts of the larger biosphere and human individuals as members of a moral community. Seeking either a vampirish absorption or an infantile fusion with nature, deep ecologists reveal that their sense of "self" differs from the web-like self of cultural ecofeminists, who want neither to fuse with, nor to absorb, nor to be atomistically isolated from Others and from nature, but instead seek to sustain satisfying relations among interdependent individuals.

Cheney defines a truly moral community as one "in which individuals are what they are in virtue of the trust, love, care, and friendships that bind the community together, not as an organism but as a community of individuals."[30] As Warren has suggested, such decisions are made consensually among individuals who are part of such a community. Such decision making neither reduces individuals to subordinate parts of a whole, nor pits them against each other as social atoms fighting for survival. This kind of moral community cannot be defined in terms of rights, though the idea of rights may be useful for dealing with strangers and others who are in a disadvantaged position.[31]

Despite the fact that Naess rejects hierarchy and defines the self in terms of its relationships and affiliations, his soul is purportedly masculinist because he uses the vocabulary of rights in connection with ecocentric egalitarianism. Cheney says that ecocentric egalitarianism cannot adjudicate disputes between rights holders without positing a holism in which individual rights are trumped by the rights of the ecosystem (an "ecological totalitarianism"). According to Cheney, extending rights to nonhuman beings is not only futile, but arrogant insofar as it attempts to reduce the "otherness" of nonhuman life by projecting onto it moral norms that are applicable only to humans. Yet Cheney does recommend that nonhuman nature be located within the "*ethical* space" of the relational, care-based moral community. The idea that people can discover how to care for nonhuman beings only insofar as they are encountered within humanity's social-linguistic space supposedly bypasses the conflicts of interests built into deep ecology's notion that all things have an equal right to live and prosper. Cheney says he doesn't trample the rights of a carrot by eating it, because his relationship to the carrot is *not* one of moral conflict.

By attempting to define deep ecology as a right-based version of environmental ethics, Cheney ignores the fact that most deep ecologists use the vocabulary of "rights" nontechnically, to describe the attitude of respect and care for nonhumans that spontaneously accompanies "ecological sensibility." Naess would agree with Cheney that he doesn't justify eating a carrot because he, Naess, has a moral "right" to do so, but rather because he is hungry. As organisms seeking to flourish, humans inevitably enter into predatory relationships with other organisms seeking to realize their own potential. Deep ecologists maintain that an ecological sensibility will foster attitudes and relationships that take into account, as much as possible, the striving of human and nonhuman alike.

Deep ecologists, then, would agree with Cheney that understanding how to deal appropriately with nonhuman beings, including those who become our food, requires an understanding of the obligations involved with the complex relationships we have both to other people and to those nonhuman beings. We gain a measure of insight into those obligations and relationships only over time, through patient observation and participation in the life of the human and the larger community, as Aldo Leopold suggests in his *Sand County Almanac*. The issues concerning our relations to the nonhuman world can only be resolved by "appropriate care, genuine, clear-sighted, sane, healthy responsiveness to a world I have come to know and cherish."[32] Cheney believes, however, that most deep ecologists, despite their talk of ecological sensibility and interconnectedness with all life, retain an alienated, atomistic masculinity that prevents them from attaining a profound connectedness with other human individuals and with the larger community of life.

Val Plumwood criticizes deep ecology for similar reasons. She argues that deep ecology is a typically masculinist ethical system that relies on reason to provide an impartial, universal account of moral obligations. Deep ecologists, we are told, argue that the act of identification by which nature becomes an object of moral concern occurs only after a long process of abstraction and disconnection. At first identifying with oneself, one's family, and one's tribe, a person gradually expands his or her sense of identification (and hence sense of moral obligation) ever wider until it embraces not only all humans, but the whole ecosphere.[33] Devall and Sessions say that after a mature, truly active person has become increasingly identified with the ecosphere and its components, he or she will preserve nature from abuse, because he or she "sees that such preservation is in one's self/Self interest."[34] Plumwood concludes that this amounts to an ecological version of rational egoism. For such egoism, self-interest—characterized by natural inclinations, personal attachments, and irrational desires—can only be checked by abstract, universal norms, as promoted by ethicists such as Kant and Rawls. Moral progress, then, involves leaving behind merely personal interests and selfish preferences, in favor of an increasingly disembodied and depersonalized state (pure practical reason) which alone makes possible just, disinterested, universally valid moral decisions.

Many feminists argue that this idea of justice stems from a masculinist, atomistic concept of selfhood. Justice requires impartial constraints to limit the competition among egos competing for scarce resources. Everything merely personal is considered self-interested, and everything emotional is a threat to fairness. Plumwood argues that although this idea of justice has some merit, it is blind to the particularist, feeling-oriented ethics of care that arise from the relational mode of selfhood reported by many women. Further, because it is grounded in humanity-nature (rational-irrational) dualism, the rationalist idea of justice cannot effectively deal with moral problems regarding natural beings. Like Cheney, Plumwood maintains that deep ecologists use the model of rational egoism to overcome humanity-nature dualism. For such egoism, there are basically only two kinds of behavior: self-interested and self-sacrificing. Regarding the latter as fruitless, deep ecologists promote the former: only now the "self" in self-interest is the ecospheric or even the cosmic Self, however that may be defined.[35] For Plumwood, however, obliterating the difference between self and Self does not necessarily promote ecologically sane practices. After all, I could posit that *my* needs are also the rainforest's; hence, if "I" need a lot of tropical lumber, the rainforest part of me would nicely serve that need.[36] Plumwood maintains that not only deep ecologists, but ecofeminists, too, must emphasize how humans are *different* from nonhuman beings, so as to avoid the dangers of undifferentiated merger with nature. Relationships are intrinsic to selfhood, but individuals cannot be reduced to those relationships; otherwise, one ends in an unhealthy "holism."

Plumwood asserts that deep ecology's universalistic, abstract love of nature discounts the importance of caring personal relationships as the *basis* for any sense of morality or ethics. One cannot care for things abstractly; rather, each thing must be understood in terms of its own particular concrete needs. Similarly, Marti Kheel maintains that absorbing everything into the greater Self obliterates the importance of individual beings.[37] Continuing to think in terms of such patriarchally ordained dualisms as reason versus emotion, universality versus particularity, and duty versus inclination, deep ecologists don't realize that by promoting an impartial or disinterested perspective from which to make moral judgments, they are reproducing those dualisms. Entering into relationships with other people and with nonhuman beings presupposes that we can acknowledge that they are somehow other, without simultaneously regarding them as wholly alien. Plumwood maintains that we can overcome anthropocentrism or human self-interest best by interpreting self in relational terms that acknowledge our distinctness from as well as our continuity with nature and others.

On this relational account, respect for the other results neither from the containment of self nor from a transcendence of self, but is an *expression* of self in relationship, not egoistic self as merged with the other but self as imbedded in a network of essential relationships with distinct others.[38]

Plumwood speaks for most cultural ecofeminists in arguing that deep ecology fails to see that dualism is profoundly linked to patriarchy. Trying to overcome humanity-nature dualism, male deep ecologists end up in monism, in which all little selves are contained within the (masculinist) cosmic Self. Deep ecologists could reply that for all nondualist traditions, where there is one, there must be two, for one cannot be understood apart from two. Hence, nondualism holds not that "all is One," but rather that there are "not two." Speaking in this way, nondualism avoids the problem of melting everything together in what Hegel called "the night in which all cows are black." Just as social atomism cannot tolerate the sense that relationships are internal to the self, so monism—as social atomism expanded to a cosmic level—also obliterates relationships by saying that everything is a part of the whole. For genuine relationships to obtain, however, there must be not only *difference,* but a measure of individual *identity.* Just as a totally relational scheme (a caricature of ecofeminist views) dissolves individual identity, so a holistic identitarian scheme (a caricature of deep ecological views) dissolves difference.

In some respects, Plumwood's distinction between deep ecology and cultural ecofeminism is similar to postmodern theorist Richard Rorty's distinction between realists seeking objectivity and pragmatists seeking solidarity. Searching for an ahistorical, objective basis for truth, realists demand more justification for their truth-claims than do pragmatists, for whom something is true if it is workable, interesting, useful, or in some other way beneficial to one's community. Pragmatic truth is both ethnocentric, since it assumes that there is no universal standpoint from which to compare truth-claims, and constructivist, since it claims that truth involves practices (in principle revisable) that change the world in interesting and useful ways. Truth involves activity, not discovery. Rorty recommends that we take seriously Nietzsche's famous description of truth and language as

a mobile army of metaphors, metonyms, and anthropomorphisms—
in short a sum of human relations, which have been enhanced,
transposed, and embellished poetically and rhetorically and which
after long use seem firm, canonical, and obligatory to a people.[39]

Seeking to avoid pragmatism's relativism and parochialism, realists presuppose "a transcultural human ability to correspond to reality," an ability that springs "from human nature itself, and [is] made possible by a link between that part of nature and the rest of nature."[40] By detaching oneself "from any particular community and look[ing] down at it from a more universal standpoint," the realist hopes to promote justice and fairness.[41] Rorty argues that this striving for metaphysical certainty is motivated by anxiety about the death of one's own historical community. Plato spawned this attempt "to avoid facing up to contingency, to escape from time and chance."[42] Ecofeminists like Cheney and Plumwood are pragmatists, for whom truth is always local, negotiated, historical, revisable, and rooted in community. For them, detached and timeless statements are not only impossible, but also either useless or—worse still—harmful, since they ignore the particular in favor of the allegedly universal.

Deep ecologists do not see Rorty as a friend of radical ecology. Viewing "our" community as Enlightenment liberalism, he affirms Bacon's view that science aims to promote human welfare by dominating nature. Incapable of knowing anything true about nature apart from how it happens to be disclosed by the liberal community, that community offers no place (apart from prudential concerns about destroying itself) from which to resist treating nature in wholly instrumental terms. Plumwood and Cheney would presumably argue that adopting Rorty's insight about the perspectival character of community does not entail accepting his preference for Enlightenment liberalism's instrumentalist attitude toward the nonhuman.

Seeking to combine universalist moral principles with a concern for the perspectives of particular, Seyla Benhabib would agree with some of ecofeminism's criticisms of deep ecology, but not with others. Consider deep ecology's view that wider identification follows from a maturation process that increases impartiality in moral judgment. According to Lawrence Kohlberg, such moral development involves moving from conventional to postconventional morality, which involves acting according to the principles of justice: equity, fairness, and reciprocity. Like Warwick Fox, Kohlberg says that care, in the form of love, friendship, and family matters, involves particular interests that limit one's capacity to make impartial judgments about people who are not part of one's immediate circle of family and friends. Though agreeing that universal moral principles are important, Benhabib adds that the invidious distinction between justice and care presupposes the validity of modernity's distinction between *moral questions of justice* and *evaluative questions of the good life.*[43]

Hobbes and other early modern philosophers introduced this distinction as the teleological Christian-Aristotelian cosmology crumbled in the face of modern science and new economic formations. According to the displaced cosmology, "the good life, the telos of man, is defined ontologically with reference to man's place in the cosmos."[44] According to the new mechanistic cosmology, no one knows the purpose of the cosmos, even if it had one: "Morality is thus emancipated from cosmology and from an all-encompassing worldview that normatively limits man's relation to nature."[45] In a disenchanted world, bourgeois subjects conclude that the "ought" is "what all would have rationally to agree to in order to ensure civil peace and prosperity (Hobbes, Locke), or the 'ought' is derived from the rational form of moral law alone (Rousseau, Kant)."[46] Merely "personal" matters, including family relationships, nurture, love, reproduction, emotions, are relegated to the private, that is, the merely "natural" realm, governed by conventional morality. "Public" matters, principally the affairs of political economy, are governed by postconventional, impartial, universal justice. In emphasizing impartiality, Fox seems to adopt a conception of justice that (1) became prominent in a world objectified by science and commodified by capitalism, and that (2) presupposes the man/culture versus female/nature dualism. This view of justice, in other words, would seem compatible with views that many radical ecologists hold responsible for the ecological crisis.

Another apparent problem for Fox is that by viewing justice as impartiality, he seems to reinforce ecofeminism's suspicion that the expanded self ignores difference and absorbs the other. Benhabib notes that Kohlberg is sympathetic to John Rawls's idea that we should derive the principles of justice while operating behind a veil of ignorance that conceals how we ourselves would be situated in the world to which those principles would apply. Despite his admirable motives, Rawls ignores the fact that one cannot fully appreciate the other without taking into account one's own concrete situatedness. Like a number of other feminists, Benhabib argues that Rawls's neo-Kantian "substitionalist universalism" operates according to the "rational choice model," which contains no moral injunction "to face the 'otherness of the other,' one might even say to face their 'altereity,' their irreducible distinctness and difference from the self."[47] Asserting that only confrontation, engagement, and dialogue can reveal this "otherness," yet seeking to overcome the false dichotomy of justice versus care, Benhabib calls for an "interactive universalism" that "acknowledges that every generalized other is also a concrete other."[48] If Benhabib is right, as I believe she is, Fox could combine his legitimate concern for impartiality with recognition that the concrete voice of the other must be taken into account in moral judgment. By resisting this move, Fox reinforces suspicion that his "wider identification" operates according to a masculinist model of moral maturity, which holds that impartiality must trump particularist care.

At this point, Fox and other deep ecologists might remind us that because deep ecology is *not* an instance of environmental ethics, the disputes examined above tend to deflect attention from deep ecology's major recommendation: self-realization through wider identification. Jim Cheney has conceded that deep ecology cannot adequately be understood as a type of environmental ethics. In "The Neo-Stoicism of Radical Environmentalism," he criticizes a version of deep ecology, Ecosophy S, which is his own distillation of the views of Devall, Sessions, and Fox. Cheney distinguishes Ecosophy S from Naess's Ecosophy T, which Cheney regards as more attuned to the concerns that he raises in his Neo-Stoicism essay. Cheney maintains that beneath Ecosophy S's explicit pronouncements lies a neo-Stoic "subtext" that expresses a longing for oneness with nature in a time of social uncertainty, specifically the passage from the modern to the postmodern world. Yearning for conversion to what Rorty calls a "New Being," or to what counterculturalists might call a New Age, Ecosopy-S theorists deny their own mortality and that of their culture by identifying with an allegedly timeless Self. Just as the ancient Stoics sought to achieve salvation and to overcome alienation in a crumbling social order by aligning themselves with the cosmos, so Ecosophy-S theorists seek the same goals by a wider identification with nonhuman beings. It is no accident that many deep ecologists show such interest in Spinoza's neo-Stoicism, or that Sessions was interested in Robinson Jeffers's "tower beyond tragedy." If for the ancient Stoics the tragedy was the rising Alexandrian world of "difference" that replaced the unified world of "Athenian supremacy," the tragedy for Ecosophy-S theorists is

the demise of modernism, its shattering into a world of difference, the postmodern world. [Ecosophy-S] expresses a yearning for embedment coupled with a refusal to forgo the ultimate hegemony so characteristic of modernism. . . . Subtextually, the central operative idea at work in these ideas [of Self-realization, identification, and ecological consciousness] is the idea of *containment,* containment of the other, of difference, rather than genuine *recognition* of the other, genuine acknowledgement and embracing of the other.[49]

The modernism of Ecosophy S can be seen in its claim to have "a privileged account of the experiences underlying a great multiplicity of widely differing voices."[50] Ecosophy S maintains not only that Greeks, American Indians, and Buddhists assert that humans are profoundly related to nature, but even more, that the essential core of these diverse traditions amounts to what Ecosophy S means by self-realization. Claiming to have grasped this core, Ecosophy-S theorists clearly remain committed to the possibility of ahistorical, eternal truths, thereby rejecting postmodern theory's contention that truth is contingent, contextual, historical, and subject to negotiation. Like Stoics, Ecosophy-S theorists presuppose that they are part of an elite group, which can intuit the interrelationship of all things and can read the "grammar of the cosmos." Despite all talk of dwelling in particular bioregions, Ecosophy-S theorists "bootstrap" themselves to universality so as to avoid negotiating with alternative visions of ecological consciousness. The effort by Ecosophy-S theorists to achieve a hegemonic position results from the same masculinist sense of self that gave rise to modern science's quest for absolute, ahistorical truth. Driven by a "static autonomy," they can relate to the other only by assimilating it into their totalizing theoretical framework. Yearning for wholeness and healing, but simultaneously refusing to give up the safety of their alienated condition, the Ecosophy-S male avoids the possibility that his alienated ego might be radically transformed by what is truly other.

According to Cheney, the process of absorbing other into self plays out an unhealthy control fantasy, which presumably resulted from problematic early childhood experiences of Ecosophy-S theorists. (Since Cheney probably has no access to clinical information to substantiate such claims, one can understand why those theorists resent his assertions!) In a healthy mother-baby relationship, the mother establishes a relationship with the baby that provides a "holding space" or "matrix" in which the baby can turn its drives into its own desires and develop confidence in its own abilities. Paul Shepard suggests that in healthy cultures, children gradually move from this maternal matrix to the "earth matrix," in which they gain a sense of their own capacities within a complex set of natural beings with which they can establish lifelong relationships. In this way, ambivalence toward the mother—as the being with whom a child may wish to merge, but at the same time to dominate—never solidifies into the subtext that governs the attitude most Western men have toward women and toward nature. In this unhealthy subtext, men see women and nature alike as things either to be dominated or merged with. In either case, an adult's behavior is governed by regressive, primitive, sadomasochistic childhood fantasies. In their account of self-realization, Ecosophy-S types simply bury this problematic "reaction formation." Having contained nature in a totalizing vision, deep ecologists can safely eulogize "Mother Earth" in the insulated, alienated, and impersonal voice of metaphysics.[51]

In privileging their version of ecological consciousness, Ecosophy-S supporters allegedly develop a "paternalistic and condescending" attitude to all those benighted people who have not yet gained the correct view of the universe and who have thus not yet achieved "ecological consciousness."[52] Despite all talk of respecting diversity and difference, then, the concerns of people who cannot agree with Ecosophy S

are colonized, deflected, ultimately delegitimized. *Difference* is not made a central dimension of a revolutionary politics of difference which might hope to eliminate *all* forms of domination, including the domination of nature; rather, difference is colonized, assimilated into a "higher," more "enlightened" discourse.[53]

As an alternative to Ecosophy S's method of developing ecological consciousness, an alternative that would contribute to "a true revolution," Cheney mentions Aldo Leopold's encounter with the *radical otherness* of nonhuman inhabitants of the land, whose plurality of perspectives undermined the presupposition that Leopold's was somehow privileged.[54] Instead of the one, true story imposed by Ecosophy S, Cheney says that we must seek "storied residences," bioregional ways of dwelling that are informed by narratives arising from experiences in a particular place and relationships with specific beings. As an example of such a storied residence, Cheney (citing Tom Jay) refers to the culture of Northwest Coast Indians, for whom salmon are

literal *embodiments* of the wisdom of the *locale*, the resource. . . . They are the old souls, worshipful children of the land. *Psychology without ecology is lonely* and vice versa. The salmon is not merely a projection, a symbol of some inner process, it is rather the embodiment of the soul that nourishes us all.[55]

Since such "storied residences" are not exportable, they cannot become abstract, totalizing narratives to which others must conform. These local narratives do not regard nature as a monolithic Self with which one is to identify or merge, but rather as an unpredictable, differentiated, and quirky Other, such as the coyote of Native American lore. The multitudinous narratives arising out of conversation with the coyote cannot be reconciled with each other.

The ragtag of such a method of doing "metaphysics" sacrifices unity to the authenticity of the voices heard in its ragbag of tales, myths, stories; but this is all to the good—totalizing accounts have a way of achieving unity at the cost of silencing those voices which cannot be heard in the official jargon. What is needed is a *grass-roots* conception of metaphysics, a notion of metaphysics as bioregional narrative, a metaphysics, directly responsive to genuine encounter.[56]

For Cheney, the value of these conflicting narratives lies precisely in the fact that they never come to a final agreement. Instead, they constitute a continuously unfolding negotiation that presupposes the capacity to listen to the other as other. This willingness to take part in weaving a complex fabric without demanding a unifying or totalizing center shapes feminist attitudes not only toward theory, but also toward identity politics and positionality, which encourage the development of "healthy voices" on the part of oppressed people.

A CRITICAL APPRAISAL OF ECOFEMINISM'S CRITIQUE OF DEEP ECOLOGY   Ecofeminists such as Salleh, Plumwood, and Cheney raise important questions about the masculinist bias of deep ecology. Feminists know how painful it is to discover that one's most deeply held convictions may be flawed by unexamined prejudices, such as racism, so they can hardly be surprised if deep ecologists resist ecofeminist criticism. As I discovered a decade ago, however, what once looked normal to me as a middle-class white man began to look very different through the lens of feminist theory. This discovery disposed me to be sympathetic to ecofeminism. Like any effective social analysis, however, ecofeminism does not provide *the* truth, but is *one* powerful way of disclosing oppressive social structures and relations. Ecofeminism's critique of deep ecology deserves careful study and reflection on the part of deep ecologists. Unfortunately, apart from essays by Warwick Fox and myself, deep ecologists have dealt only superficially with the challenges posed by ecofeminism, particularly in its postmodern version.

As noted earlier, Fox responded to Cheney's initial essay by noting that deep ecology is *not* a version of environmental ethics. Rejecting the social atomism associated with rights-based ethics, deep ecologists maintain that humans are interrelated in a myriad of ways with everything else in the universe. Fox calls on Cheney to meet deep ecology on its own terms, that is, as a movement calling for wider identification with nonhuman beings. Given Cheney's emphasis on the importance of particularized, caring, nurturing relationships with nonhuman beings, the difference between Cheney's ecofeminism and deep ecology seems to boil down to this: the former favors a personally based identification, whereas the latter favors a cosmologically based identification.[57] In criticizing ecofeminism, however, Fox maintains that "a purely personal basis for identification (*my* self first, *my* family next, and so on), looks more like the cause of possessiveness, war, and ecological destruction than the solution to these seemingly intractable problems."[58]

Roger J. H. King argues that although cultural ecofeminists are right in emphasizing the importance of care for changing exploitative attitudes toward nature, they have not yet successfully explained how the caring appropriate to members of a family can be successfully extended to a community of strangers, much less to plants and animals, rivers and biomes.[59] Further, although Cheney claims that we are to "locate nature within the social space of community," he does not present a persuasive discussion of the specifics of this claim. Is he offering a new version of Marx's view that nature is a "social category"? If nature is thus located, one can imagine that it will always take second place to more pressing interhuman relationships, as it has both in Marxism and capitalism. Moreover, even in an ecofeminist social space, one is hard-pressed to see how the wild otherness and difference of nature could be preserved, as Cheney proposes. Located within the human community, nature would tend to be tamed, because it would *inevitably* be interpreted in terms of categories originally drawn from the social realm.

King also asks whether the personal narratives about "lived experience" emphasized by Karen Warren can do the work required for founding a nondomineering attitude toward nature. Since many people lack such lived experience in nature, how can they be expected to "care" about it? In attempting to do without an abstract, universal ethics, Warren emphasizes the alternative of local ethical narratives that are voiced by particular people involved in a given situation. King asks, however,

whose voice should we be listening to: the resort developer's, the agribusiness entrepreneur's, the hunter's, the tourist's, the weekend athlete? These voices are not all compatible with one another, nor are they all interested in the well-being of the natural world.[60]

The limitations of the personal narrative as a guide for "caring" for nonhuman beings and thus for locating them within human "social space" is discernible in Warren's first-person account of climbing a cliff. She reports that she suddenly felt that she and the cliff were old friends, partners in a silent conversation. Warren does not explain, however, how a rock cliff can in any sense be understood as a *conversational partner* or as a friend. King poses the problem very well:

Warren's narrative does not clarify what care means or what its moral significance is. She contrasts a climber who cares about the rock with one who seeks to conquer it, yet for the rock, it is all the same thing; the rock does not care. Indeed, the fact that the climber cares for the rock appears to have no practical consequences for the rock itself. What, then, is gained by the metaphors of conversation, partnership, and friendship when these are taken out of their human context and when the only speaker and ultimate beneficiary is still the human climber?[61]

Warren's account of her relationship with the cliff invites the following question: if the masculinist character of a deep ecologist is revealed in his desire (silently) to identify or to merge with the cliff, does the feminist character of a female ecofeminist revealed itself in her desire to have a conversation with the cliff? Perhaps a cliff is just too problematically "other" to sustain a relationship that doesn't consist solely of human projections, however. Ecofeminists are right that the abstract rationalism of modern ethical theory omits the element of friendship, caring, feeling, love, personal relationship, and narrative that are so crucial in socializing children and sensitizing them to moral issues. Such personal human interaction is important for moral development, but it may not suffice for developing concern about nonhuman beings. Many ecofeminists would argue, however, that such concern can be encouraged by childhood experiential encounters, which reveal that many nonhumans have needs, wants, and viewpoints, too.

Experiences I had as a boy in a small country town helped me to understand how Arne Naess's early encounters with little creatures shaped his subsequent concern for and sense of relationship with the natural world. In long hours spent climbing glacial cliffs, playing in creeks full of minnows and frogs, and wandering through forests and fields, I "communed" with the vegetation and animal life, the water and hills, and the sun and wind. I spoke with things, and I liked to think that they replied to me in their own ways. Surely fantasy and projection played a role here. My experiences were probably colored by a lack of satisfying interpersonal relationships at home. Naess has described how in his youth a mountain became the strong, stable father that he lacked. Some ecofeminists might say that if Naess and I (and Thoreau and Muir) had better family relationships, we would not have attempted to find solace and relationship by projecting ourselves upon and identifying with nature.

But such projection, in the sense of a *participation mystique,* is likely involved in the animism of native peoples who are often admired by ecofeminists. Val Plumwood argues that emotional attachment to and concern for specific persons, places, and things is an important, though often neglected dimension of morality.[62] If my boyhood experiences in the woods were *simply* a matter of projection, then in identifying with the plants and animals, trees and streams, I would have been—as Cheney says—absorbing them into myself, not letting them be in their otherness. Given my personal isolation, I may have done this at times. At other times, however, I think my identification with the woods was elicited by what Cheney calls a shift in perception that let me see "*other subjects,* ones with their *own* purposes, their *own* perspectives, their *own* goods."[63] In my own fumbling way, I conversed with the forest creatures and befriended them. Though perceiving a kinship with these nonhuman creatures, I nevertheless realized that conversing with nonhuman creatures was not fully satisfying; I needed closer ties to and conversation with my own kind. In exploring my beloved woods, I learned something about the difference between my kind and the squirrels, though I treasured our secret kinship. I say "secret," for at the time I knew no one with whom I could have shared these experiences, even if I could have articulated them. To find such experiences brought to language, I had to wait for Wordsworth's poetry and Annie Dillard's matchless prose.[64] Like her, I was a pilgrim at the woods on the outskirts of Newcomerstown.

For the five-year old Naess, a new mode of perception occurred when he encountered tiny animals, insects, and fish, sometimes in a state of suffering from which he could not rescue them. In feeling a profound *identification* with them, he did not absorb or cancel out their "otherness." Instead, he began encountering them as subjects with lives and purposes of their *own,* independent of his. Before that moment of identification, he could not let those things "be" what they were, because he could not experience their otherness *as* subjects somehow analogous to himself. Aldo Leopold's accounts of the land as experienced from the perspective of its nonhuman inhabitants— accounts that Cheney cites approvingly—presuppose that the animals are not *radically* other. If so, we could make little sense of them; hence, our capacity for caring would not be elicited.

In some respects, deep ecologists and ecofeminists seem to disagree about what constitutes caring. For the latter, caring seems to be grounded in a context of relationships that personally matter to me; for the former, although personal caring is important, it cannot provide an impartial basis for dealing with beings with whom or with which I have no personal relationship. Ecofeminists cannot simply dismiss the importance of impartiality in moral affairs. Cheney himself admits that most of the people with whom we deal are total strangers.[65] My own experience suggests that concrete relationships with family members, friends, and with woodland denizens helped to develop my capacity to have a measure of care and respect for strangers. Contextual caring and impartial respect are not mutually exclusive; instead, both are necessary for coping with the complex demands of our lives.

Cheney argues that unlike modern emancipation movements, which focus on freeing people in specific historical circumstances, deep ecology is an ahistorical salvation movement.[66] But Naess's hero, Gandhi, was partly successful in combining salvational aims with historically specific emancipatory goals. Although Spinoza did tend to take a neo-Stoic, salvational view, even he explained how his views on freedom pertained to contemporary political problems. Though criticizing the social atomism of modern moral theory, Fox emphasizes that the capacity for universality and impartiality indicates maturity in moral relationships with human and nonhuman beings. In his view, a cosmologically based identification reveals that all beings are "relatively autonomous modes of a single, unfolding process, that all entities are leaves on the tree of life."[67] Only this wider, cosmological identification will move us to show increasing concern for all life on planet earth. Rejecting Cheney's claim that this striving for cosmological identification is an example of an alienated masculinist voice, Fox contends that the experience of cosmological identification does not respect gender boundaries. Similarly, ecofeminist Charlene Spretnak speaks of experiencing a nondual awareness of profound connectedness with all things.[68]

In "Man Apart," the late Norwegian deep ecologist, Peter Reed, counters both Fox's impartial self-realization and Cheney and Warren's personalized caring.[69] Reed argues that what Rudolf Otto meant by the Holy, that is, the stupendous Other that inspires awe and humility, provides a better basis for deep ecology than does its norm of wider identification. We want to "do right" by nature, not because of our increasing knowledge of how we are interrelated with it, but rather because of our intuition that nature *differs* from us and has intrinsic value. Encountering the "austere mystery" of dominant nature can reveal our relative insignificance. Echoing Jeffers's inhumanism, Reed asserts that the "towering reality" of nature solicits from us a response of humility, compassion, and concern for this Other in all its manifestations.[70] Unlike Jeffers, however, who says that "man" is a part of larger nature, Reed insists that he differs from and exists apart from nature as that which dwarfs him. Only by cultivating this difference, rather than seeking to overcome it through wider identification, can people retain appropriate respect for the wholly Other.

Cheney might concede Reed does accentuate nature's otherness, but only in terms of a masculinist abstractness characteristic not only of deep ecology, but of Rudolf Otto's transcendent, aloof, and wholly other Divine. In reply, Reed might have said that Cheney's hope that a bioregional narrative can help establish communal relations with the salmon or some other natural feature, while preserving its otherness, is misguided, for such narratives try to domesticate and to anthropomorphize nature's awesome Otherness. If attempting to grasp the Other in a metaphysical scheme indicates a lack of respect for the Other, so does attempting to include it in the human community by virtue of local narratives. *All* attempts adequately to specify and to preserve nature's difference, including Chency's attempt to establish caring relationships with it, have some shortcomings.

For example, Cheney seems to presuppose the universal validity of Gilligan's distinction: that the feminine sense of self is relational whereas the male sense of self is atomistic. Other feminists have criticized this distinction. Moreover, since he assumes that males in gift/exchange societies have a relational self, his original distinction between the male and female types of self apparently holds only for people in *modern* society—and quite possibly not even then, since Gilligan's types are only one way of constructing gender distinctions. Apparently, Cheney does not see the problem of analyzing the social/gender structure of tribal societies in terms of categories applicable (if then) to women and men in modern society. Further, he speaks as if there are only two types of economies: gift/exchange and market, whereas in fact economic history is far more complex than such a dichotomy would suggest.

Many examples can be found to support Fox's contention that women as well as men seek a wider identification with nature. Elizabeth Dodson Gray's claims that understanding our profound interrelationship with the larger whole leads me to realize that "what hurts any part of my larger system hurts me."[71] Given Gray's insistence on relationships and caring, Cheney could hardly describe her as an "alienated masculinist soul," although as an educated, middle-class woman she may have inadvertently absorbed some patriarchal views. Perhaps he would say the same of the ecofeminist Carol P. Christ, who promotes biocentric egalitarianism:

God/Goddess/Earth/Life/It, the whole of which we are a part, the unnameable beneath naming, serves a profoundly relativizing function. The supreme relativizing is to know that we are no more valuable to the life of the universe than a field flowering in the color purple, than rivers flowing, than a crab picking its way across the sand—and no less.[72]

In her prize-winning novel, *The Color Purple*, Alice Walker describes how a Southern, rural black woman arrives at what amounts to a cosmologically based identification. Concluding that God "ain't a he or a she, but a It," the woman says:

I believe God is everything, say Shug. Everything that is or ever was or ever will be. And when you can feel that, and be happy to feel that, you've found it. . . . My first step away from the old white man was trees. Then air. Then birds. Then other people. But one day when I was sitting quiet and feeling like a motherless child, which, I was, it come to me: that feeling of being part of everything, not separate at all. I knew that if I cut a tree, my arm would bleed. And I laughed and I cried and I run all around the house. I knew just what it was. In fact, when it happen, you can't miss it.[73]

Is this the expression of an alienated, masculinist soul, yearning to merge with Mother Nature in order to control her during a time of social upheaval? Or is this the expression of an ancient human experience of wider identification with the cosmos? Are we to join Freud in reducing this "oceanic feeling" to a yearning for the infantile state of oneness with mother? Or are we to rely on wisdom traditions that distinguish between psychological regression and moments of authentic illumination in which the limiting boundaries of the ego-subject dissolve so as to make possible more integrated, nondualistic awareness? A sense of identity with the cosmic whole does not have to come at the expense of relationships to particular things, but instead grows out of and remains nurtured by those relationships. Again, personal relationship and wider identification are not mutually exclusive; both are needed for mature moral experience.

Ecofeminists rightly say, however, that deep ecologists sometimes emphasize impartial identification at the cost of particular relationships. For example, Freya Matthews believes that the idea of self-realization "requires that the universe be a self," that is, a teleological system characterized by conatus (will-to-exist) and a striving to realize value in itself.[74] Insofar as the human self is nested within ever more complex selves, including ecosystems and beyond, an individual's conatus helps to shape the wider self-system, which in turn sustains the environment needed for the emergence of self-realizing forms of life.[75] As my identification widens, what I consider to be my interests widen, too.

Since I am ontologically at one with Nature, my conatus actually feeds the cosmic conatus, actually helps to maintain the ecocosm in existence! It is in this human participation in the cosmic process that the meaningfulness of our relation to Nature may be found.[76]

According to Matthews, cosmic conatus is expressed through affirmative, joyful actions. Our lives attain meaning by our "*spiritual* capacity to keep the ecocosm on course, by teaching our hearts to practise affirmation, and by awakening our faculty of active, out-reaching, world-directed love."[77] Just as Cheney calls on the narratives of Northwest coastal Native Americans to justify his idea of storied residences, Matthews calls on the Hopi to justify her idea of wider identification. As described by anthropologist Laura Thomson, the central ideas of Hopi culture are

the unity and rhythm of nature; the correlating interdependence of nature and man; natural law as the basis for human law; the pervading power of prayer, ritual, art, and concentration on the "good."

. . . Order and rhythm are in the nature of things. It behooves man
to study them to bring his life into harmony with them. Only so
may he be free.[78]

For the Hopi, as well as for many other tribal people, establishing
the appropriate relationship with the greater Whole, or with the
cosmic Grandparents (or however else this may be described),
through rituals and prayers is not only necessary to insure salvation
and survival, but also to sustain the very being of the cosmos. Many,
tribal peoples regard it as an existential responsibility to perform tribal
rituals faithfully, for deviations would prevent the sustaining power
from the hidden, eternal, "sacred" world from flowing down through
the totem (located at the "world navel") into the tribe's world.
Without this cosmic energy, the chaos that lies outside the domains
of the tribe would begin to destroy the world-order. Tribal peoples
do *not* regard their world-founding myths and rituals as one of many
countless narratives, but instead as the "Truth." As totalizing, foundationalist thinkers, they are notoriously intolerant of strangers
coming from the chaotic domain *outside* the one, true world. Tribal
peoples whose very *identity* is grounded in the veracity of their
mythic systems would not regard such myth as a matter of negotiation with the many different voices of other tribes. Tribal people
often regard nonmembers not just as different, but as less than
human—as fearsome demons.[79]

Recognizing that otherness and difference often generate fear and
hostility, Enlightenment thinkers (influenced by Christianity) postulated a *universal* human nature that was embodied by people in
particular tribes, nations, or religious sects. Insofar as all people are
human, they are endowed with rights that must be respected, even
if a person is a total stranger, or a member of a competing group.
So long as Serbs, Croatians, and Muslims refuse to recognize the
humanity (however that may be defined) of the other party, and so
long as they feel threatened by these allegedly inhuman others, they
will feel justified in murdering them. Conceding that his contextualist ethic must deal with the fact that most of our social contacts

are with strangers, Cheney says that a contextualist ethic "must also make provisions for the specific problems to which it itself is prone, most obviously the loss of autonomy and degeneration into fascism. Such a contextualist ethic has yet to be developed."[80]

For Cheney's politics of difference to succeed, it must presuppose that each participant presupposes that every other participant deserves to be heard *simply by virtue of being human.* Given anxieties that the human will be defined in an exclusionary way (as it was, unfortunately, by many Enlightenment thinkers), however, proponents of the politics of difference usually reject such universal notions as essentialist and totalizing. But difference seems intrinsically related to identity. We can speak of *different* sorts of human beings only because we assume that there is something that all humans have in common. Problems arise in attempting to *specify* what is common, for specifying groups have often defined the human in a way that excludes or marginalizes those who don't belong to that group. The definition of the "human" should remain contested, but with a bias in favor of the widest possible definition.

While rejecting Ecosophy S's claim to being a privileged discourse, Cheney himself privileges the voices of oppressed people who can allegedly "spot distortions, mystifications, and colonizing and totalizing tendencies within other discourses."[81] Presumably, these oppressed people are somehow more human than their oppressors. According to Cheney, the "genuine encounters" embodied in storied residences provide a healthy alternative to Richard Rorty's view of language as a nonreferring free play of conversations that are either useful or frivolous.[82] Rorty's problem is that, although he dismantles the correspondence theory of truth, he leaves in place the now worldless transcendental subject, whose view of nature is summarized by the slogan "It's language all the way down." As an alternative to Rorty's view, an alternative that also finishes off the worldless transcendental subject, Cheney calls on none other than Heidegger's thought! Here, he conveniently forgets that some deep ecologists have already called on Heidegger's thought to articulate their own views. Moreover, Cheney fails to mention that Heidegger used his own thought to promote a political movement that was inconsistent with Cheney's own preference for respecting "otherness." In view of the dire political consequences of Heidegger's condemnation of Enlightenment universalism, I am skeptical of Cheney's appeal to Heidegger's thought to find a way of anchoring linguistic reference in the face of the postmodern theory that Cheney himself otherwise so admires.

Cheney extols Heidegger's differentiation between "fallen" and "primordial" language. The former, purporting to mirror nature for the sake of human ends, is uprooted from the world, whereas the latter, eschewing any total view, arises from "experiential embedment in the world."[83] Our "mother tongue" is contextualized, embedded discourse, whereas totalizing, essentializing language is the voice of the alienated, gnostic, dissociated subject. Cheney maintains that by adopting the stance of what Heidegger calls "meditative openness," we allow the world to speak through us. Hence, the notion that "It's language all the way down" is counterbalanced by the notion that "It's world all the way up." Not *the* world, of course, but the specific world constituted by the continually unfolding interplay of people and bioregion. Such a narrative amounts to a myth, a teleological story that binds together self and geography in healthy ways, wholly unlike the linear narrative of the self-grounding, alienated subject. Cheney observes that "we in the postmodern West are only beginning to see such possibilities in language."[84]

Whomever Cheney means by "we," a number of people have already experienced the terrible results of extolling regional dialectics while simultaneously condemning the "rootless" language of abstract modern universalism. During the 1930s, Heidegger praised the dialectic of his Alemannian region while supporting Hitler's attempt to save Germany from modernity's nihilistic, universalistic cosmopolitanism (code words for the "Jewish" ideals animating the dreaded League of Nations). National Socialism established the identity of the German Volk in part by so radically differentiating it from the Jews, whom they labeled subhuman vermin. In connection with anxieties about National Socialist myths of the *Volk's* rootedness in

German soil, language, and custom, Ynestra King has expressed concern about bioregionalists seeking to root people in an authentic language:

Although many of the people who work on bioregional projects are women (as is the case with most locally based movements), bioregionalism is problematic from an ecofeminist perspective. There are no social ethics in bioregionalism, so there is no a priori commitment to the liberation of women, or to opposing racism or to any other particular program. . . .

[B]ioregionalism is one piece of an overall Green strategy, but it does not in and of itself suggest a structure for a free society, especially for women—the goal of any feminist, eco- or otherwise.[85]

In support for his claim that storied residences provide moral orientation in a bioregional community, Cheney cites approvingly Tom Jay's claim that salmon are "literal *embodiments* of the wisdom of the land," "the embodiment of the soul that nourishes us all."[86] What, however, can be meant by "the soul"? Is this a cosmic wisdom principle, a unifying (dare one say the word?) power of which all things are manifestations? The salmon was a totem animal, a magical being through which transcendental power flowed in order to nourish and order tribal life. Establishing appropriate relationships with the totem animal meant not only receiving food for survival, but participating in rituals that contribute to cosmic regeneration.

Cheney does not explain how the coastal landscape of Northwest Native Americans became a "democracy of spirits." At times, he suggests that their experience was typical of all native peoples. As we saw earlier, however, Peggy Sanday has argued that only people living in bioregions with a plentiful food supply generate myths of origins that lend themselves to a democratic "partnership" society, similar to the one discussed by Cheney and Jay. People living in environments (bioregions) with less plentiful food supplies develop very different mythologies and more oppressive, patriarchal cultures. If Sanday is right, the storied residence of tribal people does reflect that people's natural environment, but in ways that are *not* necessarily conducive to Cheney's idyllic, neoromantic society in which "healthy" natives interact in terms of "healthy" social practices grounded in their "healthy" land. An uncharitable reading of Cheney's work would conclude that his obsession with "health" mirrors the fanaticism about "purity" and "health" exhibited by proponents of Nazism's religion of nature, as well as by contemporary reactionaries who extol the innocence of nature and condemn the tawdriness of urban life. Health cannot be conceived apart from disease, life apart from death, good apart from evil. Despite his critique of dualism, then, Cheney seems to retain the following binary oppositions: deep ecology versus his own ecofeminism; healthy versus unhealthy societies; fallen versus authentic language; inauthentic versus authentic existence; dominant versus oppressed discourse; masculinist versus feminist; storied residences versus abstract schemes; world versus word. Dualism is also evident in his account of the agrarian revolution, where he says that "contextualized discourse seems to emerge as our *mother tongue;* totalizing, essentializing language emerges as the voice of *the constructed subjective self,* the voice of dissociated, gnostic alienation."[87]

Cheney calls on postmodern theory's critique of foundationalism, totalizing narratives, and correspondence theories of truth to deconstruct deep ecology, but he does not appreciate the extent to which postmodern theory's critique of linguistic reference and truth undermines his own "storied residences." Why believe that narratives of tribal peoples are somehow more genuine or closer to the phenomena than the languages of science, law, contemporary fiction, or television documentaries? Postmodern theorists would quickly shoot down Cheney's claim that bioregional narrative is a "'gift' in which things come to presence," because this claim: upholds the metaphysics of presence; supposes that such a narrative is somehow closer to experience; asserts that authentic language grows from and articulates experience (instead of seeing that experience is always articulated by language); presumes that a bioregional narrative lacks its own hidden power-interests; and holds that such a narrative has somehow escaped being contaminated by the totalizing discourse of the dominant society.[88]

Cheney's selective adoption of postmodern theory is visible in the fact that, despite insisting on the perspectival character of knowing, he does not regard *his* perspective as just one among others, but rather as closer to the truth. Only by following his recommendations will "genuine revolution" (whatever that means) and "healthy" societies be possible. Having found the truth, he shows a condescending attitude toward misguided male deep ecologists, who can't tell a profound intuition from a repressed reaction formation. As Cheney admits elsewhere, the belief that one's own narrative is somehow "naturally" grounded tends to make one intolerant of the views of others. Cheney traps deep ecology within his own conceptual scheme, denying it any authentic voice of its own. Moreover, he offers a totalizing narrative of the past twelve thousand years of history. Ever since the agrarian revolution, we are told, things have been going downhill. "Totalizing" and "essentializing pressure" was set in motion when gatherer-hunters became the first farmers, who achieved a "centered" point of view in a "diminished" landscape ten thousand years ago, an era that antedates by several thousand years the start of Heidegger's history of being.[89] Offering an anachronistic interpretation of early farmers as totalizing essentialists (!), Cheney gives no account of the *motivation* that led people to support such a project. Although Griffin and Ruether point to death denial, Cheney seems to conclude that death anxiety would play no role in "healthy" societies.

Posing as a postmodern theorist who criticizes deep ecology for being a modernist (totalizing) movement that disguises itself as an antimodernist one, Cheney himself seems to be a premodernist posing as a postmodernist. The postmodern world he describes looks very much like one inhabited by tribal societies eradicated by urbanized humanity. Although critical of the machismo attitude displayed by some Earth First!ers, Cheney shares their nostalgia for an earlier epoch in which people supposedly lived "closer" to nature. In today's technological world, however, where does he think new storied residences would arise? Contemporary *tech noir* films hardly portray as socially tolerant and nature-loving the tribes who emerge from the rubble of industrial modernity. Even if we manage to avoid nuclear war, the salmon may well become extinct before the human inhabitants of Washington State generate a storied residence in which the salmon "literally *embodies*" the soul of the world.

Although Cheney frequently cites Donna Haraway's work, including her idea that discarding totalizing theories doesn't mean that we cannot develop large-scale theories (e.g., regarding ecosystemic functions), he does not grapple with her cyborg myth, which offers a far more disturbing, but possibly more realistic vision of the future. As we shall see in the next chapter, Haraway calls for new images and narratives to inspire imaginative responses by women and men to currently oppressive technological circumstances. In saying that she'd rather be a cyborg than a goddess, in claiming that there are no "privileged" perspectives even for the oppressed, and in taking an unblinking look at the technological possibilities unfolding around and through us, Haraway risks goring the sacred cows of some feminists and ecofeminists alike, in order to offer what she thinks may be a more effective political stance on postmodernity.

A BUDDHIST PROPOSAL   Before turning to the final chapter, I should like to examine briefly Cheney's claim that Ecosophy-S proponents—instead of calling on a totalizing position drawn from the *Upanishads,* "Thou art That" (*atman purusa Brahman*), to support their ideal of wider identification—would do better by turning to Buddhism's notion that enlightenment consists in "experiencing the *emptiness* of all *dharmas.*" According to Cheney,

The agnosticism expressed in the Buddha's "four-cornered negation" and the relentlessly "deconstructive" technique employed, for example, in Nagarjuna's dialectic are at odds with the Orientalism preferred by proponents of Ecosophy S.[90]

Among alleged proponents of Ecosophy S, Sessions and Devall mention but do not deal extensively with Asian religions. Fox's idea of psychological identification is similar to the *Upanishads'* insight that "thou art that," but he does *not* adhere to the idea of Brahman as an all-embracing, nondualistic absolute that includes but transcends creation. Because Arne Naess has been most influenced by Advaita Vedanta, perhaps his notion of wider identification involves the totalizing monism criticized by Cheney, but he himself praises Naess's emphasis on diversity and pluralism. Moreover, as we saw earlier, Naess was influenced by Mahayana Buddhism's contention that there are no enduring essences or substances. In addition to Naess, Gary Snyder and I have also interpreted wider identification as a process of self-emptying, rather than of self-expansion. Because ontological phenomenalism's deconstruction of the self seems to offer a nonmasculinist approach to the issue of identity and difference, I am puzzled by the fact that Cheney ignores this aspect of the deep ecology literature.

A long-time Zen student, Snyder takes seriously the critique of the "inflated-self" idea of enlightenment. For Zen, insight into the Buddha-nature (absolute emptiness) of all creatures eliminates identification with the self, because such insight reveals the self to be empty. Enlightenment means discovering that *nirvana* and *samsara* are "the same." Such a transformational insight enables one to enter ever more deeply into the uncertainties of everyday life. Ordinary activities like chopping wood and carrying water come alive by the paradoxical insight that one is *both* this embodied person-in-relationship-to-all-other-phenomena (dependent coproduction) *and* the "openness/emptiness" (*sunyata*) in which all those spatiotemporal phenomena can unfold into manifestness. The greater the surrender to emptiness, the greater the liberation from the anxiety, insecurity, and defensiveness produced by the illusion of separateness that arises from identifying with the ego. As Wilber would argue, however, gaining such insight is not a conceptual matter for the mental ego, but rather involves achieving higher, more integrated levels of awareness that transcend mental-egoic consciousness.

Mahayana Buddhism maintains that suffering arises from clinging. Cessation of clinging not only ends suffering, but also leads spontaneously to compassion for all beings. Such cessation can be misunderstood as the problematic type of "detachment" which some ecofeminists accuse deep ecologists of promoting. In Fox's recommendation that people develop a wider identification that would make possible more impartial judgments regarding family, other people, and nonhuman beings, some ecofeminists read him as saying that one should detach oneself from personal relationships in order to forge abstract relationships with nature. In my view, if Fox were to adopt Buddhism's ontological identification, instead of his own cosmological identification, he might avoid such criticism. Let me explain.

It is true that many men (and women) have sought a wider, impartial identification with the cosmos in order to find a "tower beyond tragedy," including the pain involved with close personal relationships. Indeed, many critics charge that the nondualistic "perennial philosophy" is a masculinist form of spiritual escapism. Although fear of dependency, betrayal, and loss is particularly problematic for men, women, however, also have such fear. Even for the apparently more relational mode of self-consciousness reported by many women, defensiveness and anxiety are often a problem. The latter are inevitable features of self-consciousness and individuation. People often adopt one of two pathological solutions to such anxiety: one involves identifying with the ego, a move often ascribed to men; the other involves identifying with others, a move often ascribed to women. Defending an isolated ego is one way to deny mortality; denying the ego in favor of others is another way to do so. Neither move is satisfying; both produce missing or deeply flawed relationships.[91]

The Buddhist deep ecologist, Joanna Macy, emphasizes that the solution to anxiety and defensiveness lies in discovering the radical emptiness of all phenomena, including the ego. This awakening involves neither smashing nor despising the ego, but rather disclosing its insubstantiality, as well as the emptiness of all other beings. Such insight melts the apparent solidity of ego, others, and things. Awakened, a person discovers that the world is constituted by a myriad of interrelated phenomena that manifest themselves moment by moment. No one and no thing is radically other. Although dualism vanishes, the result is not a pathological or regressive merging of self and other, but rather a higher order affirmation of relationships at all levels. Fully integrated and no longer terrified about death, a person spontaneously seeks to alleviate the suffering of all other sentient beings, which for Mahayana Buddhism includes virtually everything. Ceasing to identify with the ego (or with anything else) does not lead to distancing or to detaching oneself from personal relationships, but rather makes possible deeper and more particularized relationships.

Fear impedes love. Fear arises from separateness. Separateness occurs when we identify with something incomplete, partial, separate. Love follows from allowing ourselves to be opened up in a way that can allow things to be what they are. There is no abstract table of ethical judgments to guide compassionate behavior, nor is compassion itself abstract. Instead, it is guided by insight into the particular needs of those who are suffering. Compassion differs from pity, which encourages the suffering other to remain in the very condition that induces suffering. Compassion becomes more concrete and specific as one becomes increasingly open to one's family, friends, and larger social matrix, as well as to one's own particular ecological context. Snyder's Buddhist version of reinhabitation has many similarities to Cheney's storied residence. Discovering one's Buddha-nature, then, enables one to enter more deeply into *concrete relationships* not only with the human beings who constitute the moral community, but also with the other sentient creatures who constitute the larger family of life of which humanity is an integral moment.

Insight into particular needs and relationships, however, is complemented by a larger understanding of the complex processes involved in generating suffering. Being awakened means being capable of attending to minute detail, including the crying of a child, while simultaneously being cognizant of the bigger picture, including how particular social and economic structures encourage ecological and social devastation. An awakened person is neither aloof nor abstract, but individuated, concrete, capable of attending to things, able to perceive in unusual ways, and open to profound relationships with others. Paradoxically, such concreteness has something to do with affirming one's own corporeality, even while affirming the emptiness of all things. This very body, so the Mahayana tradition states, is the body of the Buddha. Becoming fully embodied means entering into relationship with all phenomena, but such embodiment requires ceasing to cling to any particular phenomenon.

Critics doubt that Buddhism can be of much help in easing the ecological crisis. For one thing, through much of its history Buddhism exhibited little interest in protecting wild nature in the way recommended by deep ecologists. Hinayana Buddhists believed that sentient beings included only humans and many animals. Further, the prevalence of Buddhism in China and Japan did not impede ecologically destructive practices, any more than peace-loving Christianity tamed the militaristic bent of Europe. The recent rise of "ecologized" Buddhism in the West can be attributed to the influence of people raised in a Christian and progressive context, for whom "compassion" means: (1) acting to prevent humankind from destroying itself by accidentally destroying the web of life; and (2) acting positively to create a less violent, more loving world for all. Certainly, social-oriented Buddhist sects have existed in various Asian countries, but in general Buddhism has exhibited little confidence in historical "progress." Westernized Buddhism, and here I think of a recent volume called *Dharma Gaia,* may constitute a new synthesis uniting compassionate insight into the interrelationship/emptiness of all things, with a commitment to democratic social transformation aimed at improving the situation for all life on earth.[92] Whether such an ecologized Buddhism, constituting a new narrative in modernity/postmodernity, could have a significant effect on current trends remains to be seen.

As we have seen, although deep ecologists criticize modernity's anthropocentric view of progress, most of them have broadly progressive views.[1] They seek to liberate all life; they laud ecological sensibility, but also believe that scientific rationality provides trustworthy knowledge; they offer narratives about humanity's developing maturity; they criticize authoritarian social structures; and they envision decentralized, democratic, ecological communities. Though disappointed with the consequences of modernity, social ecologists are even more explicit in affirming its emancipatory aims and defending its methods against the irrationalism allegedly discernible in aspects of deep ecology. Social ecology's grand narrative of human liberation affirms that reason can understand the potentiality being actualized in human and cosmic history. By virtue of such understanding, humans can generate ecologically harmonious societies. Despite differences, deep ecology and social ecology are offshoots of the utopian strain of counterculturalism.

Like other radical ecologists, most ecofeminists have reservations about modernity's ideal of progress, which is tainted by patriarchal attitudes. As progressive counterculturalists, however, ecofeminists envision a postpatriarchal (better) future; they devise their own grand narratives about the rise and potential disappearance of patriarchy's subjugation of women and nature; and they appeal to contemporary scientific accounts of interrelatedness to support their critique of modernity's atomistic, mechanistic, dualistic paradigm. Some ecofeminists join progressive theorists in arguing that postmodern theory's deconstruction of gender, identity, history, and agency makes radical criticism and social change inconceivable. But other ecofeminists support postmodern theory's criticism of the essentialist, teleological, potency-act metaphysics that has justified Western man's domineering grand narrative. Despite their hope for an improved future, then, many ecofeminists are suspicious of those progressive narratives that may be closely tied to the patriarchal ego's yearning for closure, unity, security, and control.

Such reservations notwithstanding, many ecofeminists agree with deep and social ecologists that large-scale critiques are needed to plan coherent socioeconomic alternatives to a rapacious capitalism, just as large-scale narratives are needed to inspire people to take part in realizing those alternatives. The question is, what sort of "planning" could conceivably address today's enormously complex social and ecological problems? The fact that the command economies of Eastern Europe not only wreaked massive ecological damage, but also generated social oppression and material deprivation, shows the serious limitations of centralized planning.[2] If centralized socialism is no longer a viable option for progressives, the interlocking forces of transnational capitalism seem little more appealing. In view of the ecologically destructive and culturally homogenizing trends of those forces, postmodern theorists call for a politics that emphasizes heterogeneity, difference, fracture, dynamic instability, and the local. Although agreeing that transnational corporations lead to many of the same environmental problems produced by centralized socialist economies, some radical ecologists nevertheless believe that only decentralized market economies are consistent with an ecologically sustainable, politically progressive future. Perhaps such local market economies, if infused with regional narratives promoting ecological attitudes, could (unpredictably) trigger off global shifts.

Recently, Wendell Berry and Alan AtKisson have debated the issue of local versus global ecological activism. Berry argues that planetary activism is impossible.[3] Everything important, we are told, involves relations with the local, and successful relations involve personal, subtle, concrete knowledge of particulars.[4] One does not converse with people using the abstract language of social causes, such as the civil rights movement or the women's movement, though initially such rhetoric may have been helpful for personal relations. By using the term "planetary," ecoactivists show that they have been seduced by the abstract. Acknowledging that no single place can be fully healthy until all others are, Berry nevertheless claims that it is "preposterous" for anyone to think that he or she can "heal the planet." From his viewpoint, there are in fact no planetary problems, only local ones. Since our problems stem from the fact that we are living wrongly, personally and communally, we must look for new, locally devised economic and political solutions to our local problems. The question

is not how to care for the planet but how to care for each of the planet's millions of human and natural neighborhoods, each of its millions of small pieces and parcels of land, each one of which is in some precious way different from all others.[5]

Only love can establish the relationship with a particular place needed to heal it, but love is absent in large-scale organizations and bureaucracies. We let them continue to wreak ecological destruction because we are not willing to live the simpler lives required to end our parasitical treatment of nature and poor people. The horrifying ecological "accidents" of the industrial age, such as Chernobyl and Bhopal, are in fact nature's revenge against human hubris. Only by humbly accepting our limited role in a particular place on Earth can we learn to live according to the limits imposed by Nature.

Alan AtKisson, though sharing Berry's conviction that local action is vital, and though acknowledging the fact that we don't have the competence to manage planets, argues that we do in fact have planetary problems that must be addressed.[6] Though ecological problems can be attributed to the action of specific individuals,

[m]any of the systems in which these individuals and households are embedded are global. Some of the individuals making those decisions and demands are controlling organizations whose reach, indeed whose very identity, is often global. To ignore this is to misrepresent the reality—a *global* reality, that is, admittedly hugely complex and beyond the ability of any one mind to comprehend fully. But that does not mean we should abandon the attempt.[7]

AtKisson maintains that the abstract language of civil rights has benefited social relationships, just as the Endangered Species Act has helped to protect rare flora and fauna. That these movements have not been more successful can be attributed in part to the inertia of existing social structures. For the city dweller who lacks Berry's proximity to land, loving the planet (and thus thinking globally) may be a crucial motivation for learning to act locally. As the Earth becomes girdled by electronic media, people everywhere can be in instantaneous contact and can thus effect local changes that have a global impact. Perhaps we must learn to think globally in order to act effectively at the local level.

Berry insists, however, that a good action must be "scaled and designed so that it fits harmoniously into the [local] natural conditions."[8] Unmoved by satellite photos of planet Earth, he insists that only his own neighborhood—"large, mysterious, painful, joyful, and lovely"—can inspire him. But AtKisson says that the same photos inspire in him a profound sense of appreciation for the beauty and complexity of planet Earth.[9] Such appreciation can inspire action at all levels. I agree with AtKisson that even if people cannot achieve a unified grasp of global ecological problems, macroscale analyses are helpful in coordinating local actions, whose combined effect may have global consequences. No one knows whether local actions, global actions, or a combination of the two will generate a new social constellation capable of forestalling the grim social and ecological consequences predicted by many different studies; no one really understands how major social changes occur; no one really knows whether the inertia of industrial modernity is so great that it will inevitably lead to ecological catastrophe, or whether a combination of luck, unexpected developments, and concerted action can avert disaster.

I retain hope for improving human affairs and humanity's treatment of nature, and I remain committed to democratic political principles. Yet Heidegger's yearning for a "new beginning" has made me skeptical both about modernity's utopian project of mastering nature and about the counterculture's yearning for a paradigm shift. Heidegger's wholesale condemnation of modernity went too far, for he ignored its emancipatory achievements and ideals. Nevertheless, he was right that modernity failed to see that every historical epoch conceals some things while revealing others. Modernity's conviction that science alone can reveal the truth has led moderns to marginalize the wisdom of tribal and non-Western cultures, women and lower-class males, along with insights drawn from religion, art, intuition, and the human body. The predictive success of science reinforced modernity's commitment to the project of mastering nature for the sake of human progress. But as many ecofeminists, Wilber, and Heidegger have suggested—though each in their own ways—modernity's drive for control is tied to death-denying, control-obsessed, mental-egoic consciousness. Insofar as many deep and social ecologists do not adequately expose the role played by death anxiety and the rage against finitude in modernity's domineering impulse, they are prone to replicating it. Hence, all radical ecologists must be wary of the potential consequences of calls for "global ecological zoning" and "centralized ecological planning."

Tempered by considerations of the difficulties facing life on this planet, chastened by recognition of the profound psychological, spiritual, and socioeconomic issues that impede personal, political, and institutional change, and wary of utopian movements, I still find myself intrigued by the possibility that humankind might evolve to a more integrative, less control-obsessed level of consciousness. Hope for such an evolutionary development dies hard in someone like myself, who has been influenced by the visions of radical ecological and New Paradigm counterculturalism. Even if such development does occur, however, I do not expect it to happen in the near future. Recent historical experience gives rise to skepticism about movements proclaiming humanity's entrance into a blissful era of social harmony and unmediated "oneness" with nature. Like postmodern theorists, I suspect that such movements risk becoming dogmatic and oppressive, despite their good intentions. And like Ken Wilber, I suspect that such movements often confuse progress toward a more integrated level of awareness with regress to a less integrated level.

In addition to the aforementioned considerations, my hopes for progressive social changes must take into account the fact that postmodern theory questions the essentialist, teleological, potency-act metaphysics to which so many modernists and counterculturalists alike have appealed to support their hopes for evolutionary social progress. Like Wilber, Bookchin, and certain deep ecologists, I remain attracted to the idea that there is a gradual, fitful, but generally progressive development of consciousness and society. Yet I recognize that the potency-act metaphysics explaining such development has also been used to justify hierarchy, androcentrism, and anthropocentrism. In place of neo-Hegelian analyses, according to which existing sociopolitical circumstances are the consequence of actualizing potential constituted by humanity's origin, postmodern theorists develop genealogical histories, according to which there is no "origin," "direction" or "goal" to history. Genealogical histories deny that social circumstances lack metaphysical necessity. Renouncing the nostalgic yearning for the One True Story, they argue that history is determined by manifold accidental, heterogeneous events, whose interconnections can never be fully grasped. Things *could* have been other than they are, but the complexity of historical circumstances and the lack of metaphysical necessity resist all attempts to find "reason" in history.

Despite the force of these claims, I find it worthwhile to explore self-critical versions of progressive narratives about cosmic and human evolutionary history. Far less optimistic than New Paradigmers are about the near-term prospects for radical social change, proponents of such self-critical narratives modify neo-Hegelian, progressive metaphysics in light of contemporary insight into organic and social evolution. There is a growing consensus among physical and social scientists that dynamic phenomena have inherent self-organizational tendencies. Many counterculturalists, radical ecologists, and postmodern theorists look to theories about self-organization and chaos as a way of explaining historical change. Chaos theory has the virtue of reconciling two apparently conflicting claims about human action. The first asserts social and ecological problems must be addressed at local levels; the second says that because many such problems do not respect national borders, those problems must *also* be addressed at a higher, more coordinated level, perhaps even global level. Chaos theory suggests that during stressful periods, particular changes at the *microlevel* of a given system can generate *macrolevel* changes involving a massive phase shift. In other words, local perturbations can trigger off global changes.

Some believe that chaos theory supports a genealogical, nondirectional explanation for such change, but others (including myself) believe that chaos theory may be consistent with a more developmental account of natural and human history. I join those who speculate that cosmos-generating, nondual awareness constitutes a "lure" that somehow cooperates with chaotic processes in a way that lends to the universe (and perhaps to human society) its apparent movement toward greater complexity, differentiation, and self-consciousness. Though constituting the non-thing like "origin" of all phenomena, nondual awareness does not act "externally" on those phenomena, but instead is an inherent ontological principle that conditions possible developmental trends. Something like mental-egoic consciousness may be a stage through which self-conscious life forms of whatever variety pass in their drift toward more integrated levels of awareness, though there is no necessity that such consciousness assume the highly dissociative, patriarchal, nature-dominating form it has taken in Western history. In the long run, increasing numbers of individuals may move to higher levels of awareness, an event that would presumably help to generate more liberating social structures and less-domineering attitudes toward nonhuman life. Such human development will fail, however, if such a huge percentage of humankind continues to be deprived of the material resources, emotional security, political freedoms, and education necessary to develop and to sustain a critical mass of self-conscious individuals, who are less dissociated and patriarchal than contemporary Western "man."

Hence, I agree with Greens that links must be strengthened among the social justice, nonviolence, ecological, and feminist movements. Moreover, I agree with those radical ecologists who propose new cosmic narratives that articulate humanity's kinship with all life, and which postulate that humankind is not forever doomed to continue to repeat the tragic errors that have caused such social misery and ecological destruction. Buddhism promised that individuals could free themselves from the ignorance that produces such suffering. Early Christianity proved attractive because it promised that divine providence, which was higher than natural necessity, could free people from the crushing power of fate. Tragically, modern Western "man" confused himself with this providential power. I regard humankind not as the lord of history, but rather as an active element in a historical process of awakening.

I can well understand why others would be skeptical of this interpretation. Nevertheless, if it is the case that something like an evolution of consciousness is occurring, if this process involves in part the development of levels of awareness that transcend the mental-egoic, and if the avatars of many spiritual traditions have evolved to those higher levels, then it behooves progressive and postmodern theorists alike to consider that such avatars would be dismayed, though hardly surprised, by the fact that mental-egoic society often turns the emancipatory insights of great avatars into religions justifying domination, patriarchy, superstition, and dogmatism. The tendency to use the concept of "providential" history as an excuse to justify ethnocentric, patriarchal violence (e.g., see the concept of "Manifest Destiny") can be resisted only by humility regarding humankind's relative insignificance in "the greater scheme of things," by awareness of mental-egoic humankind's tendency to portray its own death-denying Atman projects as the realization of that scheme, and by admission that finite humans are incapable of understanding this "greater scheme." Arguably, such humility, awareness, and admission would emerge only in connection with a shift beyond dissociative, patriarchal, death-denying mental-egoic consciousness.

Many postmodern theorists might agree that arrogance and death denial have promoted the totalizing grand narratives that, both in their religious and utopian-social versions, have produced untold social violence for centuries. In preferring a *genealogical* account of history, however, and in thus rejecting a directional account, some postmodern theorists would seem to have little reason to expect that a chaos-generated "phase shift" would generate a society that is less arrogant and death denying. The new society would simply be *different,* not necessarily "better" in terms of the emancipatory categories shared not only by modernists, but also by many postmodernists. Consider the following possibility. Some people argue that biological evolution tends to give rise to organisms and ecosystems capable of processing ever-greater quantities of energy/information in ever more efficient ways. Chaos theory says that phase shifts often occur when an existing system is faced either with collapsing or else with transforming itself so as to process energy/information more efficiently. Hence, chaos theory may be able to shed some light on evolutionary processes. Arguably, a major shift in *social* evolution might follow from advances in biotechnology, computerization, and electronic media, which are making possible extraordinary increases in processing energy/information more efficiently. But if a cultural phase shift were triggered off by such advances, why expect that the emerging culture would be emancipatory, meliorative, or environmentally sound? In fact, a chaos-generated future *may* be far more like a dystopian technological nightmare than the ecotopian world of radical ecologists, the utopian world of counterculturalists, or even the less ambitious "pluralistic" and less domineering worlds of some postmodern theorists. In a dystopian future, the demand for efficiency might reach such a pitch that concerns about freedom, individual well-being, self-realization, and ending domination would vanish, just as medieval concerns about otherworldly salvation disappeared with the advent of modern rationalism and materialism.

Since the massive social changes envisioned by radical ecology are unlikely to occur in the near future, perhaps the best that can be hoped for in the coming century is the emergence of society of the sort envisioned by some "critical postmodernists." Such postmodernism shares modernity's hope for meliorative social change, but shares postmodern theory's suspicion that utopian movements often lead to oppression, not liberation. Critical postmodernism often dispenses with a directional view of history, but is not necessarily incompatible with such a view. In section one of this chapter, we examine Gus diZerega's claim that an ecologically sustainable society could arise from ecologically informed versions of market liberalism, which can be understood as a chaotic system. In section two, we study the possibility that chaos theory and deconstructive postmodern theory point to a future consistent neither with postmodern theory's pessimism nor with radical ecology's utopianism, but rather with a critical postmodernism. Finally, in the last section, we investigate Donna Haraway's speculation that future humankind will overcome existing dualisms by becoming half-animal monsters and half-technological cyborgs. The reader will see that these three sections constitute, in part, critical postmodern rejoinders to deep ecology, social ecology, and ecofeminism.

CHAOS THEORY, EVOLUTIONARY LIBERALISM, AND RADICAL ECOLOGY Although most radical ecologists hold that liberal market systems lead to ecological suicide, some—including many Greens—argue that only a nonmonopolistic, de-centered market system, in conjunction with grassroots political pressure, can respond effectively to ecological problems without resorting to authoritarian measures. Recently,

Gus diZerega has attempted to reconcile chaos theory, the self-organizational procedures of market liberalism, and ecocentrism. DiZerega distinguishes between anthropocentric, Promethean, individual liberalism, on the one hand, and evolutionary liberalism, on the other. Individual liberalism, descended from Thomas Hobbes, John Locke, Jeremy Bentham, and J. S. Mill, and represented by contemporary authors as diverse as Robert Dahl, Murray Rothbard, and the Robert Nozick of *Anarchy, State and Utopia*, portrays the individual as the basic social unit. Evolutionary liberalism, descended from David Hume, Adam Smith, and John Ferguson, and represented today by authors like F. A. Hayek, Michael Polanyi, and Peter Berger, "conceives individuals in significant degree to be social products, even though society itself is the result of individual volition and creativity."[10] Unlike Promethean liberalism, evolutionary liberalism maintains that "self-organizing processes [are] as fundamental to social phenomena as the beings whose actions generate them."[11] What unites evolutionary liberalism with evolutionary theory "is that ordered relations can arise without anyone deliberately devising that order."[12] Self-organizing processes are at work in both the biological and the social realm.

DiZerega differentiates ecologically beneficial, evolutionary liberalism from the individualist liberalism that forms the basis of free market environmentalism.[13] In fact, free market environmentalism could help to solve some major ecological problems, particularly those attributable to centralized economic planning, by privatizing publicly held land and by developing new forms of ownership of "common" resources, including air, water, and oceans. Because individualist liberalism accords only instrumental value to nonhuman beings, however, it generates at least as many ecological problems as it may be able to solve. Conceding that evolutionary liberals like Hayek were anthropocentric in outlook, diZerega maintains that evolutionary liberalism's modest assessment of the capacities of individuals and its emphasis on self-organization lets him reinterpret it in a way largely consistent with ecocentric principles.[14]

Liberalism is usually noted for emphasizing individual liberty. Evolutionary liberalism retains that emphasis, but refuses to portray the individual as the basic unit of all social phenomena. Rather, evolutionary liberalism portrays individuals as participants in processes that transcend individual motive and understanding. Hence, diZerega resists attempts by animal rights activists to extend the principles of liberal individualism to nonhuman beings, as well as efforts to explain deep ecology as an extension of liberal individualism. He believes that such well-intended plans are "environmentally absurd," for ecological well-being follows not so much from emphasizing the well-being of individual organisms, but from encouraging species and their larger communities to flourish.[15] Individuals are important, but because they arise from larger communities, individuals cannot be legitimately portrayed as radically separate from and morally superior to those communities. In some sense, diZerega's version of evolutionary liberalism attempts to negotiate a course between old-style ecosystem ecology and contemporary population ecology. For the former, individuals are functions of ecosystemic processes; for the latter, ecosystemic phenomena are often the consequence of the activity of individual organisms. For diZerega, systems and individuals are not reducible to one another; rather, they exist and evolve by virtue of an unstable, dynamic, creative tension.

DiZerega would note that Bookchin's claim to being an ecological thinker is undermined by his emphasis on individual autonomy, which derives from Aristotle's doctrine of substances striving to realize themselves, or to actualize their potential. As we have seen, the Aristotelean-Spinozistic idea of self-realization is a major link between social and deep ecology. Though social and deep ecologists alike claim that individuals are constituted by internal relations, diZerega and many cultural ecofeminists complain that social and deep ecologists define individual organisms in a way that is too dependent on a masculinist atomism that is primarily concerned with protecting its autonomy and fulfilling its goals. DiZerega suggests that Bookchin's affinity-constituted ecological municipalities risk becoming self-enclosed communal atoms, interacting with other communal atoms primarily on the basis of suspicion and hostility. Postmodern theorists and many ecofeminists, who believe that democracy must be contentious, dynamic, and uncertain, would prefer that Bookchin's like-minded organic communities be fractured and thus opened to ongoing contestation over identity and values.

Many people in control-obsessed modernity have been drawn to *individual* liberalism not only because of its emphasis on individual autonomy and freedom, but also because its abstractions, including "economic man," provide greater predictive power than does evolutionary liberalism, which operates according to "rules of thumb" and does not pretend to provide an intellectual framework for solving all moral and political disputes. As opposed to social engineers who use the predictability of abstract economic man to enhance their planning ability, *evolutionary* liberals "seek to *cultivate* the conditions for desirable change rather than to plan, manage, direct, or control such change—either by engineering it or by subjecting action to absolute standards of individual justice."[16] DiZerega agrees with deep ecology that cultivating an ecological sensibility is an important condition for ecologically sound social changes. Yet he would also warn deep ecologists not to replicate modernity's control impulse, such as, by calling for a U.N.-sponsored "unified integrated ecosystem approach" in order to prevent wilderness destruction.[17] Like deep ecologist Gary Snyder, diZerega feels that calling for the United Nations or some other centralized organization to protect the planet is like inviting foxes to guard the henhouse.[18] Though a centrally controlled movement "from above" would be counterproductive, diZerega maintains that local, grassroots action is most effective when undertaken in the light of available information about the larger social, economic, and ecological context.

Ecosystems and human societies are so complex, however, that no amount of information can hope fully to understand or to predict their workings. Since control is predicated on knowledge, and since such knowledge is lacking in many cases, efforts to control things often generate "solutions" that are worse than the "problems" supposedly being solved. Attempts to control human interaction are often motivated by the desire to harmonize human relationships. The recent collapse of Eastern European socialist countries indicates that centralized planning cannot produce the desired harmony, not least because the requisite knowledge for central planning is *always* lacking. DiZerega believes that the market order, more so than any alternative, can effectively, though not perfectly, harmonize the plans of many different individuals with different values and goals.[19] DiZerega uses Hayek's term "catallaxy" to describe an economic system that serves not a single set of ends, as in a corporation's budget, but rather the great host of different and incommensurable ends of the members of a given community.[20] Many ecologists use equilibrium thermodynamics to describe ecosystems in terms of energy flows, budgets, productivity, efficiency, yield, and so on. Such "bionomics," according to diZerega, "is ecology as 'economy,' not 'catallaxy'."[21]

As opposed to reductionistic bionomics, which is consistent with an anthropocentric nature-management ethos, a holistic view of ecology, which emphasizes the vast complexity and interrelatedness of terrestrial life, is a catallaxy that takes into account the aims of many different forms of life. Because this self-organizing, self-generating web of life cannot be evaluated in terms of any one goal or standard, it makes no sense to speak of making the system more "efficient." Yet just as Hayek sought to encourage in the socioeconomic domain those conditions that would make possible the harmonious realization of the greatest number of individual aims, so diZerega recommends promoting in the ecological domain those conditions that would encourage the flourishing of the greatest variety of organisms.[22]

DiZerega contrasts his views with those of Bookchin, who contends that cooperation and mutual assistance alone can create healthy communities. Emphasizing the link between limited competition and the Bookchin's prized individuation, diZerega notes that the Greek *polis,* so admired by Bookchin, was itself a hotbed of rivalry. Such rivalry may have been the social context necessary for the Greeks' extraordinary creativity.[23] DiZerega denies that market competition necessarily fosters sociopathic economic man, that is, an abstract, wholly self-interested economic agent. The abstractness of the market lies not in individuals, who rarely resemble economic man, but rather in impersonal *procedures* that necessarily proceed on the basis of abstract and general rules if they are to apply equally to all. Although social Darwinists tried to justify raw capitalism by overemphasizing competition and downplaying cooperation in nature, Bookchin overreacts by virtually denying a place for competition in nature. Agreeing with Bookchin's critique of monopoly capitalism, diZerega nevertheless argues that the competition at work in market economies is analogous to the competition occurring in nature. He cites Holmes Rolston III, who writes that

like business, politics, and sports, ecosystems thrive on competition. In a natural community the cougars are the critics (if we may put it so) that catch the flawed deer, and thereby build better ones, as well as gain a meal. Alternatively, the fleet footed deer test out any cougars slow enough to starve. . . . [I]n both [human and natural] communities, helping is subtly intwined with competition. There is a biological, though not a cultural, sense in which deer and cougar cooperate, and the integrity, beauty, and stability of each is bound up with their coactions.[24]

Liberal market societies channel competition in terms of abstract procedures that minimize antagonism and promote the cooperation required for markets to work. Bookchin himself acknowledges that his utopian vision is threatened by the fact that historically, most small organic societies have been either indifferent or hostile toward strangers and have engaged in constant wars and feuds (here, one again thinks of ancient Greece).[25] He offers no plausible evidence for why the situation would be any different in a world of ecomunicipalities, however, nor does he explain convincingly how the current world would devolve into the decentralized one he envisages. An advantage of liberal democracy is that it calls for guarantees (in principle, at least) that protect minorities from the tyranny of the majority. Clearly, such guarantees would need to be included in Bookchin's ecomunicipalities.

Anticentrist liberals note that the impersonal procedures of the market offer a context in which people of different ethnic, religious, and political affiliations can interact in ways that moderate local conflicts. Market systems presuppose that the activities of individual agents produce unintended, but socially beneficent consequences. From Adam Smith's notion of the "invisible hand," Hegel apparently derived his notion of the cunning of Reason, according to which the efforts of individuals lead to an outcome that is both unknown to them and also more universal than their own particular goals. DiZerega emphasizes that self-organization is the spontaneous and unintended consequence of the actions and interactions of countless individuals. Hence, when Bookchin speaks of self-organization as the consequence of intentional, face-to-face decisions made by autonomous individuals cooperating to achieve a common goal, he fails to grasp what ecologists, economists, and chaos theorists mean by self-organization. Ilya Prigogine's concept of order out of chaos refers to how ordered structure—in chemical processes, ecosystems, language, society—arises spontaneously and unintentionally from the apparently chaotic processes of many particulars. The enormous variety of terrestrial organisms has arisen not because the biosphere is following a plan, but rather because the interaction of millions of organisms, species, and their environments creates conditions that foster the emergence of new and diverse types of organisms. Rolston remarks that

there is a kind of order that arises spontaneously and systematically when many self-concerned units jostle and seek their own programs. . . . In culture, the logic of language and the integrated efficiency of the market are examples. . . . In nature, our ecosystem systematically generates a spontaneous order, an order that exceeds in richness, beauty, integrity, and stability the order of any of the component parts, an order that feeds (and is fed by) the richness, beauty, and integrity of these component parts.[26]

As we saw in an earlier chapter, Fritjof Capra maintains that chaos theory can explain how order, interaction, and evolutionary development occur at virtually all levels, from the molecular to the social and galactic. Drawing on the work of Prigogine, according to whom new levels of complexity are spontaneously achieved (through "broken symmetry") when an existing dissipative structure is subjected to energy flows or such perturbations that extant structural arrangements cannot process, Capra maintains that nature is characterized by "the progressive increase of complexity, coordination, and interdependence." The science of chaos lets us conclude that

evolution is basically open and indeterminate. There is no goal in it, or purpose, and yet there is a recognizable pattern of development. The details of this pattern are unpredictable because of the autonomy living systems possess in their evolution as in other aspects of their organization. In the systems view the process of evolution is not dominated by "blind chance" but represents an unfolding of order and complexity that can be seen as a kind of learning process, involving autonomy and freedom of choice.[27]

Such talk of the progressive evolution of complexity, autonomy, and freedom is music to Bookchin's ears, but he argues that neither systems theory nor chaos theory can explain evolutionary developments, that is, why one organizational level "supersedes or incorporates another one."[28] Needed for such an explanation is the idea that the universe has an inherent tendency to develop higher levels of complexity, differentiation, order, spontaneity, and freedom.[29] There would seem to be only a vanishing difference, however, between Bookchin's view that there is a cosmic *nisus* toward complexity and chaos theory's view that the cosmos has a *tendency* to generate order. Both views seem inadequate to me, however, insofar as they lack the idea that generative, nondual awareness acts as a "lure" which helps to give a measure of direction to chaotic development.

Though agreeing with Prigogine that unstable societies evolve fastest and that market societies involve dynamic instability, diZerega maintains that the market system alone is not a sufficient condition for promoting the (r)evolutionary changes needed to confront ecological problems.[30] Bookchin criticizes capitalism for its restless expansionism, but he also asserts that "in nature, balance and harmony are achieved by ever-changing differentiation, by *ever-expanding* diversity."[31] Although "diversity" in market societies is often restricted to an array of repetitive consumables, market societies do in fact encourage extraordinary diversity in many areas. Indeed, without the diversity generated by the market's unpredictable free play and self-organization, material abundance would not be possible in Bookchin's ecomunicipalities.

DiZerega attributes Bookchin's failure to comprehend self-organization's role in ecology, economics, and evolution to two problems: "his Promethean ideal of humankind's taking control of its own evolution and his opposition to mediation of any sort between one person and another."[32] Bookchin's preference for face-to-face communities is admirable as a defense against a collectivist oppression of individuals, but underemphasizes the extent to which humans can neither foresee nor control the consequences of their interactions. Bookchin's concern with personal control undermines his effort to wed anarchist humanism with ecology. DiZerega asserts that market societies are not only more consistent with ecological principles and freer from the threat of fascism than face-to-face municipalities, but also that people in such like-minded municipalities usually suffer from stifling conformity.[33] The anonymous, abstract, and cosmopolitan environments of large cities have often helped to generate enormous creativity. Bookchin himself values cities because their large populations provide enough like-minded individuals for affinity groups and viable communities, committed to community well-being, instead of militarism, consumerism, and exploitation. But diZerega maintains that the face-to-face relations in Bookchin's ecological municipalities would inevitably give way to impersonal market relations, when trade is established among confederated communities. Trade of any magnitude requires complex transportation, banking, and communication networks that are incompatible with face-to-face relationships. Further, trade and markets generate consequences that are not intended by, and thus are not in the control of, the individuals who trade on the market.

Seeking to surpass the anthropocentrism of Hayek's liberalism, diZerega's version of evolutionary liberalism calls on ecological science, Aldo Leopold, and deep ecology to emphasize that humans are part of a larger life community. In a way consistent with some postmodern theorists, diZerega explains that ethical obligations are shaped by the types of relationships that obtain in a given community. People show respect for other members of the community and regard it as immoral to treat any member solely as a resource. Hence, if people acknowledged that they were part of a larger life community, they could not ethically treat nonhuman forms of life merely as raw material. Evolutionary liberalism holds, then, that liberal *institutions* are not what gives rise to the ecological crisis. Instead, the crisis follows from the fact that anthropocentric, power-craving, modern individuals understand those institutions primarily as ways of enhancing personal wealth and gaining control over nature.[34] Shifting to an ecological sensibility, one that discloses humans as part of a larger life community, would not change the impersonal character of market procedures, but it would place certain limits on market practices, just as prohibitions against slavery did more than a century ago.

Market mechanisms can be used by individuals and groups inspired by ecological sensibility, nurtured by new cosmic narratives, and motivated by concerns that are not merely private, anthropocentric, or prudential. For example, the Nature Conservancy preserves protect ecologically important land by purchasing it on the marketplace.[35] Nevertheless, such individuals and groups must decline opportunities, offered by the market, to maximize their financial incomes. Such opportunities are *not* ignored, however, by people who deny that they are part of a larger life community. Agreeing with ecologists that neoclassical, anthropocentric, liberal economics is leading to ecological catastrophe,[36] diZerega asserts that

we cannot simply accept the libertarian argument that whatever happens within the market is better than any practicable alternative. The market has biases that, if left to themselves, are profoundly destructive to certain nonanthropocentric values. Certain things need to be protected from full exposure to market forces, particularly maintaining the viability of species and ecosystems.[37]

According to diZerega, individual liberalism's concepts of *property* and *ownership* are what give rise to so much ecological destruction. The despotic idea that one has the absolute right to control one's property, even to the point of destroying all life on it, must be curbed. Rights to property "should reflect not just efficiency in meeting human desires, but should also take account of our place in communities other than the purely human."[38] Moreover, in addition to requiring that "utilization of a renewable resource must maintain fertility required for an indefinite period," new laws would require that property must be used so as to preserve biological diversity: hence, causing the extinction of a plant or animal could be justified only in the most extreme cases.[39] Recalling Hayek's standard for public policy, namely, that it must seek to increase for any given person "the prospects that the overall effect of all changes required by that [public policy] order will increase his chances of attaining his ends," diZerega says that since the "ecological community values species rather than individuals, the needed modification here is only that each species should generally have its opportunity to flourish relatively unhindered by human activities."[40]

If diZerega is right, if a cultural paradigm shift consistent with democratic ideals and ecological sensibility *does* occur, it will happen as the unpredictable outcome of the actions of many individuals, who agree that enhancing human life cannot be accomplished at the expense of the rest of life on earth:

Given the incredible diversity of both ecosystems and human activity, allowing many people to work out an indefinite number of approaches is likely the wisest approach. Successes will be emulated and failures will be shunned, but the inevitable failures will cover a far smaller area than [those put at risk by] attempts at national planning.[41]

To gain credibility among radical ecologists, diZerega would have to explain how evolutionary liberalism's different views about property and its more respectful attitude toward nature could possibly displace the anthropocentric, nature-dominating attitudes of *individual* liberalism. Wilber maintains that individual liberalism's concepts of property are necessary correlates of the mental-egoic level of consciousness. He argues that mental-egoic consciousness will eventually evolve into a more integrated level of consciousness, which will have a far less despotic concept of property and a more satisfying, less dissociative relationship with the larger life community. DiZerega would probably regard Wilber's views of human evolution not as a catallaxy taking into account the aims of many different forms of life, however, but rather as a restrictive spiritual economy that focuses solely on the human. Yet by not adopting Wilber's directional view of history, diZerega leaves himself without an adequate account of *why* people might move toward an ecological sensibility.

Today, people are becoming more aware of humanity's interdependence with life on earth. But far from leading to an ecological sensibility that might help to trigger a social "phase shift," such growing ecological awareness could be factored into market decision making and government planning in a way that simply reinforces anthropocentric mental-egoic consciousness. For Wilber, there is no necessity that the shift to level five consciousness will occur in *human* history, though it is inevitable that such a shift will occur for lifeforms *somewhere* in the universe. Moreover, even if the shift to level five consciousness *does* occur in human history, there is no reason to think that it will happen before mental-egoic humans have first turned the entire planet into a functioning artifact. If a move toward a more integrated level of consciousness does occur in human history, that move might not take place until humans are beginning to take control of other planets in the solar system. Neither chaos theory nor neo-Hegelian metaphysics offers any certainty that humankind will move toward a society of the kind favored by radical ecologists.

Despite such considerations, I find much of value in diZerega's evolutionary liberalism. Karl Hess, Herman Daly and John Cobb, Jr.,

Robyn Eckersley, and Lester Milbrath have also devised interesting approaches to pluralistic, democratic, decentralized, market-oriented, Green societies.[42] It is also worth noting that Arne Naess's rejection of a "single 'postmodern' paradigm, . . . that humans on this planet have in common," and his corresponding emphasis on pluralism, seem consistent with evolutionary liberalism's claim that major systemic shifts occur by virtue of many individuals pursuing sometimes conflicting courses.[43] Just as Naess regards it as a virtue that great philosophical texts inspire many divergent interpretations, so he welcomes the proliferation of total views ("useful fictions") and ecosophies, since diversity adds to the richness of possible solutions. He sides with moral pluralists like Christopher Stone and Eugene C. Hargrove against J. Baird Callicott, who supposedly seeks "the [one] coherent, adequate theory" for environmental ethics.[44] Although presupposing that ecological activists would agree that the natural world has some "intrinsic value," Naess leaves this idea so open that it could be embraced by people from a multitude of different viewpoints, including evolutionary liberals. He opposes a "gigantic quasi-green movement," for a

trend towards a uniform, not to say monolithic, way of conceiving reality, may be an ominous sign of stagnation of the total human enterprise on this planet, a sign of cultural conformity. Environmentalism and the quest for a greener society will not, I hope, contribute to conformity, but it might! *This is the reason I take these abstract themes seriously and wish many others will do the same.*[45]

Recently, Naess distanced himself from the view that a "dramatic, sudden turn-around in social and political variables" will be necessary to deal with the still-growing ecological crisis.[46] He is optimistic that the increasingly influential, pluralistic ecology movement will let humanity muddle through its current problems. By the twenty-second century, an increasing number of "mature" people may identify more widely with and expand their capacity for caring to nature, but Naess argues that the widespread emergence of such maturity will be a longer-term process. For many years to come, "intensively energetic people . . . will tend to aspire to bigness rather than to greatness: Creativeness, even 'fortitude and generosity' (Spinoza), but without pretension of greatness in the cultural sphere."[47] Somewhat surprisingly, he insists that energetic, creative entrepreneurs be allowed "ample elbow room," because their controversial and sometimes destructive work is required "in any dynamic society."[48] He recommends that entrepreneurial activity and conspicuous consumption be limited by a strong ecological and ethical framework, that political tolerance for grave social injustice should be minimized, and that there be opportunities for people to explore remaining free nature. But he goes on to ask:

Why portray a society which seemingly needs no big entrepreneurs, only organic farmers, modern artists, and mild naturalists. A capitalist society is in a certain sense a rather *wild* society. We need some degree of wildness, but not exactly the capitalist sort. The usual utopian green societies seem so sober and tame. We shall need enthusiasts of the extravagant, the luxuriant, the big. But they must not dominate.[49]

Instead of trying to eliminate wild spirit, then, we should try to cultivate it, broaden it, cross-fertilize it with more affirmative, less predatory kinds of exuberance and excessiveness. Bookchin might conclude that such remarks show the real social poverty of deep ecology. In fact, however, Naess's wild entrepreneurial spirit and diZerega's evolutionary liberalism would in some respects seem consistent with Bookchin's praise for the excess, abundance, excessiveness, and eroticism that characterized the anarchist avant-garde, in comparison with which his ecological municipalities seem rather tame.

CHAOS THEORY, RADICAL ECOLOGY, POSTMODERN THEORY, AND CRITICAL POST-MODERNISM   For chaos theorists, chaos does not mean sheer disorder, endless differentiation, and irrationality, though some postmodern theorists seem to interpret it in this way. At one time, for example,

Foucault viewed madness as the "other" of domineering modern rationality. Moreover, he saw Georges Bataille's de-centered sensuality, polymorphous aestheticism, and economy of excess as a possible avenue of resistance to and even an alternative to modernity's control-obsession. Yet there are dangers involved in Bataille's celebration of the "sacred" dimension of horror, death, madness, chaos, and profligacy. Opposing the homogenizing power of rationalist modernity, he affirmed the heterogeneous: what is marginal, different, disorderly, demented, and erotic. Like Nietzsche, Bataille complained that the bourgeoisie are governed by utilitarian, survival-oriented considerations. Out of touch with the wastefulness of the capitalism that had originally generated great wealth, the early twentieth-century bourgeoisie preferred frugality and limits. To those who think that a mature humanity would live in harmony with nature, Bataille replied that "*conscious humanity has remained a minor;* humanity recognizes the right to acquire, to conserve, and to consume rationally, but it excludes in principle *nonproductive expenditure.*"[50] Such expenditures include "luxury, mourning, war cults, the construction of sumptuary monuments, games, spectacles, arts, perverse sexual activity," all of which have no end beyond themselves.[51] Only such expenditures can violate and transgress the hardened boundaries that stifle life in the rationalist order of modernity. Bataille interpreted the Native American potlatch ritual as an instance of this nonutilitarian excessiveness. The potlatch replaces the stability of hereditary fortunes with the "excessive exchange" of a "deliriously formed ritual poker."[52]

According to Bataille, a bourgeois man is like a son whose patriarchal father expects him to live prudently, except for "a little harmless recreation." Not permitted to speak about what really fires him up, however, the son "is obliged to give people the impression that for him no *horror* can enter into consideration."[53] A fully alive, emancipated man would act "in a way that allows for the satisfaction of disarmingly savage needs, and it seems able to subsist only at the limits of horror." For such a man, drawn to destroy all established authority, "a peaceful world, conforming to his interests," would be little more than a "convenient fiction."[54] Despite its capacity for generating and squandering wealth, however, capitalism represses the terrifying, violent, and impure dimensions of human nature, and thus splits humanity into two classes: bourgeoisie and worker. Bearing the dissociated aspects of humanity, the working class exists in an ignoble, repressed, and apathetic—that is, inhuman—condition. A workers' revolution would consist not so much in seizing control of the means of production, but rather in overthrowing the constricting, prudential, survival-oriented vision that characterizes the dehumanized, denaturalized modern world. "Human life," Bataille writes, "cannot in any way be limited to the closed systems assigned to it by reasonable conceptions."[55] Supposedly, only by giving way to the illogical impulse to squander what might rationally have been preserved, only by entering into insubordination against the recurring demand that life must balance its accounts and satisfy "needs," can humanity create "unproductive values." Although such talk has a recurrent appeal, we must be clear that—at least for Bataille—such values include extravagance, sacrifice, violence, horror, sacred ritual, and unbounded desire, but "the most absurd of these values, and the one that makes people the most rapacious, is *glory.*"[56]

Rapacious glory is tied to the most prodigious form of waste and sacrifice, war, so highly praised by the reactionary modernist, Nietzschean aesthete, and masculinist fantasizer Ernst Jünger. Bataille's apparent support for the workers' revolution cannot disguise his problematic affiliation with Jünger's protofascist thinking. Given that postmodern theory is so indebted to the writings of Sade, Nietzsche, Bataille, Artaud, and Blanchot, it is little wonder that critics suspect that it flirts with fascist aestheticism and celebrates a problematic attitude toward unleashing the "affective forces." Habermas, for instance, wonders "how the subversively spontaneous expression of these forces and the fascist canalizing of them really differ."[57] Celebrating the limitless appetite of the schizophrenic "desiring machine" in *Anti-Oedipus,* Félix Guattari and Gilles Deleuze attacked the bourgeois subject and its craving for controls, norms, and systems. But rejecting all normative limits while urging maximum expression of desire may end in a type of fascism.[58]

For Jünger, glorying in the intense aesthetic pleasures of war was an opportunity for those elite few who showed no pity for those who clutched pointlessly to their senseless little bourgeois lives. Some vestige of historical memory is required to recall the consequences to which such aestheticism, purged of every trace of the compassion characteristic of the "degenerate" biblical traditions, led in a previous generation. Many radical ecologists are not tempted by such aestheticism, since they focus not on human imagination, but rather on the manifold expressions of creativity in the whole community of life. Deep ecologists often emphasize Buddhism's ideal of compassion. Ecofeminist Charlene Spretnak argues that Christian mercy and justice can play a vital role in inspiring ecological activism.[59] Social ecologists like Bookchin, who emphasizes the avant-garde, unconstrained sensuality, and the ideal of the individual as a self-creating work of art, come closest to Bataille's aesthetic vision. Bookchin's appeal to social justice and his critique of authoritarianism, however, clearly distance him from the fascist dimensions of that vision. Like Bookchin, John Clark refuses to concede that exploring the imaginative aesthetic domain involves flirting with fascism. Arne Naess would agree that gaining access to the "wild" dimension of the human involves, in part, giving rein to the aesthetic imagination. It would be a big mistake, then, to assume that nonrational practices inevitably lead toward fascist or authoritarian politics. Indeed, without imagination people could not envision *alternatives* to existing social arrangements and cultural attitudes. Those who overemphasize "rationality" may themselves be gripped by a masculinist control impulse that promotes authoritarian attitudes.

Given the tendency of religions to squelch desire in the name of allegedly higher virtue, proponents of erotic aestheticism suspect that mercy, justice, and compassion are really code words for renunciation of desire. Alice Holzhey-Kunz argues that desire is so problematic because acknowledging it exposes one to anxiety about the fact that humans seem to lack an ontological foundation. Being human means to be mortal, groundless, linked to nothingness. Since desire itself is groundless and thus unjustifiable, its presence elicits anxiety. Further, desire generates a sense of guilt, because desire usually puts one at odds with social expectations. Modern emancipatory movements helped to alleviate these problems by reconceiving desire as basic biological and social *needs,* the satisfaction of which one had a *right* to demand, without incurring either anxiety or guilt.[60] Deep ecology's claim that humans have a right to satisfy their "vital needs" is indebted to emancipation ideologies. Arguing that "need is the perverted form of desire," Holzhey-Kunz says that the aim of "authentic human emancipation, is not to give up desire but rather to learn to desire."[61] By turning desire into need, people hope for a kind of fulfillment and wholeness that will overcome the futility of existing as mortals who desire without justification. Affirming desire and mortality requires recognizing the death-denying, world-controlling tendencies of the narcissistic ego bent on satisfying its "justifiable" needs. Acknowledging the suffering produced by the ego does not call for violence against it, but rather for compassion borne of understanding the difficulties involved in being human. By way of contrast, the violent, glory-worshipping aestheticism of Bataille seems to say that affirming desire involves annihilation of the ego. There are problematic masculinist overtones in this regressive craving to alleviate the pangs of individual existence, and to regain a lost prior unity, by unleashing a chaotic frenzy that transgresses all limits.

In reviewing Norman O. Brown's recent book, *Apocalypse and/Or Metamorphosis,* the "sur(reg)ionalist" Max Cafard suggests that chaos, understood as sensual abundance and life-affirming excess, is consistent with an emancipatory vision. By regarding humanity as part of nature's "self-manifesting, outpouring, effusion," Cafard reports, Brown "is implicitly attacking the myth of scarcity that has been so indispensable to all systems of domination. As Bataille maintains, the basic problem for all societies has been how to expend the excess, the surplus."[62] Brown says that "capitalism has proven itself more dynamic—i.e., Dionysian—than socialism. Its essential nature is to be out of control: exuberant energy, exploiting every opportunity, to extract a surplus."[63] Interpreting Spinoza as calling for "an identification with the exuberant life of the whole," Brown seems to reveal an affinity with Naess's version of deep ecology. Yet deep ecologists also call for asceticism, satisfying only vital needs, limits to growth, and conservation in a way that seems inconsistent with the idea of nature's prodigality and extravagance. To avoid the interrelated errors of need-based asceticism and utilitarianism, Cafard argues, radical ecologists will have to develop an *authentic* Dionysianism to replace the pseudo-Dionysianism of capitalism: "If the Left is to have a future, it must begin thinking again about the taboo concept of freedom and about the wonders of power."[64] Like many postmodern theorists influenced by Bataille, Artaud, and Sade, Brown condemns modernity for having excluded from the world the threatening Other of death, madness, chaos, and excess. In attempting to control the Other life and reason, as many critics have argued, people end up magnifying that Other. Supposedly, only by fusing madness and reason, life and death, in a Heraclitean unity of opposites can modern humanity overcome its crippling dualisms.

At first glance, Brown's emphasis on overcoming such binary dualisms would seem to be consistent with Wilber's claim that level five consciousness would reintegrate what mental-egoic consciousness has dissociated. Wilber would not agree with this interpretation of Brown's work, however. For Wilber, a more integrated level of awareness continues to distinguish between different types of phenomena and different levels of awareness, even while it integrates them. Brown's call for a fusion of madness and reason threatens to collapse such levels, thereby encouraging psychological regression. Although perhaps not as much as in *Life Against Death,* Brown still verges on committing the "pre-trans-fallacy," in that he encourages the mental ego to recover the blissful, prerational, or even irrational states of early childhood. These states are characterized not only by a lack of ego boundaries, but simultaneously by a limitless narcissism.

In some ways, Brown's critique of control-obsessed rationality resembles the critique made by French postmodern theorists influenced by Bataille, Artaud, and Blanchot. According to Martin Jay, Bataille's attacks on vision (symbol of rationality) and his celebration of headlessness and the "solar anus" were only one instance of a more generalized revolt against reason on the part of many twentieth-century French intellectuals.[65] If rationality is linked with God, but if the God of reason is dead, then the only access to the sacred and the ecstatic would seem to involve exploring forbidden bodily pleasures and emotional realms. Some contemporary French feminists have also moved in this direction.

Like Wilber, however, I would say that much is put at risk in moving in this direction. The control-obsessed rationality of mental-egoic consciousness is not to be sacrificed in favor of, or even "fused" with, bodily-orgiastic madness. Postmodern celebrations of madness and bodily ecstasy, despite their more contemporary vocabulary, are reminiscent of themes voiced by early twentieth-century, proto-fascist, European intellectuals. Rather than calling for replacing solar rationality with neo-Nietzschean, neo-Dionysian bodily intoxication and excess, I recommend that people explore meditation and other practices that encourage a shift to an increasingly nondual level of awareness, one that neither obliterates nor fuses with mental-egoic consciousness, but rather simultaneously transcends and preserves it, in what Hegel might call an *Aufhebung*. Because people at this more integrated level of awareness increasingly recognize the eternal dimension that permeates all life, and because they are thereby increasingly freed from the death anxiety that generates an obsession with controlling the body, emotions, and nature, such people can begin to experience bodily and emotional ecstasy in a way that does not require the obliteration of ego and reason.

Though Foucault never entirely ceased being suspicious of rationality, and though he would not have agreed with Wilber's idea of consciousness evolution, he gradually began to think of chaos not as madness that constitutes the liberating opposite of constraining order, but rather as an order-generating principle. In 1979, he led a seminar on Friedrich Hayek's *Individualism and Economic Order* and Ludwig Von Mises, *The Anti-Capitalist Mentality*. These economists maintained that the lack of central controls and the presence of apparent disorder in liberal market economies create maximum possibilities for the emergence of new social formations and economic relationships, especially in stressful circumstances that might undermine a centralized system. The intentional activities of individuals in market systems do not govern the outcome of their collective behavior; markets generate order out of apparent chaos. Similarly, Foucault argued that power must be grasped in its productive and formative dimensions. Power structures are not global forms imposed from above; rather, they arise from and are sustained by the unintended interactions of myriad agents operating at the microlevel.

Other postmodern theorists have also tried to derive from chaos theory an interpretation of how people acting at the local level could achieve a measure of freedom despite the centralizing power of technological modernity. Lyotard's vision of a de-centered, de-totalized subject operating according to paralogy, that is, a nonlinear, nontotalizing logic akin to that which guides chaos theory and catastrophe theory, presupposes a liberal democratic commitment to universalism.[66] But how could multiple little narratives of local groups relate themselves to larger narratives justifying universal emancipation?[67] Further, if the historical periodization scheme (prehistoric, ancient, medieval, modern) proposed by progressive narratives is invalid, as Lyotard maintains, would it make sense to regard de-centered social groups as an *improvement* over what has gone before, or simply as something *different?* Postmodern social theorists, like radical ecologists and New Paradigmers, continue to grapple not only with the issue of the relation between the local and the general, or between the particular and the universal, but also with the question of how constructive change can arise in a world that is increasingly understood to be constituted at all levels by chaotic processes.

Critical postmodernist N. Katherine Hayles has made a fascinating attempt to reconcile chaos theory and information theory with deconstructive postmodern theory. She maintains that Derrida's notion that there is nothing outside the text gains support from scientists who believe

that the fundamental structure of both matter and energy can be reduced to flows of information. To [Edward] Fredkin *the world is quite literally a text,* a physical embodiment of information markers. . . . Across a wide spectrum of disciplines, information is emerging as a synthesizing concept that changes how we see the world.[68]

Claude Shannon helped to create the information revolution— and hence chaos theory—by defining entropy not as the absence of order, but rather as the presence of information. Influenced by Shannon, Lila Gatlin defines life as an "information-processing system" capable of reproducing itself, and language—instantiated in the genetic code—as "the basis of all life."[69] Chaos, understood as information-bearing dis-organization, becomes "the source of all that is new in the world."[70] Chaotic phenomena involve determinate structures that can be expressed quantitatively, but are nevertheless in principle unpredictable, such as weather. Chaos theory reveals that there is a "deep structure" of order, or "orderly disorder," in chaos.[71] For instance, there is a universal pattern in the relation between large- and small-scale features. The best-known example of this relation is that of coastlines, which repeat the same rugged features at every scale of measurement. Recursive, iterative patterns also characterize other chaotic phenomena, such as Mandelbrot's fractals. Although Lyotard once hoped that chaos theory, fractal geometry, and other instances of "paralogy" would help postmodern theory "wage a war on totality," Hayles counters that chaos theory arises from and thus can contribute to the globalizing impulse of modern science, for chaos theory shows *universal* structures in apparent disorder. Nevertheless, she asserts that by destabilizing the binary opposition between order and disorder, chaos theory has opened up a "major fault line" in the foundations of Western culture.[72]

An ancient fault line is the distinction between nature and culture. Derrida shows that although Rousseau pretends that nature is pure and complete in itself, he admits that nature (in people) must be "supplemented" by education. But describing education as a supplement suggests that education is merely a cultural accretion, not a constitutive aspect of the natural. Hayles remarks that

in every case the first term, nature for example, is "naturally" deficient, making the supplement indispensable. In what sense then is the supplement more "unnatural" than nature? In this implicit contradiction, Derrida shows that the supplement is in fact *what allows the privileged term to be constituted.* The originary precedence of the privileged term is revealed as an illusion, a myth or longing for origin rather than an origin as such.[73]

Texts produce meaning by postulating an originary differentiating concept, which Hayles terms a "fold," that serves as the origin from which other differences—binary oppositions—are supposed to flow. In *Of Grammatology,* Derrida unfolds the fold, thus revealing that this apparently stable difference is uncertain and indecidable, a fact that makes all subsequent distinctions equally unstable. Texts resemble chaotic phenomena in that both are inherently unpredictable. Chaos theorists argue that

iteration produces chaos because it magnifies and brings into view . . . initial uncertainties. Similarly, Derrida attributes textual indeterminacy to the inherent inability of linguistic systems to create an origin. In Derrida, the fold marks the absence of an origin, just as the inability to specify initial conditions with infinite accuracy marks the onset of chaos for Feigenbaum.[74]

Hayles emphasizes the following parallels between chaos theory and deconstruction: (1) just as chaos theory undermines the primacy of ordered systems, so deconstructive theory reveals the relation between customary concepts of order and oppressive ideologies; (2) chaos theory shifts attention from the individual unit to "recursive symmetries," whereas deconstruction stresses the death of the subject, and writes about "the replicating, self-similar processes that constitute individuals"; (3) chaos theory discloses a domain "that cannot be assimilable to either order or disorder; deconstruction detects a trace that cannot be assimilated to the binary oppositions it deconstructs."[75]

Another critical postmodernist, Alexander J. Argyros, however, maintains that even though deconstruction and chaos theory exhibit a parallel interest in nonlinearity, the differences between the two outweigh their similarities. Hayles herself admits that, whereas Derrida proclaims that chaos goes all the way down in every text, scientists confirm that some systems are ordered and predictable. Further, scientists admire the order-, beauty-, and structure-producing capacity of chaos, whereas Derrida emphasizes its randomness and disorder since he wishes to undermine metaphysical absolutes. Hence, Argyros says that "for deconstructionists, chaos repudiates order; for scientists, chaos makes order possible."[76] By privileging his own literary methodology, Argyros says, Derrida either ignores or distorts the extraordinary developments in "postpositivistic" science, including chaos theory.[77] Like many radical ecologists, Argyros regards deconstructive postmodern theory as a linguistic idealism. The problem is not the claim that there is nothing outside the text, but rather the attempt to limit "text" to linguistic phenomena associated with recent human history. Argyros argues that humanity and language originate within the far older, self-evolving, self-differentiating, and order-generating "text" of the universe, as described in evolutionary cosmic narratives associated with Big Bang cosmology.[78] Deconstructive postmodern theory ignores that "being is a palimpsest of its history, a complex and multilayered onion whose layers are its past."[79]

Although sharing Derrida's critique of the rigid, eternal, foundations preferred by logocentrism, Argyros maintains that Derrida errs by privileging the other pole of the binary dualism, discord or difference. Derrida's dissemination involves not productive chaos, but rather what Hegel called bad infinity: endless heterogeneity and fragmentation. Needed is a new metaphysics that explains that the universe can generate a relatively stable ontological hierarchy, but one that can always surpass itself by bringing forth new levels of organization with their own emergent properties. For instance, the molecular level gave rise to the cellular level, which later generated the organismic level, which itself relates to earlier levels in increasingly complex feedback loops. Conceding that there is no linear necessity at work in history, Argyros nevertheless asserts that "Hegel's dialectical eschatology is much closer to the preferred strategies of nature than Derridean dissemination."[80] Mind and culture, then, are complex products of their own evolutionary history. Such a view provides

both a needed conservative ballast on rampant reference and the tools necessary for innovation. Evolution is the history of previous successful solutions to the problem of existence. In a fundamentally Hegelian way, evolution does not abandon inherited inventions, but incorporates them into subsequent levels as their skeleton.[81]

Although Derrida emphasizes the difference-pole of the identity versus difference, or order versus randomness dualism, chaos theorists emphasize that chaos is a nondualistic "third term, a kind of dynamic disorder able to balance determinism with freedom."[82] Fearful of the power of stable structures, Derrida overemphasizes the destabilizing power of the endless play of difference. His chaotic dissemination supposedly leads to decentralized, agonistic, nontotalizing local worlds, but Prigogine's chaos promotes new forms of global order and cooperation consistent with growing freedom.[83] Argyros even suggests that Derrida and Lyotard fear uncertainty and change:

Derrida's "always already" precludes genuine innovation, and Lyotard's general agonistics would guarantee that local perturbations remain locked in place by the pressure of other, warring language games. In both cases, . . . an essentially rigid cosmology prevents such local fluctuations from generating genuine global innovation. . . . [I]n the absence of a mechanism allowing for global communication and transformation, the system spends itself in the creation of local pockets of energy differentials.[84]

Rejecting blanket critiques of totalizing narratives, Argyros maintains that they are needed both for maintaining and for changing human society.[85] Fascism and other evil systems cannot simply be "declared out of existence," for the price of freedom in a dynamic world is the possibility of generating evil. The way to combat evil systems, he argues, is to propose systems that are better—because freer, more flexible, more inclusive.[86] Systems with such traits are more consistent with the principles of chaotic self-organization preferred by evolutionary liberals.

As I mentioned earlier, counterculturalists and some radical ecologists are attracted to chaos theory because it helps to explain how large-scale social change can occur. In a complex system, Hayles postulates that local areas reproduce the recursive, self-similar traits of the larger cultural system. Thus, local is to global as microcosm is to macrocosm. In chaotic systems, when symmetries between various levels are aligned, movement between levels is possible. In moments of alignment, systems become highly sensitive to tiny fluctuations or perturbations, a phenomenon known as "the butterfly effect," referring to the (perhaps farfetched) possibility that air stirred by a butterfly's wings may eventually trigger off a major storm far away. Analogously, disparate groups operating at the local level to deconstruct metaphysical dualisms, could trigger off major macro-level cultural shifts. Hayles says that

change arrives not as a monolithic unity, but as complex vortices of local turbulence. Not to see that the agitation is general is to miss the fact that there are significant changes in the underlying cultural currents; not to notice that the turbulence follows different dynamics at different sites is to miss the complexities that the new views of chaos both initiate and signify.[87]

As noted earlier, however, even if chaos theory provides a model for *how* a cultural shift might occur, chaos theory does *not* guarantee that such a shift would lead to a society that progressives, New Paradigmers, or radical ecologists would recognize as better than the one it replaces. Though some people fear that the dawning information/communication era will dissolve the personality structure, thereby promoting passivity and "soft" totalitarianism, others maintain that the new era will foster greater social interaction and tolerance. For example, Argyros predicts that the broadly progressive emerging era will increase lifespan; heighten individuation; increase the capacity for differentiating information; lead to a complex global state that undermines violent nationalism, increases reverence for art that combines classicism and experimentation, revitalizes sex and kinship roles in a flexible, aesthetic way, and institutes new forms of sacred devotion. The new era, we are told, would be "the setting for a new Eden."[88] Yet if Argyros differs from postmodern theorists in his relative optimism, he differs from New Paradigmers in his greater realism. For him, the envisioned Eden "would have its contingent of snakes. . . . But with the snakes would come astonishing new possibilities for human freedom, imaginative transcendence, and creativity."[89] Hence, Argyros's critical postmodernism takes into account the virtues and limitations of liberal democracy, the pluses and minuses of postmodern theory's defense of difference against the logic of identity, and the promises and problems of chaos theory and narratives of cosmic evolution.[90]

Argyros might agree with Erich Jantsch that the information (novelty) accumulated by countless individual human decisions and interactions is guided by "the urge toward higher autonomy which may be interpreted as an urge toward higher consciousness."[91] For Wilber, this urge is the ontological "lure" drawing consciousness toward ever more integrated levels. Hence, Argyros may be read as combining chaos theory, aspects of Naess's concept of self-realization, Bookchin's idea of the cosmic *nisus* toward greater freedom, diZerega's evolutionary liberalism, and Wilber's neo-Hegelianism. One thing that differentiates his vision from that of the radical ecologists and diZerega, and which links him more with Wilber, is that Argyros does not seem particularly concerned about the fate of nonhuman life, though he recognizes that ecological breakdown would undermine the informational era. Most deep ecologists, then, would fear that Argyros—like Eric Chaisson and Eric Lerner—uses chaos theory and new evolutionary cosmology as a dissimulating garb to conceal his real commitment to modernity's and New Age's projects of controlling nature for human ends.

Similarly to Jim Cheney, but without his nostalgia for bioregional communities, Argyros would reply that deep ecologists are motivated by fear of the phase change occurring as the matter-oriented modern world gives way to a postmodern world in which matter is seen as a "particular manifestation of an evolving hierarchy of information."[92] Anxiety about such transformations motivates deep ecology's attempt not only to halt modern technology from destroying the natural world, but also to characterize the natural world "imperialistically" as "stable and static whereas it has, in fact, always burgeoned with creativity."[93] A dynamic, evolving universe is simultaneously destructive and constructive. Unfortunately, the dynamics of multinational capitalism may also generate an increasingly homogeneous, culturally impoverished, and ecologically unstable era, whose worldwide TV networks cannot prevent people from retreating into a multiplicity of xenophobic armed camps. Metaphors about self-organization, chaos, differentiation, encoding, information, language, and data cannot conceal the possibility that a paradigm shift might produce a world that radical ecologists would describe as technological nihilism.

Baudrillard has argued that current fascination with the genetic code and other sign-systems is preparing the way for the "neo-capitalist cybernetic order that aims now at total control."[94] Modern historical narratives presupposing the distinction between surface and depth, such as, between cultural superstructure and economic base, are annihilated when everyone becomes consumers of *signs:* simulation, model, code, and signifier precede and even produce "reality."[95] As Stephen Watt explains, Baudrillard was influenced by Jacques Monod's views about DNA, whose processes can be altered by interaction between mechanical necessity and chance mutation. Sharing Monod's emphasis on entropy, Baudrillard declares that far from there being a dialectical direction to organic evolution, or a human potential to be realized, we are faced with a futureless history in which no decisive events will occur. Representing the exhausted, cynical, bored, and melancholic side of postmodern theory, Baudrillard seems to be writing a dystopic fiction based on the questionable assumption that current trends are finalities.[96] Some see Baudrillard's work as typical of the disillusionment, apolitical cynicism, and conservative tendencies that followed from the failure of a certain type of French ultra-radical postmodern theory to produce social change.[97]

Baudrillard views humans as biological mutants, freaky consequences of "noise" in the genetic code. Trapped in a world of surfaces, images, and signs, humans are functions of a metastasizing social system, whose internal tensions could at any moment trigger off a terrifying catastrophic shift that would abolish the already problematic hyped-up media-reality, while generating a nihilistic, ecologically insane, ecstatic, and scarcely imaginable domain. This grim view is hardly consistent with the hopeful idea that the information/communication era will help to trigger the shift to an ecologically sound society. We are again reminded that we cannot simply "read off" progressive political views from contemporary trends in science. Yet in view of the changes being wrought by informational technology, we may ask: what is meant by "progressive"?

THE POSTMODERN WORLD OF THE CYBORG   Recalling Argyros's contention that the coming phase change will combine "astoundingly imaginative" and "potentially hideously monstrous" developments,[98] we now explore for a moment the views of the critical postmodernist and feminist, Donna Haraway. She has articulated a provocative account of a cybernetic future in which women and men explore the imaginative/creative and monstrous/transgressive possibilities of the informational era. Advocating a view alien to mainstream feminism and ecofeminism, Haraway seeks to redefine progress in a way consistent with the world now emerging. Refusing to be nostalgic for an unrecoverable (and probably unreal) past, she seeks instead to foster creativity and freedom in the informational age. Though sympathetic to ecofeminism's interest in the "natural" body and the Goddess, Haraway urges women not to fear the technological future, but to face it with resolve and imagination. Only by becoming technologically skilled "cyborgs" can women help lead society away from ecocide.

Haraway adapts postmodern theory's critique of the centered subject, totalizing narratives, objective knowledge, the longing for origins and final reconciliation of self and other, dualisms, and privileged perspectives (including those of oppressed groups), without letting postmodern theory's corrosive side cripple her political imagination. Her vision of the future relations between human and nonhuman (organic and artificial) is sometimes harrowing, sometimes exhilarating, and always challenging. As a socialist feminist, she at first criticized the disembodied, abstract knowledge-claims of "objective" Western science, which constructs nature as a site of control and labor, a site that includes the female body.[99] Although her encounter with postmodern theory shook many of her presuppositions about socialism as well as feminism, she remains a political activist. Hence, she speaks not of the "death of the subject," as do the disempowering "boys" in postmodern theory, but rather of "the opening of non-isomorphic subjects, agents, and territories of stories unimaginable from the vantage point of the cyclopian, self-satiated eye of the master subject."[100] The disturbing and powerful myth she narrates in "A Cyborg Manifesto" explores the implications of post-modernity's "fractured identities."

Although understanding the desire of cultural ecofeminists to restore an appropriate relation to the female body and to Earthbody, Haraway maintains that the real opportunity for women (and for men as well) lies *not* in recovering an unrecoverable origin, but rather in taking the risk of imaginatively exploring multiple identities that transgress the boundaries between the human, the natural, and the mechanical, thereby opening up unexpected alternatives to the deadly path forged by technological society. Conversant with the trends of high-tech capitalism, she concludes that there is no way to stop the unfolding of astonishing new technological configurations. If women become engaged in this technological future, however, they can help prevent it from reinforcing racism, sexism, capitalism, and "the tradition of the appropriation of nature as a resource for the productions of culture."[101] Given her cyborgian vision, however, some radical ecologists do not see how Haraway could avoid promoting precisely such appropriation.

A cyborg is an artifact: part-human, part-machine. Although cyborgs are usually associated with science fiction, Haraway asserts that because we are intricately involved with, dependent on, and shaped by an enormous complex of technological systems, we are *already* cyborgs: "chimeras, theorized and fabricated hybrids of machines and organism" (CM, 150). (Note "CM" = "Cyborg Manifesto"; quotations from it will be cited as "CM" followed by page number.) She regards the cyborg as an emancipatory political symbol, encouraging women and men to participate in the struggle now taking place: to redefine relations between production and reproduction, human organism and machine, humankind and nature. Exploring and enjoying the "monstrous" possibilities of crossing boundaries (and of establishing them) in a high-tech world of splintered identities and vanished essences, the cyborg does not shy away from the "unnatural." Promoting a postgender world, the cyborg "has no truck with bisexuality, pre-oedipal symbiosis, unalienated labor, or other seductions to organic wholeness through a final appropriation of all the powers of the parts into a higher unity" (CM, 150). Away with Hegelian-Marxist master narratives envisioning the final *Aufhebung* that reconciles the alienated subject with its object!

Like some cultural feminists, Haraway discerns the seeds of patriarchy in the biological and cultural factors that make women responsible for reproduction. This responsibility insures that women become the object for the subsequent psychological fantasies of their sons, and daughters, too. Freud provided the personal version and Marx the social version of Western humanism's saga of self-realization: original unity, the phallic mother, separation, individuation, development, final reconciliation with and appropriation of the Other. In Haraway's account, this mythic journey culminates in omnicide: nuclear war. The individuated patriarchal self, longing for a return to original innocence and blissful unity, strives to control and absorb the presumed site of bliss: Woman, Mother, Nature. Western dualisms reflect the One's domination of the Others: women, lower class people, nonwhites, and all those "whose task is to mirror the [unitary] self" (CM, 177). In nuclear war, the control-obsessed patriarchal subject would finally erase the other who reminds him of his dependence and insecurity. By annihilating the other, the One simultaneously vanishes, thereby "overcoming" the separation of self and other in a final spasm of rage about not being able "to name the Enemy" (CM, 151, 177).

Although the ultimate product of the masculinist subject's drive toward independence, the cyborg abjures any claim to organic origin, Garden of Eden, oedipal ties, natural bonds, nuclear family, and related factors that originally helped to give rise to that desperate drive. Ironic, relation-seeking, perverse, perspectival, utopian, and noninnocent, cyborgs "are not reverent; they do not re-member the cosmos. They are wary of holism, but needy for connection" (CM, 151). Having rebuffed ecofeminists who claim that women are organically closer to nature, Haraway also negates the idea that the oppressed female has a more innocent view of nature. In giving up their own longing for organic wholeness and innocence, women renounce not only patriarchy's constraining self-understanding, but also nature feminism's limiting idea of what counts as the "friendly body" and legitimate political discourse (CM, 174).

Haraway argues that in the late twentieth century the possibility has arisen for overcoming several dualisms. Ecofeminists have been concerned about one of them, the dualism between humans and animals, but cyborgs revel in transgressing the boundaries involved in other dualisms as well. Since contemporary biology and evolutionary theory have virtually obliterated the distinction people used to make between humans and animals, the task is "to contest the meanings of the breached boundary" (CM, 174). Cyborgs share with cultural ecofeminists the importance of affirming and reintegrating our animality, but go even further in "monstrous" possibilities of unnatural human-animal relationships. Another dualism involves the physical versus the nonphysical. Computers and other microelectronic devices deal in the rapid exchange of signals and waves whose "existence" is tenuous and elusive. Cyborgs admire the fluidity and evanescence of the electronic signal, even while opposing the horrendous military purposes to which that signal is put.

A third dualism concerns that of women and men. With the cyborg's renunciation of the myth of natural origins, and with the fracturing of identities in the postmodern world, the whole distinction between "female" and "male" is up for grabs. Indeed, since gender is a construction forced upon women (and men) by patriarchy, colonialism, and capitalism, what is the point of retaining such a distinction? Instead of trying to find the conceptual glue holding the multifarious aspects of "woman" together, it is time to explore and to celebrate interesting, empowering, contemporary boundary formations—and transgressions. In other words, in the postmodern world cyborgs must avoid the temptation of

lapsing into boundless difference and giving up on the confusing task of making partial, real connections. Some differences are playful; some are poles of world historical systems of domination. "Epistemology" is about knowing the difference. (CM, 161–162).

A final dualism involves human organism versus machine. Computer technology is producing devices that are surprisingly lively and that may eventually become self-conscious and even "autonomous," though this is a hotly disputed topic. Haraway's celebrates the merging of the organic with the mechanical, the natural with the artificial, so as to code the world in a way that undermines the integrity and innocence of the "organic whole." Conceiving of machine and organism as coded texts to be playfully reinterpreted would shock ecofeminists who protest that postmodern theory's "textualizing" disregards "the lived relations of domination that ground the 'play' of arbitrary readings" (CM, 161–162). Haraway insists, however, that resistance cannot rely on appeals made to an "imagined organic body" (CM, 154). It is now time to renounce "the certainty of what counts as nature," for "the transcendent authorization of interpretation is lost, and with it the ontology grounding 'Western' epistemology" (CM, 152–153). The loss of such grounding should not lead to despair, but to transgressing and constituting boundaries in ways that promote survival in the face of future developments.

Such developments include "the informatics of domination," a worldwide system of production/reproduction and communication that currently integrates and exploits women (CM, 163). The comfortable hierarchies of industrial capitalism are giving way to the scary new networks of polymorphous information systems, a shift so great that it requires reconceptualizing issues of oppression and exploitation, as well as of race, gender, and class. Communications technology and biotechnology constitute an enormously complex and powerful system that transforms the body into a set of interchangeable and alterable biotic components, none of which are sacred. Sounding much like Heidegger describing modern technology, Haraway says that the aim of this system is

the translation of the world into a problem of coding, a search for a common language in which all resistance to instrumental control disappears and all heterogeneity can be submitted to disassembly, reassembly, investment, and exchange. (CM, 164)

In the near future, life threatens to vanish into electronic bits in computer programs, the configurations of which are open to infinite variations. In his novels, William Gibson explores this drive to overcome the limitations of materiality. His characters "jack in" to "cyberspace," the electronic-informational realm on the other side of the computer screen.[102] In view of all this, the cyborg stands before two possible paths. The first involves inventing new "social and bodily realities in which people are not afraid of their joint kinship with animals and machines not afraid of permanently partial identities and contradictory standpoints" (CM, 164). On this path, the machine is not an "it" to be either worshiped or dominated, but rather an aspect of ourselves, working with which we can take pleasure. Regarding the undervalued daily activities that some feminists portray as the ground of life, Haraway dares to ask: "What about all the ignorance of women, all the exclusions and failures of knowledge and skill? What about men's access to daily competence, to knowing how to build things, to take them apart, to play?" (CM, 181). For many women working in electronics plants, the cyborgian transformation remains gruesome, but it can be transformed into something affirmative if women can invent empowering narratives (like the Cyborg Manifesto) which lead to a transformation of the very character of "production." Unflinchingly, Haraway describes the challenges posed by the high-tech future in major institutions, including home, market, paid workplace, state, school, clinic-hospital, and church (CM, 170–173).

The second path is the completion of patriarchy's aim of gaining total control of the planet, by virtue of the common language—the ultimate Code—that reduces everything to interchangeable raw material. Ecofeminists like Mary Daly fear that Haraway, despite her protests to the contrary, is in fact treading this grim path. Daly proclaims that "the projected manufacture by men of artificial wombs, of cyborgs, which will be part flesh, part robot . . . all are manifestations of phallotechnic boundary violations."[103] The urge to turn warm flesh into cold steel has long been a dream of men like Ernst Jünger, whose fantasies of the humanized robot—a monstrous hybrid of soft flesh and cold steel, organic tissue and copper wiring—so influenced Heidegger's dark vision of the coming technological world. In recommending that women become cyborgs capable of directing the technological flow, Haraway may seem to embrace aspects of that vision.

Similarly, Baudrillard describes hyperreality as a situation in which subject-object dualism is overcome by the triumph of technological objects over human subjects. Lyotard offers yet another approach to the technological future. In his early writings, he emphasized desire, corporeality, the nonrational, and anarchy. In *The Postmodern Condition,* however, exhibiting an increasing interest in contemporary scientific and technological trends, he argued that catastrophe theory, chaos theory, self-organizing systems theory, electronic media, and open access to computer memory banks would end hierarchy and promote practices consistent with decentralized, pluralistic democracy. Commentators have noted the affinity between such paralogical (i.e., nonlinear, order-out-of-chaos generating) phenomena and the self-organizing processes associated with liberal democratic economies.

Given Lyotard's emphasis on the transformational potentiality of open systems, one could imagine him moving toward a view consistent with diZerega's evolutionary liberalism. Recently, however, Lyotard made a remark that brings him closer to modernity's project of denying death by conquering nature. Lyotard comments that the most pressing task facing us is "to consider life as a technology, to consider technology on a cosmic scale."[104] The human brain is perhaps the most highly efficient open system, since it uses symbolic technology. The most effective type of community formed by these individual open systems (i.e., human brains) is another type of open system: "political democracy and socioeconomic liberalism (based on the pursuit of competition for optimum performativity)." Since the brain is still dependent on the energy supply provided by the body, Lyotard concludes that all contemporary research in every discipline seeks

to emancipate the human brain from constraints common to living systems on the earth; or to manufacture a system, one at least as complex as the brain, independent of these constraints. It is a question of one or the other 'surviving' the destruction of the solar system and continuing to function in the ordinary conditions of the cosmos. There are 4.5 billion solar years in which to attain this result. In cosmic time, this is nothing.[105]

For Lyotard, apparently, the liberal market economy is beneficial because it promotes the projects of the death-defying of egos bent on survival at all costs. Such projects include turning flesh-and-blood mortals into enormously complex data banks sustained "forever" by self-replicating computers. Allowing metaphors drawn from codes and data to displace modernity's metaphors drawn from machines, Lyotard suggests that humans are simply an extraordinarily complex instance of the codes generating all natural phenomena. Cultural ecofeminists would point out that this way of overcoming humanity-nature dualism is consistent with ancient masculinist fantasies about overcoming mortality by gaining control over nature, the body, and the female. Revulsion is a common response to fusing the human body with technical devices, but Haraway insists that such revulsion prevents women from offering creative, affirmative, playful responses that could help redirect the emerging postmodern/electronic society so that it does not realize the most horrendous and oppressive possibilities.

Critics charge that Haraway is a technological determinist, who does not fully appreciate the economic interests lying behind the metaphors of "code" and "data" that give rise to bioengineering and other high-tech developments, which are transforming and destroying persons, human society, and much of life on earth. Given her socialist background, however, she is well aware of arguments that explain such developments in terms of society's economic base. Her point is not just that economic trends and technological developments are dialectically interrelated, but that the very idea of interrelation between the cultural superstructure and economic base of society needs to be reexamined in light of technological developments unimaginable to Marx. Again, the problem is not only how to conceive what "progress" would mean in a world that undermines basic concepts of identity and difference, but also how to define politics processes needed to achieve such progress.

Haraway believes that feminist dream of a unified female culture freed from patriarchy's technology reasserts the dualism of organism versus machine, feminine versus masculine. Her crucial insight is that *the longing for unity always produces duality:* "One is too few, but two are too many" (CM, 177). In deconstructing One and duality, she is in effect calling for the emergence of *nondualism.* Containing no pastoral images of mystics blissfully communing with "nature" in pretechnological bioregions, her truly radical nondualism calls on us to cease clinging to our identity as gendered, organic, and human, and to participate in the dangerous, boundary-crossing, technological play that is our destiny, whether we like it or not. In a striking passage, Haraway proclaims:

This is a dream not of a common language, but of a powerful infidel heteroglossia. It is an imagination of a feminist speaking in tongues to strike fear into the circuits of the supersavers of the new right. It means both building and destroying machines, identities, categories, relationships, space stories. Though both are bound in the spiral dance, I would rather be a cyborg than a goddess. (CM, 181)

With their image of the Goddess, some ecofeminists have attempted to conceive of nature not as a passive resource, but rather as an active subject. But conceiving of nature as the caring Goddess also means conceiving of her as the threatening and withholding Mother. Hence, for Haraway, a major task is to redefine nature. Nature is "not a treasure to be fenced in," as some radical ecologists seem to think; not an "essence to be saved or violated"; not a "text to be read in the codes of mathematics and biomedicine"; and not "the 'other' who offers origin, replenishment, and service. Neither mother, nurse, nor slave, nature is not matrix, resource, or tool for the reproduction of man."[106] Stressing the interactive, generative aspect of nature, Haraway defines it as "figure, construction, artifact, movement, displacement."[107] To say that nature is a construct does not reduce it to a version of Baudrillard's hyperreality, but emphasizes that nature is an ongoing coproduction, generated by humans as well as by organic, material, linguistic, and technical nonhumans. In her quest to reanimate nature, Haraway opposes the two leading alternative views of nature. The first, the "hyper-productionism" of white, phallocentric, Western rationalism, regards nature solely as a resource for his own self-reproduction, and thus "refuses the witty agency of all the actors but One; that is a dangerous strategy—for everyone."[108] The second, "transcendental naturalism," preferred by some radical ecologists, "also refuses a world full of cacophonous agencies and settles for a mirror image sameness that only pretends to difference."[109]

If we are going to project nature as an active subject, why not picture nature as having a sense of humor, as being playful and unpredictable? Why not think of nature not as "mother/matter/Mutter," but rather as the native American Coyote or Trickster? In relating to the Coyote, "we give up mastery, but keep searching for fidelity, knowing all the while that we will be hoodwinked."[110] In "revisioning the world as coding trickster with whom we must learn to converse," instead of as a Mother with whom we long to be reunited, humanity would enter into a playful and responsible era in which the idea of maturity, culmination, and completion would wither away. If we approach nature as Trickster, we must stop envisioning organisms as "preexisting plants, animals, protistes, etc., with boundaries already established and awaiting the right kind of instrument to note them correctly."[111] Instead, we must conclude that organisms are "natural-technical entities" that emerge in the complex discourses occurring among biological, material, scientific, and technical agents. Here, Haraway comes close to Naess's and Mahayana Buddhism's "ontological phenomenalism," which holds that entities lack fixed essences and are instead complex gestalts constituted by interactive perceptual and discursive processes. Haraway goes further than Naess, however, in examining more closely the politically charged contests that help both to generate and to sustain those gestalts.

According to Haraway, conceiving nature as a "construction" of science and nature does *not* mean locating "all agency firmly on the side of humanity,"[112] but it does mean forgoing the idea of a pristine nature that must be "protected" from human intervention. Haraway seeks not to save nature in walled-off reserves, but rather to generate a politics of "social nature," that is, "of a different organization of land and people, where *the practice of justice restructures the concept of nature.* "[113] She maintains that the idea of an "empty" nature, one devoid of people, could only have emerged after so many native Americans were killed by the disease and violence that accompanied the "discovery" of the New World. In fact, the Amazonian rainforest, for example, often heralded as the last natural refuge untouched by human hands, has been shaped for many centuries by various human groups.

Haraway's assertion that "the Amazonian Biosphere is an irreducibly human/non-human collective entity" that cannot survive without social justice, shapes her reply to deep ecology's question, "Who speaks for the jaguar?" Expressing concern about species nearing extinction, Haraway refuses to accept the question as posed, for it rests on "a political semiotics of representation."[114] In such a semiotics, the entity represented is removed from its own context, so as to be spoken for by the one claiming authority to speak. In this way, "the represented is reduced to the permanent status of the recipient of action, never to be a co-actor in an articulated practice among unlike, but joined, social partners."[115] Supposedly acting in the role of a disinterested party, but in fact projecting his own fond dreams onto the jaguar and acting as a ventriloquist, the spokesman seeks to protect the animal from those who are threatening it, that is, the people who are closest to it in the forest. Just as disinterested objectivity has justified problematic scientific-technical attempts to "control" nature, so the objectivity of the deep ecologist can serve to justify an attitude of arrogance to indigenous people whom he would like to control. If the Amazonian forest is to be saved, "all the people who care, cognitively, emotionally, and politically, must articulate their position in a field constrained by a new collective entity, made up of indigenous people and other human and nonhuman actors."[116]

Forsaking the idea of a pristine nature as the origin from which humans arose, Haraway also recommends abandoning the idea of a goal toward which we are headed, such as the goal of "rational progress of science, in potential league with progressive politics, patiently unveiling a grounding nature."[117] The geometry of Haraway's "amodern" (neither modern nor postmodern) history will be "permanent and multi-patterned interaction through which lives and worlds get built, human and unhuman."[118] What we need is not a "happy ending," but a "non-ending," consistent with the idea of a self-articulating world, an unpredictable Trickster constantly generating itself anew, with no final purpose. In this discourse, some will recognize echoes of the Nietzschean aestheticism that proved so attractive to German conservative revolutionaries early in this century. Spengler and Jünger denied that there is any progress or *telos* to human or cosmic history; instead, there is an endless and ultimately meaningless sequence of cultural gestalts, which organize humanity and nature in determinate ways.

As opposed to such political aesthetes, who anticipated a brilliant and dangerous new world run by technological monsters, half-human, half-mechanical hybrids, Haraway's reference to the idea of "social justice" shows how committed she remains to the progressive discourse of Enlightenment modernity, which was itself in part the secular expression of moral themes drawn from Judaism and Christianity. Yet she abandons progressive narratives, whether Hegelian-Marxist or perennial philosophical, in terms of which people often feel either blessedly or cursedly enmeshed in webs of "cosmic meaning." Renouncing the need for an overarching cosmic narrative, and insisting that all knowledge and practices are inevitably local and historical, her immersion in "worldliness" and her profound commitment to social justice amount to an admirable act of faith.[119]

Haraway explores some of these complex issues in examining Ridley Scott's movie, *Blade Runner*. Here, I expand upon her analysis. Scott's *tech noir* film, loosely based on a short story by Philip K. Dick, projects a grim future world of ecological catastrophe and authoritarianism, where astonishing wealth and technical achievement starkly contrast with barbarous hordes living in squalid urban areas (in short, a possible future for American cities). *Blade Runner*'s protagonist is Rick Decard, a reluctant bounty hunter whose targets are replicants, that is, cyborgs usually constructed for dangerous missions beyond planet Earth. A replicant named Rachel, Haraway remarks, "stands as the image of a cyborg culture's fear, love, and confusion" (CM, 178). Decard is assigned to hunt down and destroy a group of renegade replicants (Rachel herself is not a renegade) who have disobeyed strict orders against returning to Earth.

Replication has become so advanced that only highly trained experts can distinguish replicants from organic humans. Because of their power and increasing autonomy, they are programmed to "die," usually after only a few years. The owner of the replication company is a domineering, aggressive, boundary-defending male. But the gender, age, and identity boundaries of the creative genius who designs the replicants is indeterminate and elusive. Perhaps only such a being could envision the transgressions needed to develop the perfect replicant. His workshop is filled with amazing mechanical creations, many of which resemble toys. Indeed, one of the female cyborgs who has returned to Earth looks and moves somewhat like a doll. In *Blade Runner*, the fascination felt by early modern Europeans in the face of clocks and mechanical automatons is mirrored in the fascination of the genius before his own creatures—one of whom returns to murder him.

The renegade replicants have returned to vent their rage at having been created as conscious beings without human prerogatives. A charismatic replicant slays both the owner of the company that manufactures replicants and the brilliant man who designs them, while avoiding Decard, who barely manages to kill the replicant's comrades. In the climactic struggle, Decard hangs by his fingertips from a tall building while the replicant leader, grief-stricken by and angry at the loss of his friends, looms over him. Inexplicably, just as the replicant's preprogrammed "lifespan" comes to an end, he saves Decard. Dying, the replicant gives a haunting soliloquy of his brief life, recounting the extraordinary things he had seen and done far out in space, things which no human could have accomplished or has ever witnessed. Confronted with the replicant's achievements, his capacity for such mercy, and his heightened self-consciousness in the face of mortality, the audience is invited to conclude that this creature is more than a mere replica of a human being.

In the course of hunting down the renegades, Decard falls in love with Rachel, the greatest achievement of the murdered genius. Intelligent, beautiful, and poised, she is even preprogrammed with childhood memories that convince her that she is *human*. When informed otherwise, her confusion and agony are palpable. As they jet away from a polluted and treacherous Los Angeles, Decard reflects on his love for Rachel. Once a jaded killer, he has been transformed by his encounter with the replicants whom he was hired to destroy. Emerging from his defensive shell, he risks loving a replicant whose "lifespan" is unknown to both of them. Crossing the boundary between human and machine, he invites the audience to reconsider their own attitude toward the nonhuman.

Disturbing to such reflection, however, is the fact that the lovers' aircraft takes them over a glorious tree-clad, snow-capped mountainous region that could scarcely exist in a world filled with such polluted cities. Not surprisingly, this happy ending was imposed by Hollywood producers. The ending in Scott's "director's cut" is more consistent with the film's dark tone. Still, the Hollywood ending is worth commenting on. Although the portrayal of the living earth seems to voice the yearning for reunion with Mother Nature against which Haraway has warned, it may also represent an alternative to the ecological crisis, of which Los Angeles (then and now) is a symptom. If this crisis stems from dualism, including man versus machine, then the solution involves not boundaryless blending, but nondualism as symbolized by the love between Rachel and the protagonist. If the Earth is to live, in other words, humans must develop a radically different attitude toward themselves and technology.

This reading may be countered by noting that men have long had a love affair with machines. For example, the automobile symbolizes everything that cultural feminists abhor about masculinist technology: the yearning for greater speed to escape finitude, the flesh, and the female. But Rachel is no passive instrument, responsive only to the whims of the master. To love her requires that Decard develop a capacity for conversing with what/whom he loves. Moreover, the fact that she is mortal means that he must abandon his fantasy that a machine (or a female/lover/mother) will grant him immortality. Faced with the fact that everything is limited, partial, and uncertain, Decard must come to terms with his own mortality, thereby halting the desperate quest that gave rise to rapacious technology.

Overall, I have high regard for Haraway's remarkable Cyborg Manifesto. In her "implosion" of the material, metaphoric, literal, figurative, organic, technical textual, political, and mythic, she has summoned a powerful Trickster, who revels in unsettling and confusing established boundaries and norms. In decentering and transgressing the categories now defining personal identities, she moves at least partly in the circuit of postmodern theory. Yet her socialist background makes her less willing than some postmodern theorists to abandon such critical concepts as social hegemony, political accountability, and systematic exploitation, the latter of which is "practiced particularly ferociously by the transnationals in the free trade zones, such as the US-Mexican border and elsewhere." Denying that she seeks to replace social struggle with "the politics of narrative," she asserts that people must find better ways to articulate their social struggles, "including those that occur in narrative and its fiercely materialized metaphor."[120] These newly articulated struggles may help to serve as the "interference" necessary to disrupt the Ultimate Code, symbolic of the patriarchal quest to turn everything into fungible raw material. Although some critics say she favors replacing fleshly bodies with "shining technobodies," her point is that today many people already inhabit domains in which flesh and code, mortal body and technical apparatus are no longer readily distinguishable. In view of this fact, she poses the following questions for political progressives: how to become aware of and to articulate what is occurring in those domains; how to assess the real and potential damage (personal, social, ecological) occurring in and spreading out from them; and how to develop effective means for publicly disclosing, personally and collectively resisting, and creatively transforming the astonishing high-tech practices, devices, attitudes, power structures, and production methods that are already coming on line? Haraway rightly urges women and men, at all levels and walks of life, to become better educated about and involved with technical developments, rather than being either passive consumers or unthinking opponents of them.

Unfortunately, those at the forefront of fast-breaking technological developments are often men driven by adolescent, death-denying fantasies. Consider "Virtual Reality," an example of how postmodernism privileges the image, or even better, the simulacrum: a representation of something that doesn't itself exist. Virtual Reality attempts to unite recent breakthroughs in the interface between computers and human perception. Virtual Reality requires a "bioapparatus," which creates audio-visual-kinesthethic experiences catering to the participant's fantasies. A bioapparatus may include: a helmet outfitted with a television screen that completely surrounds the wearer's field of vision; and special gloves wired to a computer, which represents on the TV screen the movements one makes with one's own hands. These movements can then be coordinated with events taking place on the screen. Still relatively primitive, the possibilities seem limitless. People are already hard at work on body suits that respond to slight leg muscle movements in such a way that the wearer will feel as if he or she is running, and all this would be coordinated with events happening on one's artificial "visual field." The goal is to create a technology so satisfying that one could become completely absorbed in an artificial world lacking any reference whatsoever to the "real" world.

Sallie Tisdale reports on Cyberthon, a convention that brought together Virtual Reality enthusiasts and representatives of the companies who stand to make millions from it. The motto of one such company is: "Reality isn't enough anymore."[121] Many of the leading figures in the new industry have had extensive experience with hallucinogenic drugs, a contention supported by the presence of Timothy Leary as a speaker. Some Virtual Reality proponents are attempting to create a technologically induced version of the fantastic experiences triggered off by the brain on LSD. Not all that impressed by the grainy images she saw inside the virtual-reality helmet, Tisdale focuses on the self-understanding of those committed to this new technology. People attending the convention are mostly white and overwhelmingly male. In some sense, they want to transgress the boundaries between machine and human, image and reality. A number of participants are conversant with the lingo of postmodernism. One man remarks that Virtual Reality could enable people to "experience what it is to be human in a more diverse, less centered, higher bandwidth sort of way."[122] Eric Gullichsen, co-founder of Sense8, says: "The time will come when you will go to look at something and there won't be any way to distinguish whether it's something that's living, whether it's artificial, whether it's controlled by another person or an artificial intelligence."[123] Gullichsen is apparently dumbfounded by the question: "What's the point of that?"

Virtual Reality fans generally lack any satisfying narrative or cosmology. They simply assume that the fantastic possibilities lying ahead will open up a future that will inevitably be positive. At the convention, no one mentions the comparison between Virtual Reality and drug-induced experiences that may pacify the masses, as described in Huxley's *Brave New World*. For many proponents, Virtual Reality is nothing more than an escape from reality, a chance to explore and do unheard of things, without any risk or commitment. The men are like gleeful kids "in the driver's seat again, and no one can see over the steering wheel."[124] The automotive metaphor is apt, reminding us of Susan Griffin's warning about man's yearning for speed. Tisdale remarks: "Imagine a technology that allows us to do anything—to do what is illegal, immoral, lost in time, physically impossible, lethal."[125] Imagine, in other words, a technology that satisfies the patriarchal craving for immortality. Imagine this powerful technology "stuck in the tiny paradigm of the white American male."[126]

According to Jaron Lanier, however, founder of VPL Research, Virtual Reality could help solve the ecological crisis. He maintains that men have been raping the planet because they have had nothing "virtual" to act out their desires to mold and shape. Virtual Reality will let them rape and murder, control and exploit without leaving the comfort of their own living rooms. Lanier fails to mention, however, that the high-tech equipment necessary for such "trips" is not only expensive, and thus out of reach of most people, but also requires sustaining the technological empire that seems to be making the planet uninhabitable. The Virtual Reality tripper—world-conquering modern man transformed into imagination-dwelling postmodern man—seems oblivious to all of this, as he slays dragons, wins virgins, and gains immortality in galaxies long ago and far away. Or perhaps he is not so oblivious after all. Perhaps he has concluded that as life on the planet chokes on radioactive and chemical wastes, heats up because of production of CO_2, becomes increasingly simplified because of loss of species, and otherwise loses its capacity to sustain soft, organic flesh, the solution is to abandon such old-fashioned mortal tissue and escape into a potentially immortal identity living in a silicon-grounded cyberspace.

In my view, this fantasy is the latest version of the death-denying, masculinist ego's denial of mortality, limitation, and corporeality. Some may fear that Haraway's Cyborg Manifesto, in the very process of attempting to shift the informational age in a liberatory direction, concedes too much to technological possibilities whose "logic" may be inherently masculinist and suicidal. She herself interprets cyberspace as a "communal hallucination" that arises from too much complexity, articulation, and connection. Those who are overwhelmed by such connection retreat into paranoia, where they defend themselves "unto death."[127] Just as Spretnak concludes that a well-defended masculinist ego is at work in postmodern theorists who emphasize the infinity of differential relationships, so too Haraway concludes that "the defended self re-emerges at the heart of relationality."[128] Further, "in virtual space, the virtue of articulation— i.e., the power to produce connection—threatens to overwhelm and finally to engulf all possibility of effective action to change the world."[129]

Unlike Haraway, I am unwilling to abandon the idea that there is some direction to cosmic history, including human affairs. I believe that nondual awareness plays the role of what Whitehead called a metaphysical lure that draws the universe forward in the process of generating ever more complex forms of awareness. Like many adherents of the perennial philosophy, I believe that only by experiencing one's relationship to the eternal, or to what Jean Gebser called "the ever-present origin," can self-conscious individuals begin to accept the mortality of their incarnate status, and thus begin to surrender the obsession with control. In light of my own experience, in view of many centuries of testimony from those who have explored the further reaches of consciousness, and by virtue of the increasingly accepted idea that the universe is in the process of generating ever-greater orders of complexity and consciousness, I am attracted to the "myth" that there is a purpose—scarcely fathomable by humans—to the unfolding infinite complexity of the universe. These days, then, I would describe myself as an adherent to the perennial philosophy who is significantly influenced by critical postmodernism and radical ecology.[130]

The future is not something lying ahead of us; rather, it will be the consequence of what we do today. No one can know how our striving, planning, and dreaming will turn out. The interplay of countless actions will have unanticipated consequences. Increasingly, modernity's project of controlling the cosmos is encountering ecological limits, though many people still cling to that project. In contrast, radical ecologists and many New Paradigmers renounce modernity's ecologically devastating, high-technology project and call instead for an ecologically sustainable society that celebrates and protects human *and* nonhuman life. Critical postmodernists look askance at aspects of radical ecology, but even more so at modernity's identity-based metaphysics. Although sharing some progressive aspirations with radical ecologists, New Paradigmers, and many critical postmodernists, the cybernetic postmodernists urge us to transgress the boundaries between human, animal, and mechanical, so as to create an imaginative, though dangerous informational world, in which organic nature would have no special consideration, that is, would not be revered as pristine and original. In such a world, everything would become virtually interchangeable, since electronic codes and patterns can interact in ways impossible for bulky matter. Deprived of Haraway's concern for social justice, this world corresponds not only with Heidegger's fearsome vision of the emerging technological era, but also with nature feminism's vision of the triumph of body-despising patriarchy. If radical ecology's ecotopia represents one end of the spectrum of possible postmodern futures, and if the de-differentiated, cybernetic, informational world represents the other end, then the coming century may lie somewhere in between.

Although continuing to work for programs that promote social and ecological well-being, and although taking inspiration from the thought that what I do may make a tiny contribution to evolutionary aims that I cannot fully fathom, I acknowledge that other paths stand open. At one time I felt sure that a Heideggerean-oriented deep ecology was the right path, but my dialogue with social ecology and ecofeminism, and my scrutiny of the reactionary dimension of Heidegger's thought, revealed the limitations of that path. In turn, critical postmodernism has disclosed to me the limitations of radical ecology. I remain a friend of deep ecology and social ecology, but I suspect that their aspirations will be disappointed by future developments. I remain attracted to the cultural ecofeminism of authors like Charlene Spretnak, who simultaneously emphasizes the role played by death denial in the domination of women and nature and acknowledges that death denial can be overcome only by virtue of developing nondual awareness.

Though not optimistic about the future, neither am I pessimistic. I am saddened when I learn that old-growth forests are falling to the axe, fearful when I read reports about radioactive contamination seeping into the Arctic Ocean, and angry when I learn that South American natives continue to be slaughtered by the guns and poisoned by the mercury of men seized by the ancient lust for gold. But I am encouraged by movements that encourage sustainable development, uplifted by the courage of those risking their lives to protest senseless whaling and logging, and brightened by countless women and men working at the local level to enhance their own lives by preserving the land that sustains them. I am both fascinated and appalled by the technological marvels invented by the dangerous and witty ape who speaks. The "progress" made possible by such innovations is not what radical ecologists have in mind, largely because this clever ape believed for so long that he was the only animal able to speak. In portraying himself as the potentially all-powerful master of nature, the clever ape—terrified of death—expressed his fantasies about immortality. So long as technological innovation is driven by a revulsion against corporeality and mortality, and by a craving to make the clever ape's ego into an immortal god, those innovations will contain an unintegrated dark side that will threaten to undermine every achievement, including efforts by the prosthetic god to flee from a planet poisoned by man's rage against mortality.

But how are these clever apes, we humans, male and female, going to come to terms with our mortal condition? According to the perennial philosophy, the sorrow of finitude can only be healed by discovering one's participation in the eternal. Mortals have a sense that they somehow share in the eternal, but they often wrongly assume that their own egos, possessions, or achievements are themselves immortal. All creatures are finite as creatures, however. Hence, the desperation that characterizes the efforts of those who think they can evade death by controlling other people, their bodies, or non-human beings. The perennial philosophy says that a person who has awakened to the eternal can identify with his or her mortal form, for the eternal simultaneously transcends the world and is present within it. No longer seeking to defend that form at all costs, an awakened person can relate to other people and nonhuman forms of life in compassionate, creative ways. Dwelling in eternity does not mean fleeing into an otherworldly heaven; far less does it mean attempting to construct a heaven on earth by controlling nature. Rather, dwelling in eternity means celebrating its presence in the here and now. Relieved of the press of death-surmounting purposiveness, one may let things be, thus adopting an attitude that lies beyond the binary of activity versus passivity. As Spinoza remarked, however, "all things excellent are as difficult as they are rare."[131]

Citing the fact that "enlightened" people have engaged in practices that seem inconsistent with such an allegedly awakened condition, critics charge that there is neither an eternal domain, nor an "evolution" of consciousness that involves greater participation in that domain. Though my sympathies are with the perennial philosophy, I do not deny that such critics may be right. Other critics maintain that the perennial philosophy emphasizes consciousness evolution, yet ignores the political-economic structures that shape consciousness. But perennial philosophers certainly agree that repressive political-economic structures can drastically impede consciousness evolution, just as those structures can destroy many of the species that have evolved in the past several millions years. Put more positively: perennial philosophers assert that certain noncoercive and materially sufficient political-economic arrangements are necessary if more and more contemporary people are to become aware of further possibilities in the development of consciousness. Perennial philosophers, however, add that those arrangements in and of themselves do not "generate" higher consciousness, but instead simply unimpede the evolutionary tendencies of consciousness itself. Current political-economic arrangements tend to reflect and to reinforce the state of consciousness already achieved, which is why modern history has been characterized by such violence. Yet within those same arrangements, many people have become aware that there are alternatives to masculinist mental-egoic consciousness. I cannot predict whether humankind will evolve to the point that dramatic improvements in social and ecological well-being will ever occur, though I hold this out as a possibility. I am convinced, however, that unless contemporary people act to alleviate widespread social oppression, to halt senseless ecological destruction, and to articulate creative and critical responses to oncoming technological developments, the human phase of evolutionary history may soon come to an end.

INTRODUCTION

1. See Michael E. Zimmerman, "Beyond Humanism: Heidegger's Under-standing of Technology," *Listening* 12 (Fall 1977): 74–83; "Heidegger and Marcuse: Technology as Ideology," *Research in Philosophy and Technology* 2 (1977): 245–261; "Dewey, Heidegger, and the Quest for Certainty," *The Southwestern Journal of Philosophy* 9, 1 (1978): 87–95; "Marx and Heidegger on the Technological Domination of Nature," *Philosophy Today* 23 (Summer 1979): 99–112; "Humanism, Ontology, and the Nuclear Arms Race," *Research in Philosophy and Technology* 6 (1983): 157–172; "Toward a Heideggerean *Ethos* for Radical Environmentalism," *Environmental Ethics* 5, no. 2 (Summer 1983): 99–131; "Anthropocentric Humanism and the Arms Race," in *Nuclear War: Philosophical Perspectives,* ed. Michael Fox and Leo Groarke (New York: Peter Lang Publishers, 1985); "The Role of Spiritual Discipline in Learning to Dwell on Earth," in *Dwelling, Place and Environment,* ed. David Seamons and Robert Mugerauer (The Hague: Martinus Nijhoff, 1985); "Implications of Heidegger's Thought for Deep Ecology," in *The Modern Schoolman* 64 (November 1986): 19–43.
2. Michael E. Zimmerman, "Heidegger and Marcuse: Technology as Ideology," *Research in Philosophy and Technology* 2 (1977): 245–261.
3. See Victor Farias, *Heidegger et le nazisme,* trans. Myriam Benarroch and Jean-Baptiste Grasset (Paris: Verdier, 1987); Farias, *Heidegger and Nazism,*

trans. Paul Burrell, Dominic Di Bernardi, and Gabriel R. Ricci (Philadelphia: Temple University Press, 1989); Hugo Ott, *Martin Heidegger. Unterwegs zu seiner Biographie* (Frankfurt am Main: Campus Verlag, 1988).

4. Michael E. Zimmerman, *Heidegger's Confrontation with Modernity* (Bloomington: Indiana University Press, 1990).

5. To be sure, Derrida and the late Foucault both declined to be called "postmodern theorists," but neither did they appreciate the more common name of "poststructuralist." In "Le moment français de Nietzsche," in *Pourquoi nous ne sommes pas nietzschéens,* ed. Luc Ferry and Alain Renaut (Paris: Bernard Grasset, 1991): 116, Vincent Descombes says that what most Americans mean by "poststructuralism" is the Nietzschean version of structuralism developed in France during the late 1960s. See Luc Ferry and Alain Renaut, *French Philosophy of the Sixties: An Essay on Antihumanism,* trans. Mary H. S. Cattani (Amherst: The University of Massachusetts Press, 1990) for a critical account of this French Nietzscheanism.

6. It is worth noting that Max Horkheimer and Theodor Adorno, despite obvious political differences with Heidegger, shared in some ways his "levelling gaze," that is, his tendency to ignore significant differences between political regimes. Hence, in the 1940s Horkheimer and Adorno tended to define all modern societies as gripped by a control obsession that reduces all life, including humankind, to instrumental means for an irrational end: the achievement of ever-more power, solely for its own sake.

7. Theodore Roszak, *Person/Planet* (Garden City, N.Y.: Anchor Press/Doubleday, 1978); *The Making of a Counter Culture* (Garden City, N.Y.: Doubleday, 1969); and *Where the Wasteland Ends* (Garden City, N.Y.: Doubleday, 1972).

8. For example, see Christopher Norris, *What's Wrong with Postmodernism* (Baltimore: The Johns Hopkins University Press, 1990), 40.

9. Boris Frankel, "Beyond Abstract Environmentalism," *Island Magazine* 38: 22–25; citation is from 24; cited in Nigel Clark's excellent, but unpublished essay, "Nature, Modernity and Postmodernism," 26.

10. See Carl Rapp, "The Crisis of Reason in Contemporary Thought: Some Reflections on the Arguments of Postmodernism," *Critical Review* 5, 2 (Spring 1991): 261–290.

11. Ariel Kay Salleh, "Deeper than Deep Ecology: The Eco-Feminist Connection," *Environmental Ethics* 6, no. 4 (Winter 1984): 339–345.

12. Michael E. Zimmerman, "Ecofeminism, Deep Ecology, and Environmental Ethics," *Environmental Ethics* 9, 1 (Spring 1987): 21–44. My attempts have been criticized by Ariel Kay Salleh. See her essays, "The Ecofeminism/Deep Ecology Debate," *Environmental Ethics* 14, no. 3 (Fall 1992): 195–216, and "Class, Race, and Gender Discourse in the Ecofeminism/Deep Ecology Debate," *Environmental Ethics* 15, no. 3 (Fall 1993): 225–244.

13. See Warwick Fox, "The Deep Ecology-Ecofeminism Debate and Its Parallels," *Environmental Ethics* 11, no. 1 (Spring 1980), 5–26.

14. Albrecht Wellmer, *The Persistence of Modernity*, trans. David Midgley (Cambridge: The MIT Press, 1991), 86.

15. See Donald Kuspit, "The Contradictory Character of Postmodernism," in *Postmodernism—Philosophy and the Arts*, ed. Hugh J. Silverman (New York and London: Routledge, 1990).

16. In *The Postmodern Condition* (Minneapolis: The University of Minnesota Press, 1984), Jean-François Lyotard emphasizes that the postmodern is part of the modern. Likewise, in *The New Constellation* (Cambridge: The MIT Press, 1991), Richard Bernstein suggests using "modernity/postmodernity" to emphasize that modernity has not simply come to an end. A number of insightful books have addressed the complex social, artistic, and political phenomena associated with the gradual shift from modernity to postmodernity and postmodernism. For example, see David Harvey, *The Condition of Postmodernity* (Cambridge, Mass.: Basil Blackwell, 1989); Margaret A. Rose, *The Post-Modern and the Post-Industrial* (Cambridge: Cambridge University Press, 1991); and Steven Best and Douglas Kellner, *Postmodern Theory: Critical Interrogations* (New York: Guilford Press, 1991). See also Charles Jencks's helpful anthology, *The Post-Modern Reader* (New York: St. Martin's Press, 1992).

17. As Richard Bernstein has noted in his introduction to *The New Constellation* (Cambridge: The MIT Press, 1991), American pragmatists criticized modernity's philosophical categories in a way quite similar to postmodern theorists. In this book, however, I focus on postmodern theory, which owes much to Heidegger's thought, which in turn has played a role in deep ecology theory.

18. Postmodern theorist Jean Baudrillard maintains that postmodern experience is structured by a reversal of the relation between reality and representation. For Baudrillard, signs—including language and art—once sought to "represent" a preexisting external reality. Today, however, layers of self-referring electronic images and signs form a "hyperreality," in which

representations themselves take on the status of reality. Baudrillard maintains that the "cultural superstructure" has eclipsed the "economic base" of society. Hence, the substance of things has been evacuated into images: people consume signs, not things; reality is a series of simulacra; history has been reduced to a flood of diverting images. In effect, for Baudrillard, we have all become Max Headroom, existing solely as images on the infinitely ironic and self-reflective cosmic TV screen. According to Morris Berman, in *Coming to Our Senses: Body and Spirit in the Hidden History of the West* (New York: Bantam Books, 1990), 305–307, postmodernity amounts to a "cybernetic holism," a society totally administered by computers and electronic media. Critics contend, however, that Baudrillard fails to see that postmodern "hyperreality" is not a radical departure from modernity, but instead a manifestation of a late capitalist phase of it. See Douglas Kellner's excellent book, *Jean Baudrillard* (Stanford: Stanford University Press, 1990).

19. In this essay, every time I use the term "man" instead of the gender neutral "humanity" or "humankind," my intention is to emphasize the masculinist dimension of the issue in question.

20. See Alan W. Watts, *Nature, Man and Woman* (New York: Vintage Books, 1970).

21. On the problems posed by the proliferation of perspectives available to the "postmodern" self, see Kenneth J. Gergen, *The Saturated Self: Dilemmas of Identity in Contemporary Life* (New York: Basic Books, 1991).

CHAPTER ONE

1. See Arne Naess in cooperation with David Rothenberg, *Ecology, Community and Lifestyle* (Cambridge: Cambridge University Press, 1989); and George Sessions, "Deep Ecology as World View," *The Bucknell Review*, forthcoming.

2. See chapter 6 of Devall and Sessions, *Deep Ecology* (Salt Lake City: Peregrine Smith, 1984).

3. Arne Naess, "The Deep Ecological Movement: Some Philosophical Aspects," *Philosophical Inquiry* 8, no. 1–2 (1986): 11–31; see p. 18.

4. Arne Naess, "Deep Ecology and Ultimate Premises," *Society and Nature* I, no. 2 (September/December, 1992): 108–119; citation is from p. 108.

5. Ibid., 113.

6. Arne Naess, "Identification as a Source of Deep Ecological Attitudes," in *Deep Ecology*, ed. Michael Tobias (San Diego: Avant Books, 1985): 256.

7. Naess, "The Deep Ecological Movement," 25–26.
8. See Warwick Fox, *Toward a Transpersonal Ecology* (Boston: Shambhala, 1990). Along with works by Naess, Sessions, Devall, and myself, see Alan Drengson, author of *Beyond Environmental Crisis: From Technocratic to Planetary Person* (New York: Peter Lang, 1989); Andrew McLaughlin, *Regarding Nature: Industrialism and Deep Ecology* (Albany: SUNY Press, 1993); and Dolores LaChapelle, *Sacred Land, Sacred Sex, Rapture of the Deep: Concerning Deep Ecology—and Celebrating Life* (Durango: Kivaki Press, 1988).
9. See McLaughlin, *Regarding Nature.*
10. On this topic, see Harold Glasser, "The Distinctiveness of the Deep Ecology Approach to Ecophilosophy," unpublished MS.
11. Devall and Sessions, *Deep Ecology,* 70.
12. Glasser, "The Distinctiveness of the Deep Ecology Approach."
13. Naess, "The Deep Ecological Movement," 14–15.
14. Ibid, 14.
15. George Sessions, "Ecocentrism, Wilderness and Global Ecosystem Protection," in Michael E. Zimmerman et al., *Environmental Philosophy: From Animals Rights to Radical Ecology* (Englewood Cliffs, N.J.: Prentice Hall, 1993). See Michael Soulé, *Research Priorities for Conservation Biology* (Washington, D.C.: Island Press, 1989); and Edward O. Wilson, *The Diversity of Life* (Cambridge: Harvard University Press, 1992).
16. See Paul R. Ehrlich and Anne H. Ehrlich, *The Population Explosion* (New York: Touchstone, 1991).
17. The controversy generated by J. Baird Callicott's essay, "The Wilderness Idea Revisited: The Sustainable Development Alternative," *The Environmental Professional* 13 (1991): 235–247, illustrates the conflicts involving how best to save wilderness from economic "development." See Holmes Rolston III, "The Wilderness Idea Reaffirmed," *The Environmental Professional* 13 (1991): 370–377, and Callicott's reply, "That Good Old-Time Wilderness Religion," 378–379.
18. Naess, "Deep Ecology and Lifestyle," in *The Paradox of Environmentalism,* ed. Neil Everndon (Ontario: York University, 1983): 57.
19. George Sessions, "Ecological Governments: A Restructuring Proposal" (1992), unpublished MS.
20. George Sessions, "Deep Ecology as World View."
21. Arne Naess, "Politics and the Ecological Crisis: An Introductory Note," in the special issue "From Anthropocentrism to Deep Ecology," ed. Warwick Fox, of *ReVision* 3, no. 3 (Winter 1991): 142–146.

22. Naess, "Politics and the Ecological Crisis," 143.

23. Ibid., 146.

24. On this topic, see David M. Johns's excellent essay, "The Relevance of Deep Ecology to the Third World," *Environmental Ethics* 12, no. 3 (Fall 1990): 233–253.

25. Warwick Fox, "Deep Ecology: Too Thin as Theory?", unpublished MS, December 1992.

26. See Michael Cohen, *The Pathless Way: John Muir and American Wilderness* (Madison: University of Wisconsin Press, 1984); and Max Oelschlaeger's readings of Muir, Thoreau, and Leopold in *The Idea of Wilderness* (New Haven: Yale University Press, 1991).

27. See Gary Snyder's 1969 essay, "Four Changes," revised in *Turtle Island* (New York: New Directions, 1974); and *The Practice of the Wild* (San Francisco: City Light Books, 1990). On the difference between reform environmentalism and deep ecology, see George Sessions, "Shallow and Deep Ecology: A Review of the Philosophical Literature," in Robert C. Hughes and J. Donald Schultz, *Ecological Consciousness* (Washington, D.C.: University Press of America, 1981); John Rodman, "The Four Forms of Ecological Consciousness Reconsidered," in *Ethics and the Environment*, ed. Donald Scherer and Thomas Attig (Englewood Cliffs: Prentice-Hall, Inc., 1983); Bill Devall, "Reform Environmentalism," *Humboldt Journal of Social Relations* 6, no. 2 (Spring/Summer 1979): 129–158; Fox, *Toward a Transpersonal Ecology;* and Christopher Manes, *Green Rage* (Boston: Little, Brown, 1990).

28. Albert Gore, *Earth in the Balance* (Boston: Houghton Mifflin Company, 1992).

29. Devall, "Reform Environmentalism," 148; Christopher Manes, "Deep Ecology as Revolutionary Thought (Action)," *The Trumpeter* 4, no. 2 (Spring 1987): 12–14.

30. Naess and Rothenberg, *Ecology, Community, and Lifestyle,* 33.

31. George Sessions, "Ecological Consciousness and Paradigm Change," in *Deep Ecology,* ed. Tobias, 30.

32. Devall and Sessions, *Deep Ecology,* 48.

33. Arne Naess, "Identification as a Source of Deep Ecological Attitudes," 269.

34. See Arne Naess, "Deep Ecology for the 22nd Century," *The Trumpeter* 9, no. 2 (Spring 1992): 87–88.

35. Bill Devall, "The Deep Ecology Movement," *Natural Resources Journal* 20 (Spring 1980): 299–322; quotation is from p. 299.

36. Charles Krauthammer, "Saving Nature, but Only for Man," *Time* 17 June 1991: 56. My emphasis. Thanks to Betty Pérez for sending me this essay.

37. On how the idea of "man's progress" justifies economic decisions favoring select groups, see C. S. Lewis, *The Abolition of Man* (New York: The Macmillan Company, 1947).

38. David Ehrenfeld, *The Arrogance of Humanism* (New York: Oxford University Press, 1978): 259–260; my emphasis. See also Christopher Plant and Judith Plant, *Green Business: Hope or Hoax?* (Philadelphia: New Society Publishers, 1991): 3: "[T]he very best thing for the planet might be a massive world-wide economic depression."

39. Ehrenfeld, *The Arrogance of Humanism,* 260.

40. Theodore Roszak, *Person/Planet: The Creative Disintegration of Industrial Society* (Garden City, N.Y.: Anchor Press/Doubleday, 1978).

41. Martin W. Lewis, *Green Delusions: An Environmentalist Critique of Radical Environmentalism* (Durham: Duke University Press, 1992): 12. This is an excellent book. For a damning indictment of the environmental movement, see Ronald Bailey and Michael Fumento, *Eco-Scam: The False Prophets of Ecological Apocalypse* (New York: St. Martin's Press, 1992).

42. Robert Paehlke, *Environmentalism and the Future of Progressive Politics* (New Haven: Yale University Press, 1989).

43. See William Godfrey-Smith (now Grey), "The Value of Wilderness," *Environmental Ethics* 1 (1979): 309–319. See also Fox, *Toward a Transpersonal Ecology,* 154–161.

44. See James Lovelock, *Gaia: A New Look at Life on Earth* (New York: Oxford University Press, 1979); and Lawrence E. Joseph, *Gaia* (New York: St. Martin's Press, 1990).

45. Rodman, "The Four Forms of Ecological Consciousness Reconsidered."

46. Ibid., 85.

47. Ibid., 86.

48. Though often taken as a pantheist, Muir may have been a *panentheist,* one who regards nature as a manifestation of but not exhaustive of the divine.

49. Paul Shepard, *Thinking Animals* (New York: Viking, 1978); *Nature and Madness* (San Francisco: Sierra Club Books, 1984); Edward O. Wilson, *Biophilia* (Cambridge: Harvard University Press, 1984).

50. See Michael McCloskey, "No Special Revelations," *Sierra* (January/February 1989): 160–165.

51. For a critical look at this movement, see William Poole, "Neither Wise nor Well," *Sierra* 77, no. 6 (November/December 1992): 58–61, 88–93.

52. See Herman Daly and John B. Cobb, Jr., *For the Common Good* (Boston: Beacon Press, 1989); Paul R. Ehrlich and Anne H. Ehrlich, *Healing the Planet* (Reading: Addison Wesley Publishing Company, Inc., 1991); Robert Costanza, ed., *Ecological Economics* (New York: Columbia University Press, 1991); and Clive Ponting, *A Green History of the World* (New York: St. Martin's, 1991).

53. See Terry L. Anderson and Donald R. Leal, *Free Market Environmentalism* (Boulder: Westview Press, 1991). For critiques of this book, see Herman Daly "Free Market Environmentalism: Turning a Good Servant into a Bad Master," and Mark Sagoff, "Free-Market versus Libertarian Environmentalism," in pp. 171–183 and 211–230 of *Critical Review*'s excellent special issue on market liberalism and environmentalism, vol. 6, no. 2–3 (Spring-Summer 1993).

54. Bill Devall, "Political Activism in a Time of War," in the special issue "From Anthropocentrism to Deep Ecology," ed. Warwick Fox, of *ReVision* 3, no. 3 (Winter 1991): 135–141; citation is from p. 137.

55. See Naess, "Simple in Means, Rich in Ends: A Conversation with Arne Naess," in Zimmerman, *Environmental Philosophy.*

56. See Michael E. Zimmerman, "The Blessing of Otherness: Wilderness and the Human Condition," in *The Wilderness Condition,* ed. Max Oelschlaeger (San Francisco: Sierra Club Books, 1992).

57. Arne Naess, "Deep Ecology in Good Conceptual Health," *The Trumpeter* 3, no. 4 (Fall 1986): 20.

58. Naess said this at the "Human in Nature" conference in Boulder, Colorado during May, 1991.

59. Naess and Rothenberg, *Ecology, Community and Lifestyle,* 72–73.

60. Naess, "The Shallow and the Deep, Long-Range Ecology Movement," 99. See also Naess, "Self-realization in Mixed Communities of Humans, Bears, Sheep, and Wolves," *Inquiry* 22 (1979): 231–241.

61. Naess, "Simple in Means, Rich in Ends."

62. Naess and Rothenberg, *Ecology, Community, and Lifestyle,* 69.

63. Naess is by no means a rigid person whose behavior is wholly consistent with a well-defined view. See Fox, *Toward a Transpersonal Ecology,* 87–88.

64. Ibid.

65. Arne Naess, "Self-Realization: An Ecological Approach to Being in the World," *The Trumpeter* 4, no. 3 (Summer 1987): 35–42; citation is from p. 39.

66. Paul Wienpahl in *The Radical Spinoza* (New York: New York University Press, 1979) depicts Spinoza as a radical ecological thinker whose views are similar to Mahayana Buddhism.

67. George Sessions, "Spinoza and Jeffers on Man in Nature," *Inquiry* 20 (1977): 481–528; citation is from pp. 494–495.

68. Naess, "Self-Realization in Mixed Communities of Humans, Bears, Sheep, and Wolves," 233.

69. Ibid., 236.

70. See Genevieve Lloyd, "Spinoza's Environmental Ethics," *Inquiry* 23 (September 1980): 293–311, and Naess, "Environmental Ethics and Spinoza's Ethics. Comments on Genevieve Lloyd's Article," *Inquiry* 23, (September 1980): 313–325.

71. Yovel's comments were made in response to Arne Naess's paper at "The Green Revolution" conference at Michigan State University.

72. See Alan R. Drengson, "Shifting Paradigms: From the Technocratic to the Person-Planetary," *Environmental Ethics* 2, no. 3 (Fall 1980): 221–240.

73. Arne Naess, "The Shallow and the Deep, Long-Range Ecology Movement," 95.

74. John Seed, "Deep Ecology Down Under," an interview in *Turtle Talk: Voices for a Sustainable Future,* ed. Christopher Plant and Judith Plant (Philadelphia, Santa Cruz, Lillooet, B.C.: New Society Publishers, 1990).

75. See Paul Shepard, "Ecology and Man—A Viewpoint," *The Subversive Science* (New York: Houghton Mifflin Co., 1969): 3.

76. See for example, J. Baird Callicott, "Animal Liberation: A Triangular Affair," *Environmental Ethics* 2, no. 4 (Winter 1980): 311–338.

77. See Karen J. Warren and Jim Cheney, "Ecosystem Ecology and Metaphysical Ecology: A Case Study," *Environmental Ethics* 15, no. 2 (Summer 1993): 99–116.

78. Naess, "Simple in Means, Rich in Ends," 12.

79. The risk involved in using scientific models to support normative views is revealed by Sessions's experience. In "Spinoza and Jeffers on Man in Nature," p. 505, he affirmed a mechanistic cosmology, but he soon recognized that mechanism has often justified disrespectful treatment of non-human beings. Hence, he began reading Spinoza as a *process* philosopher. See Sessions, "Western Process Metaphysics (Heraclitus, Whitehead, and Spinoza)," in Devall and Sessions, *Deep Ecology.*

80. Freya Matthews, *The Ecological Self* (London: Routledge, 1990). See also Ted Peters, *The Cosmic Self* (San Francisco: HarperSan Francisco, 1991).

81. C. J. Graves, *The Conceptual Foundations of Contemporary Relativity Theory* (Cambridge: MIT Press, 1971): 314; cited by Matthews, *The Ecological Self,* 68.

82. Graves, *The Conceptual Foundations,* 315.

83. Matthews, *The Ecological Self,* 143ff.

84. Ibid., 144.

85. Ibid., 148.

86. Ibid., 162. In some ways an anti-anthropocentrist and Spinozist, Bertrand Russell would have criticized Matthews's attempt to develop a progressive cosmology. See Russell, *Mysticism and Logic* (Garden City, N.Y.: Anchor Doubleday, 1957).

87. For neo-Kantian support for the idea that nonhuman life deserves moral respect, see Paul W. Taylor, *Respect for Nature* (Princeton: Princeton University Press, 1986). See also *The Monist* 75, no. 2 (April 1992), which is devoted to the topic of "The Intrinsic Value of Nature."

88. For a review of some of these arguments, see my essay, "The Critique of Natural Rights and the Search for a Non-Anthropocentric Basis for Moral Behavior," *Journal of Value Inquiry* 19 (1985): 43–53.

89. John Rodman, "Animal Justice: The Counter-revolution in Natural Right and Law," *Inquiry* 22 (Summer 1979): 3–22; citation is from p. 10.

90. John Rodman, "The Liberation of Nature?" *Inquiry* 20 (1977): 83–145; citation is from p. 94.

91. Ibid.

92. For a good critique of atomistic metaphysics, see Matthews, *The Ecological Self.*

93. Fox, *Toward a Transpersonal Ecology*, 259.

94. See Michael E. Zimmerman, "Implications of Heidegger's Thought for Deep Ecology," *The Modern Schoolman* LXIV (November 1986): 19–43.

95. Naess, "Identification as a Source of Deep Ecological Attitudes," 268.

96. Naess made this statement at "The Green Revolution" conference in 1992.

97. Naess, "Deep Ecology and Ultimate Premises," 110.

98. See Stephen Jay Gould, "A Humongous Fungus Among Us," *Natural History* (July 1992): 10–18.

99. Holmes Rolston III, *Philosophy Gone Wild* (Buffalo: Prometheus Books, 1986) and *Environmental Philosophy* (Philadelphia: Temple University Press, 1988).

100. Naess, "Self-Realization," 36.

101. See Naess and Rothenberg, *Ecology, Community and Lifestyle*, 85–86; and Naess, "Self-Realization," 40.

102. Although Naess would agree with many of these points, he is not as willing as Fox seems to be to abandon the terminology of the intrinsic worth of human and nonhuman beings.

103. See Henryk Skolimowski, "In Defense of Ecophilosophy and of Intrinsic Value: A Call for Conceptual Clarity," *The Trumpeter* 3, no. 4 (Fall 1987): 9–12.

104. See Harold Fromm, "Ecology and Ideology," *The Hudson Review* 45, no. 1 (Spring 1992): 23–36; reference is to p. 30.

105. Warwick Fox, "Post-Skolimowski Reflections on Deep Ecology," *The Trumpeter* 3, no. 4 (Fall 1986): 16.

106. Many of Callicott's excellent essays are collected in *In Defense of the Land Ethic* (Albany: SUNY Press, 1989). Leopold and Callicott view the expansion of moral concern as an evolutionary development within Euro-American culture, but since Native Americans long regarded humans and nonhumans as part of a larger family, this Eurocentric view needs reexamining. The relation between Native American culture and radical ecology is controversial. Some, including Callicott, say that we have much to learn from Native Americans. Others warn, however, that viewing Native Americans as proto-ecologists is but another instance of Western "colonization." See Michael Castro, *Interpreting the Indian* (Albuquerque: University of New Mexico Press, 1983); and Michael Fischer, "Ethnicity and the Post-Modern Arts of Memory," in *Writing Culture: The Poetics and Politics of Ethnography*, ed. J. Clifford and G. Marcus (Berkeley, Los Angeles, London: University of California Press, 1984).

107. Fox, *Toward a Transpersonal Ecology*, 264–265.

108. Naess, "Identification as a Source of Deep Ecological Attitudes," 263.

109. Fox, *Toward a Transpersonal Ecology*, 133–137. The way I develop the ultimate norm "Obey God!" is my own, not Fox's.

110. Glasser, "The Distinctiveness of the Deep Ecology Approach."

111. See, for example, Matthew Fox, *The Coming of the Cosmic Christ* (New York: Harper & Row, 1989).

112. Glasser argues that wider "identification," not self-realization, is crucial to deep ecology, but even though there may be textual grounds for this claim, Glasser himself notes that the DEP's first two points, which emphasize the "flourishing" and "realization" of all beings, seem more consistent with the norm of self-realization than with wider identification.

113. Fox, *Toward a Transpersonal Ecology*.

114. Jim Cheney, "The Neo-Stoicism of Radical Ecology," *Environmental Ethics* 11, no. 4 (Winter 1989): 293–325.

115. Ibid., 297–298.

116. Cited in Fox, *Toward a Transpersonal Ecology*, 200–201.

117. Ibid., 204ff.

118. Warwick Fox, "Deep Ecology: A New Philosophy for Our Time?" *The Ecologist* 14 no. 5–6 (1984): 194–200; citation is from p. 196. Despite Fox's claim that this essay no longer fully reflects his views, aspects of it—including the point under consideration—would seem to retain their validity for him.

119. Naess's Ecosophy T seems to combine ontological with cosmological identification.

120. Fox, *Toward a Transpersonal Psychology,* 265.

121. Roderick Nash, *The Rights of Nature* (Madison: The University of Wisconsin Press, 1990).

122. Manes, "Deep Ecology as Revolutionary Thought (Action)," 13.

123. Manes, *Green Rage,* 172–173.

124. Kelly Bulkley, in "The Quest for Transformational Experience: Dreams and Environmental Ethics," *Environmental Ethics* 13, no. 2 (Summer 1991): 151–163, answers this question in terms of the "dream" work associated with depth psychology.

125. See Irvin D. Yalom, *Existential Psychotherapy* (New York: Basic Books, 1980).

126. On this topic, see Erich Fromm, *Escape from Freedom* (New York: Avon Books, 1964).

CHAPTER TWO

1. See Norman Cohn's classic, *The Pursuit of the Millennium* (New York: Oxford University Press, 1981).

2. See William Irwin Thompson, "Sixteen Years of the New Age," in David Spangler and William Irwin Thompson, *Reimagination of the World* (Santa Fe: Bear & Company, 1991): 19.

3. Ibid., 18–19.

4. Charles Jencks, "Preface: Post-Modernism—The Third Force," in Jencks, ed., *The Post-Modern Reader* (New York: St. Martin's Press, 1992): 6–7.

5. Rachel Carson, *Silent Spring* (New York: Houghton Mifflin, 1962): 261.

6. See Klaus Eder, "The Rise of Counter-culture Movements Against Modernity: Nature as a New Field of Class Struggle," *Theory, Culture & Society* 7 (1990): 21–47.

7. George Sessions, "Ecological Consciousness and Paradigm Change," in *Deep Ecology,* ed. Michael Tobias (San Diego: Avant Books, 1985): 32. See Raymond F. Dassmann, "Conservation, Counter-culture, and Separate Realities," *Environmental Conservation* 1, no. 2 (Summer 1974): 133–137.

8. Sessions, "Ecological Consciousness and Paradigm Change," 28.

9. Ibid.

10. Ibid.

11. Ibid., 39. In *Beyond Counterculture* (Pullman; Washington State University Press, 1990), Jentri Anders describes Mateel, a countercultural, ecologically

oriented community that arose in the 1970s in Humboldt County, California.

12. Theodore Roszak, *Where the Wasteland Ends* (Garden City, N.Y.: Doubleday, 1972): 50. See also Roszak, *The Making of a Counter Culture* (Garden City, N.Y.: Doubleday Anchor, 1969).

13. Theodore Roszak, *Unfinished Animal* (New York: Harper & Row, 1975).

14. Theodore Roszak, *Person/Planet* (Garden City, N.Y.: Anchor Press/Doubleday, 1978): 317.

15. Theodore Roszak, *The Voice of the Earth* (New York: Simon & Schuster, 1992).

16. Ibid, 321.

17. The reference to Berger comes from p. 41 of Hans-Jürgen Ruppert, *Durchbruch zur Innenwelt: Spirituelle Impulse aus New Age und Esoterik in kritischer Beleuchtung* (Stuttgart: Quell Verlag, 1988).

18. Fritjof Capra, *The Tao of Physics* (New York: Bantam Books, 1976): xix.

19. Paul Shepard, *Nature and Madness* (San Francisco: Sierra Books, 1982). On the ecological and cultural implications of the agricultural revolution, see Max Oelschlaeger, *The Idea of Wilderness* (New Haven: Yale University Press, 1991).

20. Shepard, *Nature and Madness*, 80.

21. Ibid., 70.

22. Lynn White, Jr., "The Religious Roots of Our Ecologic Crisis," in *Philosophy and Technology*, ed. Carl Mitcham and Robert Mackey (New York: The Free Press, 1972): 259–265.

23. For a critical account of the role played by patriarchy in the conquest of "virgin" wilderness in America, see Annette Kolodny, *The Lay of the Land* (Chapel Hill: University of North Carolina Press, 1975).

24. See Dolores LaChapelle and Janet Bourque, *Earth Festivals* (Silverton, Colo.: Finn Hill Arts, 1976).

25. Roszak, *The Voice of the Earth*, 320–321.

26. David R. Williams, personal communication.

27. David R. Williams, *Wilderness Lost: The Religious Origins of the American Mind* (Selinsgrove: Susquehanna University Press, 1987): 15; emphases in quotation are mine. Regarding this issue, I have benefited from conversations with Williams and with Teresa Toulouse, who for years has stressed the importance of Edwards's Puritanism for deep ecology.

28. Williams, *Wilderness Lost*, 48.

29. In *Desert Solitaire* (Tucson: University of Arizona Press, 1988), Edward Abbey suggests that regeneration is possible if one removes oneself into the

desert, far from the temptations of a corrupt, anthropocentric, urban humanity. This idea is rooted not only in Puritanism, but in the "desert fathers" of early Christianity.

30. Williams, *Wilderness Lost,* 108; emphasis mine.

31. In *The Coming of the Cosmic Christ* (San Francisco: Harper & Row, 1988), Matthew Fox describes what amounts to a Christian nature-mysticism in the form of creation-centered spirituality.

32. Thanks to Teresa Toulouse for helpful discussions about the development of Thoreau's work.

33. John Muir, cited by Frederick Turner, *Rediscovering America: John Muir in His Time and Ours* (New York: Viking Press, 1985): 147–148.

34. See *Critical Questions About New Paradigm Thinking,* a special issue of *ReVision* 9, no. 1 (Summer/Fall 1986).

35. Williams, *Wilderness Lost,* 92.

36. Ibid., 117.

37. Fritjof Capra, *The Turning Point* (New York: Simon & Schuster, 1982). But see his recent dialogue with Christian monk, David Steindl-Rost, *Belonging to the Universe* (San Francisco: HarperSan Francisco, 1991).

38. David Spangler, "Images of the New Age," in *Reimagination of the World,* 25.

39. See Andrew Ross's insightful essay, "New Age—A Kinder, Gentler Science?" in *Strange Weather* (New York: Verso, 1991).

40. George Sessions, "Deep Ecology as World View," forthcoming in *Bucknell Review.*

41. Hazel Henderson, "A Guide to Riding the Tiger of Change," in *Gaia: A Way of Knowing,* ed. William Irwin Thompson (Great Barrington, Mass.: Lindisfarne Association, Inc., 1987): 158; my emphasis.

42. George Sessions, "Deep Ecology as World View"; Marilyn Ferguson, *The Aquarian Conspiracy* (Los Angeles: J. P. Tarcher, 1980).

43. R. Buckminster Fuller, *Operating Manual for Spaceship Earth* (New York: Simon & Schuster, 1979): 36.

44. Conrad Bonfanti, cited by Sessions, pp. 9–10, "Deep Ecology, New Age, and Gaian Consciousness," unpublished MS.

45. Peter Russell, *The Global Brain: Speculations on the Evolutionary Leap to Planetary Consciousness* (Los Angeles: J. P. Tarcher, 1983). See also *Gaian Consciousness,* a special issue of *ReVision* 9, no. 2 (Winter/Spring 1987).

46. As cited by Sessions in "Deep Ecology as World View," 10.

47. As cited by Sessions, in "Deep Ecology, New Age, and Gaian Consciousness," 11.

48. Ibid., 12.

49. James Lovelock, *Gaia: A New Look at Life on Earth* (New York: Oxford University Press, 1979).

50. See Bill Devall, "New Age and Deep Ecology: Contrasting Paradigms," unpublished essay (1981).

51. Ibid.

52. David Spangler, *Reimagination of the World*, 57.

53. Lovelock, *Gaia*, 148, as cited by Devall, "New Age and Deep Ecology," 6.

54. Ibid.

55. Michael Allaby and James Lovelock, *The Greening of Mars* (London: Andre Deutsch, 1984).

56. Edward O. Wilson, *Biophilia* (Cambridge: Harvard University Press, 1984): 117.

57. J. Peter Vayk, *Doomsday Has Been Cancelled* (Culver City, Calif.: Peace Press, 1978): 61, as cited in Devall, "Deep Ecology and New Age," 8–9.

58. See Neil Evernden, *The Natural Alien* (Toronto: The University of Toronto Press, 1985); and Bill Devall and George Sessions, "The Development of Natural Resources and the Integrity of Nature," *Environmental Ethics* 6, no. 4 (Winter 1984): 293–322.

59. Morris Berman, "The Cybernetic Dream of the 21st Century," in *Renewing the Earth*, ed. John Clark (London: Green Print, 1990): 12–32.

60. Capra, *The Turning Point*, 412. On the Capra-deep ecology link, see Steffen Link, "Ein Neues Lied, ein bessres Lied . . . ?" in *Zwischen den Zeiten: Das New Age in der Diskussion*, ed. Matthias Pilger and Steffen Rink (Marburg: Diagonal-Verlag, 1989): 11–24.

61. Capra, *The Turning Point*, 412.

62. Ibid., 266–267.

63. Ibid., 35–40.

64. Ibid., 292.

65. Jaakov Jerome Garb, "The Use and Misuse of the Whole Earth Image," *Whole Earth Review* (March 1985): 18–25. See also Garb, "Perspective or Escape? Ecofeminists Musings on Contemporary Earth Imagery," in *Reweaving the Earth: The Emergence of Ecofeminism*, ed. Irene Diamond and Gloria Feman Orenstein (San Francisco: Sierra Club Books, 1990): 264–278.

66. Martin Heidegger, "The Age of the World Picture," in *The Question Concerning Technology*, trans. William Lovitt (New York: Harper & Row, 1977).

67. Martin Heidegger, "Only a God can save us: *Der Spiegel*'s interview with Martin Heidegger," trans. Maria P. Alter and John D. Caputo, *Philosophy Today* XX (Winter 1976): 267–284; citation is from p. 277.

68. On Reagan's media presidency, see Walter Truett Anderson's insightful book, *Reality Isn't What It Used To Be* (San Francisco: Harper & Row, 1990).

69. See Lawrence Tribe, "Ways Not to Think About Plastic Trees," in *When Values Conflict,* ed. Lawrence Tribe et al. (Cambridge: Harvard University Press, 1976): 61–91.

70. Henryk Skolimowski, *Eco-Philosophy* (Boston/London: Marion Boyars, 1981); and *Living Philosophy: Eco-Philosophy as a Tree of Life* (London and New York: Arkana, 1992).

71. Skolimowski, *Eco-Philosophy,* 69.

72. Ibid.

73. Ibid., 74.

74. Ibid., 78.

75. Henry Skolimowski, "Eco-Philosophy and Deep Ecology," *Society and Nature* I, no. 2 (September/December 1992): 98–107.

76. Arne Naess, "Deep Ecology and Ultimate Premises," *Society and Nature* I, no. 2 (September/December 1992): 108–119.

77. George Sessions, review of Skolimowski's *Eco-Philosophy, Environmental Ethics* 6, no. 2 (Summer 1984): 167–174; citation is from p. 174.

78. Henryk Skolimowski, "The Dogma of Anti-Anthropocentrism and Eco-philosophy," *Environmental Ethics* 6, no. 3 (Fall 1984): 283–288. The controversy continued in *The Trumpeter* in 1986 and 1987.

79. Sessions, review of Bonifazi's *The Soul of the World,* in *Environmental Ethics* 3, no. 3 (Fall 1981): 275–281; citation from p. 276.

80. Roszak, *Person/Planet,* 54.

81. Ibid. My emphasis.

82. Ibid., 55.

83. Ibid.

84. Ibid.

85. Roszak, *Unfinished Animal,* 91.

86. Ibid., 91–92. My emphasis.

87. Paul Shepard, *The Tender Carnivore and the Sacred Game* (New York: Charles Scribner's Sons, 1983): 103.

88. Ibid.

89. Roszak, *The Voice of the Earth,* 185.

90. Jencks, *The Post-Modern Reader,* 7.

91. See Matthias Pilger, "New Age in der Bildungsarbeit," in Pilger and Rink, *Zwischen den Zeiten,* 197. See also James R. Lewis and J. Gordon Melton, *Perspectives on the New Age* (Albany: SUNY Press, 1992); Daniel Sillescu, "Was ist 'New Age?'," in *Zwischen den Zeiten,* 25–36.

92. Mark Satin, *New Age Politics* (New York: Dell Publishing Co., Inc., 1979): 11.

93. Some serious scholars argue that recent sightings of the Virgin Mary, Bigfoot, and UFOs are symptoms of humanity's unconscious effort to restore balance to the unbalanced masculinist psyche, which emphasizes abstract rationality, separateness, and control, at the expense of concrete, feminine insight into interconnectedness and cooperation. See Keith Thompson's excellent book, *Angels and Aliens* (Reading, Mass.: Addison-Wesley, 1991); Michael Grosso, "UFOs and the Myth of the New Age," *ReVision* 11, no. 3 (Winter 1989): 5–13; and Kenneth Ring, *The Omega Project* (New York: William Morrow and Company, Inc., 1992). See also John Mack, *Abduction: Alien Encounters and Human Evolution* (New York: Scribners, 1994).

94. Ruppert, *Durchbruch zur Innenwelt*, 37.

95. Fritjof Capra and Charlene Spretnak, *Green Politics* (New York: Dutton, 1984).

96. Roszak, *Unfinished Animal*, 11; see pp. 26–29 for a chart of the constituents of "the Aquarian Frontier."

97. Ibid., 113.

98. Hans Sebald, "Wiederverzauberte Nature, Versöhnung, neue Spiritutali-tät," in *Geist und Natur*, ed. Hans-Peter Dürr and Walther Ch. Zimerli (Bern/München/Wien: Scherz Verlag, 1991): 327.

99. See Ross, *Strange Weather*, 43.

100. Ibid., 44.

101. Roszak, *Unfinished Animal*, 239.

102. Ibid., 249.

103. Peter Russell, *The Global Brain*, as cited in Daniel Sillescu, "Was ist 'New Age?'," in Pilger and Rink, *Zwischen den Zeiten*, 33.

104. Sessions, "Deep Ecology, New Age, and Gaian Consciousness."

105. On this topic, see Sillescu, "Was ist 'New Age?'," 25–36. For a sophisticated discussion of New Age medicine, see Larry Dossey, *Space, Time, and Medicine* (Boulder: Shambhala, 1982).

106. Küenzlen, "New Age und grüne Bewegung," 131.

107. Ross, *Strange Weather*, 53ff.

108. Ibid.

109. Fritjof Capra, foreword to Rüdiger Lutz, *Die sanfte Wende* (Frankfurt am Main: Ullstein Sachbuch, 1987), 7.

110. Roszak, *The Unfinished Animal*, 93.

111. Ibid., 85.

112. Wallace Black Elk and William S. Lyon, *Black Elk: The Sacred Ways of a Lakota* (New York: Harper & Row, 1990).

113. Harman, *Global Mind Change* (New York: Warner Books, 1990).

114. Ibid., 112.

115. Ibid., 83–89.

116. Ibid., 121. My emphasis.

117. Ibid., 117.

118. Ibid., 119.

119. Ibid., 147. My emphasis.

120. Ibid., 149.

121. Ibid., 160.

122. But see William Irwin Thompson's important essay, "The Big Picture and Messianic Delusion," in *Reimagination of the World,* 73–81.

123. Frederic Jameson, *Postmodernism* (Durham: Duke University Press, 1992): 159. Highly recommended for insight into the political implications of cultural and artistic postmodernism.

124. Arthur Mendel, *Vision and Violence* (Ann Arbor: University of Michigan Press, 1992): 250–251.

125. Oswald Spengler, *Der Mensch und der Technik* (München: 1932): 82; cited by Hans-Jürgen Ruppert, "Neues Denken auf alten Wegen: New Age und Esoterik," in *Die Rückkehr der Zauberer,* ed. Hansjörg Hemminger (Hamburg: Rowohlt Verlag, 1987): 84.

CHAPTER THREE

1. Luc Ferry and Alain Renaut, *French Philosophy of the Sixties,* trans. Mary H. S. Cattani (Amherst: University of Massachusetts Press, 1990).

2. Claude Lévi-Strauss, *The Savage Mind* (Chicago: The University of Chicago Press, 1962). See Robert Young's critique of Sartre's view of history in *White Mythologies: Writing History and the West* (New York: Routledge, 1990): 28–47.

3. Lévi-Strauss as cited in David Pace, *Claude Lévi-Strauss: The Bearer of Ashes* (London: Routledge & Kegan Paul, 1983): 179.

4. Ibid., 247.

5. Ibid., 250.

6. Ibid., 247

7. Rainer Nägele, "The Scene of the Other: Theodor W. Adorno's Negative Dialectic in the Context of Poststructuralism," in *Postmodernism and Pol-*

itics, ed. Jonathan Arac (Minneapolis: University of Minnesota Press, 1986): 102.

8. Ibid.

9. Jacques Derrida, "White Mythology," in *Margins of Philosophy,* trans. Alan Bass (Chicago: The University of Chicago Press, 1982).

10. See Kenneth J. Gergen's fascinating and disturbing book, *The Saturated Self* (New York: Basic Books, 1991).

11. For instance, see the special issue on art and ecology, *Art Journal,* ed. Jackie Brookner, 51,2 (Summer, 1992). See also Nigel Clark's insightful essay, "The Hyperenchantment of the World? Ecology, Aesthetics and the Postmodern," *Sites* 22 (Autumn 1991), 21–33, and Suzi Gablik, *The Reenchantment of Art* (New York: Thomas and Hudson, Inc., 1991).

12. See George Sessions, "Spinoza and Jeffers on Man in Nature," *Inquiry* 20, no. 4 (1977): 481–528.

13. Ibid., 508–509.

14. Brian Steverson, "Ecocentrism and Ecological Modeling," forthcoming in *Environmental Ethics.*

15. See Donald Worster's informative essay, "The Ecology of Order and Chaos," in *Environmental Ethics: Divergence and Convergence,* ed. Susan J. Armstrong and Richard G. Botzler (New York: McGraw-Hill, 1993): 39–49. On nature "knowing best," see Sessions, "Spinoza and Jeffers on Man in Nature," 491.

16. Worster, "The Ecology of Order and Chaos," 39–40.

17. Ibid., 40–41.

18. Ibid., 43.

19. See Harley Cahen, "Against the Moral Considerability of Ecosystems," *Environmental Ethics* 10, no. 3 (Fall 1988): 195–216; and Stanley N. and Barbara M. Saithe, "Ecosystem Moral Considerability: A Reply to Cahen," *Environmental Ethics* 11, no. 4 (Winter 1989): 355–362.

20. Cited in Worster, "The Ecology of Order and Chaos," 45.

21. For a critique of such environmental holism, see Karen J. Warren and Jim Cheney, "Ecosystem Ecology and Metaphysical Ecology: A Case Study," *Environmental Ethics* 15, no. 2 (Summer 1993): 99–116.

22. Worster, "The Ecology of Order and Chaos," 47.

23. Karen Warren and Jim Cheney, "Ecological Feminism and Ecosystem Ecology," *Hypatia* 5, no. 1 (Spring 1991): 179–197.

24. Max Hallman, "Nietzsche's Environmental Ethics," *Environmental Ethics* 13, no. 2 (Summer 1991): 99–125.

25. My Heidegger-deep ecology essays are listed in n. 1, Introduction. See also Laura Westra, "Let it Be: Heidegger and Future Generations," *Environmental Ethics* VII, no. 7 (Winter 1985): 341–350; Bruce V. Foltz, "On Heidegger and the Interpretation of Environmental Crisis," *Environmental Ethics* VI, no. 4 (Winter 1984): 323–338; and Kah Kyung Cho, "Ökologische Suggestibilität in der Spätphilosophie Heideggers," in *Bewusstsein und Natursein* (München: Verlag Karl Alber, 1987).

26. As Warwick Fox points out, according to this skewed "logic," the following argument is also valid: some Christians have supported inquisitions; Christianity has been proposed as a possible source for deep ecology; therefore, some deep ecologist will probably propose inquisitions.

27. Bill Devall and George Sessions, *Deep Ecology*, (Salt Lake City: Peregrine Smith, 1985): 98.

28. Martin Heidegger, "Letter on Humanism," trans. Frank A. Capuzzi in collaboration with J. Glenn Gray, in *Basic Writings*, ed. David Farrell Krell (New York: Harper & Row, 1977).

29. Martin Heidegger, *Nietzsche*, vol. 2 (Pfullingen: Günther Neske, 1961): 145.

30. Martin Heidegger, *Discourse on Thinking*, trans. John M. Anderson and E. Hans Freund (New York: Harper & Row, 1966).

31. Martin Heidegger, "On the Essence of Truth," trans. John Sallis, in *Basic Writings*, 127.

32. Alan Watts, *Psychotherapy East and West* (New York: Ballantine Books, 1969): 14. Decades ago, this far-sighted book already applied the perennial philosophy to the ecological crisis.

33. Martin Heidegger, *An Introduction to Metaphysics*, trans. Ralph Mannheim (Garden City, N.Y.: Anchor Doubleday, 1961): 130–148.

34. See Michael E. Zimmerman, "Marx and Heidegger on the Technological Domination of Nature," *Philosophy Today* 33 (Summer 1979): 99–112; and John Clark, "Marx's Inorganic Body," *Environmental Ethics* 11, no. 3 (Fall 1989): 243–258.

35. See Michael E. Zimmerman, *Heidegger's Confrontation with Modernity* (Bloomington: Indiana University Press, 1990); Richard Wolin, *The Politics of Being* (New York: Columbia University Press, 1990); and Tom Rockmore, *On Heidegger's Nazism and Philosophy* (Berkeley and Los Angeles: University of California Press, 1992).

36. See Luc Ferry and Alain Renaut, *Heidegger and Modernity*, trans. Franklin Phillip (Chicago: The University of Chicago Press, 1990). For an inter-

esting defense of Heidegger's political thought, see Frank Schalow, "A Question Concerning Heidegger's Involvement in National Socialism," *Journal of the British Society for Phenomenology* 24, no. 2 (May 1993): 121–139.

37. Martin Heidegger, *Die Grundbegriffe der Metaphysik,* ed. Friedrich-Wilhelm von Herrmann, *Gesamtausgabe* Vol. 29–30 (Frankfurt am Main: Vittorio Klostermann, 1983).

38. Ibid., 278, 282.

39. Martin Heidegger, *Grundbegriffe,* ed. Petra Jaeger, *Gesamtausgabe* Vol. 51 (Frankfurt am Main: Vittorio Klostermann, 1981): 4–5.

40. Martin Heidegger, *On the Way to Language,* trans. Peter D. Hertz (New York: Harper & Row, 1971): 107.

41. Martin Heidegger, "Letter on Humanism," in *Basic Writings,* 204.

42. Lévi-Strauss as cited in Claude Pace, *Claude Lévi-Strauss* (London: Routledge & Kegan Paul, 1983): 250.

43. Ibid., 248.

44. Paolo Caruso, "Exploring Lévi-Strauss: Interview," *Atlas* 11 (April 1966): 245; cited by Pace, *Claude Lévi-Strauss,* 200.

45. Hans Jonas, *The Phenomenon of Life* (New York: Harper & Row, 1966): 227–233.

46. Jonas, *The Phenomenon of Life,* 232. In *Deep Ecology,* 69, Devall and Sessions portray Heidegger as a biocentrist.

47. Jonas, *The Phenomenon of Life,* 234.

48. Ibid., 283–284.

49. Werner Marx, *Is There a Measure on Earth?,* trans. Thomas Nenon and Reginald Lilly (Chicago: University of Chicago Press, 1987); Hans Jonas, *The Imperative of Responsibility,* trans. Hans Jonas, with David Herr (Chicago: University of Chicago Press, 1984).

50. Ibid., 200.

51. Sessions, "Spinoza and Jeffers on Man in Nature," 484–485.

52. George Sessions, "Anthropocentrism and the Environmental Crisis," *Humboldt Journal of Social Relations* 2 (Fall/Winter 1974).

53. Heidegger, "What Are Poets For?", *Poetry, Language, Thought,* trans. Albert Hofstadter (New York: Harper & Row, 1971): 116.

54. Martin Heidegger, *Discourse on Thinking,* 55–56.

55. Murray Bookchin offers an alternative to Heidegger's view: "The greatest danger we face apart from nuclear immolation is the homogenization of the world by a market society and its objectification of all human rela-

tionships and experiences." See Bookchin, *The Philosophy of Social Ecology* (Montréal/New York: Black Rose Books, 1990): 130.

56. *Discourse on Thinking*, 52. Heidegger associates the goal of material happiness with Nietzsche's miserable "last man."

57. See Martin Heidegger, *Beiträge zur Philosophie*, ed. Friedrich-Wilhelm von Herrmann, *Gesamtausgabe* Vol. 65 (Frankfrut am Main: Vittorio Klostermann, 1989); and Manfred Frank, *Der kommende Gott* (Frankfurt am Main: Suhrkamp, 1982).

58. Martin Heidegger, "Only a God Can Save Us Now," *Der Spiegel*'s interview with Heidegger, trans. Maria P. Alter and John D. Caputo, *Philosophy Today* 20 (Winter 1976): 267–284.

59. See Michael E. Zimmerman, "The Blessing of Otherness," in *After Earth Day*, ed. Max Oelschlaeger (Denton: The University of North Texas Press, 1992).

60. Arne Naess, "A Defense of the Deep Ecology Movement," *Environmental Ethics* 6, no. 3 (Fall 1984): 265–270; citation is from p. 270, emphasis in original.

61. Arne Naess, "The Arrogance of Antihumanism?", *Ecophilosophy* VI (1984): 8.

62. Martin Heidegger, *Identity and Difference*, trans. Joan Stambaugh (New York: Harper & Row, 1969): 31.

63. T. L. S. Sprigge, "Non-human Rights: An Idealist Perspective," *Inquiry* 20 (1984): 439–461; cited by Naess in "The World of Concrete Contents," *Inquiry* 28 (1985): 417–428. See also Naess, "A Defence of the Deep Ecology Movement," *Environmental Ethics* 6, no. 3 (Fall 1984): 265–270.

64. Evernden, *The Natural Alien* (Toronto: The University of Toronto Press, 1985).

65. Holmes Rolston III, "Challenges in Environmental Ethics," in Zimmerman et al., *Environmental Philosophy* (Englewood Cliffs, N.J.: Prentice Hall, 1993).

66. Heidegger, *Discourse on Thinking*, 64.

67. Naess, "The World of Concrete Contents," 419.

68. Ibid., 424.

69. The example is taken from Naess, "Ecosophy and Gestalt Ontology," *The Trumpeter* 6, no. 4 (Fall 1989): 134–136.

70. Naess and Rothenberg, *Ecology, Community and Lifestyle* (New York: Cambridge University Press, 1989): 60–61.

71. Naess, "The World of Concrete Contents," 420; emphasis in original.

72. Naess, "Ecosophy and Gestalt Ontology," 136.

73. Ibid., 419.

74. Naess and Rothenberg, *Ecology, Community and Lifestyle,* 50.

75. Ibid., 425.

76. Martin Heidegger, *What Is a Thing?,* trans. W. B. Barton, Jr. and Vera Deutsch (Chicago: Henry Regnery Co., 1967): 41.

77. Heidegger, *Being and Time,* trans. John Macquarrie and Edward Robinson (New York: Harper & Row, 1962): 228.

78. William F. Vallicella, "Heidegger and the Problem of the Thing in Itself," *International Philosophical Quarterly* 23 (1983): 35–43, especially p. 42.

79. William F. Vallicella, "Heidegger's Reduction of Being to Truth," *The New Scholasticism* 59 (1985): 156–171.

80. Hubert L. Dreyfus, *Being-in-the-World* (Cambridge: The MIT Press, 1992): 251–265.

81. Martin Heidegger, *Phänomenologische Interpretation von Kants Kritik der reinen Vernunft,* ed. Intraud Görland, *Gesamtausgabe* Vol. 25 (Frankfurt am Main: Vittoria Klostermann, 1977): 26.

82. Michel Haar, *Le chant de la terre* (Paris: l'Herne, 1987): 39. See Reginald Lilly's translation, *The Song of the Earth* (Bloomington: Indiana University Press, 1993).

83. See Heidegger, *Poetry Language Thought,* 91.

84. These hopes dimmed somewhat because of his political experience.

85. Ibid., 182.

86. Dolores LaChapelle, noted as a skier, mountaineer, and deep ecologist, maintains that skiing can be such a practice that unites mortal with earth, sky, and gods by "letting the mountain be." See LaChapelle, *Earth Wisdom* (Silverton: Fill Hill Arts, 1978), available from LaChapelle at P.O. Box 542, Silverton, Colo. 81433.

87. Martin Heidegger, *Erläuterung zu Hölderins Dichtung,* ed. Friedrich Wilhelm von Herrmann, *Gesamtausgabe* Vol. 4 (Frankfurt am Main: Vittorio Klostermann, 1981).

88. Martin Heidegger, *The End of Philosophy,* trans. Joan Stambaugh (New York: Harper & Row, 1973), 109.

89. Heidegger, *On the Way to Language,* 92.

90. Martin Heidegger, *The Question Concerning Technology,* trans. William Lovitt (New York: Harper & Row, 1977), 15.

91. Martin Heidegger, *An Introduction to Metaphysics,* trans. Ralph Mannheim (Garden City, N.Y.: Anchor Doubleday, 1961): 130.

92. A deep ecologist might say that unless wilderness management occurs in light of an ecological sensibility, such areas will be reduced to the status of mere parks. See "Natural Resource Conservation or Protection of the Integrity of Nature: Contrasting Views of Management," chapter 8 of Devall and Sessions, *Deep Ecology*.

93. To be faithful to the insight that being and nothingness, form and emptiness, are "the same," I should speak of the nothingness *as which* things come into presence, but such an expression defies good English.

94. Joanna Macy, "The Greening of the Self," *Dharma Gaia*, ed. Allan Hunt Badiner (Berkeley: Parallax Press, 1990).

95. See Arne Naess, *Freedom, Emotion and Self-Subsistence* (Oslo: University of Oslo Press, 1975); Naess, "Spinoza and Ecology," *Philosophia* VII (1977): 45–54; Naess, "Environmental Ethics and Spinoza's Ethics" *Inquiry* 23 (1980): 313–325.

96. See my essay, "Ontological Aestheticism: Heidegger, Jünger, and National Socialism," in *The Heidegger Case*, ed. Tom Rockmore and Joseph Margolis (Philadelphia: Temple University Press, 1992); and John D. Caputo, *Deconstructing Heidegger* (Bloomington: Indiana University Press, 1993).

97. Holmes Rolston III, "Can the East Help the West to Value Nature?", *Philosophy East and West* 37, no. 2 (April 1987): 172–190.

98. Ty Cashman, "Epistemology and the Extinction of Species," in *Revisioning Philosophy*, ed. James Ogilvy (Albany: SUNY Press, 1992): 8.

99. Ibid., 13.

100. Ibid., 13.

101. Ibid., 16.

102. Ibid., 292.

103. Jacques Derrida, "Structure, Sign, and Play in the Discourse of the Human Sciences," in *Writing and Difference*, trans. Alan Bass (Chicago: The University of Chicago Press, 1978): 278.

104. Jacques Derrida, "Différance," in *Margins of Philosophy*, trans. Alan Bass (Chicago: The University of Chicago Press, 1982): 26–27.

105. Stefano Rosso and Umberto Eco, "A Correspondence on Postmodernism," in *Zeitgeist in Babel*, ed. Ingeborg Hoesterey (Bloomington: Indiana University Press, 1991): 251.

106. Derrida, "Différance," 12.

107. Peter Engelmann, "Jacques Derridas Randgänge der Philosophie," an interview with Derrida, in *Semiotica Austriaca*, special issue, ed. Jeff Bernard, 9, no. 1 (1987): 96–110; citation from pp. 107–108; my emphasis.

108. Ibid.

109. See David Lee Griffin, ed., *The Reenchantment of Science* (Albany: SUNY Press, 1988).

110. According to Fritjof Capra, physicist Geoffrey Chew's S-matrix or "bootstrap" theory describes the constituents of the subatomic realm as being constituted by a constantly shifting play, in which there are no fundamental entities and in which everything refers to everything else. In some ways, this play resembles Derrida's differential play of texts. See Capra, *The Turning Point* (New York: Bantam, 1983): 92–97. For criticism of Capra, see Ken Wilber, *Quantum Questions* (Boulder: Shambhala, 1984); Robert K. Clifton and Marilyn G. Regehr, "Toward a Sound Perspective on Modern Physics," *Zygon* 25, no. 1 (March 1990): 73–104; and Michael E. Zimmerman, "Quantum Theory, Intrinsic Value, and Non-Dualism," *Environmental Ethics* 10, no. 1 (Spring 1988): 3–30.

111. David Loy, "The Deconstruction of Buddhism," *Derrida and Negative Theology*, ed. Harold Coward and Toby Foshay (Albany: SUNY Press, 1992): 235; stress in original. See also David Loy, "The Non-Duality of Life and Death: A Buddhist View of Repression," *Philosophy East and West* 40, no. 2 (April 1990): 151–174.

112. Francis H. Cook, *Hua-yen Buddhism: The Jewel Net of Indra* (University Park: Pennsylvania State University, 1977): 2; as cited in Loy, "The Deconstruction of Buddhism," 236.

113. Loy, "The Deconstruction of Buddhism," 230.

114. David Loy, *Nonduality: A Study in Comparative Philosophy* (New Haven: Yale University Press, 1988): 259. This is an outstanding book.

115. Ibid., 256.

116. Ibid., 249.

117. Loy, "The Deconstruction of Buddhism," 247–249.

118. Ibid., 250.

119. Ibid.

120. For defenses of Derrida's politics, see John D. Caputo, *Radical Hermeneutics* (Bloomington: Indiana University Press, 1989); and Richard Bernstein, *The New Constellation* (Cambridge: The MIT Press, 1992). For criticism, see Thomas McCarthy, "The Politics of the Ineffable: Derrida's Deconstructionism," *The Philosophical Forum* 21, nos. 1–2 (Fall/Winter 1989–1990): 146–168.

121. Jacques Derrida, "Of an Apocalyptic Tone Newly Adopted in Philosophy," trans. John P. Leavey, Jr., in *Derrida and Negative Theology*, 51.

122. Ibid.

123. Jürgen Habermas, *The Philosophical Discourse of Modernity,* trans. Frederick Lawrence (Cambridge: The MIT Press, 1990): 43.

124. Ibid., 44.

125. Harold Coward, "A Hindu Response to Derrida's View of Negative Theology," in *Derrida and Negative Theology,* 209.

126. Ibid., 210.

127. Ibid., 216; my emphasis.

128. Naess, "Self Realization: An Ecological Approach to Being in the World," *The Trumpeter* 4, no. 3 (Summer 1987): 35–42; citation is from p. 40. See also Naess, "Identification as a Source of Deep Ecological Attitudes," *Deep Ecology,* ed. Michael Tobias (San Diego: Avant Books, 1984): 260.

129. Naess and Rothenberg, *Ecology, Community and Lifestyle,* 85; my emphasis.

130. Loy, *Nonduality,* 197.

131. Naess, "Identification as a Source of Deep Ecological Attitudes," 261. Warwick Fox makes a similar claim in "Self and World," *ReVision* 13, no. 3 (Winter 1991): 116–122.

132. Naess and Rothenberg, *Ecology, Community and Lifestyle,* 79.

133. T. R. V. Murti, *The Central Philosophy of Buddhism* (London: Allen and Unwin, 1969): 217; cited in Loy, *Nondualism,* 202.

134. Loy, *Nondualism,* 214–215.

135. For a critique of the view that modernity is a secularized version of Christian eschatology, see Hans Blumenberg, *The Legitimacy of the Modern Age,* trans. Robert M. Wallace (Cambridge: The MIT Press, 1983).

136. See Roderick Nash, *The Rights of Nature* (Madison: University of Wisconsin Press, 1989).

137. Thomas H. Birch, "The Incarceration of Wildness: Wilderness Areas as Prisons," *Environmental Ethics* 12, no. 1 (Spring 1990): 3–36; citation is from p. 6.

CHAPTER FOUR

1. Readers familiar with Bookchin's thought will see his debt to Mumford in Robert Casillo's essay, "Lewis Mumford and the Organicist Concept in Social Thought," *Journal of the History of Ideas* LIII, no. 1 (January–March 1992): 91–116, even though Casillo does not mention Bookchin's name.

2. Lewis Herber (pseudonym), *Our Synthetic Environment* (New York: Alfred A. Knopf, 1963); republished under Bookchin's real name by Harper & Row in 1974.

3. Murray Bookchin, *Post-Scarcity Anarchism* (Palo Alto: Ramparts Press, 1971): 59–60.

4. Ibid., 64, 67–68.

5. Murray Bookchin, *Remaking Society* (Boston: South End Press, 1990): 124, 128.

6. Ibid., 94; see also *The Ecology of Freedom* (Palo Alto: Chesire Books, 1982): 363.

7. Ibid., 128–129. On Jünger's thought, see Zimmerman, *Heidegger's Confrontation with Modernity* (Bloomington: Indiana University Press, 1990).

8. Bookchin, *Remaking Society*, 126.

9. Bookchin, *The Ecology of Freedom*, 322.

10. Murray Bookchin, "The Greening of Politics: Toward a New Kind of Political Practice," *Green Perspectives* no. 1 (January 1986).

11. Murray Bookchin, "Municipalization: Community Ownership of the Economy," *Green Perspectives* no. 2 (February 1986). See also Bookchin, *The Limits of the City* (Montréal: Black Rose Books, 1986).

12. Bookchin, "Municipalization: Community Ownership of the Economy," 82; my emphasis.

13. Ibid., 113.

14. Bookchin, *The Ecology of Freedom*, 48.

15. Ibid., 47.

16. Bookchin, *Remaking Society*, 50–51. But in *Female Power and Male Dominance* (Cambridge: Cambridge University Press, 1981), Peggy Reeves Sanday says that people living in harsh climates not only tend to regard nature as difficult and stingy, but also construct societies that are hierarchical and patriarchal.

17. Bookchin, *Remaking Society*, 50.

18. Bookchin, *The Ecology of Freedom*, 80ff. See also *Remaking Society*, 54.

19. Ibid., 121; my emphasis.

20. Bookchin, *The Ecology of Freedom*, 120; see also *Post-Scarcity Anarchism*, 113.

21. Bookchin, *Remaking Society*, 76.

22. Bookchin, *The Ecology of Freedom*, 81.

23. For a critique of Bookchin's views on the origin of hierarchy, see Mary Meleor, *Breaking the Boundaries: Toward a Green Feminist Socialism* (London: Virago Press, 1992).

24. In "Marx's Inorganic Body," *Environmental Ethics* 11, no. 3 (Fall 1989): 243–258, John Clark effectively criticizes Marx's instrumentalist view of nature.

25. Ibid., 60.

26. Fox, "The Deep Ecology-Ecofeminism Debate and Its Parallels," *Environmental Ethics* 11, no 1 (Spring 1989): 5–25.

27. John Clark, "Social Ecology: A Philosophy of Dialectical Naturalism," in Zimmerman et al., *Environmental Philosophy* (Englewood Cliffs: Prentice-Hall, 1993). See also Murray Bookchin, "Recovering Evolution: A Reply to Eckersley and Fox," *Environmental Ethics* 12, no. 3 (Fall 1990): 253–274.

28. Bookchin, *The Ecology of Freedom*, 317.

29. John Clark suggests that both Bookchin and Heidegger do not sufficiently emphasize the importance of the *creative* power of imagination, which goes beyond "drawing out" the potential of the material with which one is working.

30. Bookchin, *The Ecology of Freedom*, 330.

31. Bookchin, *Remaking Society*, 139–152, 148.

32. Ibid., 16–17.

33. Bookchin, *Remaking Society*, 8.

34. See Steven Vogel's helpful essay, "Reification and the Non-Identical: On the Problem of Nature in Lukács and Adorno," to appear in a volume of the Society for Phenomenology and Existential Philosophy.

35. John Ely, "Lukács Construction of Nature," *Capitalism, Nature, Socialism* no. 1 (Fall 1988): 107–116; citation is from p. 111.

36. Ely, "Lukac's Construction of Nature," 112.

37. Theodore W. Adorno, *Negative Dialectics,* trans. E. B. Ashton (New York: Continuum, 1987): 22.

38. Ibid., 13.

39. Bookchin, "Thinking Ecologically," 38.

40. Ibid., 39.

41. Ibid., 58.

42. Ibid.

43. Ibid., 60. The Heraclitean tension of opposites is reminiscent of Taoism, which John Clark portrays as a version of social ecology in "On Taoism and Politics," *Journal of Chinese Philosophy* 10, no. 1 (March 1983): 65–87. Bookchin complains that Taoism was consistent with an oppressive social order, but Heraclitus' views could be read in the same way.

44. John Rodman, "Animal Justice: The Counter-revolution in Natural Right and Law," *Inquiry* 22 (Summer 1979): 3–22.

45. Ibid., 186–218.

46. Bookchin, *The Philosophy of Social Ecology*, 65.

47. Ibid., 176; my emphasis. See also p. 32 of Murray Bookchin, "Thinking Ecologically: A Dialectical Approach," *Our Generation* 18 (Spring/Summer 1987): 3–40.

48. Bookchin, *The Philosophy of Social Ecology*, 42–43.

49. Bookchin, "Thinking Ecologically," 33.

50. Cited by Robyn Eckersley, "Divining Evolution," *Environmental Ethics* 11, no. 2 (Summer 1989): 99–116; see p. 111.

51. Bookchin, "Recovering Evolution."

52. References to Bookchin are from *Remaking Society*, 31, 204. For a critique of genetic engineering, see Jeremy Rifkin, in collaboration with Nicanor Perlas, *Algeny* (New York: Penguin Books, 1984).

53. Bookchin, "Recovering Evolution," 272.

54. Arne Naess, "Politics and the Ecological Crisis: An Introductory Note," in the special issue "From Anthropocentrism to Deep Ecology," ed. Warwick Fox, of *ReVision* 13, no. 3 (Winter 1991): 142–146; citation is from p. 144.

55. Naess made this distinction in an interview with George Sessions and Harold Glasser in the spring of 1992.

56. Bookchin, "Recovering Evolution," 274.

57. Bookchin, "Thinking Ecologically," 32–33.

58. See Sessions, "Ecocentrism, Wilderness, and Global Ecosystem Protection," in *Environmental Philosophy*.

59. See David Abram, "The Perceptual Implications of Gaia," *ReVision* 9, no. 2 (Winter/Spring 1987): 7–16.

60. Bookchin, *The Philosophy of Social Ecology*, 45.

61. Murray Bookchin, "Social Ecology versus 'Deep Ecology'," *Green Perspectives* nos. 4 & 5 (Summer 1987).

62. Bookchin, *Remaking Society*, 18.

63. Ibid., 163.

64. Ibid., 164.

65. Charlene Spretnak, "Radical Nonduality in Ecofeminist Philosophy," to appear in Karen J. Warren, *Ecological Feminism* (Bloomington: Indiana University Press, 1994).

66. Cited by Bookchin in *The Philosophy of Social Ecology*, 159.

67. Bookchin is right, however, to ask why Bill Devall did not challenge such remarks in the course of interviewing Foreman.

68. Murray Bookchin, "Will Ecology Become the Dismal Science?", *The Progressive* (December 1991): 18–21. In its March 1992 issue, *The Progressive* published many letters responding critically to Bookchin.

69. Murray Bookchin and Dave Foreman, *Defending the Earth,* ed. Steve Chase (Boston: South End Press, 1991). Highly recommended.

70. See Joel Kovel, "The Marriage of Radical Ecologies," and George Bradford, "Toward a Deep Social Ecology," in *Environmental Philosophy;* see also David M. Johns, "The Relevance of Deep Ecology to the Third World," *Environmental Ethics* 12, no. 3 (Fall 1990): 233–252; and Andrew McLaughlin, *Regarding Nature: Industrialism and Deep Ecology* (Albany: SUNY Press, 1993).

71. Bill Devall, "Political Activism in a Time of War," in *ReVision* 13, no. 3 (Winter 1991): 135–141; citation from p. 137.

72. Bookchin, *The Philosophy of Social Ecology,* 197.

73. Bookchin in *Defending the Earth,* 130.

74. On this topic, see "Paradise Now: The Counterculture," in Arthur P. Mendel, *Vision and Violence* (Ann Arbor: University of Michigan Press, 1992).

75. Ramachandra Guha, "Radical American Environmentalism and Wilderness Preservation: A Third World Critique," *Environmental Ethics* 11, no. 1 (Spring 1989): 71–83.

76. See Sessions, "Ecocentrism, Wilderness, and Global Ecosystem Protection," in *Environmental Philosophy.*

77. Johns, "The Relevance of Deep Ecology for the Third World."

78. Devall and Sessions, *Deep Ecology,* 65. Sessions and Devall cite William R. Catton, Jr., *Overshoot: The Ecological Basis of Revolutionary Change* (Urbana: University of Illinois Press, 1980).

79. See Murray Bookchin, "Social Ecology versus 'Deep Ecology'," *Green Perspectives* nos. 4 & 5 (1987): 1–23; "The Crisis in the Ecology Movement," *Green Perspectives* no. 6 (May 1988); "Yes!—Whither Earth First?" *Green Perspectives* no. 10 (September 1988). For an excellent criticism of the neo-Malthusianism of certain strains of deep ecology, see George Bradford, "Toward a Deep Social Ecology," in *Environmental Philosophy.*

80. Dave Foreman, in "Beyond the Wilderness," *Harper's Magazine* 280, no. 1679 (April 1990): 48.

81. The quote is from *Post-Scarcity Anarchism,* 61; see also *Remaking Society,* 32.

82. Bookchin, "Will Ecology Become the Dismal Science?", 20.

83. Bookchin, *The Ecology of Freedom,* 228.

84. Robert A. Pois, *National Socialism and the Religion of Nature* (London & Sydney: Croom Helm Publishers, 1986). This is an important and disturbing book.

85. See Manfred Frank, *Der kommende Gott* (Frankfurt am Main: Suhrkamp, 1982); Frank, *Gott im Exil* (Frankfurt am Main: Suhrkamp, 1988); Karl Heinz Bohrer, ed., *Mythos und Moderne* (Frankfurt am Main: Suhrkamp, 1983); and Peter Kemper, ed., *Macht des Mythos—Ohnmacht der Vernunft* (Frankfurt am Main: Fischer Taschenbuch Verlag, 1989).

86. Jürgen Habermas, *The Philosophical Discourse of Modernity*, trans. Frederick Lawrence (Cambridge: The MIT Press, 1987): 92.

87. Frank, *Der kommende Gott*, 160.

88. Ibid., 155ff.

89. Ibid., 14.

90. See Friedrich Wolfzettel, "Utopien des Frühsozialismus oder Fortschritt als Erlosung," in *Macht des Mythos*.

91. Frank, *Gott im Exil*, 212–313.

92. George L. Mosse, *The Crisis of German Ideology* (New York: Grosset & Dunlap, 1964): 15.

93. Raymond H. Dominick III, *The Environmental Movement in Germany* (Bloomington: Indiana University Press, 1992): 115.

94. Ibid., 90.

95. See Jeffrey Herf's outstanding book, *Reactionary Modernism* (New York: Cambridge University Press, 1984).

96. Pois, *National Socialism and the Religion of Nature*.

97. George Steiner, "Through that Glass Darkly," *Salmagundi* no. 93 (Winter 1992): 32–50; citation is from p. 45. See also Jean-François Lyotard, *Heidegger and "the Jews"*, trans. Andreas Michel and Mark S. Roberts (Minneapolis: University of Minnesota Press, 1990).

98. Pois, *National Socialism and the Religion of Nature*, 118.

99. Ibid., 41–42. See also the chapter on Rosenberg's *Der Mythus des 20. Jahrhunderts* in Frank, *Gott im Exil*.

00. Pois, *National Socialism and the Religion of Nature*, 52. In *Coming to Our Senses* (New York: Bantam Books, 1989), Morris Berman offers an excellent treatment of the occult dimension of National Socialism.

01. Pois, *National Socialism and the Religion of Nature*, 30; emphasis mine.

02. In "Revolution als Ritual: Der Mythos des Nationalsozialsmus," *Revolution und Mythos*, ed. Dietrich Harth and Jan Assmann (Frankfurt am Main: Fischer, 1992), Klaus Vondung says that Hitler's elaborate annual ceremonies sought to encourage a sense of "revolutionary immortality" on the part of his followers, who would "live eternally in the blood of new National Socialist men."

103. Pois, *National Socialism and the Religion of Nature,* 43ff.

104. As cited in ibid., 117.

105. Ibid., 40.

106. Ibid., 38.

107. As cited in ibid., 42–43.

108. Ibid., 39; emphasis mine.

109. Ibid., 123ff.

110. Philippe Lacoue-Labarthe, *La fiction du politique* (Paris: Christian Bourgeois, 1987).

111. Pois, *National Socialism and the Religion of Nature,* 151.

112. Pois, *National Socialism as a Religion of Nature,* 151. Pois argues that Ronald Reagan's nationalism, involving an irrationalist flight from history, also echoed fascist ideology.

113. Tim Lukes, "The Dreams of Deep Ecology," *Telos* no. 76 (Summer 1988): 65–92; citation is from p. 78.

114. Cited by Jessica Matthews of World Resources Institute, in *The International Herald Tribune,* Tuesday, 25 February 1992: 6.

115. Christopher Manes, *Green Rage: Radical Environmentalism and the Unmaking of Civilization* (Boston: Little, Brown & Company, 1990), 226, 237. In *The Idea of Wilderness* (New Haven: Yale University Press, 1991), Max Oelschlaeger offers a more nuanced analysis than does Manes of the difficulties facing the "post-modern primitive."

116. Ibid., 228.

117. Manes, *Green Rage,* 239.

118. Ibid., 37. See Heilbroner, *An Inquiry into the Human Prospect* (New York: W. W. Norton & Company, Inc., 1974): 26. Even Arne Naess, no friend of totalitarianism, states that within fifty years we will either have adopted deep ecological attitudes, or else we will be faced with a dictatorship purporting to solve dire ecological crises. See Naess, "Simple in Means, Rich in Ends," in Zimmerman, ed., *Environmental Philosophy,* 184.

119. Manes, *Green Rage,* 37.

120. For a critique of the idea that discarding universal conceptions of humanity will lead to the peaceful coexistence of fragmented ethnic groups, see Thomas McCarthy, "The Politics of the Ineffable: Derrida's Deconstructionism," *The Philosophical Forum* XXI, nos. 1–2 (Fall-Winter 1989–1990): 146–168.

121. This remark is from the unedited version of an interview with Sessions, "Wilderness: Back to Basics." The edited version was published in *Creation* V, no. 2 (May/June 1989): 17–19, 33.

22. In "Regenerate Culture!", in *Turtle Talk,* ed. Christopher Plant and Judith Plant (Philadelphia, Santa Cruz, Lillooet, B.C.: New Society Publishers, 1990): 16, Gary Snyder warns of the fascist potential of bioregionalism.

23. Warwick Fox, *Toward a Transpersonal Ecology* (Boston: Shambhala, 1990): 19–20.

24. On this topic, see Frances Moore Lappé and Joseph Collins, *World Hunger: Twelve Myths* (New York: Grove Press, Inc., 1986).

25. Warwick Fox, "The Deep Ecology-Ecofeminism Debate and Its Parallels," *Environmental Ethics* 11, no. 1 (Spring 1989): 5–25.

26. Fox, *Toward a Transpersonal Ecology,* 178–179.

27. See Betsy Hartmann, *Reproductive Rights and Wrongs* (New York: Harper & Row, 1987). For a liberal critique of Malthusian doctrines, see H. J. McCloskey, *Ecological Ethics and Politics* (Totowa, N.J.: Rowman and Littlefield, 1983), chap. 3.

28. Paul R. Ehrlich and Anne H. Ehrlich, *The Population Explosion* (New York: Touchstone, 1990).

29. For a defense from an ecological perspective of the problematic social holism in Plato's *Republic,* see J. Baird Callicott, "Animal Liberation: A Triangular Affair," *Environmental Ethics* 2, no. 4 (Winter 1981): 311–338. Callicott now distances himself from some of the claims made in this polemical essay.

30. Bookchin, *Post-Scarcity Anarchism,* 145; see also p. 27.

31. Ibid., 78.

32. Bookchin, *The Philosophy of Social Ecology,* 127–128.

33. Bookchin, *Post-Scarcity Anarchism,* 139.

CHAPTER FIVE

1. In *Revisioning Environmental Ethics* (Albany: SUNY Press, 1990), Daniel A. Kealey approaches radical ecology in light of Jean Gebser's "integralism," a view of consciousness evolution promoted by Ken Wilber.

2. Christopher D. Stone, *Should Trees Have Standing? Toward Legal Rights for Natural Objects* (Los Altos: William Kaufmann, Inc., 1974).

3. Christopher D. Stone, *Earth and Other Ethics* (New York: Harper & Row, 1987).

4. J. Baird Callicott, "The Case Against Moral Pluralism," *Environmental Ethics* 12, no. 2 (Summer 1990): 99–124. See also Callicott, "Rolston on Intrinsic Value: A Deconstruction," *Environmental Ethics* 14, no. 2 (Summer 1992): 129–144.

5. Murray Bookchin, *The Philosophy of Social Ecology* (Montréal: Black Rose Books, 1990): 22ff.

6. Ibid., 148ff. See also Stephan Elkins, "The Politics of Mystical Ecology," *Telos* no. 82 (Winter 1989–1990): 52–70.

7. Ibid., 66ff. In *Mutual Causality in Buddhism and General Systems Theory* (Albany: SUNY Press, 1991), however, the deep ecological Buddhist, Joanna Macy, argues for the relevance of systems theory and Buddhism.

8. Bookchin, *The Philosophy of Social Ecology,* 10ff.

9. Morris Berman, "The Cybernetic Dream of the 21st Century," in *Renewing the Earth: The Promise of Social Ecology,* ed. John Clark (London: Merlin Press, 1990): 24. See also Berman, *The Reenchantment of the World* (Ithaca: Cornell University Press, 1980).

10. *The Philosophy of Social Ecology,* 27.

11. Bookchin, "Thinking Ecologically," 36.

12. G. W. F. Hegel, *Philosophy of Nature,* in *The Essential Writings,* ed. Frederick G. Weiss (New York: Harper & Row, 1974): 214–220.

13. Bookchin, *The Ecology of Freedom,* 236.

14. Bookchin, "Recovering Evolution," 266–268.

15. Bookchin, *The Philosophy of Social Ecology,* 182–183.

16. I have drawn this account from "The New Evolutionary Tree: Five Kingdoms of Life," *Green Earth Observer* no. 4 (Summer 1991): 1–2.

17. Stephen Jay Gould, *Wonderful Life* (New York: Norton, 1989).

18. Ibid., 44, 45.

19. Bookchin, *The Ecology of Freedom,* 14, and *The Philosophy of Social Ecology,* 40.

20. Eric Lerner, *The Big Bang Never Happened* (New York: Times Books/Random House, 1991): 401.

21. Jeffrey S. Levinton, "The Big Bang of Animal Evolution," *Scientific American* 267, no. 5 (November 1992): 84–91; citation is from p. 91. See also Robert J. Richard's book, *The Meaning of Evolution: The Morphological Construction and Ideological Reconstruction of Darwin's Theory* (Chicago: University of Chicago Press, 1992), which argues that Darwin held "progressive" views about evolution.

22. John Maynard Smith, "Taking a Chance on Evolution," *The New York Review of Books* XXXIX, no. 9 (14 May 1992): 34.

23. Paul Davies, *The Cosmic Blueprint* (New York: Touchstone/Simon & Schuster, 1988): 291. More recently, in *The Mind of God* (New York: Simon and Schuster, 1992), Davies argues that the universe is a manifes-

tation of divine consciousness. See also Erich Jantsch, *The Self-Organizing Universe* (Oxford: Pergamon, 1980). More recently, see Stuart A. Kauffman, "Antichaos and Adaptation," *Scientific American* (August 1991): 78–84; Frank Tipler and John Barrow, *The Cosmological Anthropic Principle* (New York: Oxford University Press, 1986); David F. Peat, *Science, Order, and Creativity* (New York: Bantam Books, 1987).

24. Stephen Jay Gould, "On Replacing the Idea of Progress with on Operational Notion of Directionality," in *Evolutionary Progress?*, ed. Matthew H. Nitecki (Chicago: The University of Chicago Press, 1988): 326–327.

25. Thomas Berry and Brian Swimme, *The Universe Story* (San Francisco: HarperCollins, 1992). See also Berry, *The Dream of the Earth* (San Francisco: Sierra Club Books, 1989); Swimme, "The Resurgence of Cosmic Storytellers," *ReVision* 9, no. 2 (Winter/Spring 1987): 83–88; Duane Elgin, "The Living Cosmos: A Theory of Continuous Creation," *ReVision* 11, no. 1 (Summer 1988): 3–22; and in the same issue, Roger W. Sperry, "Structure and Significance of the Consciousness Revolution," 39–56.

26. Berry and Swimme, *The Universe Story,* 86; emphasis in original.

27. Ibid.

28. Brian Swimme, *The Universe is a Green Dragon: A Cosmic Creation Story* (Santa Fe: Bear & Company, 1985), 170.

29. Arne Naess, "The Arrogance of Antihumanism?", *Ecophilosophy* VI (1984): 8.

30. Alexander F. Skutch, *Life Ascending* (Austin: The University of Texas Press, 1985): x, agrees that the "immanent or unconscious purpose" of the universe, achieved only after billions of years and "immense suffering," is "to bring forth beauty along with beings able to enjoy it." But, he adds on p. 230, "the Universe does not exist for us, but man exists for the Universe."

31. Warwick Fox, *Toward a Transpersonal Ecology* (Boston: Shambhala, 1989): 179–184.

32. Levinton, "The Big Bang of Animal Evolution," 88.

33. Eric Chaisson, *The Life Era: Cosmic Selection and Conscious Evolution* (New York: W. W. Norton & Company, 1987). In *Gaia: The Human Journey from Chaos to Cosmos* (New York: Pocket Books, 1989), Elisabet Sahtouris offers an account similar to Chaisson's, without the same level of commitment to a human takeover of the solar system and beyond.

34. Eric Lerner, *The Big Bang Never Happened* (New York: Times Books/Random House, 1991).

35. Ibid., 181–182.

36. Ibid., 189.
37. The 1992 edition of Lerner's book rebuts claims that recent discoveries about cosmic background radiation strongly support the Big Bang theory.
38. See David Layzer, *Cosmogenesis* (New York: Oxford University Press, 1990), 154ff., for another critique of Big Bang theory.
39. Lerner, *The Big Bang Never Happened,* 392.
40. Ibid., 310.
41. Ibid., 325–326.
42. Ibid., 415.
43. Ibid., 420.
44. Ibid., 379–380; emphasis mine.
45. Ibid., 419.
46. Bookchin, *The Ecology of Freedom,* 24.
47. Ken Wilber, *Up From Eden: A Transpersonal View of Human Evolution* (Boulder: Shambhala, 1983): 4.
48. Ibid., 21.
49. George Wald, "Life and Mind in the Universe," in *The Evolution of Consciousness,* ed. Kishore Gandhi (New York: Paragon House, 1983): 23.
50. On the Western concept of progress, see Robert Nisbet, *History of the Idea of Progress* (New York: Basic Books, 1980); and Nannerl O. Keohane, "The Enlightenment Idea of Progress Revisited," *Progress and Its Discontents,* ed. Gabriel A. Almond, Marvin Chodorow, and Roy Harvey Pearce (Berkeley: University of California Press, 1982).
51. Bhikshu Sangharakshita, however, in *A Survey of Buddhism* (Boulder: Shambhala, 1980): 36ff., agrees that there are stages of enlightenment, but claims that Buddhism sees human history as declining, not progressing.
52. Wilber, *Up From Eden,* 12.
53. Morris Berman, *Coming to Our Senses* (New York: Bantam Books, 1989).
54. Wilber, *Up From Eden,* 13.
55. Ibid., 15.
56. Ibid., 112.
57. Carl Becker, *Escape From Evil* (New York: Free Press, 1975), cited by Wilber, *Up From Eden,* 67.
58. Ibid., 118ff.
59. Ibid., 154.
60. Wilber, *Up From Eden,* 231.
61. Ibid.
62. Jean Gebser, "Foundations of the Aperspective World," *Main Currents* 29, no. 2 (1972), cited in Wilber, *Up From Eden,* 183.

63. Wilber, *Up From Eden,* 187; my emphasis.
64. Ibid., 287.
65. Ibid., 204; emphasis in original.
66. Berman, *Coming to Our Senses,* 98.
67. Wilber, *Up From Eden,* 286.
68. Ibid.
69. Ibid., 260.
70. Ibid., 166.
71. Ibid., 325–326; my emphasis.
72. Ibid., 204.
73. Bill Devall, "Deep Ecology and New Age," unpublished MS, 9.
74. Ibid., 13.
75. Dolores LaChapelle, *Sacred Land, Sacred Sex, Rapture of the Deep* (Durango: Kivaki Press, 1988).
76. Christopher Manes, "Nature and Silence," *Environmental Ethics* 14, no. 1 (Winter 1992): 339–350; citation is from p. 347.
77. Quoted by Sessions, "Spinoza and Jeffers on Man in Nature," 512.
78. Robinson Jeffers, cited by Sessions, "Spinoza and Jeffers on Man in Nature," 513.
79. Ibid., 513. Today, Sessions maintains that he never really identified with Jeffers' "tower beyond tragedy."
80. Ibid., 511. My emphasis.
81. Lacoue-Labarthe, *La fiction du politique* (Paris: Christian Bourgeois, 1987).
82. Morris, *Coming To Our Senses,* 271, 293.
83. Slavoj Žižek, *The Sublime Object of Ideology* (London/New York: Verso, 1990): 5; my emphasis. On this topic, see also Berman, *Coming to Our Senses,* 289.
84. Žižek, *The Sublime Object of Ideology,* 5.
85. Wilber, *Up From Eden,* 68.
86. Bookchin, *The Ecology of Freedom,* 177.
87. Murray Bookchin, "What Is Social Ecology?", in *Environmental Philosophy* (Englewood Cliffs, N.J.: Prentice Hall, 1992): 362.
88. In *Escape from Freedom* (New York: Avon Books, 1964), Erich Fromm offers a similar account of the connection among capitalism, the Reformation, social isolation, and growing anxiety.
89. Joel Kovel, *History and Spirit* (Boston: Beacon Press, 1991): 236.
90. Bookchin, *The Philosophy of Social Ecology,* 30.
91. Ibid., 28.
92. Ibid., 37.

93. Ibid., 38.

94. Biehl, *Rethinking Ecofeminist Politics,* 117.

95. J. Baird Callicott, "The Metaphysical Implications of Ecology," *Environmental Ethics* 8, no. 4 (Winter 1986): 301–316.

96. Ibid., 312.

97. Ibid., 313.

98. Bookchin, "Toward a Philosophy of Nature—The Basis for an Ecological Ethic," in *Deep Ecology,* ed. Michael Tobias (San Diego: Avant Books, 1985): 235.

99. Bookchin, *Remaking Society,* 103.

100. Bookchin, *The Philosophy of Social Ecology,* 10–11. Paradoxically, many members of the proto-Nazi *Freikorps* revealed a hyper-masculinist fear about having their ego-boundaries penetrated by the flowing, indeterminate, female principle, symbolized by the Bolshevik "red tide." See Klaus Theweleit, *Male Fantasies,* vol. 1, trans. Stephen Conway (Minneapolis: University of Minnesota Press, 1987).

101. Alan E. Wittbecker, "Metaphysical Implications from Physics and Ecology," *Environmental Ethics* 12, no. 3 (Fall 1990): 275–282; citation from p. 277; my emphasis.

102. Ibid., 279.

103. Ibid., 280.

104. Bookchin, *The Ecology of Freedom,* 324.

105. Because Bookchin speaks of aesthetic self-fashioning, critics maintain that he remains committed to Marx's productionist metaphysics: for something "to be" means for it to be produced by the human subject. Despite debts to this tradition, Bookchin's work cannot be satisfactorily understood solely in terms of it.

106. Richard Rorty, "Solidarity or Objectivity?", in *Post-Analytic Philosophy,* ed. John Rajchman and Cornel West (New York: Columbia University Press, 1985): 10.

107. Ibid., 11–12.

108. Ibid., 13.

109. Becker, *The Denial of Death.*

110. Wilber, *Up From Eden,* 98.

111. Richard Rorty, *Contingency, Irony, Solidarity* (Princeton: Princeton University Press, 1989): 20–21.

112. *C. S. Peirce: A Chronological Edition,* vol. 2, ed. Max H. Fisch et al. (Bloomington: Indiana University Press, 1984): 33.

113. Ibid., 4.

114. See Manfred Frank, *Was ist Neostrukturalismus?* (Frankfurt am Main: Suhr-kamp, 1983): 103–104.

115. Ibid., 116ff.

116. Michel Foucault, *Les mots et les choses*, 15; cited by Frank, p. 146.

117. Ibid., 147.

118. Martin Jay, "Habermas and Postmodernism," in *Zeitgeist in Babel: The Postmodernist Controversy*, ed. Ingeborg Hoesterey (Bloomington: Indiana University Press, 1991): 99. For an insightful critical review of attempts to ground progressive views of history on the basis of some invariant factor in nature or humankind, see Joseph Margolis, *The Flux of History and the Flux of Science* (Berkeley, Los Angeles, London: University of California Press, 1993).

119. Jay, "Habermas and Postmodernism," 108.

120. See Frederic Jameson, "Postmodernism, or the Cultural Logic of Late Capitalism," *New Left Review* no. 146 (July–August 1984): 53–91.

121. Ibid., 56.

122. Jameson, "Postmodernism, or the Cultural Logic of Late Capitalism," 63.

123. For another leftist critique of postmodernism, see David Harvey, *The Condition of Postmodernity* (Cambridge, Mass.: Basil Blackwell, 1989). Regarding whether postmodernism is a reactionary moment within modernity, or whether it constitutes a genuine rupture requiring new social theory, see Douglas Kellner, "Postmodernism as Social Theory: Some Challenges and Problems," *Theory, Culture & Society* 5 (1988): 239–269.

124. Bookchin, *Remaking Society*, 72–73.

125. Terry Eagleton, "Capitalism, Modernism and Postmodernism," *New Left Review* no. 146 (July–August 1984): 53–91; citation is from p. 70.

126. Adorno, *Negative Dialectic*, 319ff., as cited and translated by Rainer Nägele in "The Scene of the Other: Theodor W. Adorno's Negative Dialectic in the Context of Poststructuralism," in *Postmodernism and Politics*, ed. Jonathan Arac (Minneapolis: University of Minnesota Press, 1986).

127. Steven Best, "Jameson, Totality, and the Poststructuralist Critique," in *Postmodernism, Jameson, Critique*, ed. Douglas Kellner (Washington, D.C.: Maisonneuve Press, 1989): 356. This is an insightful essay.

128. Ibid., 361.

129. See "Foucault: Critique as a Philosophical Ethos," in Richard J. Bernstein, *The New Constellations* (Cambridge: The MIT Press, 1992).

130. Thomas McCarthy, "The Politics of the Ineffable: Derrida's Deconstruction," *The Philosophical Forum* 21, nos. 1–2 (1989): 146–168.

131. Ibid., 156.

132. Ibid., 158.

133. Ibid., 155; the phrase "monstrous mutation" is from Derrida's *Of Grammatology,* trans. Gayatri Chakravorty Spivak (Baltimore: Johns Hopkins University Press, 1976): 123.

134. McCarthy, "The Politics of the Ineffable," 162. For another approach to these issues, see Ernesto Laclau, "Universalism, Particularism, and the Question of Identity," *October* 61 (Summer 1992): 83–90.

135. See Bertrand Russell, *Mysticism and Logic,* 30.

136. Roderick Frazier Nash, *The Rights of Nature* (Madison: The University of Wisconsin Press, 1989): 11–12. As noted earlier, Fox and Naess use "rights" nontechnically to avoid disputes that have arisen about this term in environmental ethics.

137. Robyn Eckersley, "Emancipation Writ Large: Toward an Ecocentric Green Political Theory," University of Tasmania, Ph.D. diss., 1990. Cited in Fox, *Toward a Transpersonal Ecology,* 265.

138. See Sessions, "Spinoza and Jeffers on Man in Nature." See also Fox's critique of "cosmic purpose ethics" in *Toward a Transpersonal Ecology,* 179–184.

139. Arne Naess, "A Defence of the Deep Ecology Movement," *Environmental Ethics* 6 (Fall 1984): 265–270; citation is from p. 270; emphasis in original.

140. Sessions, "Wilderness: Back to Basic," unedited version.

141. Ibid., 19.

142. Bookchin, *The Philosophy of Social Ecology,* 44.

143. Ibid.

CHAPTER SIX

1. Agnes Heller, "Existentialism, Alienation, Postmodernism," in *Postmodern Conditions,* ed. Andrew Milner, Philip Thomson, and Chris Worth (New York: Berg Publishers, 1990): 13.

2. For an excellent survey of contemporary feminist theory, see Rosemary Tong, *Feminist Thought* (Boulder: Westview, 1989).

3. Carolyn Merchant argues, however, that these types of feminism have made important contributions to the ecology movement. Unfortunately, I encountered her informative book, *Radical Ecology* (New York: Routledge, 1992), too late to be of much use in the present study. For an evaluation of the four kinds of feminism from an ecofeminist perspective, see Karen J. Warren, "Feminism and Ecology: Making Connections," *Environmental Ethics* 9, no. 1 (Spring 1987): 3–20. See also Janis Birkland, "Ecofeminist: Linking Theory and Practice," in *Ecofeminism: Women, Animals, Nature,* ed. Greta Gaard (Philadelphia: Temple University Press, 1993).

4. Alison Jaggar, "Political Philosophies of Women's Liberation," in *Feminist Frontiers,* ed. Laurel Richardson and Veita Taylor (Reading, Mass.: Addison-Wesley Publishing Company, 1983): 323.

5. Shulamith Firestone, *The Dialectic of Sex: The Case for Feminist Revolution* (New York: Morrow, 1970).

6. Ibid., as cited by Judith Halberstam in "Automating Gender: Postmodern Feminism in the Age of the Intelligent Machine," *Feminist Studies* 17, no. 3 (Fall 1991): 439–460; citation is from p. 450.

7. See Linda Alcoff's excellent essay, "Cultural Feminism versus Post-Structuralism: The Identity Crisis in Feminist Theory," *Signs* 13, no. 3 (Spring 1988): 405–436. In "Curves Along the Road," in *Reweaving the World: The Emergence of Ecofeminism,* ed. Irene Diamond and Gloria Feman Orenstein (San Francisco: Sierra Club Books, 1990), Susan Griffin makes clear that not only women, but men too can be attuned to nature's rhythms. For a defense of Griffin against the charge of biological essentialism, see Carol P. Christ, "Rethinking Theology and Nature," in *Reweaving the World.*

8. Virginia Held, "Feminism and Epistemology: Recent Work on the Connection between Gender and Knowledge," *Philosophy and Public Affairs* 14 (1985): 296–307.

9. Alcoff, "Cultural Feminism versus Post-Structuralism," 407. See Renate Hof's critique of essentialist ecofeminism, "'But what if the object began to speak?'—Einige Gedanken über den Zusammenhang von Feminismus und Ökologie," *Amerikastudien/American Studies* 32: 327–337.

10. Alcoff, "Cultural Feminism versus Post-Structuralism," 415.

11. Nancy Fraser and Linda Nicholson, "Social Criticism without Philosophy: An Encounter between Feminism and Postmodernism," *Theory, Culture & Society* 5 (1988): 373–394; citations from p. 391. This is an insightful essay.

12. For essays critical of essentialist ecofeminism, see Karen J. Warren, "Feminism and Ecology: Making Connections," *Environmental Ethics* 9, no. 1 (Spring 1987): 3–20; Michael E. Zimmerman, "Feminism, Deep Ecology, and Environmental Ethics," *Environmental Ethics* 9, no. 1 (Spring 1987): 21–44; Warwick Fox, "The Deep Ecology-Ecofeminism Debate and Its Parallels," *Environmental Ethics* 11, no. 1 (Spring 1989): 5–25.

13. Ariel Kay Salleh, "Deeper than Deep Ecology: The Eco-Feminist Connection," *Environmental Ethics* 6, no. 4 (Winter 1984): 339–345; citation is from p. 340.

14. Ariel Salleh, "Stirrings of a New Renaissance," *Island Magazine* no. 38 (1989): 26–31; citation is from p. 26; my emphasis. This quote is from Robyn Eckersley's unpublished essay, "The Paradox of Ecofeminism," 14.

15. Ariel Salleh, "The Ecofeminism/Deep Ecology Debate: A Reply to Patriarchal Reason," *Environmental Ethics* 14, no. 3 (Fall 1992): 195–216.

16. See Elizabeth B. Spelman, *Inessential Woman: Problems of Exclusion in Feminist Thought* (Boston: Beacon Press, 1988).

17. Ibid., 173.

18. Ibid., 156.

19. Haraway, "Situated Knowledges," 191.

20. Ibid., 193.

21. See Kenneth E. Goodpaster, "On Being Morally Considerable," *Journal of Philosophy* 75 (1978): 308–325, and J. Baird Callicott's review of Tom Regan, *The Case for Animal Rights,* in *Environmental Ethics* 7, no. 4 (1985): 365–372.

22. Locke argued that labor transforms natural things from valueless stuff to valuable commodities. That Marx shared Locke's labor theory of value and his instrumental view of nature, although nevertheless rejecting Locke's social and metaphysical atomism, shows that an instrumental attitude toward nature is compatible with a metaphysics of internal relationships.

23. Naomi Scheman, "Individualism and the Objects of Psychology," in *Discovering Reality,* ed. Sandra Harding and Merrill Hintikka (Boston: D. Reidel Publishing Company, 1983): 234–235.

24. See Ruth Hubbard, "Have Only Men Evolved?", in *Discovering Reality.* For a nonfeminist critique of the circularity of Darwin's reasoning about "natural" competition, see Jeremy Rifkin, *Algeny* (New York: Penguin Books, 1984).

25. Michael Gross and Mary Beth Averill, "Evolution and Patriarchal Myths of Scarcity and Competition," *Discovering Reality.* See Jane Flax, "Political Philosophy and the Patriarchal Unconscious," in *Discovering Reality,* 245–281, for a feminist critique of Hobbesian anthropology.

26. Scheman, "Individualism and the Objects of Psychology," 240.

27. Nancy Chodorow, *The Reproduction of Mothering* (Berkeley, Los Angeles, London: University of California Press, 1978); Isaac Balbous, *Marxism and Domination* (Princeton: Princeton University Press, 1982).

28. For example, see Robin Morgan, *The Anatomy of Freedom* (Garden City, N.Y.: Anchor/Doubleday, 1982).

29. As Jean Grimshaw observes in *Philosophy and Feminist Thinking* (Minneapolis: Minnesota University Press, 1986), some of Mary Daly's writings affirm the lifestyle of the loner.

30. Carol Gilligan, *In a Different Voice* (Cambridge: Harvard University Press, 1981).

31. Carole Pateman, "'The Disorder of Women': Women, Love, and the Sense of Justice," *Ethics* 91 (1980): 20–34; citation is from p. 33.

32. Ibid.

33. Gilligan, *In a Different Voice.*

34. Flax, "Political Philosophy and the Patriarchal Unconscious," 270.

35. Marti Kheel, "The Liberation of Nature: A Circular Affair," *Environmental Ethics* 7, no. 2 (Summer 1985): 135–150; citation is from p. 140.

36. Peggy Reeves Sanday, *Female Power and Male Dominance* (Cambridge: Cambridge University Press, 1981).

37. See Sherry B. Ortner's classic essay, "Is Female to Male as Nature is to Culture?", in *Woman, Culture, and Society,* ed. Michelle Rosaldo and Louise Lamphere (Standford: Stanford University Press, 1974); Joan Bamberger, "The Myth of Matriarchy: Why Men Rule in Primitive Society," in *Woman, Culture, and Society;* and Barbara Diane Miller, ed., *Sex and Gender Hierarchies* (New York: Cambridge University Press, 1993).

38. Ibid., 57.

39. Carolyn Merchant, *The Death of Nature* (New York: Harper & Row, 1980).

40. Susan Bordo, "The Cartesian Masculinization of Thought," *Signs* 11, no. 3 (Spring 1986): 439–456; citation is from pp. 442–443.

41. See Evelyn Fox Keller, *Reflections on Gender and Science* (New Haven: Yale University Press, 1985); Genevieve Lloyd, *The Man of Reason* (Minneapolis: University of Minnesota Press, 1984).

42. Bordo, "The Cartesian Masculinization of Thought," 447.

43. Ibid., 452.

44. Brian Easlea, *Witch-Hunting, Magic and the New Philosophy* (Atlantic Highlands, N.J.: Humanities Press, 1980).

45. Ibid., 453.

46. Elizabeth Dodson Gray, *Green Paradise Lost* (Wellesley, Mass.: Roundtable Press, 1981): 113–114.

47. Charlene Spretnak, *States of Grace* (New York: Harper & Row, 1991): 119.

48. See Catherine Roach, "Loving Your Mother: On the Woman-Nature Relationship," in the special issue on Ecological Feminism, ed. Karen J. Warren, of *Hypatia* 6, no. 1 (Spring 1991): 46–59.

49. Mary Daly, *Gyn/Ecology* (Boston: Beacon Press, 1978).

50. Marilyn French, *Beyond Power: Women, Men, and Morality,* (New York: Summit Books, 1985): 341.

51. Ibid.

52. Susan Griffin, *Woman and Nature: The Roaring Inside Her* (New York: Harper & Row, 1978): 104.

53. Ibid., 190.
54. It is interesting to compare Hans Peter Duerr's book, *Dreamtime: Concerning the Boundary between Wilderness and Civilization,* trans. Felicitas Goodman (New York: Basil Blackwell, 1985), with Griffin's. Duerr argues that witches were feared because they reminded people of the wildness that reason could not control. Instead of trying to repress the "other," we must learn to appreciate its otherness *as such.* Being truly "civilized" involves integrating the wild side of oneself, instead of *dissociating* oneself from it. See my essay, "The Blessing of Otherness," in *The Wilderness Condition,* ed. Max Oelschlaeger (San Francisco: Sierra Club Books, 1992).
55. Rosemary Radford Ruether, *New Woman, New Earth* (New York: Seabury Press, 1975).
56. I explore this theme from a Heideggerian perspective in "Humanism, Ontology, and the Nuclear Arms Race," *Research in Philosophy and Technology* 6 (1983): 151–172; and in "Anthropocentric Humanism and the Arms Race," *Nuclear War: Philosophical Perspectives,* ed. Michael Fox and Leo Groarke (New York: Peter Lang Publishers, 1985).
57. Ibid., 154. More recently, see Rosemary Radford Ruether, *Gaia and God: An Ecofeminist Theology of Earth Healing* (New York: Harper & Row, 1992).
58. See Warren Farrell, *Why Men Are the Way They Are* (New York: Berkeley Books, 1988).
59. Marija Gimbutas, *The Goddesses and Gods of Old Europe,* rev. ed. (London: Thomas & Hudson, 1982); Riane Eisler, *The Chalice and the Blade* (San Francisco: Harper & Row, 1987); Charlene Spretnak, *The Spiritual Dimension of Green Politics* (Santa Fe: Bear & Co., 1986); Spretnak, *States of Grace;* and Spretnak, "Ecofeminism: Our Roots and Flowering," in *Reweaving the World.*
60. See Riane Eisler, "The Gaia Tradition and the Partnership Future," in *Reweaving the World.*
61. Starhawk, "Power, Authority, and Mystery: Ecofeminism and Earth-Based Spirituality," in *Reweaving the World,* 73.
62. Eisler, "The Gaia Tradition and the Partnership Future," 43.
63. Paula Gunn Allen, "The Woman I Love Is a Planet; the Planet I Love Is a Tree," in *Reweaving the World.*
64. Spretnak, *States of Grace,* 136.
65. Patricia Jagentowicz Mills, "Feminism and Ecology: On the Domination of Nature," *Hypatia,* Special Issue on Ecological Feminism 6, no. 1 (Spring 1991): 162–177; citation is from p. 167.

66. Ibid., 163.
67. Also see Spretnak's essay, "Postmodern Directions" and the other essays in David Ray Griffin's collection, *Spirituality and Society,* ed. (Albany: SUNY Press, 1988).
68. See Judith Butler's challenging book, *Gender Trouble: Feminism and the Subversion of Identity* (New York: Routledge, 1990).
69. See Seyla Benhabib's fine book, *Situating the Self: Gender, Community and Postmodernism in Contemporary Ethics* (New York: Routledge, 1992): 213–218.
70. Ibid., 218–223.
71. Ibid., 223–228. See also Linda Vance, "Ecofeminism and the Politics of Reality," *Ecofeminism: Women, Animals, Nature,* ed. Greta Gaard (Philadelphia: Temple University Press, 1993).
72. Spretnak, *States of Grace,* 121. In *The Body in the Mind* (Chicago: University of Chicago Press, 1987), Mark Johnson argues persuasively that the human imagination links intellectual and bodily structures, thereby showing a bodily grounding for much of languge. See also George Lakoff, *Women, Fire and Dangerous Things* (Chicago: University of Chicago Press, 1987).
73. See Genevieve Lloyd, *The Man of Reason in Western Thought* (Minneapolis: University of Minnesota Press, 1984).
74. For a defense of Foucault, see Lois McNay, *Foucault and Feminism* (Boston: Northeastern University Press, 1993).
75. Spretnak, *States of Grace,* 122.
76. Ibid., 125.
77. Ibid. Emphasis mine.
78. On this topic, see my *Heidegger's Confrontation with Modernity* (Bloomington: Indiana University Press, 1990).
79. Janet Biehl, *Rethinking Ecofeminist Politics* (Boston: South End Press, 1991): 117.
80. Janet Biehl, "What is Social Ecofeminism?", *Green Perspectives* no. 11 (October 1988): p. 3.
81. Ibid., 4.
82. Warren, "Feminism and Ecology."
83. Karen J. Warren, "The Power and the Promise of Ecological Feminism," *Environmental Ethics* 12 (Summer 1990): 125–146.
84. Ibid., 128.
85. Janet Biehl, "The Politics of Myth," *Green Perspectives* no. 7 (June 1988): 1.
86. Ibid, 2.

87. Huey-li Li, "A Cross Cultural Critique of Ecofeminism," in *Ecofeminism,* ed. Gaard, pp. 273–274.

88. Ibid., 276.

89. Ibid., 5. For a more temperate critique of Goddess ecofeminism, see Greta Gaard, "Ecofeminism and Native American Cultures: Pushing the Limits of Cultural Imperialism?", in *Ecofeminism,* ed. Gaard.

90. Ibid., 3.

91. Biehl, *Rethinking Ecofeminist Politics,* 63–64.

92. Biehl, "The Politics of Myth," 4.

93. Charlene Spretnak (personal communication) points out, for example, that in "The Politics of Myth," Biehl represents as a commentary about Green Politics a passage from Spretnak that originally referred to the ERA and abortion rights.

94. See Spretnak, *States of Grace,* for an examination of the progressive dimension of Judaism and Christianity.

95. Spretnak, personal communication.

96. Spretnak, *States of Grace.*

97. Spretnak, personal communication.

98. See Lorna Salzman, "The U.S. Greens: A Dream Ends, A Nightmare Begins," a privately circulated open letter, p. 2. Salzman's highly critical remarks cannot be taken as disinterested.

99. Diana Fuss, *Essentially Speaking* (New York: Routledge, 1989). See Elizabeth Carlassare's excellent master's thesis, *An Exploration of Ecofeminism,* (Berkeley: Energy and Resources Group, 1992).

100. Carlassare, *An Exploration of Ecofeminism,* 43.

101. Ibid.

102. Fuss, *Essentially Speaking,* xi; cited by Carlassare, *An Exploration of Ecofeminism,* 33.

103. Ynestra King, "Healing the Wounds: Feminism, Ecology, and the Nature/Culture Dualism," in *Reweaving the World,* 112.

104. Ibid., 115.

105. Ibid., 117.

106. Spretnak, *States of Grace,* 120.

107. Michel Foucault, "Film and Popular Memory," in *Foucault Live,* trans. John Johnston, ed. Sylère Lotringer (New York: Semiotext(e), 1989): 100.

108. Ibid., 101.

109. In *Reactionary Modernism* (Cambridge: Cambridge University Press, 1986), Jeffrey Herf maintains that National Socialism cannot be understood

simply as an instance of capitalism using racist myths to promote its own ends.

10. Ernest Becker, in *Life Against Death* (New York: Free Press, 1973), asserts that no culture can thrive without a profound story that gives a heroic dimension to the lives of ordinary people.

11. Paula Allen Gunn, *The Sacred Hoop* (Boston: Beacon Press, 1986): 103–105; as cited by Jim Cheney, "Postmodern Environmental Ethics: Ethics as Bioregional Narrative," *Environmental Ethics* 11, no. 2 (Summer 1989): 117–134.

12. Spretnak, *The Spiritual Dimension of Green Politics,* 16; emphasis in original.

13. Manfred Frank, "Die Dichtung als 'Neue Mythologie'," in *Mythos und Moderne,* ed. Karl Heinz Bohrer (Frankfurt am Main: Suhrkamp Verlag, 1983): 35.

14. David Michael Levin, *The Opening of Vision: Nihilism and the Postmodern Situation* (New York: Routledge, 1988). This is an excellent book.

15. See Leszek Kolakowski, *Modernity on Endless Trial* (Chicago and London: The University of Chicago Press, 1990).

16. See *International Society for Environmental Ethics Newsletter* 4, no. 2 (Summer 1993): 24.

CHAPTER SEVEN

1. Salleh, "Deeper than Deep Ecology: The Eco-Feminist Connection," *Environmental Ethics* 6 (Winter 1984): 339–345; citation is from p. 340.

2. Ibid.

3. Ibid., 342.

4. Ibid., 343.

5. Ibid.

6. Ibid., 344–345.

7. Michael E. Zimmerman, "Feminism, Deep Ecology, and Environmental Ethics," *Environmental Ethics* 9, no. 1 (Spring 1987): 21–44.

8. Ariel Salleh, "The Ecofeminism/Deep Ecology Debate: A Reply to Patriarchal Reason," *Environmental Ethics* 14, no. 3 (Fall 1992): 195–216; and Salleh, "Class, Race, and Gender Discourse in the Ecofeminism/Deep Ecology Debate," *Environmental Ethics* 15, no. 3 (Fall 1993): 225–244. This latter essay appeared too late to be discussed in this book.

9. See Karen J. Warren, "Feminism and Ecology: Making Connections," *Environmental Ethics* 9, no. 1 (Spring 1987): 3–20.

10. See Warwick Fox, "The Deep Ecology-Ecofeminism Debate and its Parallels," *Environmental Ethics* 11, no. 1 (Spring 1989): 5–25.

11. Ibid., 24.

12. Huey-li Li, "A Cross Cultural Critique of Ecofeminism," in *Ecofeminism,* ed. Greta Gaard, 287.

13. Ibid., 287–288.

14. On this point, see Robert Sessions, "Deep Ecology versus Ecofeminism: Healthy Difference or Incompatible Philosophies?", in the Special Issue on Ecological Feminism, ed. Karen J. Warren, of *Hypatia* 6, no. 1 (Spring 1991): 90–107.

15. See Ariel Salleh, "Working with Nature: Reciprocity or Control?", in *Environmental Philosophy,* ed. Michael E. Zimmerman et al., (Englewood Cliffs, N.J.: Prentice-Hall, 1993).

16. See Roger J. H. King, "Caring about Nature: Feminist Ethics and the Environment," in the Special Issue on Ecofeminism, ed. Karen J. Warren, of *Hypatia* 6, no. 1 (Spring 1991): 75–89.

17. See George Sessions, "Radical Environmentalism in the 90s," *Wild Earth* 2, no. 2 (Fall 1992): 64–70.

18. See Vandana Shiva, *Staying Alive: Women, Ecology and Development* (London: Zed Books, 1988).

19. See Irvin D. Yalom, *Existential Psychotherapy* (New York: Basic Books, 1980), for an excellent analysis of the role played by death anxiety in neurotic and even psychotic conditions.

20. See Robert Sessions' insightful essay, "Deep Ecology versus Ecofeminism: Healthy Differences or Incompatible Philosophies," in the Special Issue on Ecological Feminism of *Hypatia* 6, no. 1 (Spring 1991): 90–107.

21. Ibid., 102.

22. Bill Devall, "Political Activism in a Time of War," in *From Anthropocentrism to Deep Ecology, ReVision* 13, no. 3 (Winter 1991): 135–141; citation is from p. 137.

23. Renate Hof, " 'But what if the object began to speak?'—Einige Gedanken über den Zusammenhang von Feminismus und Ökologie," *Amrikastudien/ American Studies* 32 (1987): 327–337.

24. Jim Cheney, "Ecofeminism and Deep Ecology," *Environmental Ethics* 9, no. 2 (Summer 1987): 115–145; citation is from pp. 117–118.

25. Ibid., p. 121.

26. Ibid., p. 124.

27. In *The I and the Not-I* (Princeton: Princeton/Bollingen, 1964), Jungian scholar M. Esther Harding notes that because most people live in a self-

contained, egoic world, they face difficulties in distinguishing self from not-self. Hence, in attempting to achieve wider identification, deep ecologists must be wary of confusing egoic self with other.

28. Cheney, "Eco-Feminism and Deep Ecology," 124.

29. Ibid., 125.

30. Ibid., 129.

31. Ibid., 133.

32. Ibid., 144.

33. Devall and Sessions, *Deep Ecology*, 67.

34. Ibid., 82.

35. See Val Plumwood's perceptive essay, "Nature, Self, and Gender: Feminism, Environmental Philosophy, and the Critique of Rationalism," in the Special Issue on Ecological Feminism of *Hypatia* 6, no. 1 (Spring 1991): 3–27; citation is from pp. 14–15.

36. Ibid., 12–13.

37. Marti Kheel, "Ecofeminism and Deep Ecology: Reflections on Identity and Difference," in *Reweaving the World*.

38. Ibid., 20.

39. Friedrich, Nietzsche, "On Truth and Lie in an Extra-Moral Sense," ed. and trans. Walter Kaufmann, *The Portable Nietzsche* (New York: Viking, 1968): 46–47; cited by Rorty, p. 14.

40. Richard Rorty, "Solidarity or Objectivity?", in *Post-Analytic Philosophy*, ed. John Rajchman and Cornel West (New York: Columbia University Press, 1985): 5, 11.

41. Ibid., 13.

42. Ibid., 14.

43. Seyla Benhabib, "The Debate Over Women and Moral Theory Revisited," in *Situating the Self* (New York: Routledge, 1992).

44. Ibid., 154.

45. Ibid.

46. Ibid.

47. Ibid., 167.

48. Ibid., 165.

49. Jim Cheney, "The Neo-Stoicism of Radical Environmentalism," *Environmental Ethics* 11, no. 4 (Winter 1989): 293–325; see especially p. 302.

50. Ibid., 298.

51. Ibid., 300–301.

52. Ibid., 315.

53. Ibid.

54. Jim Cheney, "Nature and the Theorizing of Difference," *Contemporary Philosophy* XIII, no. 1: 1–12.

55. Tom Jay, "The Salmon of the Heart," in *Working the Woods, Working the Self,* ed. Finn Wilcox and Jeremiah Gorsline (Port Townsend: Empty Bowl, 1986): 116; cited by Jim Cheney in "Postmodern Environmental Ethics: Ethics as Bioregional Narrative," *Environmental Ethics* 11, no. 2 (Summer 1989): 117–134; see especially p. 122.

56. Cheney, "The Neo-Stoicism of Radical Environmentalism," 319.

57. Fox, "The Deep Ecology-Ecofeminism Debate and its Parallels," 12.

58. Ibid.

59. Roger J. H. King, "Caring About Nature: Feminist Ethics and the Environment," in the Special Issue on Ecofeminism of *Hypatia* 6, no. 1 (Spring 1991): 75–89.

60. Ibid., 84.

61. Ibid., 85.

62. Plumwood, "Nature, Self, and Gender."

63. Cheney, "Nature and the Politics of Difference," ms., 18.

64. Annie Dillard, *Pilgrim at Tinker's Creek* (New York: Bantam Books, 1975).

65. Cheney, "The Neo-Stoicism of Radical Environmentalism," 325, n. 94.

66. Jim Cheney, "Nature and the Theorizing of Difference;" citation is from p. 4.

67. Ibid.

68. In "Radical Nonduality in Ecofeminist Philosophy," *Ecological Feminism: Multidisciplinary Perspectives,* ed. Karen Warren (Bloomington: Indiana University Press, 1994), Spretnak insightfully discusses the criticism advanced by some postmodern ecofeminists toward the allegedly hegemonic concept of "unity."

69. Peter Reed, "Man Apart: An Alternative to the Self-Realization Approach," *Environmental Ethics* 11, no. 1 (Spring 1989): 53–70.

70. Ibid., 63–64.

71. Elizabeth Dodson Gray, *Green Paradise Lost* (Wellesley, Mass.: Roundtable Press, 1981): 85.

72. Carol P. Christ, "Rethinking Theology and Nature," *Reweaving the World,* 66.

73. Alice Walker, *The Color Purple* (New York: Harcourt Brace Jovanovich, 1982): 167; cited in Spretnak, *The Spiritual Dimension of Green Politics,* 55.

74. Matthews, *The Ecological Self,* 154.

75. Ibid., 155.

76. Ibid.
77. Ibid., 160.
78. Cited by Matthews, ibid., 160.
79. See Joseph Campbell, *The Flight of the Wild Condor* (South Bend, Ind.: Regnery/Gateway, Inc., 1979). On tribal prejudice, see Claude-Lévi Strauss, "Race and History," in *Structural Anthropology*, vol. 2, trans. Monique Layton (New York: Basic Books, 1976).
80. Cheney, "The Neo-Stoicism of Radical Environmentalism," 325.
81. Cheney, "Postmodern Environmental Ethics," 118.
82. Ibid., 118–119.
83. Ibid., 119.
84. Ibid., 123.
85. Ynestra King, letter to *The Nation* (12 December 1987): 730.
86. Cheney, "Postmodern Environmental Ethics," 122.
87. Ibid., 122; my emphasis.
88. See Mick Smith, "Cheney and the Myth of Postmodernism," *Environmental Ethics* 15, no. 1 (Spring 1993): 3–17.
89. Cheney, "Postmodern Environmental Ethics," 133. See Smith, "Cheney and the Myth of Postmodernism."
90. Cheney, "The Neo-Stoicism of Environmental Ethics," 312.
91. See Yalom, *Existential Psychotherapy*.
92. Allan Hunt Badiner, *Dharma Gaia: A Harvest of Essays in Buddhism and Ecology* (Berkeley: Parallax Press, 1990).

CHAPTER EIGHT

1. See Laurent Dobuzinskis, "Is Progressive Environmentalism an Oxymoron?", in *Critical Review* 6, no. 2–3 (Spring/Summer 1993): 283–303, for a helpful examination of environmentalism's "progressive" status.
2. See Murray Feshback and Alfred Friendly, Jr., *Ecocide in the USSR: Health and Nature Under Siege* (New York: Basic Books, 1992).
3. Wendell Berry, *The Unsettling of America: Culture and Agriculture* (New York: Avon Books, 1977); Berry, *The Gift of Good Land* (San Francisco: North Point Press, 1981).
4. Berry, "The Futility of Global Thinking," *Harper's* (September 1989): 16–22. See also "Out of Your Car, Off Your Horse," *Atlantic Monthly* (February 1991): 61–63.
5. Berry, "The Futility of Global Thinking," 18.

6. Alan AtKisson, "The Utility of Global Thinking," *In Context* no. 25 (Late Spring 1990): 55–57. I have benefited from personal discussion with Alan AtKisson about these issues.

7. Ibid., 56.

8. Letter by Wendell Berry, *In Context* no. 27 (Winter 1991): 4.

9. See Alan AtKisson's letter replying to Berry, ibid.

10. Gus DiZerega, "Unexpected Harmonies: Self-Organization in Liberal Modernity and Ecology," *The Trumpeter* 10, no. 1 (Winter 1993): 25–32; citation from p. 25. I am much indebted to diZerega's insightful essays.

11. Ibid.

12. Ibid.

13. See Terry L. Anderson and Donald R. Leal, *Free Market Environmentalism* (Boulder: Westview Press, 1991).

14. DiZerega, "Unexpected Harmonies," 26.

15. Ibid.

16. Ibid.

17. George Sessions makes such a proposal in "Wilderness and Global Ecosystem Protection," in Zimmerman et al., ed., *Environmental Philosophy* (Englewood Cliffs, N.J.: Prentice-Hall, 1993): 246.

18. Snyder objected to Sessions's proposal at the Wilderness and Civilization Conference, August 1989, in Estes Park, Colorado. On Gary Snyder's animosity toward the state, see *The Practice of the Wild* (San Francisco: North Point Press, 1990): 41.

19. DiZerega, "Unexpected Harmonies," 27.

20. Ibid., 28.

21. Ibid.

22. Ibid.

23. See Gus DiZerega, "Social Ecology, Deep Ecology, and Liberalism," in the Special Issue on Environmentalism and The Market of *Critical Review* 6, no. 2–3 (Spring/Summer 1993): 305–370.

24. Holmes Rolston III, "Duties to Ecosystems," in *Companion to a Sand County Almanac,* ed. J. Baird Callicott (Madison: University of Wisconsin Press, 1987): 250; cited by diZerega, p. 22.

25. Murray Bookchin, *The Ecology of Freedom* (Palo Alto: Chesire Books, 1983): 149ff.

26. Rolston, "Duties to Ecosystems," 256–257; cited by diZerega, pp. 25–26.

27. Capra, *The Turning Point* (New York: Bantam Books, 1982): 288.

28. *The Philosophy of Social Ecology,* 71–72.

29. Ibid., 37ff.
30. Ibid., 419.
31. Bookchin, *The Ecology of Freedom*, 24.
32. Ibid., 15.
33. Gus diZerega, "Social Ecology, Deep Ecology, and Liberalism," 314. See also diZerega, "Green Politics and Post-Modern Liberalism," *Critical Review* (Spring 1987): 17–41. In *Ecological Ethics and Politics* (Totowa, N.J.: Rowman and Littlefield, 1983), H. J. McCloseky offers a liberal reformist approach to ecological problems.
34. DiZerega, "Unexpected Harmonies," 29.
35. Ibid.
36. See Joel Jay Kassiola, *The Death of Industrial Civilization* (Albany: SUNY Press, 1992); Andrew Bard Schmookler, *The Illusion of Choice* (Albany: SUNY Press, 1992); Robyn Eckersley, *Environmentalism and Political Theory* (Albany: SUNY Press, 1992); Paul R. Ehrlich and Anne H. Ehrlich, *Healing the Planet* (Reading, Mass.: Addison Wesley, 1991); Andrew Dobson, *Green Political Thought* (London: HarperCollins, 1991).
37. Gus diZerega, personal communication.
38. DiZerega, "Unexpected Harmonies," 31.
39. Ibid.
40. Ibid.
41. Ibid. On the role played by chance and cultural diversity in human "progress," see Claude Lévi-Strauss, "Race and History," in *Cultural Anthropology*, vol. 2, trans. Monique Layton (New York: Basic Books, 1976).
42. See Karl Hess, *Visions Upon the Land* (Washington, D.C.: Island Press, 1992); Herman Daly and John B. Cobb, Jr., *For the Common Good* (Boston: Beacon Press, 1989); Eckersley, *Environmentalism and Political Theory;* Lester W. Milbrath, *Envisioning a Sustainable Society* (Albany: SUNY Press, 1989).
43. Arne Naess, "The Encouraging Richness and Diversity of Ultimate Premisses in Environmental Philosophy," *The Trumpeter* 9, no. 2 (Spring 1992): 53–60; citation is from p. 53.
44. Ibid., 57.
45. Ibid., 55; my emphasis.
46. Arne Naess, "Deep Ecology for the 22nd Century," *The Trumpeter* 9, no. 2 (Spring 1992): 87–88; reference is to p. 88.
47. Ibid., 87.
48. Ibid.

49. Ibid., 88.

50. Georges Bataille, "The Notion of Expenditure," in *Visions of Excess,* trans. Allan Stoekl, Carl R. Lovitt, and Donald M. Leslie, Jr. (Minneapolis: University of Minnesota Press, 1985): 117; emphasis in original.

51. Ibid., 118.

52. Ibid., 122–123.

53. Ibid.

54. Ibid., 117–118.

55. Ibid., 128.

56. Ibid.

57. Habermas, *The Philosophical Discourse of Modernity,* 220.

58. See Manfred Frank, *Was ist Neostrukturalismus?* (Frankfurt am Main: Suhrkamp, 1984): 422–437.

59. Charlene Spretnak, *States of Grace* (New York: Harper & Row, 1991).

60. Alice Holzhey-Kunz, "Emancipation and Narcissism: On the Meaning of Desire," special issue, *Psychotherapy for Freedom,* ed. Erik Craig, of *The Humanistic Psychologist* 16, no. 1 (Spring 1988): 186–202.

61. Ibid., 191.

62. Max Cafard, *"Apocalypse And/Or Metamorphosis:* A Surregional View," *Exquisite Corpse* no. 37 (1992): 15–16.

63. Norman O. Brown, *Apocalypse And/Or Metamorphosis* (Berkeley, Los Angeles, London: University of California Press, 1991): 189.

64. Cafard, *"Apocalypse And/Or Metamorphosis:* A Surregional View."

65. See Martin Jay, *Downcast Eyes* (Berkeley, Los Angeles, London: University of California Press, 1993). See also Rosalind E. Kraus, *The Optical Unconscious* (Cambridge: The MIT Press, 1993).

66. See for example Herta Nagl-Docekal, "Das Heimliche Subjekt Lyotards," in *Die Frage nach dem Subjekt,* ed. Manfred Frank, Gerard Raulet, and Willem van Reijen (Frankfurt am Main: Suhrkamp, 1988).

67. See also Robert Weimann and Hans Ulrich Gumbrecht, with Benno Wagner, ed., *Postmoderne-globale Differenz* (Frankfurt am Main: Suhrkamp, 1991): 33.

68. N. Katherine Hayles, "Chaos as Orderly Disorder: Shifting Ground in Contemporary Literature and Science," *New Literary History* 20, no. 2 (Winter 1989): 305–322; citation is from p. 305. See also Hayles's excellent book, *Chaos Bound: Orderly Disorder in Contemporary Literature and Science* (Ithaca: Cornell University Press, 1990).

69. Lila Gatlin, *Information Theory and the Living System* (New York: Columbia University Press, 1972): 1–4.

70. Ibid., 306. On chaos theory, see Ilya Prigogine and Isabelle Stengers, *Order Out of Chaos* (New York; Bantam Books, 1984); James Gleick, *Chaos: Making a New Science* (New York: Penguin Books, 1987); Paul Davies, *The Cosmic Blueprint* (New York: Touchstone, 1989).

71. Hayles, "Chaos as Orderly Disorder," 307.

72. Ibid., 313.

73. Ibid., 315.

74. Ibid., 317.

75. Ibid.

76. Ibid.

77. Alexander J. Argyros, *A Blessed Rage for Order: Deconstruction, Evolution, and Chaos* (Ann Arbor: University of Michigan Press, 1992): 94. This is a superb book.

78. Ibid., 282.

79. Ibid., 228.

80. Ibid., 117.

81. Ibid., 179.

82. Ibid., 234.

83. Ibid.

84. Ibid., 236.

85. Ibid., 143.

86. Ibid., 236.

87. Hayles, "Chaos as Disorderly Order," 321.

88. Argyros, *A Blessed Rage for Order,* 327–328.

89. Ibid.

90. Others who are attempting to develop a critical postmodernism include Ernesto Laclau and Chantal Mouffe, *Hegemony and Socialist Strategy: Toward a Radical Democratic Politics* (London: Verso Books, 1985); Robyn Eckersley, *Environmentalism and Political Theory;* and Bill Martin, *Matrix and the Line: Derrida and the Possibilities of Postmodern Social Theory* (Albany: SUNY Press, 1992). For a sympathetic critique of *Hegemony and Socialist Strategy,* see Steven Best and Douglas Kellner, *Postmodern Theory: Critical Interrogations* (New York: The Guilford Press, 1991): 192–204.

91. Eric Jantsch, *The Self-Organizing Universe* (New York: Pergamon Press, 1980): 142.

92. Argyros, *A Blessed Rage for Order,* 327.

93. Ibid., 326.

94. Jean Baudrillard, *Simulations,* trans. Paul Foss, Paul Patton, and Philip Beitchman (New York: Semiotext(e), 1983): 111.

95. On this point, see Stephen Watt's fine essay, "Baudrillard's America (and Ours?): Image, Virus, Catastrophe," in *Modernity and Mass Culture,* ed. James Naremore and Patrick Brantlinger (Bloomington: Indiana University Press, 1991): 142–143.

96. See Kellner, *Jean Baudrillard,* 203–210.

97. Ibid., 216.

98. Argyros, *A Blessed Rage for Order,* 116.

99. See Donna Haraway, *Simians, Cyborgs, and Women: The Reinvention of Nature* (New York: Routledge, 1991). See *Coming to Terms: Feminism, Theory, Politics,* ed. Elizabeth Weed (New York/London: Routledge, 1989), for three critical appraisals of Haraway's cyborgian myth: Christina Crosky, "Allies and Enemies"; Mary Ann Doone, "Cyborgs, Origins, and Subjectivity"; and Joan W. Scott, "Cyborgian Socialists."

100. Haraway, "Situated Knowledges: The Science Question in Feminism and the Privilege of Partial Perspective," *Simians, Cyborgs, and Women,* 192.

101. Haraway, "A Cyborg Manifesto," *Simians, Cyborgs, and Women,* 150; hereafter, CM.

102. William Gibson, *Neuromancer* (West Bloomfield, Minn.: Phantasia Press, 1987); *Count Zero* (Hastings-on-Hudson, N.Y.: Ultramarine Publishers, 1987); *Mona Lisa Overdrive* (New York: Bantam, 1988).

103. Mary Daly, *Gyn/Ecology,* as cited by Judith Halberstam, "Automating Gender: Postmodern Feminism in the Age of the Intelligent Machine," *Feminist Studies* 17, no. 3 (Fall 1991): 439–460; citation is on p. 445.

104. Jean-François Lyotard, in *Virtual Seminar on the Bioapparatus,* ed. Mary Anne Moster, seminar led by Catherine Richards and Nell Tenhaaf (Banff: The Banff Center for the Arts, 1991): 28.

105. Ibid.

106. Donna Haraway, "The Promises of Monsters: A Regenerative Politics for Inappropriate/d Others," in *Cultural Studies,* ed. Lawrence Grossberg, Cary Nelson, Paula Treichler (New York: Routledge, 1992): 295–337; citation from p. 296.

107. Ibid.

108. Ibid., 297. On this topic, see also Donna Haraway, "Otherworldly Conversations; Terran Topics; Local Terms," *Science as Culture* 3, pt. 1, no. 14 (1992): 64–98; especially pp. 81–84.

109. Ibid.

110. Haraway, "Situated Knowledges," 199.

111. Haraway, "The Promises of Monsters," 298.

112. Ibid., 304.

113. Ibid., 309. Haraway recommends Susanna Hecht and Alexander Cockburn, *The Fate of the Forest* (New York: Verso, 1989).

114. Haraway, "The Promises of Monsters," 311.

115. Ibid., 313.

116. Ibid., 315.

117. Ibid., 304.

118. Ibid.

119. Haraway, personal communication.

120. Sallie Tisdale, "It's Been Real," *Esquire* (April 1991): 34–37, 145–147. See Howard Rheingold's excellent survey, *Virtual Reality* (New York: Summit Books, 1991); and David Gelernter, *Mirror Worlds* (New York: Oxford University Press, 1992).

121. Haraway, personal communication.

122. Tisdale, "It's Been Real," 146.

123. Ibid., 147.

124. Ibid., 146.

125. Ibid.

126. Ibid., 147.

127. Haraway, "The Promises of Monsters," 325.

128. Ibid.

129. Ibid.

130. See the essays by David Ray Griffin, ed. *Spirituality and Society: Postmodern Visions* (Albany: SUNY Press, 1988).

131. Benedict de Spinoza, *The Ethics* in *The Chief Works of Benedict de Spinoza*, trans. R. H. M. Elwes (New York: Dover Publications, Inc., 1951).

Designer: U.C. Press Staff
Compositor: Braun-Brumfield, Inc.
Text: Garamond
Display: M. Gill Sans
Printer: Maple-Vail Book Manufacturing Group
Binder: Maple-Vail Book Manufacturing Group